Self and Other

Self and Other

Exploring Subjectivity,
Empathy, and Shame

Dan Zahavi

OXFORD
UNIVERSITY PRESS

OXFORD
UNIVERSITY PRESS

Great Clarendon Street, Oxford, OX2 6DP,
United Kingdom

Oxford University Press is a department of the University of Oxford.
It furthers the University's objective of excellence in research, scholarship,
and education by publishing worldwide. Oxford is a registered trade mark of
Oxford University Press in the UK and in certain other countries

First Edition published in 2014

Impression: 2

Published in the United States of America by Oxford University Press
198 Madison Avenue, New York, NY 10016, United States of America

British Library Cataloguing in Publication Data
Data available

Library of Congress Control Number: 2014940243

ISBN 978-0-19-959068-1

Printed and bound by
CPI Group (UK) Ltd, Croydon, CR0 4YY

Acknowledgements

This book was written at the Center for Subjectivity Research at the University of Copenhagen. I have profited immensely from my daily interaction and discussion with staff members and visitors. I am also grateful to a number of funding sources and agencies, whose generous support over the years made the research activities of the Center for Subjectivity Research possible and allowed me to complete different parts of the book: the Danish National Research Foundation, the Velux Foundation, the Danish Council for Independent Research, the European Science Foundation, the European Commission, and the University of Copenhagen's Excellence Programme for Interdisciplinary Research.

I have had the opportunity to present material from the manuscript at many places including: the University of Osnabrück, Emory University (Atlanta), the University of Bern, the University of Edinburgh, Peking University, the University of Portsmouth, the University of Cardiff, Duquesne University (Pittsburgh), the University of Leiden, University College Dublin, the University of Barcelona, Radboud University Nijmegen, the University of Iceland (Reykjavik), the Bergische Universität Wuppertal, the École Normale Supérieure (Paris), Boston College, the University of Pavia, Humboldt University (Berlin), the Chinese University of Hong Kong, the College of Charleston, Rice University (Houston), the Katholieke Universiteit Leuven, the University of Heidelberg, the University of Oslo, the University of Fribourg, the Hebrew University (Jerusalem), Jadavpur University (Kolkata), Jawaharlal Nehru University (Delhi), Boğaziçi University (Istanbul), the University of Vienna, Tokyo University, the Freie Universität Berlin, the University of Amsterdam, the University of Milan, and the Ritsumeikan University (Kyoto). I have profited, in every instance, from the ensuing discussions and the comments I have received.

I have learned much from my discussion with the following people, many of whom have also read and commented on parts of the manuscript: Miri Albahari, Stan Klein, Anthony Rudd, Shaun Gallagher, Thor Grünbaum, Joel Krueger, Pierre Jacob, Charles Siewert, Fabrice Teroni, Joe Neisser, Glenda Satne, John Michael, Julian Kiverstein, Erik Rietveld, Sanneke de Haan, Søren Overgaard, Jay Garfield, Evan Thompson, Rasmus Thybo Jensen, Josef Parnas, Barry Dainton, Philippe Rochat, Chantal Bax, Mark Siderits, Adrian Alsmith, Hans Bernhard Schmid, Vittorio Gallese, Vasudevi Reddy, Peter Hobson, Jean Decety, Andreas Roepstorff, Thomas Fuchs, Matt MacKenzie, Thomas Szanto, Mark Steen, Michael Wallner, Sandy Berkovski, and Philipp Schmidt. Many thanks to them all.

I am particularly grateful to Galen Strawson, Marya Schechtman, Uriah Kriegel, Sophie Loidolt, and Wolfgang Fasching, whose incisive comments resulted in substantial changes. Special thanks also to Sophie Loidolt and Mark Steen for organizing workshops in Vienna and Istanbul respectively, where advanced drafts of the entire manuscript were discussed. Let me finally acknowledge my debt to two anonymous referees for Oxford University Press, who provided some exceptionally helpful and incisive comments.

Thanks to Felipe Leon for helping me with the list of references, to Adele-France Jourdan for compiling the index, to Laurien Berkeley for her excellent copy-editing, and a special thanks to Peter Momtchiloff for his impeccable editorship and for having originally encouraged me to start on the book.

While I was working on the book, early versions of some of the material found their way into stand-alone articles. Everything was then thoroughly revised and rewritten for the book, so none of the current chapters have already been published. However, relevant previous publications include: 'Self and Other: The Limits of Narrative Understanding', in D. D. Hutto (ed.), *Narrative and Understanding Persons*, Royal Institute of Philosophy Supplement 60 (Cambridge: Cambridge University Press, 2007); 'Simulation, Projection and Empathy', *Consciousness and Cognition*, 17 (2008), 514–22; 'Is the Self a Social Construct?', *Inquiry*, 52/6 (2009), 551–73; 'Empathy, Embodiment and Interpersonal Understanding: From Lipps to Schutz', *Inquiry*, 53/3 (2010), 285–306; 'Unity of Consciousness and the Problem of Self', in S. Gallagher (ed.), *The Oxford Handbook of the Self* (Oxford: Oxford University Press, 2011); 'The Experiential Self: Objections and Clarifications', in M. Siderits, E. Thompson, and D. Zahavi (eds.), *Self, No Self? Perspectives from Analytical, Phenomenological, and Indian Traditions* (Oxford: Oxford University Press, 2011); 'Empathy and Direct Social Perception: A Phenomenological Proposal', *Review of Philosophy and Psychology*, 2/3 (2011), 541–58; 'Faces and Ascriptions: Mapping Measures of the Self' (with A. Roepstorff), *Consciousness and Cognition*, 20 (2011), 141–8; 'The Uncanny Mirror: A Re-Framing of Mirror Self-Experience' (with P. Rochat), *Consciousness and Cognition*, 20 (2011), 204–13; 'Shame and the Exposed Self', in J. Webber (ed.), *Reading Sartre: On Phenomenology and Existentialism* (London: Routledge, 2011); 'The Complex Self: Empirical and Theoretical Perspectives', in J. McCurry and A. Pryor (eds.), *Phenomenology, Cognition, and Neuroscience* (Pittsburgh: Simon Silverman Phenomenology Center, 2012); 'Self, Consciousness, and Shame', in D. Zahavi (ed.), *The Oxford Handbook of Contemporary Phenomenology* (Oxford: Oxford University Press, 2012); 'Empathy and Mirroring: Husserl and Gallese', in R. Breeur and U. Melle (eds.), *Life, Subjectivity and Art: Essays in Honor of Rudolf Bernet* (Dordrecht: Springer, 2012); 'The Time of the Self', *Grazer Philosophische Studien*, 84 (2012), 143–59; 'Vindicating Husserl's Primal I', in N. de Warren and J. Bloechl (eds.), *Phenomenology in a New Key: Between Analysis and History. Essays in Honor of Richard Cobb-Stevens* (Dordrecht: Springer, 2015); 'For-me-ness: What It Is and What It Is Not' (with U. Kriegel), in D. O. Dahlstrom, A. Elpidorou, and W. Hopp (eds.), *Philosophy of Mind and Phenomenology: Conceptual and Empirical Approaches* (London: Routledge, 2015); 'You, Me and We: The Sharing of Emotional Experiences', *Journal of Consciousness Studies* (2015).

Contents

Part III. The Interpersonal Self

Introduction: Genesis and Structure

I have been working on the topics of self and other for more than twenty years. In my doctoral dissertation, *Husserl und die transzendentale Intersubjektivität*, which I began in 1992, I offered a new interpretation of Husserl's theory of intersubjectivity. I argued that one of Husserl's central motivations for devoting so much attention to intersubjectivity was his concern with the transcendental philosophical questions about what it means for something to be real and how we can experience it as such. According to Husserl, an elucidation of these questions necessitates a turn towards transcendental intersubjectivity. I also discussed the contributions of Sartre, Merleau-Ponty, and Heidegger to a phenomenological theory of intersubjectivity, and stressed the common features and virtues of such analyses when compared to the language-oriented approach to intersubjectivity that was to be found in the work of Habermas and Apel.

In my habilitation thesis, *Self-Awareness and Alterity*, which was published in 1999, I went on to examine the notion of pre-reflective self-consciousness, and defended the view that our experiential life is characterized by a form of self-consciousness that is more primitive and more fundamental than the reflective form of self-consciousness that one finds exemplified in introspection. I presented a new interpretation of Husserl's analysis of self-consciousness and inner time-consciousness, and by also drawing on the writings of Merleau-Ponty, Sartre, Henry, and Derrida, I demonstrated how central and fundamental a role the concept of self-consciousness plays in phenomenological philosophy. Phenomenology hasn't merely been interested in the question of how consciousness is involved in the manifestation of objects, but has also had to tackle the problem of how to understand the self-manifestation of consciousness.

My research since then has continued to move back and forth between these basic topics. On the one hand, I have worked on the relationship between experience, self, and self-consciousness. I have argued that all three concepts are interconnected, and that a theory of consciousness that wishes to take the subjective dimension of our experiential life seriously also needs to operate with a (minimal) notion of self. An early effort along these lines can be found in my article 'Self and Consciousness' from 2000. On the other hand, I have continued to write on intersubjectivity, empathy, and social cognition. I have defended a phenomenological account of empathy, argued in favour of the bodily and contextual character of interpersonal understanding, and criticized dominant positions within the so-called 'theory of mind' debate, including simulation theory and theory-theory. My article 'Beyond Empathy: Phenomeno-logical Approaches to Intersubjectivity', from 2001, is one representative publication.

Subjectivity and Selfhood, from 2005, gathered much of my work from the preceding years. Although I afterwards continued to work on both subjectivity and intersubjectivity, I had initially no intention of writing a new book on the topic, but in 2008 I started to think about how my core ideas could be further developed, how I might respond to some of the criticism I had encountered, and in particular how I might integrate the two lines of my research more systematically. In 2009 I finally started work on the present book. It has taken a long time to complete, longer than any of my previous books.

The book is divided into what at first might look like three distinct parts. As will become clear, however, there are a number of interlocking themes that run through it and make it into one interconnected whole. To facilitate a better grasp of the book's overarching structure, let me provide a quick overview of the steps of the argumentation:

1. Chapter 1 compares the anti-realist position defended by some philosophers with the realism about self that we find in the work of various cognitive psychologists, developmental psychologists, psychiatrists, and neuroscientists. As this initial comparison makes clear, there is a striking mismatch between the self that is rejected by some philosophers and the self that is accepted by many empirical scientists. Not only does this finding make it urgent to distinguish different notions of self, it also illustrates the importance of getting a proper grip on how to conceive of the relationship between empirical and theoretical approaches to self.

2. Chapter 2 introduces two very different conceptions of self. According to social constructivism, one cannot be a self on one's own, but only together with others. According to a more experience-based approach, selfhood is a built-in feature of experiential life. Importantly, both of these approaches reject the definition of the self espoused by many anti-realists, that is, the view that the self, if it exists, must be an unchanging and ontologically independent entity. Most of the chapter is then taken up by a closer examination of the experience-based, phenomenological proposal. In a first step, this is done through an examination of the relationship between phenomenal consciousness and self-consciousness. Next, different conceptions of experiential ownership are distinguished and discussed, and the notion of an experiential self is then defined in terms of the first-personal character of experience.

3. The core of the proposal having been outlined in Chapter 2, the following two chapters consider various objections that have been or might be raised against

it. Chapter 3 is taken up by a presentation and assessment of different versions of what might be termed the *anonymity objection*, which denies that experience per se entails subjectivity, first-personal givenness, and for-me-ness. One version of the objection argues that consciousness on the pre-reflective level is so completely and fully immersed in the world that it remains oblivious to itself. There is at that stage and on that level no room for any self-consciousness, for-me-ness, or mineness. On this view, experiential ownership is the outcome of a meta-cognitive operation that involves conceptual and linguistic resources. Another version denies that one is ever directly acquainted with one's own experiences, that is, not only pre-reflectively but also when one engages in reflection and introspection. According to those who defend the *transparency thesis*, phenomenal consciousness is strictly and exclusively world-presenting. Having replied to both of these objections, the chapter ends with a discussion of whether neuro- and psychopathology might present us with relevant exceptions to the claim that experiential episodes are first-personal, that is, with pathological cases featuring anonymous experiences that altogether lack mineness and for-me-ness.

4. Chapter 4 engages with a quite different line of attack. The target is no longer the existence or prevalence of experiential subjectivity, but rather the identification of the latter with selfhood. According to one criticism, experience might indeed be characterized by subjectivity, but this in no way warrants the claim that there is also a unified self. Indeed, to interpret the intrinsically self-reflexive stream of consciousness as an enduring self-entity is, according to some Buddhist critics, to engage in an illusory reification. The assessment of this objection once again makes it clear that the current debate is complicated by the coexistence of quite different notions of self, and that the self that is denied by these critics differs markedly from the experiential self. This is where the second objection takes over. It rejects the minimalist notion of an experiential self and argues that the self, rather than simply being equated with a built-in feature of consciousness, must instead be located and situated within a space of normativity. To put it differently, the requirements that must be met in order to qualify as a self are higher than those needed in order to be conscious. One influential version of this proposal, the so-called narrative account of self, is analysed, and the chapter ends with a discussion of whether the narrative account can stand alone or whether it necessarily presupposes the dimension of self that is targeted by the experience-based approach.

5. The narrative account of the self accentuates the temporal dimension of selfhood and is primarily addressing the issue of long-term diachronic identity and persistency. But what about the experiential self? Is it minimal in the sense of being temporally non-extended? Chapter 5 discusses the relation between temporality and selfhood, and argues that the experiential self must

possess some degree of diachronic unity. This still leaves it an open question, however, how temporally extended it is. The current proposal is compared and contrasted with two other recent experienced-based accounts, according to which the self is either very short-lived or capable of preserving its identity across periods of dreamless sleep only if it is defined in terms of its capacity to be conscious rather than as something that is essentially conscious. The chapter ends with a discussion of the extent to which the notion of an experiential self might be able to address the traditional problem of personal identity.

6. Chapter 6 departs a bit from the preceding trajectory by primarily being exegetically oriented. It discusses what at first sight seems to be an important difference between Merleau-Ponty's and Husserl's views on the relationship between self and other. Is the difference between self and other fundamental or derived and rooted in some preceding stage of undifferentiatedness? This discussion brings to the fore not merely how minimal a notion the experiential self is, but also why it is necessary to operate with more complex forms of self, including ones that are socially constructed. One decisive question is then whether an insistence on the priority of the experiential self jeopardizes or rather allows for a proper account of intersubjectivity. This question will be the topic of Part II.

7. Throughout the preceding chapters, the notion of an experiential self has been contrasted with a more normatively embedded notion of self. Chapter 7 concludes Part I by summarizing the arguments for the former and by defending a multidimensional model of self, one that sees the two notions of self as complementary notions rather than as excluding alternatives. It is also suggested, however, that it might be necessary to consider an as yet unexplored interpersonal dimension of self, one that might serve to bridge and connect the other two notions. The suggestion will be pursued further in Part III.

8. Chapter 8 starts Part II by pointing to the following challenge: Isn't the notion of an experiential self overly Cartesian, and doesn't a strong emphasis on the first-personal character of consciousness prohibit a satisfactory account of intersubjectivity? To really allow for the latter shouldn't one rather argue for the co-constitution of self and other, or perhaps opt for the view that one only obtains the self-relation constitutive of selfhood by being socialized into a publicly shared space of normativity?

9. Chapter 9 takes up the question of how we get to understand and know others. A brief introduction to the theory of mind debate having been provided, the focus is squarely on empathy. It is shown how some of the central suggestions proposed by contemporary simulationists, in particular the idea that empathy involves some combination of simulation and projection, can be traced back to Theodor Lipps's influential account at the beginning of the twentieth century. Lipps's theory preceded and influenced the analyses of the subsequent

phenomenologists, who all remained quite critical of it. An obvious question to ask is consequently whether their criticism as well as their more positive exploration of empathy still have something to offer to the current debate.

10. The longest chapter of the book, Chapter 10, offers a detailed investigation of the multilayered analyses of empathy found in the writings of Scheler, Husserl, Stein, and Schutz. It discusses the importance they assign to embodiment and expressivity, and clarifies the relation between empathy and related phenomena like emotional contagion, sympathy, and emotional sharing. Although these thinkers did not agree on everything, there is a sufficient amount of overlap between their respective theories to warrant talking about a distinct phenomenological account of empathy, one that differs rather markedly from recent attempts to explain empathy in terms of mirroring, mimicry, imitation, emotional contagion, imaginative projection, or inferential attribution. More specifically, the phenomenologists conceived of empathy as a distinct other-directed form of intentionality, one that allows the other's experiences to disclose themselves as other. One noteworthy feature of their proposal is that, while remaining firmly committed to the first-personal character of consciousness, it also highlights and respects what is distinctive about the givenness of others.

11. Chapter 11 elaborates the phenomenological account of empathy further by discussing and assessing a number of objections it has recently encountered. What does it mean to say that empathy provides direct access to the minds of others, and to what extent is such a claim compatible with the idea that social understanding is always contextual? To what extent does insistence on the experiential accessibility of other minds commit one to an untenable form of behaviourism? And to what extent is the phenomenological proposal really distinct from existing simulationist and theory-theory accounts of social cognition? The chapter also discusses whether the phenomenological analyses might be in line with recent developmental findings concerning early forms of social understanding.

12. Chapter 12 concludes Part II by arguing that an examination of empathy can serve to elucidate the self–other relationship, and that empathy, rather than entailing an overcoming or elimination of the self–other differentiation, entails preservation of it. This is precisely why any resolutely non-egological account of consciousness will be incapable of accounting convincingly for empathy, and why an emphasis on the inherent and essential first-personal character of experiential life must be regarded as a prerequisite for, rather than an impediment to, a satisfactory account of intersubjectivity. In closing, however, attention is called to an important limitation of the preceding analysis. Empathic understanding can occur without any kind of reciprocation on the part of the other, but doesn't this miss something rather crucial about the self–other

relationship? Isn't one of the unique features of other experiencing subjects the fact that they have a perspective of their own, and not just upon the world of objects, but also upon us? The final part of the book will partially address this imbalance by considering not only some examples of socially mediated and constituted types of self(-experience), but also a more reciprocal kind of self–other interdependence.

13. Chapter 13, the first chapter of Part III, discusses research on facial self-recognition. The ability to recognize one's own face, for instance by passing the mirror mark test, has often been heralded as providing empirical evidence for the presence of self-awareness. A failure to pass the test has also been seen as evidence for the absence of self-awareness. Some have even argued that creatures incapable of passing such a test lack conscious experiences altogether. These interpretations are criticized and the plausibility of an alternative interpretation of mirror self-experience is assessed, one that sees facial self-recognition as testifying to the presence of a rather special kind of self-consciousness, namely, one that in the case of human beings often has a distinctive social dimension to it.

14. Chapter 14, the central chapter of Part III, engages with the topic of shame. What does the fact that we feel shame tell us about the nature of self? Does shame testify to the presence of a self-concept, a (failed) self-ideal, and a capacity for critical self-assessment, or does it rather, as some have suggested, point to the fact that the self is in part socially constructed? Should shame primarily be classified as a self-conscious emotion, or is it rather a distinct social emotion, or is there something misleading about this very alternative? The chapter explores these questions and discusses whether the experience of shame presupposes a possession of a first-person perspective and a capacity for empathy, and whether it exemplifies an other-mediated form of self-experience and to that extent involves a more complex self than the thin experiential self.

15. The concluding chapter of the book, Chapter 15, explores the question of whether the preceding investigation of self and other can help to elucidate the structure of the we. One initial question concerns whether we-intentionality presupposes and involves self-consciousness and other-consciousness, or whether it rather abolishes the difference between self and other. Another central question concerns the relationship between the second person singular and the first person plural. Even if self-consciousness is retained in we-experience, the latter must modify the former. Might the adoption of a second-person perspective, where I am aware of the other and at the same time implicitly aware of myself in the accusative, as attended to or addressed by the other play an important role?

PART I

The Experiential Self

1

Conflicting Perspectives on Self

There has been, and continues to be, much controversy about the nature, structure, and reality of the self. Consider, for instance, two recent books on the topic, namely, Thomas Metzinger's *Being No One* and Miri Albahari's *Analytical Buddhism: The Two-Tiered Illusion of Self*. Both philosophers endorse a form of scepticism about the self: they both take the self to be non-existent, but whereas Albahari's scepticism draws on classical considerations in Buddhist philosophy, Metzinger's scepticism is primarily motivated by findings in contemporary neuroscience.

What arguments do Metzinger and Albahari provide for their radical claim? Metzinger concedes that most of us do have an experience of being a self, but he argues that it would be a fallacy to infer from the content of our self-experience to the existence of an internal non-physical object. There is no immutable, unchanging soul-substance. Rather, the self is in reality a persistent illusion created by a multitude of interrelated cognitive modules in the brain. Our self-experience, our feeling of being a conscious self, is never truthful; it merely testifies to the fact that we tend to confuse a representational construct with a really existing entity (Metzinger 2003: 370, 385, 390).

Albahari defines the self as an identical, unchanging principle of identity. It is the owner of experiences, thoughts, and feelings. This is also why she considers it to be different from and independent of the multitude of mental episodes. Most of us might have an experience of being such a self, but just like Metzinger, Albahari insists on the difference between phenomenology and metaphysics. We have to distinguish between experience and reality. Our sense of self doesn't guarantee the existence of such a self. Rather than the sense of self being grounded in an actual self, which purports to be the originator of our experiences, the sense of self is for Albahari produced and shaped by the multitude of thoughts, feelings, and sensations. But why is it then an illusion? Because of the mismatch between appearance and reality. The self appears to possess a property, namely, ontological independence, which in reality it lacks (Albahari 2006: 72).

A striking feature of Metzinger's and Albahari's ontological anti-realism about the self is that they both endorse a rather reified notion of selfhood. They both claim that the self, if it exists, must be an unchanging and ontologically independent entity. They both deny the existence of such an entity, and therefore argue that there is no self. But this conclusion would only be warranted if their definition of the self were the only one available, and that is hardly the case. In fact, the notion of the self they employ and criticize is a notion that by and large has been abandoned by most philosophers steeped in twentieth-century German and French philosophy, as well as by most of the empirical researchers who currently investigate the development, structure, function, and pathology of the self. Although one might perhaps initially assume that only philosophers would be interested in investigating the nature and existence of something as elusive as the self, this assumption is clearly mistaken. The topic of the self is intensively discussed in various scientific disciplines such as cognitive science, developmental psychology, sociology, neuropsychology, and psychiatry. In recent years, there has even been a marked increase of interest in the topic.

Consider, for instance, in the case of psychology, a very influential article from 1993 in which Ulric Neisser distinguishes five different notions of the self: the *ecological self*, the *interpersonal self*, the *conceptual self*, the *temporally extended self*, and the *private self*.[1] For Neisser, the most fundamental and primitive self is the one that, with reference to Gibson, he calls the ecological self (Neisser 1993). It denotes the individual as an active explorer of the environment, and involves a sense of oneself as a differentiated, environmentally situated, and agentive entity. When and how are we conscious of this self? For Neisser, every perception involves information about the relation between perceiver and environment. In every perception there is a co-perception of self and environment. As an illustration of this, consider the early reaching behaviour of infants. An infant as young as a few weeks old can discriminate between objects that are within his reach and objects that are just beyond his reach. The infant is far less inclined to reach out for an object that is just beyond his reach. But this discriminatory ability does not merely presuppose that the infant perceives where the object is, it also requires the infant to perceive where the object is vis-à-vis himself. This should not be understood in the sense that the infant already possesses an explicit self-representation, but, as has been claimed, the infant must be able to perceive a distinctive kind of 'affordance' involving self-specifying informa- tion. Thus, even very young infants are sensitive to information that specifies the ecological self. They respond to the 'optical flow', discriminate between themselves and other objects, and easily distinguish their own actions and their immediate consequences from events of other kinds. They experience themselves, where they are, how they are moving, what they are doing, and whether a given action is their own or not. These achievements have already appeared in the first weeks and months of life, and testify, according to Neisser, to the existence of a primitive but basic form of self-experience (Neisser 1993: 4).

---

[1] It is important to notice that Neisser explicitly distances himself from a traditional notion of an inner self. As he makes clear, the five selves he is referring to are not homunculi of any sort. The self, on his account, is not a special inner part of the person (or of the brain), but rather the whole person considered from a particular point of view (Neisser 1993: 3–4).

If we move on to emotion research, it has been customary to distinguish primary emotions like happiness, fear, anger, and sadness, and more complex emotions like shame, guilt, and jealousy. The second group of emotions is often classified as self-conscious emotions. There is currently an ongoing debate about how early in development these more complex emotions emerge, just as it is debated what kind of cognitive processing they involve. But there is widespread agreement that a proper analysis of these emotions will require an analysis of self as well. As Campos writes in the introduction to a textbook on the topic, 'One cannot study self-conscious emotions without trying to conceptualize the self and its many levels and its role in the generation of emotions' (Campos 2007, p. xi). According to a widespread view, for instance, the difference between shame and guilt is that shame involves a negative assessment of one's global or total self, whereas guilt implies a negative assessment of a specific action. There is more to be said for and against this proposal, but my point for now is merely that many psychologists would argue that, in order to understand the difference between shame and guilt, we have to employ the notion of self.

In 1913 Karl Jaspers used the notion of *Ichstörungen* (self-disorders) in his account of schizophrenia (Jaspers 1959). There is currently broad consensus that some of the most prominent schizophrenic symptoms involve fundamental changes in one's relationship to one's own thoughts, actions, sensations, and emotions. As the French psychiatrist Minkowski put it, 'The madness...does not originate in disorders of judgement, perception or will, but in a disturbance of the innermost structure of the self' (Minkowski 1997: 114). In the current debate, this approach has been defended by Josef Parnas and Louis Sass. They both claim that various forms of self-disorder, which are already present in the prodromal phase, can be ascribed a pathogenic role and can offer a partial explanation of the subsequent psychotic symptomatology (Sass and Parnas 2003).

To mention a final example, consider the case of Alzheimer's disease. This is a progressive, degenerative brain disorder that results in profound memory loss and changes in behaviour, thinking, and reasoning, as well as a significant decline in overall functioning. But it is also customary to describe the disease in terms of an increasing loss of self. As Seeley and Miller write:

Though once relegated to philosophers and mystics, the structure of the self may soon become mandatory reading for neurology, psychiatry, and neuroscience trainees. For the dementia specialist the need for this evolution is transparent, as shattered selves—of one form or another—remain a daily part of clinical practice. (Seeley and Miller 2005: 160)

One might wonder how Seeley and Miller would react to Metzinger's claim that 'nobody ever *was* or *had* a self' (Metzinger 2003: 1).

To recapitulate the current line of argument: I started out by briefly outlining two philosophical views on the self. Then I exemplified how the self is discussed and analysed in empirical research. It should have become clear that it is often approached and discussed in a way that differs significantly from how it is treated by the two philosophers I started out with, and that most empirical researchers would probably have difficulties accepting the definition and notion of selfhood that Metzinger and Albahari operate with. But what conclusion should we draw? Should we conclude that philosophy has outlived its usefulness when it comes to the study of the self, and that real progress these days happens in the domain of empirical science?

If we reconsider Seeley and Miller's observation, it is obvious that it can be interpreted in two quite different ways. Is the idea that empirical researchers should become familiar with philosophical discussions of the self, since the latter are relevant to empirical research, or is the idea rather that empirical researchers should take on the task of analysing and explaining the self themselves? It is certainly not difficult to find vocal representatives of the latter view. Consider, for instance, the following editorial by Thomas Wakley, a former editor of *The Lancet*:

From the fact that the philosophy of the human mind has been almost wholly uncultivated by those who are best fitted for its pursuit, the study has received a wrong direction, and become a subtle exercise for lawyers and casuists, and abstract reasoners, rather than a useful field of scientific observation. Accordingly, we find the views, even of the most able and clear-headed metaphysicians, coming into frequent collision with the known facts of physiology and pathology. (quoted in Hacking 1995: 221)

The editorial was printed on 25 March 1843. However, Wakley is neither the first nor the last to argue that it would be best not to leave the study of the self and consciousness to philosophers. For a more recent defender of such a view, consider Francis Crick, who in the mid-1990s wrote that 'it is hopeless to try to solve the problems of consciousness by general philosophical arguments; what is needed are suggestions for new experiments that might throw light on these problems' (Crick 1995: 19). Indeed, on Crick's view, 'the study of consciousness is a scientific problem.... There is no justification for the view that only philosophers can deal with it' (Crick 1995: 257–8). Quite the contrary, in fact, since philosophers 'have had such a poor record over the last two thousand years that they would do better to show a certain modesty rather than the lofty superiority that they usually display' (Crick 1995: 258). This is not to say that philosophers cannot contribute, but they must 'learn how to abandon their pet theories when the scientific evidence goes against them or they will only expose themselves to ridicule' (Crick 1995: 258). In short, philosophers are welcome to join the common enterprise, but only as junior partners. Indeed, one suspects that philosophy (of mind) on Crick's view will ultimately turn out to be dispensable. Whatever contribution it can make is propaedeutic and must eventually be replaced by a proper scientific account.

These polemical assertions do raise a fundamental question. What is the right way to conceive of the relationship between philosophical analysis and empirical investigation when it comes to the study of the self? One tempting reply might be that the task left to philosophy is to pose the questions, to which empirical science can then provide the answers. If philosophers want to be taken seriously, they need to formulate hypotheses that empirical science can subsequently corroborate or falsify.

This cannot quite be right, however, if only because the alleged empirical answers are often in urgent need of conceptual clarification. I don't want to deny that it is important to test theoretical hypotheses—though I think the task of transforming theoretical arguments into hypotheses that can be tested in realistic and reliable experiments is one that calls for interdisciplinary collaboration, rather than being something that should simply be left to the philosophers; they will rarely have the required expertise. No, my point is rather that the role of philosophy and theoretical reflection cannot be reduced or limited to this specific task. Philosophy can accomplish much more than that. It can also, for instance, contribute by scrutinizing the consistency and plausibility of those theoretical assumptions that are more or less tacitly at work in empirical science—assumptions that obviously influence not only the interpretation of the empirical findings, but also the very design of the experiments.

When one reads research on the self written by experimentalists, it is obvious that much effort is spent on explaining the experimental setup and on discussing and interpreting the experimental results. Much less time is typically devoted to discussing and clarifying the very notion of selfhood at work. However, a lack of clarity in the concepts used will lead to a lack of clarity in the questions posed, and thus also to a lack of clarity in the design of the experiments supposed to provide an answer to the questions. I consequently think it would be premature to conclude that the empirical exploration of the self can manage without philosophical input and theoretical reflection. Consider, by way of illustration, research on autism.

Although, to the general public, autism spectrum disorder might mainly seem to be associated with social impairments, there is, of course, a long-standing tradition—reflected in the very term 'autism', from the Greek term for the self, *autos*—of also considering it as a disorder of the self and self-understanding. However, if one examines some of the claims that have been made concerning these aspects, one will find rather conflicting views, even by the same authors. It has in turn been claimed that children with autism are mind-blind and unaware of their own mental states (Baron-Cohen 1989), but also that classical autism involves a total focus on the self (Baron-Cohen 2005). It has been argued that people with autism can judge their own inner states only by their actions (Frith and Happé 1999), but also that individuals with autism can report their inner feelings and experiences in great detail (Frith 2003). It has been said that they lack introspection and self-awareness (Frith and Happé 1999), but also that they possess self-knowledge (Frith 2003); that they have appropriate representations of the physical, psychological, and narrative self, but also that autism is characterized by an absent self (Frith 2003).

I find all of this rather confusing, and I think confusion will continue to reign as long as terms such as 'self' and 'self-consciousness' are left undefined and treated as unequivocal and monolithic notions. A rather blatant example of this can be found in a paper by Simon Baron-Cohen from 2005. At the beginning of his contribution, Baron-Cohen writes as follows:

The idea that as a result of neurological factors one might lose aspects of the self is scientifically important, in that it offers the promise of teaching us more about what the self is. In this chapter I do not tackle the thorny question of how to define the self... Rather, I accept that this word refers to something we recognize and instead raise the question: are people with autism trapped—for neurological reasons—to be totally self-focused? (Baron-Cohen 2005: 166)

But does it really make sense to discuss whether autism involves a disturbed focus on the self if one doesn't spend any time discussing and defining the concept of self at play? Perhaps one could object that the notion of the self is so univocal and obvious that it is superfluous to provide a more thematic demarcation and clarification; but that retort is easy to dismiss. As we have already seen, the current discussion of the self is quite diversified, to put it mildly.

This fact, however, has also given rise to a kind of philosophical scepticism that on some readings might be considered even more radical than Metzinger's and Albahari's. Whereas both of these philosophers deny the reality of self, Eric Olson has gone so far as to deny the very existence of a concept of the self, for which reason he finds himself unable to understand claims regarding the existence or non-existence of the self well enough to know whether he would agree or disagree (Olson 1998: 653). Olson would consequently see the existence of a multitude of conflicting definitions of self as indicative of a degenerate debate (Olson 1998: 646). In his view, matters discussed under the heading of 'self' are ultimately so varied that no one can seriously say they are all about the same thing. Thus, there 'is no such idea as the idea of self, and therefore nothing for the "problem of the self" to be a problem about' (Olson 1998: 651).

Interestingly, Olson is not out to deny that there are perfectly legitimate questions and problems bearing on, say, personal identity and diachronic persistence, the semantics of the first-person pronoun, the unity of consciousness, the nature of self-consciousness, the varieties, extent, and limitations of first-person knowledge, etc., and although he concedes that these questions are not completely unrelated to the so-called problems of the self, he would argue that all the problems just listed can be, and should be, stated (and addressed) without employing the term 'self'. Accordingly there is no reason, other than tradition, for continuing to speak of the self.

As has already become evident, however, the self is not merely a topic of interest to (some) philosophers. It is also investigated by many empirical scientists, and it is hard to see the sudden proliferation of empirical work in developmental psychology, social neuroscience, psychiatry, etc. as being predominantly motivated by veneration for the philosophical tradition. Moreover, is it really true that all the listed problems can be solved adequately without referring to the self, and that anybody who speaks about the self, and who is saying something coherent, must in reality be talking about something completely different (Olson 1998: 651)? I am not convinced by these blunt claims, and I am also sceptical of the suggested ban on the term 'self'. If we were to prohibit the use of all concepts that lack widely accepted definitions, philosophy would be much impoverished. Not only do I think an analysis and investigation of the self can be philosophically and scientifically rewarding—and it is to be hoped that the following investigation will be able to substantiate this claim—but I also wouldn't consider the coexistence of different definitions as problematic per se. It might merely reflect the fact that the self is a multidimensional and complex phenomenon. This also seems to be increasingly recognized in autism research. As Klein puts it,

What *is* warranted is that *some* aspects of self-knowledge may be impaired by an autistic disorder while others may be intact. The self...is not a *thing* that submits to all-or-nothing analysis. While aspects of autistic self-knowledge can show impairment, such findings do not warrant general conclusions about 'the self in autism'. (Klein 2010: 178)

The task, of course, is then to specify the aspects that are affected in autism spectrum disorder. Many contributors now focus on specific deficits related to the interpersonal dimension of self. In so far as this dimension is taken to refer to a dimension of self that is constitutively dependent upon others, and to a form of self-experience that is mediated through others, this is precisely where one should expect impairments in individuals with autism spectrum disorder. Such impairments might, for instance, show up in the capacity for joint attention, in the management of strategic self-presentations, in the display of certain self-conscious emotions, and in the possession of a fully developed reflective relationship to oneself.

These are topics that I shall return to in what follows. For now, let me simply point out that if it should turn out to be necessary to distinguish different types of self-experience and different facets of self, it might not only be necessary to integrate various complementary accounts and analyses if we are to do justice to the complexity at hand. Such complexity would also necessitate conceptual clarification and theoretical analysis: it wouldn't make either superfluous.

2

Consciousness, Self-Consciousness, and Selfhood

There is a long tradition in philosophy of claiming that selfhood is socially constructed and self-experience intersubjectively mediated. It is a view that has had many different voices. According to a standard reading, Hegel argued that selfhood is something that can only be achieved within a social context, within a community of minds, and that it has its ground in an intersubjective process of recognition rather than in some immediate form of self-familiarity. In the late nineteenth and early twentieth centuries related views were defended in the United States by Royce and Mead. According to Royce, 'Self-conscious functions are all of them, in their finite, human and primary aspect, social functions, due to habits of social intercourse' (Royce 1898: 196). Mead argued that the self is not something that exists first and then enters into relationship with others; rather, it is better characterized as an eddy in the social current (Mead 1962: 182), and he explicitly defined self-consciousness as a question of becoming 'an object to one's self in virtue of one's social relations to other individuals' (Mead 1962: 172).

Related ideas can also be found in German and French post-war thought, where it has been claimed—partly as a showdown with Husserlian phenomenology—that subjectivity, rather than being a given, something innate and fundamental, is a cultural and linguistic construction. That is, subjectivity was considered the result of a discursive or narrative praxis; it was something that could only be acquired by participating in a linguistic community (see Benveniste 1966: 258–66). Partly playing on the etymological roots of the term 'subject' (one is always subject to, or the subject of, something), Foucault claimed that people come to relate to themselves as selves, come to engage in practices of self-evaluation and self-regulation, within contexts of domination and subordination. Forming subjects and subjecting them to authority are, on his view, two sides of the same coin. He writes, 'the subject who is constituted as subject—who is "subjected"—is he who obeys' (Foucault 1990: 85). On such an account, subjectivity and individuality are not rooted in some free and spontaneous interiority. Rather, we are dealing with ideological categories produced in a system of social organization. By forcing and fooling us to think of ourselves in terms that might support moral categories such as guilt and responsibility, the system will be better able to control us. An example found in Althusser illustrates this idea well.

When a policeman calls out to someone in the street, 'the hailed individual will turn round', and, as Althusser continues, 'By this mere one-hundred-and-eighty-degree physical conversion, he becomes a *subject*' (Althusser 1971: 174).

Without denying that there are significant differences between these various proposals, I think it is fair to say that they are all united in their rejection of the idea that subjectivity and selfhood (and for reasons that will become apparent in the following, I shall be using the two notions interchangeably) are innate and automatic. Being a self is an achievement rather than a given, and therefore also something that one can fail at. Selves are not born, but arise in a process of social experience and interchange. Indeed, many would consider the self a construction, something more a matter of politics and culture than of science and nature.

My aim in Part I is not to dispute that there are important insights to be found in such claims. However, in so far as they are presented as accounts of the self *tout court*, rather than as accounts of certain dimensions or aspects of self, I find all of them unpersuasive. I think there is a basic yet crucial dimension of the self that they all fail to consider, let alone explain. In the following, I shall criticize the claim that the self is utterly socio-cultural in origin, that is, nothing but a social construct, and argue against social reductionism by defending a more minimalist experience-based notion of selfhood that I consider a necessary precondition for any socially constructed self. This more basic notion is one with a venerable ancestry. It has been defended by various figures in the phenomenological tradition, including Sartre and Husserl.

Consider the following quotations from Sartre's *L'Être et le néant*—three quotations that conjointly articulate a view that is widespread among phenomenologists, and which I endorse:

It is not reflection which reveals the consciousness reflected-on to itself. Quite the contrary, it is the non-reflective consciousness which renders the reflection possible; there is a pre-reflective cogito which is the condition of the Cartesian cogito. (Sartre 2003: 9)

This self-consciousness we ought to consider not as a new consciousness, but as *the only mode of existence which is possible for a consciousness of something*. (Sartre 2003: 10)

[P]re-reflective consciousness is self-consciousness. It is this same notion of *self* which must be studied, for it defines the very being of consciousness. (Sartre 2003: 100)

What is Sartre saying here? First of all, on his view, an experience does not simply exist, it exists in such a way that it is implicitly self-given, or, as Sartre puts it, it is 'for itself'. This self-givenness of experience is not simply a quality added to the experience, a mere varnish; rather, for Sartre the very *mode of being* of intentional consciousness is to be *for-itself* (*pour-soi*), that is, self-conscious (Sartre 2003: 10). Furthermore, Sartre is quite explicit in emphasizing that the self-consciousness in question is *not* a new consciousness. It is not something added to the experience, an additional experiential state, but rather an intrinsic feature of the experience.[1] When

---

[1] Let me emphasize that the choice of the term 'intrinsic' is merely meant to emphasize the difference between this view and a higher-order or reflection-based account of self-consciousness, where

speaking of self-consciousness as a permanent feature of consciousness, Sartre is consequently not referring to what is called reflective self-consciousness. Reflection (or higher-order representation) is the process whereby consciousness directs its intentional aim at itself, thereby taking itself as its own object. By contrast, Sartre considers the self-consciousness in question to be pre-reflective. It is not an addendum to, but a constitutive moment of, the original intentional experience. To rephrase, on his account, consciousness has two different modes of givenness: a pre-reflective and a reflective. The first has priority since it can prevail independently of the latter, whereas reflective self-consciousness always presupposes pre-reflective self-consciousness.

In a subsequent move, Sartre then argues that consciousness, precisely because of its ubiquitous pre-reflective self-consciousness, must be said to possess a basic dimension of selfhood, which Sartre terms *ipseity* (from the Latin term for self, *ipse*) (Sartre 2003: 126). When Sartre speaks of the self, he is consequently referring to something very basic, something characterizing (phenomenal) consciousness as such. Although it is something I can fail to articulate, it is not something I can fail to be.

At the beginning of the *Bernauer Manuskripte über das Zeitbewusstsein*, Husserl remarks that consciousness exists, it exists as a stream, and it appears to itself as a stream. But how the stream of consciousness is capable of being conscious of itself, how it is possible and comprehensible that the very being of the stream is a form of self-consciousness, is, he says, the enduring question (Husserl 2001: 44, 46). Husserl's detailed investigation of time-consciousness was to a large extent motivated by his interest in answering this question, and throughout his writings he argues that self-consciousness, rather than being something that only occurs during exceptional circumstances, namely, whenever we pay attention to our conscious life, is a feature characterizing the experiential dimension as such, no matter what worldly entities we might otherwise be intentionally directed at (Husserl 1959: 189, 412; 1973b: 316). In Husserl's words, 'every experience is "consciousness," and consciousness is consciousness *of*... But every experience is *itself experienced* (*erlebt*), and *to that extent* also "conscious" (*bewußt*)' (Husserl 1966a: 291; translation slightly modified). Husserl uses a variety of terms to characterize this pre-reflective self-consciousness, but the most frequent ones are 'inner consciousness', *Urbewußtsein*, or 'impressional consciousness' (see Zahavi 1999). Ultimately, Husserl would emphasize the ubiquitous presence of self-consciousness in experiential life, and on repeated occasions equate (1) the first-personal character of consciousness, (2) a primitive form of self-consciousness, and (3) a certain basic form of selfhood. As he writes in a research

---

self-consciousness is conceived in terms of a relation between two mental states. The term isn't meant to indicate that we are dealing with a feature that our experiences possess in complete independence of everything else. To talk of self-consciousness as an intrinsic feature of experience is not to deny that the (self-conscious) experience in question is also intentional and world-directed.

manuscript dating from 1922, 'The consciousness in which I am conscious of myself (*meiner*) is my consciousness, and my consciousness of myself and I myself are concretely considered identical. To be a subject is to be in the mode of being aware of oneself' (Husserl 1973b: 151).[2]

As might start to become clear, the account I wish to articulate and defend is one that argues for a very tight connection between experiential selfhood and self-consciousness. However, before I can directly address the former, more needs to be said about the latter, and especially about the relationship between self-consciousness and consciousness.

One persisting difficulty in discussing these matters is that the notion of 'self-consciousness' (and 'self-awareness') is notoriously ambiguous.[3] In everyday life, self-consciousness is often thought to be a matter of a person thinking about herself. But even that apparently simple definition can cover a variety of very different cognitive accomplishments. Consider, for instance, the difference between intro-spectively scrutinizing one's occurrent experience, thinking about one's past per-formance, taking pride in one's ability to fulfil a chosen social role, or anxiously appraising how others perceive one. If one ventures into the theoretical debate, the complexity only multiplies, since the philosophical, psychological, psychiatric, and neuroscientific literature is filled with competing, conflicting, and complementary definitions.

Let me just mention here a few important proposals:

- In developmental and social psychology, prominent theories understand self-consciousness as an explicit act of recognizing oneself as an embodied individ-ual. Gallup has, for example, argued that the so-called mirror-recognition task is the decisive test for self-consciousness (Gallup 1977).
- In psychopathology, it has occasionally been argued that self-awareness requires one to be in possession of a theory of mind that one then applies to oneself. Baron-Cohen, and Frith and Happé, have, for instance, all argued that one can test the presence of self-awareness in people with autism by using classical theory of mind tasks, such as the false-belief task or the appearance–reality task (Baron-Cohen 1989: 581, 591; Frith and Happé 1999: 1, 5).
- In philosophy, it has sometimes been argued that self-consciousness requires the ability to think of oneself *as* oneself. That is, one must be able to conceptualize the distinction between self and non-self (Baker 2000: 67–8). Likewise, some have claimed that for a creature to be self-conscious it is not sufficient that the creature in question is able to self-ascribe experiences on an individual basis without recognizing the identity of that to which the experiences are ascribed.

---

[2] Related claims can also be found in other phenomenologists. See, for instance, Stein (2000: 17, 100), Merleau-Ponty (2012: 424, 450), and Henry (1963: 581–5). For a more extensive discussion, see Zahavi (1999).

[3] In the following, I shall be using the two concepts synonymously.

Rather, the creature must be capable of thinking of the self-ascribed experiences as belonging to one and the same self (Cassam 1997).

While recognizing that there are kernels of truth in all these definitions—they all capture various important aspects of the phenomenon—I think we need to acknowledge the existence of a logically and ontogenetically more primitive form of self-consciousness. This would be a form of self-consciousness that precedes the mastery of language and the ability to form full-blown rational judgements and propositional attitudes. In various previous publications, I have defended what might be considered a minimalist definition of self-consciousness according to which phenomenal consciousness as such entails a thin or minimal form of self-consciousness (Zahavi 1999, 2005). According to this view, self-consciousness is not something that only comes about the moment one scrutinizes one's experiences attentively, let alone something that only comes about the moment one recognizes one's own mirror image, refers to oneself using the first-person pronoun, or is in possession of identifying knowledge of one's own character traits. Rather, self-consciousness is a many-layered phenomenon. It comes in many forms and degrees, and whereas one of the most advanced forms might involve contemplating one's life as a whole and reflecting on the kind of person one is and on the values one holds dear, the most primitive form of self-consciousness is a question of the ongoing first-personal manifestation of one's own experiential life. This kind of self-consciousness is not something unique to, or distinctive of, adult human beings, but something all phenomenally conscious creatures possess.

Such an idea is by no means unique to phenomenology. A related view has been defended by Flanagan, for instance, who not only argues that consciousness involves self-consciousness in the weak sense that there is something it is like for the subject to have the experience, but who has also spoken of the low-level self-consciousness involved in experiencing my experiences as mine (Flanagan 1992: 194). Arguing along somewhat similar lines, Uriah Kriegel has more recently claimed that we should distinguish two types of self-consciousness, namely, *transitive* and *intransitive* self-consciousness. Whereas transitive self-consciousness designates the case where a subject is self-conscious of her thought that *p* (or of her perception of *x*), intransitive self-consciousness can be captured by saying that the subject is self-consciously thinking that *p* (or perceiving *x*). What is the difference between these two types of self-consciousness? Kriegel initially lists four differences, and claims that whereas the first type is introspective, rare, voluntary, and effortful, the second is none of these. However, he then also points to another crucial difference: whereas transitive self-consciousness is a second-order state that is numerically distinct from its object, namely, the respective first-order state, intransitive self-consciousness is a property of the occurring first-order state (Kriegel 2003a: 104–5). Moreover, in so far as there would not be anything it is like for a subject to be in a mental state she is unaware of being in, intransitive self-consciousness must be considered a necessary condition for phenomenal consciousness (Kriegel 2003a: 106).

The claim that there is a tight link between phenomenal consciousness and self-consciousness is in fact altogether more widespread than one might expect. It is widely shared not only by phenomenologists such as Sartre and Husserl and self-representationalists like Kriegel, but also by higher-order representationalists. For the latter, the difference between conscious and non-conscious mental states rests upon the presence or absence of a relevant meta-mental state. One way to illustrate the guiding idea of this approach is to compare consciousness to a spotlight. Some mental states are illuminated; others do their work in the dark. What makes a mental state conscious (illuminated) is the fact that it is taken as an object by a relevant higher-order state. It is the occurrence of the higher-order representation that makes us conscious of the first-order mental state. In short, a conscious state is a state we are conscious of (Rosenthal 1997: 739). Higher-order theories have consequently typically explained phenomenal consciousness in terms of the mind's self-directedness, that is, in terms of some kind of self-consciousness. As Carruthers puts it, 'such self-awareness is a conceptually necessary condition for an organism to be a subject of phenomenal feelings, or for there to be anything that its experiences are like' (Carruthers 1996a: 152; compare Carruthers 1996a: 154).

There are similarities as well as important differences between higher-order representationalism, self-representationalism, and the phenomenological account of pre-reflective self-consciousness. One might, in short, share the view that there is a close link between phenomenal consciousness and self-consciousness and still disagree about the nature of the link. Whereas higher-order representationalists view the self-consciousness in question as one that obtains between two distinct non-conscious mental states, where the meta-state takes the first-order state as its intentional object, the phenomenologists insist that the relevant kind of self-consciousness is one that is integral and intrinsic to the mental state in question. Kriegel's distinction between transitive and intransitive self-consciousness consequently bears an obvious resemblance to the phenomenological distinction between reflective and pre-reflective self-consciousness (Zahavi 2004a). However, there is also an important difference in that Kriegel ultimately persists in taking self-consciousness (even in its intransitive form) as a species of object-consciousness. As Kriegel argues, to say that a subject has a mental state self-consciously is to say that the subject is implicitly or peripherally aware of her having the state, or of the state being her own. Thus, for him the distinction between intransitive and transitive self-consciousness can also be cashed out by means of the distinction between focal and peripheral awareness. We are confronted with transitive self-consciousness when the subject is focally aware of being in a specific mental state, whereas we are dealing with intransitive self-consciousness when the subject is only peripherally aware of being in the mental state (Kriegel 2004). By arguing in this manner, Kriegel accepts Rosenthal's Transitivity Principle, that is, the principle that a 'state's being conscious involves one's being noninferentially conscious of that state' (Rosenthal 2002: 409).

Although Kriegel's self-representationalism is clearly an attempt to carve out a same-order alternative to various forms of higher-order representationalism, we should consequently not overlook the presence of some striking similarities (see Kriegel 2003b: 486–9). Both positions argue that conscious states involve two representational contents. In the case of a conscious perception of a tone, there is an outward-directed first-order content (that takes the tone as its object), and an inward-directed second-order content (that takes the perception as its object), and their main disagreement is over the question whether there are two distinct mental states, each with its own representational content, or only one mental state with a twofold representational content, which would be Kriegel's view (2003b). In short, both types of theory argue that for a state to be conscious means for it to be represented, and they only differ in whether it is represented by itself or by another state.

A conscious state is experiential and to that extent something that factors in our awareness. If it weren't, it might be a state *of* or *in* the subject, but it would be like nothing *for* the subject. By saying that a state is phenomenally conscious one is precisely committing oneself to the idea that its presence or absence makes a distinctive difference to how it is subjectively. The question, though, is whether we only have the choice between the two following options: either our mental states are given as objects or they are non-conscious. According to phenomenological orthodoxy, my experiences are not given as objects for me pre-reflectively. In short, I do not occupy the position or perspective of an observer, spectator, or in(tro)spector of these experiences. That something 'is *experienced*, and is in this sense conscious, does not and cannot mean that this is the *object* of an act of consciousness, in the sense that a perception, a presentation or a judgement is directed upon it' (Husserl 1984a: 165 [273]). In pre-reflective or non-observational self-consciousness, experience is given, not as an object, but precisely as subjectively lived through. On this view, my intentional experience is lived through (*erlebt*), but it does not appear in an objectified manner; it is neither seen nor heard nor thought about (Husserl 1984a: 399; Sartre 1957: 44–5). The more general claim that has been made is that object-consciousness necessarily entails an epistemic divide between that which appears and that to whom it appears, between the object and the subject of experience, and that this is why object-consciousness (and the transitivity principle) might be singularly unsuited as a model for *self*-consciousness proper (Zahavi 1999; Legrand 2011: 207).[4]

---

[4] Kriegel has explicitly considered and rejected the notion of a non-objectifying self-consciousness. What motivates him to make this move? In part his attempt to offer an informative reductive account. He makes the reasonable claim that for methodological reasons one should abstain from adopting a primitivist account of anything at the outset of inquiry, though, of course, one might eventually be forced to embrace it, if all plausible alternatives fail (Kriegel 2009: 102). Ultimately he rejects the view according to which the subjective character of experience is a kind of *sui generis* intrinsic glow (Kriegel 2009: 102), and offers us his neo-Brentanian self-representationalism instead. One should note, however, that Kriegel himself admits

One should be mindful of the differences between higher-order representational-ism, self-representationalism, and the phenomenological account of pre-reflective self-consciousness—differences that I have discussed *in extenso* elsewhere (Zahavi 1999, 2004a, 2005)—but important as these differences might be in other contexts, they do not need to concern us here. What is important for the present purpose is rather the shared idea that a 'mental state M of a subject S is conscious at *t* if and only if there is something it is like for S to be in M at *t*' (Janzen 2008: 34), and that this entails that self-consciousness is a constitutive feature of phenomenal consciousness. But what does all of this have to do with subjectivity and selfhood? Quite a lot, in fact.

As Galen Strawson has argued, if we wish to understand what it means to be a self, we should look at self-experience, since self-experience is what gives rise to the question in the first place by giving us a vivid sense that there is something like a self (Strawson 2000: 40). In his *Selves: An Essay in Revisionary Metaphysics* Strawson develops this idea further and argues for the following necessary condition for selfhood: If there is such a thing as a self, then it must have properties of the kind that feature in any genuine form of self-experience. In short, nothing can count as a self unless it possesses such properties. In addition, he argues for the following sufficient condition for selfhood: If there is an entity that has the properties that feature in any genuine form of self-experience, then such an entity is a self. In short, nothing can fail to count as a self if it possesses such properties. Accepting both conditions will then allow for a rejection of the following two metaphysical objec-tions: (1) Although there are entities that have the properties attributed in self-experience, it doesn't follow that they are selves, or that selves exist; (2) Although there might be selves, we have no understanding of their fundamental nature (Strawson 2009: 56–7).

The phenomenologists would concur with Strawson's necessary and sufficient condition. In fact, one finds a very similar line of reasoning in *Ideen II*, where Husserl argues that reflection on a single experience will reveal the nature of the pure ego (see also Chapter 6.2), and that it is absurd to claim that this ego doesn't really exist or that it is ultimately quite different from what it is revealed as (Husserl 1952: 104). But ultimately they would go one step further by claiming that when it comes to this most

that self-representation per se is insufficient for subjectivity. The existence of self-referring sentences and the possibility of functionally equivalent zombies might constitute relevant counter-examples. To avoid these objections, Kriegel ends up opting for the view that only non-derivative, specific, essential self-representation is sufficient for consciousness (Kriegel 2009: 162). When articulating the requirements that must be met for the self-representation to be sufficiently specific and essential, he concedes that the subject's epistemic relations to her conscious states are special (Kriegel 2009: 106), and that the relationship between the inner awareness and what it is aware of is far more intimate than the standard relationship between a representation and what it represents (Kriegel 2009: 107–8). By having to introduce all these qualifications to make the model work, Kriegel admits that the relevant type of self-representation constitutes a very unusual form of object-awareness. But at this point, one might wonder whether the difference between a highly unusual form of object-awareness and a non-objectifying form of awareness is all that substantial.

basic form of self, it is constituted in and through self-experience, that is, that the phenomenology of that kind of self just is the metaphysics of that kind of self.[5]

The phenomenological proposal can be seen as occupying a middle position between two opposing views. According to the first view, the self is some kind of unchanging soul-substance that is distinct from and ontologically independent of the worldly objects and conscious episodes it is directed at and of which it is the subject. According to the second view, there is nothing to consciousness apart from a manifold or bundle of changing experiences. There are experiences and perceptions, but no experiencer or perceiver. A third option is available, however, the moment one realizes that an understanding of what it means to be a self calls for an examination of the structure of experience, and vice versa. Thus, the self currently under consideration—and let us simply call it *the experiential self*—is not a separately existing entity—it is not something that exists independently of, in separation from, or in opposition to the stream of consciousness—but neither is it simply reducible to a specific experience or (sub)set of experiences; nor is it, for that matter, a mere social construct that evolves through time. Rather, it is taken to be an integral part of our conscious life. More precisely, the claim is that the (minimal or core) self possesses experiential reality and that it can be identified with the ubiquitous first-personal character of the experiential phenomena. Similar ideas have explicitly been defended by the Danish philosopher Erich Klawonn (1991) and by the French phenomenologist Michel Henry, who states that the most basic form of selfhood is the one constituted by the very self-manifestation of experience (Henry 1963: 581; 1965: 53).

To unpack this guiding idea, suppose that you first see a green apple and then see a yellow lemon. Your visual perception of the yellow lemon is then succeeded by a recollection of the yellow lemon. How should we describe the phenomenal complexity? One rather natural way to do so is as follows: First, we have an intentional act of a specific type (a perception) which is directed at a specific object (an apple). Then we retain the intentional act-type (the perception), but replace the apple with another object (a lemon). In a final step, we replace the perception with another act-type (a recollection) while retaining the second object. By going through these variations, we succeed in establishing that an investigation of our experiential life shouldn't merely focus on the various intentional objects we can be directed at, but that it also has to consider the different act-types or intentional attitudes we can adopt. This is all trivial. But then consider the following question. If we compare the initial situation where we perceived a green apple with the final situation where we recollected a

---

[5] Let me emphasize that when I talk here and later about the metaphysics of the self, I am referring to the question regarding the existence and reality of selfhood. I am not concerned with the question of what kind of 'stuff' a self might ultimately be made of, and I am not suggesting that a phenomenological investigation of the self can per se resolve the latter question.

yellow lemon, there has been a change of both the object and the type of intentionality. Does such a change leave nothing unchanged in the experiential flow? No, it doesn't. Not only is the first experience retained by the last experience, but there is also something that the different experiences, whatever their type, whatever their object, have in common. For every possible experience we have, each of us can say: whatever it is like for me to have this experience, it is *for me* that it is like that to have it. What-it-is-like-ness is properly speaking what-it-is-like-*for-me*-ness. Although I live through various different experiences, there is consequently something experiential that remains the same, namely, their first-personal character. All the different experiences are characterized by a dimension of *mineness*, or *for-me-ness*, and we should distinguish the plurality of changing experiences from their persisting *dative of manifestation*.

Related ideas can also be found in contemporary analytic philosophy of mind. According to Levine, there are three features that are distinctive of mental phenomena: rationality, intentionality, and consciousness (or experience) (Levine 2001: 4). When analysing the latter, however, we need to realize that there is more to it than its qualitative character, that is, the fact that the experience is painful or pleasurable. Rather, we also need to bear in mind that the experience in question is like something for me, and that conscious experience consequently involves an experiential perspective or point of view (Levine 2001: 7). Along very similar lines, Kriegel has argued that phenomenal character involves both qualitative character, for example, the bluish component, and subjective character, that is, the for-me component (Kriegel 2009: 8). Kriegel further describes the subjective character as that which remains invariant across all phenomenal characters, and argues that a phenomenally conscious state's qualitative character is what makes it the phenomenally conscious state it is, while its subjective character is what makes it a phenomenally conscious state at all (Kriegel 2009: 2, 58).

Neither Levine nor Kriegel is particularly concerned with the relation between subjectivity and selfhood; rather, for both the crucial question is whether or not subjectivity can be naturalized. As Levine asks at the beginning of *Purple Haze* (thereby pretty much repeating a question posed by Brentano in his *Psychologie vom empirischen Standpunkte*): do the 'features that distinguish minds from everything else in nature mark a fundamental division between the natural, or the physical, and the non-natural, or the immaterial? Are we, and the phenomena that constitute our mental lives, an integral part of the natural, physical world, or not?' (Levine 2001: 4). For Levine, subjectivity involves a special first-person kind of access to the contents of conscious experience, and he explicitly argues that part of the reason why subjectivity, on his view, continues to elude explanation (particularly in physical or non-mental terms) is its *self-intimating* character (Levine 2001: 24, 109). A satisfying account of consciousness should respect and acknowledge this feature. It must take the first-personal or subjective character of consciousness seriously, since an utterly essential feature of consciousness is the way in which it is experienced by the subject.[6] As Shoemaker once put it,

it is essential to a philosophical understanding of the mental that we appreciate that there *is* a first person perspective on it, a distinctive way mental states present themselves to the subjects whose states they are, and that an essential part of the philosophical task is to give an account of mind which makes intelligible the perspective mental subjects have on their own mental lives. (Shoemaker 1996: 157)

As fascinating as the question concerning the naturalizability of subjectivity might be, this is not a question I shall address in what follows (see, however, Zahavi 2004b, 2010b). But by arguing for the link between phenomenal consciousness, subjectivity of experience, for-me-ness, and some form of self-experience, the positions of Levine and Kriegel are very akin to my own.

Recently, however, various authors have criticized the proposal that there should be some unique phenomenal feature that is present in all experiences belonging to the same subject and thereby marking them out as mine and mine alone. One alleged proponent of such a view is Hopkins, who writes of

my selfbeing, my consciousness and feeling of myself, that taste of myself, of *I* and *me* above and in all things, which is more distinctive than the taste of ale or alum, more distinctive than the smell of walnutleaf or camphor, and is incommunicable by any means to another man. (Hopkins 1959: 123)

In rejecting Hopkins's description as being phenomenologically unconvincing since it just isn't plausible to claim that each and every one of my experiences possesses the same phenomenal property, a stamp or label or I-qualia that clearly and unequivocally identifies them as mine (Dainton 2004: 380; 2008: 150; compare Strawson 2009: 184; Bayne 2010: 286; Bermudez 2011: 162, 165). Dainton also takes himself to be rejecting my own proposal, namely, that experiences are characterized by mineness, or for-me-ness (Dainton 2008: 242).

One way to understand Dainton's criticism is by seeing it as insisting on the need for a distinction. One might very well accept the claim that every experience by conceptual and metaphysical necessity presupposes a subject of experience, while denying that the self itself is in any way experientially given. Versions of such a view can be found in Kant, and have more recently been defended by both Searle and Jesse Prinz.

According to Searle, the self is not a separate and distinct entity but rather a formal feature of the conscious field. Searle claims that we misdescribe the conscious field if we think of it as a field constituted only by its contents and their arrangements. The

---

[6] It is important not to conflate a claim concerning the presence of this asymmetry with related but stronger claims concerning infallibility (if x believes that he is φing, then he is in fact φing) or incorrigibility (if x believes that he is φing, then that cannot be shown by others to be mistaken).

contents require a principle of unity, but that principle, namely, the self, is not a separate thing or entity. However, Searle then also insists that the postulation of a self is like the postulation of a point of view in visual perception. Just as we cannot make sense of our perceptions unless we suppose that they occur from a point of view, even though the point of view is not itself perceived, we cannot, according to Searle, make sense of our conscious experiences, or have meaningfully structured experiences, unless we suppose that they occur to a self, even though that self is not consciously experienced. The self is not the object of consciousness, nor is it part of the content of consciousness. Indeed, according to Searle, we have no experience of the self at all, but since all (non-pathological) consciousness has to be possessed by a self, we can infer that it must exist (Searle 2005: 16–18). One way to understand Searle's argument is consequently to see him distinguishing the question whether an experience is necessarily had by a self from the question whether the self necessarily figures in experience. Whereas Searle denies the latter, he affirms the former, thereby taking ownership of experience to be a non-experiential and merely metaphysical relation rather than something experiential or phenomenological.

Arguing along somewhat similar lines, Jesse Prinz denies that there is a phenomenal I. Importantly, he is not denying the existence of a phenomenal *me*. The self can be the object of conscious experience, but he denies that it is phenomenally present qua subject of experience. Likewise, he doesn't deny that we can form judgements about ownership or that there may be experiences on the basis of which we infer ownership, but there is, on his view, no experience of ownership, there is no mineness of experience (Prinz 2012: 140). In arguing for this view, Prinz asks us to focus on the actual qualities that make up a concrete experience, and then suggests that there are three options: The first possibility is to claim that among these experiential qualities there is a specific item that we can label 'the I'. If we reject this proposal, as we should, we are left with two further possibilities that both have a distinctly Humean flavour to them. We might maintain that there is an I-qualia but then argue that it is reducible to qualia of other kinds, that is, that it is nothing above and beyond the qualities of perception, sensation, and emotion. The final possibility, which is the one that Prinz favours, is to opt for eliminativism and simply reject that there is any I-qualia at all (Prinz 2012: 123–4). Interestingly, Prinz's eliminativism should not be taken as a defence of an ontological anti-realism about the self. He is not arguing that consciousness is selfless. Rather, consciousness is, as he puts it, 'thoroughly permeated by the self' (Prinz 2012: 149). We always experience the world from a perspective or point of view. Who we are—our goals, interests, and histories—very much filters and constrains what we experience. Thus, the self might be said to be present, not as an item of experience, but as a kind of constraint (Prinz 2012: 149).

The problem with these various criticisms, however, is that they all fail to exhaust the available options. They all fail to realize that the self can be given, can be real and possess experiential reality, even if it does not appear as an object of, or item in, experience. The experiential self, that is, experiential subjectivity, doesn't denote an experiential item or object, but rather denotes the very first-personal mode of experiencing. More specifically, and contrary to what seems to be assumed by the critics, the mineness of experience is not some specific feeling or determinate quale. It is not a quality or datum of experience on a par with, say, the scent of crushed mint leaves or the taste of chocolate (which is also why one shouldn't conflate my proposal with that of Hopkins). In fact, the for-me-ness, or mineness, doesn't refer to a specific experiential content, to a specific *what*; nor does it refer to the diachronic or synchronic sum of such content, or to some other relation that might obtain between the contents in question. Rather, the mineness refers to the distinct manner, or *how*, of experiencing. It refers to the first-personal presence of all my experiential content; it refers to the experiential perspectivalness of phenomenal consciousness. It refers to the fact that the experiences I am living through present themselves differently (but not necessarily better) to me than to anybody else. When I have experiences, I, so to speak, have them minely. Their mineness is, to use an advantageous formulation by Mark Rowlands, an adverbial modification of the act rather than a property of the object of that act (Rowlands 2013). To deny that such a feature is present in our experiential life, to deny the for-me-ness, or mineness, of experience, is to fail to recognize an essential constitutive aspect of experience. It is to ignore the subjectivity of experience. It would amount to the claim that my own mind is either not given to me at all (I would be mind- or self-blind) or present to me in exactly the same way as the minds of others.[7]

Perhaps the following thought experiment might make the guiding idea somewhat clearer. Imagine two perfect twins, Mick and Mack, who are type-identical when it comes to their physical and psychological properties. Currently both of them are gazing at a white wall. In terms of content, the two streams of consciousness are type-identical. From a third-person perspective, there is no relevant qualitative difference between the two. But consider what happens the moment we leave the third-person perspective behind and instead adopt the first-person perspective. Let us assume that I am Mick. Although my mental and physical characteristics continue to be type-identical with those of Mack, there would be, for me, a crucial difference between our respective tokens of experience, a difference that would prevent any kind of conflation. What might that difference consist in? It obviously has to do with a difference in givenness. Only my tokens of experience are given first-personally to me, which is precisely what makes them mine, whereas the type-identical experiences of Mack are not given first-personally to me at all, and therefore not part of my experiential life. Given that I could come to have experiences of the very same kind as somebody else without becoming the other, just as

---

[7] As I am using the term 'self-blindness', it is not supposed to contrast with self-intimation, if self-intimation amounts to the claim that a subject who is in a phenomenal state automatically also believes that she is in that state (compare Byrne 2012: 166). Whereas I don't think you can be in a phenomenal state without that state necessarily being like something for you, I do think this can take place without necessarily giving rise to associated beliefs.

somebody else could have experiences of exactly the same type as I without being me, it seems natural to conclude that what most fundamentally distinguishes my experiential life from the experiential life of others is not the specific content of experience, but rather the for-me-ness, or how, of experiencing. In other words, and to repeat a point made earlier (for instance, in the lemon–apple example), if we want to do justice to the phenomenal character of our experiential life, it is not sufficient merely to describe the experienced object and the intentional act-type; we shouldn't overlook the first-personal character of experience. The latter amounts to a distinct but formal kind of experiential individuation. This, of course, is why (*pace* various critics) I think that the very subjectivity of experience, its first-personal character, although being quite formal, amounts to a kind of self. In fact, one virtue of the thought experiment is that it should make quite vivid precisely which aspect of consciousness the experiential notion of self is trying to target. It precisely targets that which distinguishes Mick and Mack, and is not concerned with issues like personality, character, preferences, and history.

But wait a second, the critics might object. It remains quite unclear how this first-personal character can serve as a principle of individuation, since, according to your own proposal, it is supposed to characterize all experiences, whether your own or those of others. How can something that all experiencing beings possess be what distinguishes and differentiates you from all others? If everybody's experiential life is characterized by for-me-ness, how can the fact that this also holds true for your own experiential life tell you anything informative about yourself? Have we not ended up in a position where the notion of self is so formal that, to quote Bernard Williams, there 'is absolutely nothing left to distinguish any Cartesian "I" from any other' and where it 'is impossible to see any more what would be subtracted from the universe by the removal of *me*'(Williams 1973: 42)? It is consequently doubtful whether the thought experiment succeeds in showing anything over and above the triviality that Mick and Mack are numerically distinct and consequently non-identical.

Let us consider a variation of the example. Imagine that Mick and Mack fall into deep dreamless sleep. When considered in this state—in a situation where they lack any kind of phenomenal consciousness—the difference between them is like the difference between two qualitatively identical but numerically distinct drops of water. Then Mick and Mack wake up. They now each have an ongoing perceptual experience of the same white wall. Will it still be appropriate to describe the difference between Mick's and Mack's experiential lives as a mere distinction between two numerically distinct but qualitatively identical tokens, that is, as a mere distinction between this and that experiential life? As long as we leave out the first-person perspective, and consider what is available from the third-person perspective, this would be the natural answer. If, by contrast, one does take the first-person perspective seriously, it should be evident that Mick and Mack differ in a way quite unlike the drops of water, which obviously lack any kind of self-manifestation. Although Mick and Mack will each have a type-identical experience of the white wall, each of these experiences will have its own distinct pre-reflective self-manifestation. For Mick, his experience will be quite unlike Mack's experience (and vice versa). It is this basic reflexivity, and not some singular essence or non-duplicable property, which provides Mick and Mack with an individuation quite unlike any possessed by the drops of water. This is also why there is something puzzling about Williams's conclusion. As Klawonn has pointed out, as seen from my perspective, how could the removal of me amount to nothing (Klawonn 1990a: 50)?

But, the critics might insist, if this is what the example is supposed to show, doesn't it merely highlight the—it is to be hoped—uncontroversial fact that a theory of phenomenal consciousness (in contrast to a theory of drops of water) must necessarily take subjectivity and the first-person perspective seriously? And why should accepting this trivial fact commit us to any more substantial claim regarding the presence and reality of an experiential self? The answer to this question is, of course, that the whole point behind the introduction of a minimalist notion of self is to highlight something that is essential to any attempt at addressing the subjectivity of consciousness but which has too often (and this unfortunately includes much recent work on the self) remained unnoticed and disregarded. To reject the existence of the self while endorsing the reality of subjectivity is to miss out on what subjectivity really amounts to, it is to pay lip-service to the idea that we should take the first-person perspective seriously, or to put it differently, and to quote Margolis, 'Only the utter elimination of experience could possibly vindicate the elimination of selves' (Margolis 1988: 41).

As should have become sufficiently clear by now, to highlight the for-me-ness of experience is not merely to make a grammatical or logical or metaphysical point. The point is not simply that it is part of the very concept of experience that an experience necessarily requires an experiencer. No, the point being made is also phenomenological. To speak of the for-me-ness of experience is to pinpoint something with ramifications for the subject's overall phenomenology. The for-me-ness of experience refers to the first-personal character of experience, to the fact that our acquaintance with our own experiential life differs from the acquaintance we have with the experiential life of others and vice versa. This difference in acquaintance or access obtains, not only when we reflect or introspect, but whenever we pre-reflectively live through an experience. At its most primitive, self-experience is simply a question of being pre-reflectively aware of one's own consciousness, and the experiential self in question is precisely defined as the very subjectivity of experience.

The basics of the proposal should now be clear. What I intend to do in the following two chapters is to clarify it further. I shall do so by considering two types of objection in detail. According to the first objection, it is simply wrong to claim that experience per se entails subjectivity, first-personal givenness, and for-me-ness. According to the second objection, experience might very well entail subjectivity, first-personal givenness, and for-me-ness; the problem, though, is that this is all quite irrelevant when it comes to understanding the nature of the self. Both objections need to be considered and addressed.

3

Transparency and Anonymity

Despite a variety of other differences, higher-order representationalism, self-representationalism, and phenomenological accounts share the view that phenomenal consciousness entails some kind of self-consciousness. Some, however, take this to be a highly contentious view.

On various occasions, Hubert Dreyfus has denounced the idea that our embodied coping is permeated with mindedness as a mentalistic myth that is untrue to the phenomenon. He has declared mindedness the enemy of our mindless coping (Dreyfus 2007a: 353), and compared Olympic swimmers, who are performing at their best, to sleepwalkers (Dreyfus 2013: 38).[1] Dreyfus has also spoken of subjectivity as the lingering ghost of the mental, and has denied that there is any immersed or implicit ego in absorbed coping. In fact, in total absorption one ceases to be a subject altogether (Dreyfus 2007b: 373). Thus, on his account, our immersed bodily life is so completely world-engaged that it is entirely oblivious of itself. It is only when this bodily absorption is interrupted that something like self-consciousness emerges. Dreyfus doesn't deny the existence of self-consciousness, but he definitely wants to see it as a capacity that is only exercised or actualized on special occasions. When that happens, I retroactively attach an 'I think' to the coping. Moreover, although Dreyfus doesn't deny that we have the capacity to step back and reflect, we cannot, on his view, exercise this capacity without disrupting our coping and thereby radically transforming affordances of the kind that are given to it (Dreyfus 2005: 61; 2007a: 354).[2]

---

[1] One can detect a certain tension in Dreyfus's account. On the one hand, he frequently refers to experts such as Israeli fighter aces, Olympic athletes, or chess masters when exemplifying mindless coping, but he also argues that one of the virtues of his account is that it can accommodate the non-conceptual coping skills we share with prelinguistic infants and higher animals. The tension consequently has to do with the question whether the mindless coping that Dreyfus wants to call attention to is one in which concepts no longer play any role—although they did play a role when the skill was initially acquired—or whether he rather wants to make the more radical claim that skilful coping is more basic than—and ultimately constitutes the basis for—conceptual rationality. I take it that he wants to claim both, but it is problematic to use examples taken from chess play or aeronautics as support of the more radical claim.

[2] Such a stance inevitably gives rise to the following question: How can one meaningfully speak of a phenomenology of mindless coping, as Dreyfus repeatedly does, if the coping is completely unconscious? Of course, a possible retort could be that it all depends on the kind of phenomenology one has in mind. It is probably no coincidence that Dreyfus at one point suggests that Dennett's *heterophenomenology* might be an improvement on and better alternative to the phenomenologies of Husserl and Sartre (Dreyfus and Kelly 2007: 47).

In the light of such considerations, it is not difficult to formulate a direct challenge to the view that self-consciousness is a pervasive feature in our experiential life. According to what might be termed the *anonymity objection*, there is no for-me-ness or mineness on the pre-reflective level, nor is there any I or self. To claim otherwise is to engage in a post hoc fabrication. Rather, the pre-reflective level is characterized by a certain anonymity. To suggest that experience is always characterized by pre-reflective self-consciousness would be to fall prey to the so-called *refrigerator fallacy*, that is, thinking that the light is always on simply because it is always on whenever we open the door of the refrigerator. In reality, the light is only potentially on all the time. In short, we should avoid conflating the presence of a *capacity* for self-consciousness with the *actualization* of that capacity. 'Accordingly, self-consciousness is more justly construed, on phenomenological grounds, as a potentiality—generally unactualized, but always actualizable—of the world-immersed experience of someone capable of first-person thought' (Schear 2009: 99). Thus, for Schear, self-consciousness is a capacity that is only exercised or actualized on special occasions, namely, whenever we reflect. Moreover, such an actualization requires a capacity for first-person thoughts. Indeed, Schear suggests that the possession of first-person conceptual capacity is precisely what puts one in a position to know immediately about one's own conscious mental life as one's own. It is precisely the availability of such a distinct first-personal relation to one's conscious experience (rather than some spurious notion of pre-reflective self-consciousness) that is required if we are to understand and account for both the mineness of experience and something like proper self-knowledge (Schear 2009: 98). It is only when the capacity for first-person thoughts is exercised that an occurrent consciousness of one's experiences *as* one's own emerges (Schear 2009: 101). According to Schear, this does not imply that the flow of experience was an impersonal stream prior to the exercise of the capacity. It is not impersonal precisely because (and in so far as) it is the stream of someone capable of first-person thoughts. Thus, rather than opting for the choice between actualized reflective self-consciousness and actualized pre-reflective self-conscious-ness, it is better to appeal to some form of availability and dispositionality and argue that the difference between conscious and non-conscious intentional states is that the former are available to reflective scrutiny when they occur in beings like us who have the capacity to form higher-order thoughts. One immediate and highly counter-intuitive implication of this, however, is that it restricts conscious mental states to creatures capable of reflection and thereby denies them to infants and (most) non-human animals.[3]

---

[3] Schear himself doesn't explicitly endorse such a view, but there are certainly others who have defended the idea that phenomenal consciousness requires thoughts, concepts, and language. Consider, for instance, Peter Carruthers's position in *Language, Thought and Consciousness*. For Carruthers, to speak of what an experience is like, or of its phenomenal feel, is an attempt to characterize those aspects of experience that are subjective. But to speak of the subjective aspects of experience is to speak of aspects that are available to the subject. What this means, according to Carruthers, is that they must be states of which the subject is

According to Schear, to insist on the presence of self-consciousness on the pre-reflective level is to distort phenomenology (Schear 2009: 99). Other critics have argued that it is developmentally implausible to claim that consciousness is characterized by pre-reflective givenness as long as such givenness is supposed to entail awareness rather than availability (Lyyra 2009: 68). On this alternative proposal, self-awareness proper requires higher-order conceptual capacities. It is only then that our experiential episodes can be said to be consciously given (Lyyra 2009: 80–1). As long as the infant lacks the capacity to distinguish between within and without and between appearance and reality, mind and world will remain indistinguishable for it. And in so far as the infant is not yet aware of his or her experiences *as* inner private entities, the infant does not yet enjoy any awareness of the experiences (Lyyra 2009: 79). It is only when the child comes to realize that her experiences take place from a first-person perspective that is unique to the child and inaccessible to others, it is only when she realizes that she enjoys unique access to her own experiences, and others to theirs, that her experiences are given to her *as* subjective, and hence in a first-person mode of givenness. Given this line of thought, it is hardly surprising that it has been denied that there is anything primitive about subjectivity of experience; rather, in so far as subjectivity of experience presupposes an apprehension of the distinction between one's own experiences and the experience of others, and of the existence of a plurality of points of view, intersubjectivity turns out to be the fundamental category (Praetorius 2009: 329). As Suzanne Zeedyk writes, 'subjectivity is born from the intimacy of intersubjectivity', and it is the latter that gives rise to capacities such as 'self-awareness, representation, language, and even consciousness' (Zeedyk 2006: 326).[4] Against the background of such considerations, which incidentally entail that

---

aware, and this precisely involves a certain amount of self-awareness. In fact, according to Carruthers, it requires the ability to reflect upon, think about, and conceptualize one's own mental states (Carruthers 1996a: 155, 157). Given this conceptual requirement, he argues that only creatures that are in possession of a *theory of mind* are capable of enjoying conscious experiences or of having mental states with phenomenal feels (Carruthers 1996a: 158). He consequently holds the view that most animals, children under the age of 3, and individuals with autism lack subjectivity and remain oblivious to the existence of their own mental states. They will lack phenomenally conscious mental states, and there will be nothing it is like for them to feel pain or pleasure (Carruthers 1996b: 262; 1998: 216; 2000: 203). Carruthers's position might be extreme, but he is not alone in holding such a view.

[4] A related view is endorsed by Gergely, who explicitly defends the social origins of the subjective sense of self (Gergely 2007: 71). Without going into all the specificities of his account, the basic idea is that 'it is the experience of one's current internal states being externally "mirrored" or "reflected" back through the infant-attuned contingent social reactions of the attachment environment that makes it possible to develop a subjective sense and awareness of one's primary affective self states' (Gergely 2007: 60). To put it differently, when the caregiver engages in affect-mirroring behaviour, the infant will search for the intended referent of this display and will direct her attention towards herself. In this way, a sensitive caregiver can teach the infant about the existence of her own primary emotional states by establishing cognitively accessible second-order representations for them (Gergely 2007: 68, 81). In a sense, it is the fact that the caregiver behaves as if the infant is already in possession of subjective experiences that causes the infant to acquire subjective experiences. It is because parents treat children as being more sophisticated than they really are that they eventually become so. This is why Gergely can conclude that the construction of the introspectively visible subjective self happens through the attachment environment (Gergely 2007: 59).

we ought to be very cautious in ascribing subjectivity to individuals with severe forms of autism, the very notions of pre-reflective self-consciousness and mineness have been taken to be not only theoretical aberrations but also redundant and explanatorily vacuous (Praetorius 2009: 332).

How should one respond to such criticisms? A first necessary step is to distinguish terminological from substantial disagreement (and misunderstandings). For some, to be self-conscious is to think of oneself *as* oneself or to be aware of one's states or parts or features *as* one's own. Some take this to require one to be conscious of one's identity as the subject, bearer, or owner of different experiences. Likewise, for some, self-experience amounts to having a sense of 'who one is', that is, having a sense of one's own particular character or personality. On such understandings of the terms, it would be quite implausible to suggest that self-consciousness and self-experience should be present whenever we as adults are phenomenally conscious of something, let alone be something that already characterizes the psychological life of infants. Likewise, for some, it is

not until the child can apprehend that his or her 'point of view' may differ from those of others, and furthermore, that he or she has *unique* access to his or her experiences—and vice versa for others—that it makes any sense to ascribe to the child first-person givenness of experiences, and thus subjectivity of experiences with a built-in experiential self-reference. (Praetorius 2009: 329)

On such a definition, it would again be highly implausible to ascribe subjectivity and a first-person perspective to infants, non-human animals, and even ordinary absorbed copers. However, as I hope the previous chapter has made abundantly clear, this is not at all how I am using the terms. I consequently think the controversy is partly terminological. When talking of the first-personal character or for-me-ness of experience, the target is not self-reference by means of the first-person pronoun; in fact, what is at issue here is not at all linguistic self-reference. Nor is it a question of a thematic kind of self-knowledge, one involving an awareness of oneself as a distinct individual, different from other individuals. When referring to the first-personal character of phenomenal consciousness, to pre-reflective self-consciousness, experiential selfhood, and for-me-ness, I am referring to the self-presentational character of experience and to the entailed experiential perspectivalness. I am claiming that we have a distinctly different acquaintance with our own experiential life than with the experiential life of others (and vice versa), and that this difference obtains, not only when we introspect or reflect, but already in the very having of the experience. When I say 'distinctly different', the claim is not that we are necessarily explicitly aware of the distinctiveness in question, but rather, and simply, that sensations of pain or hunger or emotions like joy and distress are characterized by an experiential givenness that makes them quite unlike mountain tops, willows, and rocking chairs, even before, say, an infant becomes explicitly aware of this difference. They have this subjective character long before the subject acquires the conceptual and linguistic skills to classify the experiences as his or her own. To phrase it differently, we ought to respect the distinction between having or embodying a first-person perspective and being able to articulate it linguistically.

P. F. Strawson famously defended the view that one cannot be said to have a subjective perspective unless one possesses a certain understanding of the objectivity condition, an understanding that environmental objects persist independently of the experiential perspective we bring to bear on them (Strawson 1959). The obvious question to ask, however, is whether the requirements that must be met in order to recognize an experience *as* subjective or categorize it *as* inner are identical to the requirements that must be met in order simply to have experiences—experiences that are essentially and by necessity characterized by what various authors have called 'pre-reflective self-consciousness', 'first-personal givenness', 'for-me-ness', 'subjective presence', 'self-presentational awareness', 'intransitive self-consciousness', or 'reflexivity'.[5]

Consider again the claim that it is phenomenologically unwarranted to insist on the pervasive experiential reality of self-consciousness. One way to understand the worry is to consider the following variety of experiences: being absorbed in a movie; being humiliated by your peers; laboriously trying to decipher a menu written in a language you hardly know; being hit in the face by a snowball; standing on the ten-metre diving board trying to persuade yourself to jump; considering whether opting for a career in the army is a wise choice. When comparing such experiences, it should be evident to most that they are self-involving and self-conscious in different ways. To deny this is indeed to distort phenomenology. Arguing that our experiential life is as such characterized by for-me-ness is, however, not to deny that we need to recognize a diversity of qualitatively different self-experiences. Indeed, the latter recognition is quite compatible with the view that there is also something that this diversity has in common.

Schear, Lyyra, and Praetorius all emphasize the dependency of experiential ownership and self-consciousness on first-person thoughts and concepts. By implication, creatures that lack such first-person thoughts—and this presumably includes infants and non-human animals—also lack self-consciousness. Some might think that this

---

[5] One slightly confusing factor in the debate is the conflicting use of the terms 'reflexive' and 'reflexivity'. Whereas the term 'reflection' is used pretty much in the same way by most authors, the term 'reflexivity' is by no means unequivocal and is in fact used by some to designate completely different phenomena. Some use the terms 'reflexive' and 'reflective' synonymously. Others use the term 'reflexivity'—and this is obviously what is confusing, particularly since reflection is called *Reflexion* in German—to designate the pre-reflective dimension. One can find this use in Mohanty, for instance, who defines reflexivity as the pre-reflective transparency of consciousness, and distinguishes it from reflection, which he takes to be a higher-order intentional act (Mohanty 1972: 159, 164, 168). More recently, Seigel has argued that whereas reflexivity has to do with something automatic, something involuntary, something like a reflex, reflection is usually considered as something intentional and wilful (something that can also establish a distance between consciousness and its content). Thus, in his view, the two terms indicate two distinct forms of self-reference, one passive and one active (Seigel 2005: 12–13). I find Seigel's comments helpful, but ultimately no consensus on the issue seems forthcoming. To some extent, one simply has to be aware of the ambiguity of the term.

implication counts in favour of the view rather than against it. But we need to recall not only how thin and basic a notion of self-consciousness I am employing, but also the preceding arguments defending the constitutive link between self-consciousness and phenomenal consciousness. In line with a long and venerable tradition in philosophy, I am using the term 'self-consciousness' to designate instances where consciousness has access to or is acquainted with itself.[6] For many thinkers (and this includes Aristotle, Descartes, Arnauld, Locke, Brentano, Husserl, Sartre, Gurwitsch, Merleau-Ponty, Henry, and Henrich) self-consciousness in this specific sense of the term is an integral part of experience; it is something that is possessed by all conscious mental states since all conscious states are necessarily experientially manifest, or, to phrase it differently, a mental state lacking this kind of self-consciousness would be a non-conscious state. The precise nature and structure of this kind of self-consciousness is obviously something that has been and continues to be debated. In Western philosophy it is debated by phenomenologists, higher-order representationalists, and self-representationalists. In classical Indian philosophy it has been an issue of controversy between reflectionist or other-illumination (*paraprakāśa*) theories and reflexivist or self-illumination (*svaprakāśa*) theories (MacKenzie 2007). Whereas the first group of positions held that self-consciousness is the product of a second-order consciousness taking a distinct first-order consciousness as its intentional object, the second group held that conscious states simultaneously disclose both the object of consciousness and the conscious state itself (MacKenzie 2008). It is not as if the latter view is universally accepted, but if one wants to criticize it, one has to engage with the relevant debate in philosophy of mind. To fail to do so, and to base one's objections, as is occasionally done, on findings in developmental psychology concerning the child's capacity to discriminate perspectives, is to miss both the target and the point of the argument. In addition, the very idea that intersubjectivity should give rise to subjectivity must be rejected as conceptually confused. Intersubjectivity designates a relation between subject(ivitie)s, and the former consequently cannot precede the latter (see Part II; Zahavi 1996). If one wants to pursue that kind of idea, one should rather opt for the claim that subjectivity is socially constructed or that subjectivity and intersubjectivity are equiprimordial. Whereas I would disagree with both these latter claims, they are at least not incoherent.

So far, I have considered the claim that experiential life frequently lacks for-me-ness and first-personal character. Let me now proceed and instead engage with another version of the anonymity objection, according to which one is never directly aware of one's own experiences, not even when one is reflecting or introspecting. As

---

[6] As Udo Thiel points out in his magisterial work *The Early Modern Subject: Self-Consciousness and Personal Identity from Descartes to Hume*, initially the English terms 'consciousness' or being 'conscious' meant a perception or knowledge of something that one shares with someone else. By the seventeenth century, however, this was no longer the standard meaning. Rather, like the Greek *syneidesis* and Latin *conscientia*, 'consciousness' changed its meaning from 'knowing together with someone else' to 'knowing something with oneself'. It came to be understood in a self-relating sense (Thiel 2011: 8).

the argument goes, experiences do not have intrinsic and non-intentional qualities of their own; rather, the qualitative character of experience is entirely constituted, as Dretske writes, 'by the properties things are represented as having' (Dretske 1995: 1). If you want to know what it is like to have a certain experience, you must look at what is being intentionally represented. Thus, 'there is no more to the quality of one's experiences in experiencing blue than there is to the color blue since the color blue *is* the color one experiences' (Dretske 1995: 85). The loudness of a sound, the smoothness of a surface, the sweetness of a taste, the pungency of a smell are not intrinsic qualities of experiences, but qualities things are represented as having. The reason an experience of a red apple differs from an experience of a yellow sunflower is consequently precisely because different kinds of object are represented.

In defending what has become known as the *transparency claim*, Michael Tye has likened visual experience to transparent sheets of glass:

Peer as hard as you like via introspection, focus your attention in any way you please, and you will only come across surfaces, volumes, films, and their apparent qualities. Visual experiences are transparent to their subjects. We are not introspectively aware of our visual experiences any more than we are perceptually aware of transparent sheets of glass. If we try to focus on our experiences, we 'see' right through them to the world outside. By being aware of the qualities apparently possessed by surfaces, volumes, etc., we become aware that we are undergoing visual experiences. But we are not aware of the experiences themselves. (Tye 2003: 24)

As Tye insists, the lesson of this transparency is that 'phenomenology ain't in the head' (Tye 1995: 151). It is consequently somewhat misleading to say that experiences have phenomenal character. In fact, the phenomenal character is something that (in veridical cases) belongs to the object of experience. For the same reason, phenomenal consciousness does not present me with aspects or dimensions of my own consciousness; rather, phenomenal consciousness is strictly world-presenting. Thus, even when we introspect, we are not conscious or aware of the experience itself. There is no subjective content to be found introspectively; rather, the properties we are introspectively aware of continue to be the publicly accessible properties of external things, if, that is, they are properties of anything at all (Tye 2009, p. xiii). By being aware of things outside, we might indirectly become aware *that* we are having such and such experiences, but we are never directly aware of the experiences themselves (Tye 2003: 24, 96–7; 2009: 145). Knowing that one is engaged in an act of perception (rather than imagination) must consequently be inferred from the way in which the world is being represented (Dretske 1999; Byrne 2005).[7] Moreover, we only acquire this indirect awareness of our experiences in so far as we bring the

---

[7] Although Tye denies that one has any direct awareness of the 'feel' of experience, he also denies that he is committed to the view that one infers the phenomenal character of one's experience from one's awareness of the external qualities. As he sees it, there is no reasoning involved, and consequently no inference (Tye 2003: 33). Rather, he takes introspection to be 'a *reliable* process that takes awareness *of* external qualities (in the case of perceptual sensations) as input and yields awareness *that* a state is present

experiences under concepts. As long as we do not apply such concepts, we remain completely oblivious of the experiences (Tye 1995: 115).

I think there is some truth to phenomenal externalism. Its account of phenomenal qualities, for instance, has the great advantage of staying clear of any kind of sense-data theory. It even bears a certain resemblance to views found in phenomenology. As Merleau-Ponty pointed out, colours 'are not sensations, they are the sensibles, and quality is not an element of consciousness, but a property of the object' (Merleau-Ponty 2012: 5). When we reflectively try to discern the experiential difference between smelling cloves and tasting chocolate or between hearing a cowbell and seeing a sunrise, we do not sever our intentional link with the world by turning some spectral gaze inwards. No, we discover these differences, and we analyse them descriptively by paying attention to how worldly objects and states of affairs appear to us.

Many of the standard examples taken to support phenomenal externalism are, however, taken from the domain of perception, but perceptual states hardly exhaust the dimension of phenomenality, and although the claim is that transparency rules, and that the phenomenal character in all cases simply is a matter of representational content,[8] the attempt to capture the phenomenal character of, say, orgasm by claiming that it is a matter of having 'sensory representations of certain physical changes in the genital region' (Tye 1995: 118), and insisting that this model can be generalized to cover the phenomenal character of all felt emotions and moods (Tye 2003: 36), has less intuitive appeal than the attempt to account in externalist terms for what it is like to smell sea air or taste liquorice. It is far from obvious how phenomenal externalism can account for the phenomenal character of distress, despair, hopelessness, relief, satisfaction, or, say, cases such as struggling to remember something, or feeling confident versus uncertain about something. To adopt an example of Evan Thompson, there is a clear phenomenological difference between first seeing a red cube and then visualizing the same red cube, but this difference (which, for instance, might include the fact that the visual perception is felt as involuntary and effortless, whereas the visualization feels voluntary and effortful) cannot be accounted for simply by referring to a difference in the features or properties the two experiences represent the object as having, since they are both taking it to have the same properties (Thompson 2007: 285).

---

with a certain phenomenal character as output' (Tye 2003: 38). As has been pointed out, however, on a standard definition such a view would precisely amount to an inferentialist one (Aydede 2003: 62).

[8] In recent publications, Tye is no longer endorsing the claim that phenomenal character is the same as representational content. One reason for this change is the case of hallucinations. As Tye argues, although no veridical and hallucinatory experiences share the same representational content, some veridical and hallucinatory experiences have the same phenomenal character; thus the latter cannot simply be identified with the former. But despite this change of mind, Tye remains firmly committed to the transparency claim (Tye 2009, p. xiii).

We need, however, to distinguish the claim that some types of phenomenality are not amenable to an externalist account from the claim that phenomenal externalism is missing something even when it comes to the most straightforward perceptual cases. When phenomenal externalism claims that we are never directly aware of our experiences, but only of the objects and properties represented by those experiences, it ignores some important distinctions. Most people are prepared to concede that there is something it is like for a subject to undergo a conscious experience (to taste an Ardbeg Uigeadail or to remember a visit to Kyoto). But we need to distinguish between the question of (1) what the object is like for the subject and (2) what the experience of the object is like for the subject. After all, we are never conscious of an object *simpliciter*, but always of the object as appearing in a certain way, say, as judged, seen, hoped, feared, remembered, smelled, anticipated, or tasted. The same object, with exactly the same worldly properties, can present itself in a variety of manners. It can be given as perceived, imagined, or recollected, etc. We need to distinguish, as Husserl did, between the intentional object in 'the how of its determinations' (*im Wie seiner Bestimmtheiten*) and in 'the how of its givenness' (*im Wie seiner Gegebenheitsweisen*) (Husserl 1976: 303–4). Not only is what it is like to perceive a blue square different from what it is like to perceive an orange triangle, but what it is like to perceive a blue square is also different from what it is like to remember or imagine a blue square. In short, there is a difference between asking about the property the object is experienced as having (how does the surface of a table feel differently from the surface of an ice cube?) and asking about the property of the experience of the object (what is the experiential difference between perceiving and imagining an ice cube?). When examining the phenomenal character of our experience, we should not overlook the subjective nature of the mental acts that enable us to experience what we experience. If we want to do justice to the phenomenal character of experience, we have to investigate both the character of the experienced object and the character of the intentional act. As Husserl once remarked:

I see phenomenological differences, especially differences of intentionality, as well as I see the difference between this white and that red as pure data of colour. If someone can absolutely not see differences of the latter kind, one would say that he is blind; if someone cannot see differences of the former sort, I cannot help myself but must once again say that he is blind, even if it is blindness in a wider sense. (Husserl 2002a: 321)

When I consciously imagine a centaur, desire a negroni, look forward to my next vacation, or remember my high school reunion, all these different intentional objects are given in correlation to a variety of different subjective experiences. I am consequently not merely presented with a variety of objects and objectual properties; rather, these objects and properties are also presented in different modes of givenness (as imagined, desired, anticipated, recollected, etc.), and it makes a difference to the phenomenal character of, say, tasting coffee whether the taste of the coffee is perceived, remembered, imagined, or anticipated. Moreover, we obviously shouldn't forget the point that was made in the previous chapter. If we wish to do justice to the phenomenal character of our experiential life, it is not sufficient to consider the intentional object and the intentional attitude, since what-it-is-likeness is properly speaking what-it-is-like-for-me-ness. Phenomenally conscious states are not states that just happen to take place *in me*, whether or not I am aware of their taking place; they are also *for me*, precisely in the sense that there is something it is like for me to have those states. This is why strong phenomenal externalism necessarily fails in its attempt to provide an exhaustive account of the phenomenal character of experience. After all, it makes rather little sense to suggest that the first-personal character of experience, the for-me-ness of experience, is a qualitative feature of the object represented (see Zahavi 2005: 119–24; Kriegel 2009: 72, 75).

But isn't this objection entirely question-begging, since phenomenal externalists like Dretske would simply contest the appeal to such descriptive findings? After all, in their view, conscious mental states are states that make us conscious of other things. That is, conscious mental states are states we are conscious with and not states we are conscious of (Dretske 1995: 100–1). There is, however, a substantial price to pay for this view. One rather obvious problem is that it isn't entirely clear how such a view will allow us to distinguish between conscious and non-conscious intentional states, all of which supposedly represent objects in the environment. As Dretske writes, that of which one is conscious is completely objective. It would be precisely the same if one weren't aware of it. Indeed, 'Everything you are aware of would be the same if you were a zombie' (Dretske 2003: 1). This seems to follow from the core claim of phenomenal externalism, namely, that experience presents us with nothing except the external objects and their properties. But if this is the case, and if for Dretske there is no significant difference between conscious intentionality and non-conscious intentionality, then it becomes unclear whether his theory really accounts for phenomenal consciousness, or whether it rather amounts to a form of eliminativism regarding experience.[9] This suspicion is further increased the moment Dretske admits that his view gives rise to the following challenge: If I am only aware of the properties represented by my mental states, and not of the mental states themselves, how then can I know at all that I do have phenomenally conscious states? As he puts it, there is nothing of which I am aware that tells me that I am aware of it, and since everything I am aware of, the world as I experience it, would be exactly the same if I were a zombie, I cannot know, at least not in any direct manner, that I am not a zombie (Dretske 2003: 1). Some might suggest that introspection is the key. By using introspection we can know that we are having experiences, and that we are consequently not zombies, but Dretske rejects this proposal, since introspection, according to him, only tells us *what* we are aware of and not *that* we are aware (Dretske 2003: 8).

---

[9] It surely is no coincidence that some defenders of the transparency view have seriously considered the 'no experience' hypothesis, that is, the view that there are no experiences in the first place (see Byrne 2009: 434–5).

Indeed, on his account, it is impossible via introspection to discern any feature of one's experience of *x* over and above what one experiences as features of *x*. We consequently do not have any direct access to the fact that we are conscious rather than non-conscious, and our conviction that we do is, according to Dretske, most likely based on a confusion (Dretske 2003: 9). The question, though, is whether this conclusion is not so counter-intuitive that it might serve as a *reductio ad absurdum* of the premises, or at the very least motivate us to look for more plausible alternatives.

I think we should opt for an account that allows us to retain and respect the difference between the case where a subject (non-consciously) perceives an object, the case where the subject is conscious of *what* she perceives, and the case where she is conscious of the fact *that* she perceives. A blindsight subject, for example, might (non-consciously) perceive something in the blind region of her visual field, as evinced from her performance on a forced-choice test, but she would not be conscious of what she perceived. Compare this to the situation where I point to a car and say 'That is a car'. I appear to say what I see, and how would I be able to do that unless I was conscious of what I perceived? But although I might be conscious of *what* I see, that is, of what a particular perception of mine is about (and how could I be that if the perception were unconscious?), it is not obvious that at the same time I must also be conscious of the fact *that* I perceive something (see Lurz 2003).

On the present proposal, we cannot be conscious of an object (a tasted apple, a seen chair, a touched piece of marble, a remembered event, an imagined creature, etc.) unless we are aware of the experience that allows the object to appear (the tasting, seeing, touching, remembering, imagining). However, this doesn't require that the experience is salient to the subject; that is, it is not as if the subject must be aware of the experiential state *as* an experiential state, nor does it have to otherwise notice or attend to or think about the state. Nor does this entail that our access to, say, the apple is *indirect*, or that it is mediated, contaminated, or blocked by our awareness of the experience, since the experience is not itself an object on a par with the apple, but instead constitutes the very access to the appearing apple. This is precisely why there is something quite misleading about the view that the only way we could become aware of an experience would be by way of some mental gymnastics, where we turned our attention inwards and replaced the ordinary object of experience with a mental object, namely, the experience itself. What this proposal overlooks is not merely the object-directed and -presenting character of experience, but also the fact that the object wouldn't appear at all if it wasn't for the experience. Had the visual episode been non-conscious, the object would not have appeared visually at all; that is, in the absence of experience, there would have been no phenomenality or phenomenal character at all.

In my everyday life, I am absorbed by and preoccupied with projects and objects in the world, and as such I do not attend to my experiential life. I tend to ignore it in favour of its object. I can, however, reflect on and attend to my experiences, I can make them the theme or object of my attention. But if I am to deliberate on and assess my beliefs and intentions, it is not enough that I have them; I must also have been aware of them; that is, prior to reflection I cannot have been 'mind-blind'. Reflection is constrained by what is pre-reflectively lived through. It is answerable to experiential facts and is not constitutively self-fulfilling. To deny that the reflective self-ascription of beliefs is based on any experiential evidence whatsoever is implausible. It is to deny that such self-ascription amounts to a cognitive achievement; it is to deny, as Boghossian puts it, that it is an information-sensitive capacity that is subject to cultivation or neglect (Boghossian 2003: 76).

Self-consciousness is not something that only emerges the moment one scrutinizes one's experiences attentively; rather, in its pre-reflective form it is present the moment I consciously experience something. It does not exist apart from the experience, as an additional experiential state. It is not brought about by some kind of reflection or introspection or higher-order monitoring, but is an intrinsic feature of the primary experience. This is also why the view in question does not amount to a form of *detectivism*, to use a label coined by Finkelstein. That is, it does not subscribe to the view that first-person authority is rooted in our ability to detect, by means of some inward observation, our own mental states, thereby making them conscious (Finkelstein 2003: 2, 9). Rather, it is the conscious states themselves, and not some internal observation of them, that provide part of the justification for any subsequent self-ascription of those very states. In short, the fact that the phenomenally conscious states are already like something for the subject is what makes those very states capable of playing a justificatory role vis-à-vis any higher-order belief regarding their very existence. Contrary to the proposal made by higher-order representationalists and self-representationalists, the phenomenological claim is not that experiences are things we persistently perceive or represent and that the relation between an experience and its first-personal givenness (subjective presence) is to be cashed out in terms of an act–object structure. The point is rather that experiential processes are intrinsically self-revealing. This is also why it might be better to say that we see, hear, or feel *consciously*, rather than saying that there is a perception of an object, and in addition an awareness of the perception (Thomasson 2000: 203). The advantage of the adverbial phrasing is that it avoids interpreting the secondary awareness as a form of object-consciousness comparable to and on a par with my peripheral awareness of the noise from the street or the soles of my shoes. This temptation will remain as long as we keep talking about conscious states as states *of* which we are conscious.

Some have objected that even if something like a non-objectifying and non-inferential self-consciousness is possible, it will be far too weak and vague to allow for or explain the distinctive character of our first-person knowledge (Caston 2006: 4; Thomasson 2006: 6). I find this a somewhat puzzling objection. I don't think pre-reflective self-consciousness in and of itself amounts to authoritative first-person knowledge (or critical self-deliberation)—which is also why Sartre, for instance, very explicitly distinguished self-consciousness (*conscience de soi*) from self-knowledge (*connaissance de soi*)—and I am not trying to obliterate the difference between the two. In order to obtain proper knowledge about one's experiences, something more than pre-reflective self-consciousness is indeed needed. Reflection does not simply reproduce the lived experiences unaltered; rather, the experiences reflected upon are transformed in the process, to various degrees and in various manners, depending upon the type of reflection at work. This transformation is precisely what makes reflection cognitively valuable. But from the fact that pre-reflective self-consciousness isn't sufficient for first-person knowledge, one can obviously not conclude that it is therefore also unnecessary if such knowledge is to obtain. The former provides for an experiential grounding of any subsequent self-ascription, reflective appropriation, and thematic self-identification, and is to that extent epistemically enabling. To rephrase, any account of first-person knowledge that denies or ignores the first-personal character of our experiential life is a non-starter. We need to explain how I can appropriate an experience as *my* experience. Had the experience been completely anonymous and impersonal when originally lived through, had it lacked first-personal givenness altogether, such an appropriation would be rather inexplicable. This is also why the obvious reply to the refrigerator objection is that it leaves it quite mysterious how our reflective gaze or monitoring stance is supposed to have that kind of effect, that is, offer that kind of illumination.

Let me try to sum up the preceding analysis by outlining what I take to be some of the main options. (1) We can deny that phenomenal consciousness entails self-consciousness and endorse a radical version of the transparency thesis. We can then argue that phenomenality is strictly and exclusively world-presenting; that is, when consciously scrutinizing the lotto coupon or when consciously admiring a portrait, we are de facto self- and mind-blind. If we deny (1) and accept the claim that phenomenal consciousness does entail self-consciousness, we then have a number of different choices (see Figure 1). We can (2) adopt a form of higher-order representationalism and argue that the phenomenality and what-it-is-likeness of our experiential states is constituted by an accompanying higher-order representation. We can also deny this and instead (3) claim that the self-consciousness that is a constitutive feature of phenomenal consciousness must be understood as an intrinsic feature of the primary experience. If we accept 3, we can then either (3a) endorse the transitivity principle and argue that the experiential episode is given to itself as a secondary peripheral object or (3b) claim that the experiential episode manifests itself pre-reflectively in a non-objectifying manner.

Before moving on, there is, however, one version of the anonymity objection that still needs to be considered and addressed. According to this objection, self and consciousness might ordinarily go together, but the relation cannot be essential and necessary since pathology presents us with relevant exceptions, that is, with cases where experiences are anonymous in that they lack mineness and for-me-ness altogether.

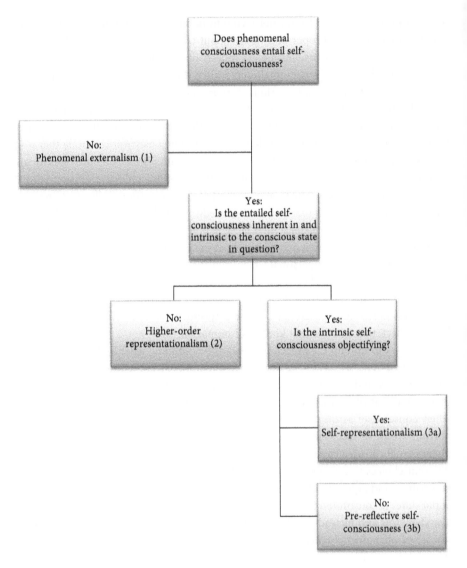

FIGURE 1

Consider, for instance, cases of schizophrenic thought-insertion, which allegedly confront us with situations in which patients experience introspectively alienated conscious thoughts for which they have no sense of agency or ownership. At least, this is how Metzinger interprets the pathology. He takes such cases to demonstrate that the phenomenal quality of mineness is not a necessary component of experience (Metzinger 2003: 334, 382, 445–6). A comparable dissociation between introspective access and felt ownership has recently been reported in a patient who suffered from hypometabolism and who, although he was able to see everything normally, did not immediately recognize that he himself was the perceiving subject. In order to become aware that it was he himself who was the perceiver, he had to undertake a subsequent inferential step. Timothy Lane has argued that that patient's experience, prior to this inferential step, lacked any quality of mineness, for which reason it was, phenomenologically speaking, nobody's. More generally speaking, Lane argues that

the mental states of organisms can be conscious states, even if they are not taken as belonging to self. Phenomenal consciousness does not entail self-awareness; it is not stamped with a *meish* quality; and, for-me-ness does not play a determining role in its constitution. Appearances notwithstanding, the awareness of a mental state's existence is never more than conditionally related to the attribution of that state to a given subject. Matters only seem otherwise, because in all ordinary situations self and consciousness are tightly interwoven. (Lane 2012: 281)

Is this conclusion warranted? I think not. Part of the problem is that Lane, like many of the previously mentioned critics, construes the notions of self-awareness and for-me-ness in a more robust sense than they are intended by authors favouring the position he is criticizing.

Let us for a moment return to schizophrenic thought-insertions. John Campbell once made the following observation in an influential paper on the topic:

The thought inserted into the subject's mind is indeed in some sense his, just because it has been successfully inserted into his mind; it has some special relation to him. He has, for example, some especially direct knowledge of it. On the other hand, there is, the patient insists, a sense in which the thought is not his, a sense in which the thought is someone else's, and not just in that someone else originated the thought and communicated it to the subject... (Campbell 1999: 610)

Despite other disagreements of all kinds, many contributions to the discussion of thought-insertion following in the wake of Campbell's paper have largely accepted the distinction between two forms of ownership: one that is linked to the fact that the experiences I am living through are given differently to me than to anybody else, and another that concerns the question whether or not the thinker of the thought recognizes himself as the agent or author of the thought. Whereas thoughts can be disowned when it comes to the latter form of ownership (or authorship), most would argue that the first kind of ownership is not lost in the case of inserted thoughts. What is the argument? When a subject who experiences thought-insertions or delusions of control reports that certain thoughts are not his thoughts, that someone else is generating these thoughts, he is also indicating that these thoughts are present, not 'over there' in someone else's head, but within *his own* stream of consciousness, a stream of consciousness for which he claims ownership. Even if the inserted thoughts or alien movements are felt as intrusive and strange, they cannot lack ownership altogether, since the afflicted subject is aware that it is he himself rather than somebody else who is experiencing these alien thoughts and movements (Zahavi

1999). As Gallagher remarks, 'For that reason the schizophrenic should provide a positive answer to what he might rightly regard as a nonsensical question: Are you sure that *you* are the one who is experiencing these thoughts? After all, this is precisely his complaint. *He* is experiencing thoughts that seem to be generated by others' (Gallagher 2000: 231). In short, some sense of ownership is still retained, and that is the basis for his complaint. Claiming that the experiences of a patient suffering from thought-insertion do not entirely lack first-personal character, and that such phenomena do not involve a complete effacement of mineness or for-me-ness, is not, however, to deny that the clinician should recognize that schizophrenia does, in fact, involve a fragile and unstable first-person perspective. But there is an important difference between claiming that thought-insertion exemplifies a state of mind with no for-me-ness, and saying that the for-me-ness that is retained is frail (see Parnas and Sass 2011: 532). Frail in what sense? In the sense that the patient no longer simply takes the for-me-ness for granted; it has lost some of its normal obviousness, familiarity, and unquestionability, and doesn't effortlessly lead to or permit reflective self-ascription (Sass and Parnas 2003: 430). In other words, we are indeed dealing with a kind of self-alienation or alienated self-consciousness, but as these phrasings also make clear, some dimension of self and self-consciousness remains intact.

Now, Lane admits that there is an utterly trivial sense in which the first-person perspective is retained even in the pathological cases, but that this has no bearing on the issue of mineness. Lane refers to a definition provided by Blanke and Metzinger according to which a weak first-person perspective merely amounts to 'a purely geometrical feature' of our visuo-spatial presentation of reality. When we perceive objects, we see objects as being to the right or left, further away or closer by. On this account, the weak first-person perspective is simply the zero-point of projection that functions as the geometrical origin of the 'seeing' organism's embodied perspective (Blanke and Metzinger 2009). I agree that this weak notion of a first-person perspective has nothing to do with subjectivity, mineness, and for-me-ness. In fact, I think one should altogether avoid using the term 'first-person perspective' as a label for this feature, since it is a feature that arguably also characterizes the input received by a video camera. But, of course, there is nothing it is like for the video camera (or, to upgrade the example a bit, the robot) to undergo such perspectival representations. The experiential perspectivalness that is retained even in the pathological cases is something altogether different. The pathological experiences are conscious, and to that extent they all entail an implicit pre-reflective, intransitive self-consciousness. This is why the experiences continue to be characterized by a subjective presence and a what-it-is-likeness that make them utterly unlike public objects that in principle are accessible in the same way to a plurality of subjects. In short, regardless of how alienated or distanced the patient feels from the experiences, the experiences do not manifest themselves entirely in the public domain. They continue to be phenomenally present to the patient in a way that is in principle unavailable to others. This is what their first-personal character amounts to, and this is why even the pathological experiences under consideration retain their mineness and for-me-ness.

Lane suggests that we ought to distinguish between *hosting* and *owning* (Lane 2012: 260). Experiences can be hosted by a subject, and that subject can be the only one who is directly conscious of them, without the experiences being lived through as the subject's own. Or, to state it differently, an experience can be *for me* in the sense that it is lived through by me and not someone else and yet the experience may not be given, even pre-reflectively, as *mine*. The problem with this distinction, however, is that it only makes sense if one operates with a more robust notion of mineness than the one I am using. If the mineness of experience simply refers to first-personal givenness and perspectival ownership, the distinction breaks down.

Still, this is not to say that there is nothing to learn from the various objections I have been considering. One lesson to learn is that we need to be quite careful when speaking of the mineness and for-me-ness of experience. We have already seen that it is necessary to distinguish a merely metaphysical claim from what is also a phenomenological claim. On a deflationary interpretation the for-me-ness of experience simply amounts to the fact that experience *occurs* in someone (a 'me'). On this view, for-me-ness is a non-experiential aspect of mental life. By contrast, a non-deflationary interpretation construes for-me-ness as an experiential feature of mental life, one with an impact on a subject's overall phenomenology. On this view, to say that an experience is *for me* is precisely to say something more than that it is *in me*. It is to state a phenomenological fact, not a merely metaphysical fact. In addition, however, I think we need to distinguish two different phenomenological claims: a minimalist one and a more robust one. On the minimalist reading, the for-me-ness and mineness of experience simply refer to the subjectivity of experience, to the fact that the experiences are pre-reflectively self-conscious and thereby present in a distinctly subjective manner, a manner that is not available to anybody else. I take it that this feature is preserved in all the cases I have discussed. On a slightly more robust reading, the for-me-ness and mineness of experience can refer to a sense of endorsement and self-familiarity, to the quality of 'warmth and intimacy' that William James claimed characterizes our own present thoughts (James 1890: 239). If this is what is meant by for-me-ness and mineness, I think it can be disturbed and perhaps even be completely absent.

4

Subjectivity or Selfhood

What if one accepted the idea of mindlessness? What if one accepted that we occasionally or perhaps even predominantly lack any kind of self-consciousness? Would that necessarily invalidate the claim concerning the existence of a minimal experiential self? Not necessarily. After all, the claim being made is that the experiential self can be identified with the subjectivity and first-personal character of experiential life. To argue that our mental life (occasionally or predominantly) lacks such first-personal character is not per se to question the identification. It merely limits its applicability and frequency. If one wants to reject the notion of an experiential self, a different line of argumentation must be employed. One might concede that there is something like a basic subjectivity of experience, but insist that we need to preserve the difference between subjectivity and selfhood. The latter cannot be reduced to the former. This is a view with many proponents, but although they share the negative thesis, when it comes to the positive view, they can be roughly divided into two very different camps. On one side, we find people who ultimately argue that the self is illusory, on the other, people who defend the reality of the self, but who claim that the real core of selfhood must be located elsewhere, namely, within the space of normativity. Let me discuss each view in turn, and let me start with the no-self challenge.

4.1 The illusory self

In her book *Analytical Buddhism: The Two-Tiered Illusion of Self*, Albahari argues that the self is an illusion. What notion of selfhood is she out to deny? She initially provides the following definition: The self should be understood as a unified, happiness-seeking, unbrokenly persisting, ontologically distinct conscious subject who is the owner of experiences, the thinker of thoughts, and the agent of actions. One of the interesting aspects of Albahari's proposal is that whereas many advocates of a no-self doctrine have denied that consciousness is characterized by unity, unbrokenness, and invariability, and have taken the denial of these features to amount to a denial of the reality of the self, Albahari considers all three to be real features of consciousness, but she nevertheless considers the self to be illusory (Albahari 2006: 3).

To get clearer on why she thinks this is the case, let us take a closer look at a distinction she introduces among different forms of ownership, namely, *possessive ownership, perspectival ownership*, and *personal ownership*. We can ignore possessive ownership, which in this context is of less interest, since it merely denotes the fact that certain objects (a car, a pair of trousers) can be regarded as mine by right of social convention. But what is the difference between personal ownership and perspectival ownership? Personal ownership is a question of identifying oneself as the personal owner of an experience, thought, action; it is a question of appropriating certain experiences, thoughts, actions, etc. as one's own, that is, a question of either thinking of them as being *mine* or apprehending them as being part of *me* (and this is something that can occur either pre-reflectively or reflectively). By contrast, for a subject to own something in a perspectival sense is simply for the experience, thought, or action in question to present itself in a distinctive manner to the subject whose experience, thought, or action it is. So the reason I can be said to own my thoughts or perceptions perspectivally is because they appear to me in a manner that is different from how they can appear to anybody else (Albahari 2006: 53–4).

Albahari argues that there is a close link between having a sense of personal ownership and having a sense of self. When the subject identifies certain items as being itself or being part of itself, it will harbour a sense of personal ownership towards the items in question. But this very process of identification generates the sense of a self–other distinction. It constitutes a felt boundary between what belongs to self and what doesn't. Thereby the self is cast as a unified and ontologically distinct entity—one that stands apart from other things (Albahari 2006: 73, 90). In this way, the subject understood as a mere point of view is turned into a substantial personalized entity (Albahari 2006: 94). According to Albahari, there is consequently more to being a self than being a point of view, than having perspectival ownership.

One way to bring out the difference between perspectival and personal ownership is to point to possible dissociations between the two. Pathology seems to provide some examples. In cases of depersonalization, we can come across thoughts, feelings, etc. that are perspectivally owned, that is, which continue to present themselves in a unique manner to the subject, without, however, being felt as the subject's own (Albahari 2006: 55). Thus, on Albahari's reading, the process of identification fails in depersonalization, and as a consequence, no sense of personal ownership regarding the experience in question is generated (Albahari 2006: 61).

Let us now consider Albahari's scepticism about the self. What does it mean for the self to lack reality? What does it mean for the self to be illusory? On Albahari's account, an illusion involves a conflict between appearance and reality: x is illusory if x does not have any appearance-independent reality but nevertheless purports to have such reality; that is, we are dealing with an illusion if x purports through its appearance to exist in a particular manner without really doing so (Albahari 2006: 122). One obvious question, though, is whether such a definition really makes that much sense when applied to the self. Does the self really purport to exist outside its own appearance? This consideration leads Albahari to redefine the notion of illusion slightly. If the self purports to be what she calls unconstructed, that is, independent of the experiences it is the subject of and the objects it is directed at, and if it should turn out that it in reality depends, even if only partially, on perspectivally ownable objects (including various experiential episodes), then the self must be regarded as being illusory (Albahari 2006: 130).

Albahari also emphasizes the need for a distinction between self and sense of self. To have a sense of x doesn't entail that x exists. Indeed, whereas Albahari takes the sense of self to exist and be real, she considers the self itself to be illusory (Albahari 2006: 17). Contrary to expectations, our sense of self is not underpinned by an actually existing ontologically independent self-entity. Rather, all that really exists is the manifold of thoughts, emotions, perceptions, etc., as well as a pure locus of apprehension, which Albahari terms *witness-consciousness*. It is the experiential flow in conjunction with this locus of apprehension that generates the sense of self. But if this is so, the self lacks an essential property of selfhood, namely, ontological independence (Albahari 2006: 72). In short, the illusory status of the self is due to the fact that the self does not have the ontological status it purports to have. Thoughts appear to be owned and initiated by an independently existing unified self, but rather than preceding the experiences, rather than thinking the thoughts, it is in reality the other way round. It is not the self that unifies our thoughts and experiences; they do so themselves with some help from the accompanying witness-consciousness (Albahari 2006: 130–2). To repeat, although it might seem to the subject as if there is a pre-existing self which identifies with various intentional states, the reality of the matter is that the self is created and constructed through these repeated acts of identification (Albahari 2006: 58).

As I mentioned earlier, an interesting aspect of Albahari's proposal is that she considers many of the features traditionally ascribed to the self to be real; it is just that, in her view, they become distorted and illusory if taken to be features of the self (Albahari 2006: 74). For instance, Albahari takes our conscious life to be characterized by an intrinsic but elusive sense of subjective presence, one that is common to all modalities of awareness, that is, one that is common to seeing, hearing, thinking, feeling, introspecting, etc. (Albahari 2006: 112, 144, 156). What does this subjective presence amount to? It includes the experience of being the perspectival owner of various experiences. It also includes diachronic and synchronic unity. Although we experience various objects, and although the objects we experience might change from one moment to the next, there still appears to be an unbroken consciousness that observes the change without itself changing (Albahari 2006: 155). Indeed, while from a first-person perspective it certainly makes sense to say that I have various experiences, we automatically feel them to belong to one and the same consciousness. For Albahari, all these features are properly ascribed to witness-consciousness, and she is adamant that we have to distinguish witness-consciousness from the self. Whereas the latter, on her definition, involves felt boundaries between self and non-self, the former doesn't.

Let me recapitulate. For Albahari, one can be conscious without being presented to oneself as an ontologically unique subject with personalized boundaries that distinguishes a *me* from the rest of the world. One can be conscious without being aware of oneself as a personal owner, a thinker of thoughts, an agent of actions. Examples that come to mind are again cases of pathology. Albahari asks us to consider both the real-life case of epileptic automatism and the hypothetical case of global depersonalization. In both cases, the person or patient would be awake and responsive to the environment, so there would be awareness present. But there would be no sense of a bounded individual self; there would be a complete lack of personal ownership; there would be no sense of me or mine (Albahari 2006: 171, 177). Albahari suggests that such a state of mind might be encountered not only in pathologies, but also in newborn infants and in primitive organisms. And, as she then points out in the conclusion of her book, and this is of course where her Buddhist orientation becomes evident, if we were to attain enlightenment, we would move from consciousness-plus-self-illusion to consciousness-*sans*-self-illusion, and the latter condition, although strictly speaking not identical with global depersonalization (after all, it correlates with highly advanced cognitive capacities), might nevertheless be compared to it (Albahari 2006: 161, 207).

The debate between advocates of self and no-self accounts is complicated by the fact that there is rather little consensus about what precisely a self amounts to, just as there is little agreement on what a no-self doctrine entails. Albahari's account in *Analytical Buddhism* constitutes a neat example of this. As we have just seen, Albahari denies the reality of the self and argues that it is illusory. To that extent, she should obviously count as a defender of a no-self account. At the same time, however, she ascribes a number of features to what she calls witness-consciousness, features including invariance, unconstructedness, and ontological independence, which many defenders of a traditional notion of the self would consider essential and defining features of selfhood. In fact, whereas I would favour replacing the traditional notion of a 'subject of experience' with the notion of a 'subjectivity of experience' (whereas the first phrasing might suggest that the self is something that exists apart from, or above, the experience and, for that reason, something that might be encountered in separation from the experience or even something the experience may occasionally lack, the second phrasing makes such misunderstandings less likely), Albahari wants to retain the former notion, since she considers the subject ontologically distinct from the experiences. Some might consequently claim that Albahari, despite her official allegiance to the no-self doctrine, is actually committed to a more robust notion of selfhood than many contemporary defenders of the self, myself included.[1] But, of course, one might also make the reverse move. I defend the

---

[1] Consider that although Albahari denies unconstructedness to the self, she ascribes it to witness-consciousness. As she puts it at one point, 'awareness must be shown to exist in the manner it purports to exist. Awareness purports to exist as a witnessing presence that is unified, unbroken and yet elusive to

reality of the self, but according to Albahari, the notion of selfhood that I operate with is so deflationary, and ultimately so revisionary in nature, that she has claimed that my position ends up being very similar to that of the no-self theorists I am criticizing (Albahari 2009: 80). When first encountering this criticism, I was somewhat puzzled, but I have subsequently come to realize that there is an obvious sense in which Albahari is right. It all comes down to what precisely a no-self doctrine amounts to. And, as Jonardon Ganeri has pointed out, there is no simple answer to the question whether the aim of the no-self doctrine (in so far as one can speak of it at all in the singular) is to identify and reject a mistaken understanding of the self—one that perpetuates suffering—or whether the point is rather to reject and dispel all notions of the self (Ganeri 2007: 185–6).[2]

Although disagreeing with a number of Albahari's positive claims, Georges Dreyfus, for instance, has explicitly argued that although the no-self view does entail a denial of a self-entity, it shouldn't be read as entailing a denial of subjectivity. There is, on his view, no enduring experiencing subject, no inner controller or homunculus. Rather, what we find is an ever changing stream of consciousness. This stream is, however, to be conceived of as a process of self-awareness. Dreyfus consequently argues that consciousness is characterized by a pervasive reflexivity, by a basic self-presencing that is part and parcel of our experiential life and not to be conceived of as an additional or separate act of cognition. But although Dreyfus by implication is prepared to accept the reality of subjectivity, he insists that distortion arises the moment we interpret this subjectivity as a bounded, unified self (Dreyfus 2011: 123). In short, the undeniable presence of a transient flow of experiences, where each is reflexively self-aware, doesn't entail the existence of an enduring self-entity; rather, the latter is, on Dreyfus's view, an illusory reification (Dreyfus 2011: 131).

Both Dreyfus and Albahari are very confident in spelling out what a self is, and having provided a univocal definition of it, they then proceed to deny its existence. The definition they provide is, however, overly simplistic. Although sceptics are often prepared to admit that the no-self option comes in a variety of different flavours and strengths (Metzinger 2011: 293), they frequently fail to realize that the same holds true for the no-no-self alternative. Now, there is no doubt that some people have defended a notion of the self similar to the one that Albahari and Dreyfus operate

---

direct observation. As something whose phenomenology purports to be unborrowed from objects of consciousness, awareness, if it exists, must exist as *completely unconstructed* by the content of any perspectivally ownable objects such as thoughts, emotions or perceptions. If *apparent* awareness... turned out to owe its existence to such object-content rather than to (unconstructed) *awareness itself*, then that would render awareness constructed and illusory and hence lacking in independent reality' (Albahari 2006: 162). This seems to commit one to viewing awareness as an ontologically independent region. It is not clear to me, however, why one would want to uphold such a view of consciousness in the first place. For further phenomenological reflections on Albahari's notion of witness-consciousness, see Fasching (2011).

[2] Needless to say, there is also a rather significant difference between claiming that experience is fundamentally selfless and claiming that a dissolution or annihilation of the self is an ultimate state we can (and should) seek to attain.

with, but I would dispute their claim that this notion is *the default notion*, that is, that it is either a particularly classical notion of self or a particularly commonsensical one, that is, one that is part of our folk psychology. Consider again the claim that the self, if it exists, is some kind of ontologically independent invariant principle of identity that stands apart from and above the stream of changing experiences: something that remains unchanging from birth to death; something that remains entirely unaffected by language acquisition, social relationships, major life events, personal commitments, projects, and values; something that cannot develop or flourish, nor be disturbed or shattered. Frankly, I don't see such a notion as being very much in line with our pre-philosophical, everyday understanding of who we are. As for the claim that the definition captures *the* (rather than *a*) traditional philosophical understanding of self, this is also highly questionable. Just consider, to take some (not entirely) randomly chosen examples, the accounts we find in Aristotle or Montaigne or Heidegger (for informative historical overviews, see Seigel 2005; Sorabji 2006). Heidegger explicitly argues that we should look at our intentional experiences if we wish to study the self. On his account, our experiential life is world-related, and there is a presence of self when we are engaged with the world; that is, self-experience is the self-experience of a world-immersed self (Heidegger 1993: 258; 1994: 95). Thus, not only does he insist that self-experience shouldn't be understood in contrast and opposition to world-experience (to have a self-experience, to be self-experiencing, doesn't involve an interruption of the experiential interaction with the world in order to turn one's gaze inwards), but it is also difficult to see him endorsing the claim that unconstructedness and boundedness are essential features of self, features that any viable notion of self must include. One can defend the reality of the self without committing oneself to the view that the self is ontologically independent of experiences and the surrounding world. In any case, when comparing the definition of selfhood provided by Albahari and Dreyfus with the definitions found in contemporary discussions of the self, it should be evident that the latter discussions are more complex, more equivocal, and that there are far more notions of self at play, including notions of ecological, experiential, dialogical, narrative, relational, embodied, and socially constructed selves. This complexity is ignored by Albahari and Dreyfus, and they thereby fail to realize that many of the contemporary notions of self are quite different from the concept they criticize. To mention just one discipline that can exemplify this, consider developmental psychology and the work of developmental psychologists like Stern (1985), Neisser (1988), Rochat (2001), Hobson (2002), or Reddy (2008). Thus, rather than saying that the self does not exist, I think the sceptics should settle for a more modest claim. They should qualify their statement and instead deny the existence of a special kind of self.

However, Albahari and Dreyfus might still insist that the contentious issue, rather than being a metaphysical and substantial one, is really a semantic and terminological one. When is it appropriate to call something a self? They might maintain that the minimalist notion of experiential selfhood is unacceptably deflationary and just too minimal to count as a genuine self (see Ganeri 2012: 154), and consequently deny that subjectivity of experience equals or amounts to a form of selfhood. I have already considered, in Chapter 2, this kind of objection, and given reasons for my own terminological preference. In addition, however, they might insist that we need to distinguish self-consciousness from consciousness of a self. Consciousness might be self-disclosing and self-revealing, but this only entails that consciousness is aware of *itself*, and not that it is aware of *an experiencing self*. Not surprisingly, this is a point that has been made by others. It matches well with Gurwitsch's classical distinction between an egological and a non-egological theory of (self-)consciousness (Gurwitsch 1941). Whereas an *egological* theory would claim that when I watch a movie by Melville, I am not only intentionally directed at the *movie*, nor merely aware of the movie being *watched*, I am also aware that it is being watched by *me*, a *non-egological* theory would omit the reference to a subject of experience and simply say that there is an awareness of the watching of the movie. Or, as Lichtenberg phrased it in his classical objection to Descartes: We only know of the existence of our sensations, ideas, and thoughts. Experiences simply take place, and that is all. To say *cogito* and to affirm the existence of an I is already to say too much (Lichtenberg 2000: 190).

The problem, though, is that this line of thinking is fuelled by too narrow a definition of what selfhood amounts to. Gurwitsch's distinction can be found in his article 'A Non-Egological Conception of Consciousness', which is a lucid reading of Sartre's *La Transcendance de l'Égo* (and incidentally the first article on Sartre published in English). But even Sartre himself came to see the distinction as being too crude. Whereas Sartre in his 1936 work had characterized non-egological consciousness as impersonal, he described this view as mistaken in both *L'Être et le néant* and his important article 'Conscience de soi et connaissance de soi', from 1948. In both cases, Sartre's crucial move is to distinguish self and ego (Sartre 2003: 263). Although no ego exists on the pre-reflective level, consciousness remains characterized by a basic dimension of selfhood precisely because of its ubiquitous self-consciousness. This is why Sartre could write, 'pre-reflective consciousness is self-consciousness. It is this same notion of *self* which must be studied, for it defines the very being of consciousness' (Sartre 2003: 100). Thus, rather than defining self-consciousness on the basis of a preconceived notion of the self, Sartre's idea was to let our notion of the self arise out of a correct understanding of self-consciousness. It is certainly true that pre-reflective self-consciousness shouldn't be understood as consciousness of a separate and distinct *self*. But pre-reflective self-consciousness is ineliminably first-personal, that is, characterized by for-me-ness. And that is all that is needed in order to warrant the notion of an experiential self.

Another way to make the same point is by arguing that the following rendering of pre-reflective self-consciousness remains imprecise: A conscious intentional episode is conscious of a certain object and at the same time also pre-reflectively given or manifested. One reason why this rendering is unfortunate is that it fails to explain our capacity to act on the basis of our experiences. If all I am conscious of when I see a fork in front of me is the fork and an (unowned) perceiving of the fork, I will not be aware that I am the one who is perceiving the fork, and consequently fail to realize that I am in a position to grasp the fork. It is partly for this reason that Greg Janzen in his own defence of a reflexivist account of consciousness has argued that we should replace 'A subject S consciously perceives x at t only if at t S is implicitly aware of perceiving x' with 'A subject S consciously perceives x at t only if at t S is implicitly aware of *herself perceiving* x' (Janzen 2008: 120–1). I think Janzen is right. The question, though, is what conclusion one should draw from this. Janzen himself favours fictionalism. As he says,

> Conscious creatures have various physical and psychological properties, and one of these latter is a sense of self. But we do not have selves, where having a self means that one is in possession of some kind of *inner psychological object*. This kind of alleged entity is, I submit, a philosophical fiction. (Janzen 2008: 131)

This would be the wrong conclusion to draw. It is much better to say that conscious experiences in so far as they are first-personal episodes cannot be selfless, but that this doesn't commit us to the idea that the self is some kind of inner object.[3]

At this point let me concede that the notion of an experiential self is indeed a quite minimal notion and that it is unable to accommodate or capture all ordinary senses of the term 'self'. Consider first something we have already touched upon, namely, that a self on some accounts is something that has or owns experiences; it is something we ascribe experiences to, and consequently something that must be ontologically distinct from the experiences themselves. The proposed notion of an experiential self differs from this conception, but, as I have also already pointed out, it is possible to offer an alternative experiential or phenomenological interpretation of ownership, where the mineness or for-me-ness of experience, rather than being a question of a non-experiential relation between the experience and a distinct owner, is a question of the experience's first-personal mode of givenness.

Consider next first-person beliefs such as 'I broke my arm' or 'I won the competition'. It might be close to incomprehensible how the referent of 'I' in those two cases could be the experiential self, that is, the for-me-ness, or first-personal character, of experience. However, it is not obvious that this really counts as an objection against the account. Consider, by comparison, the relation between the logically and ontogenetically primitive kind of self-awareness that is constitutive of phenomenal consciousness, and the more complex form of self-consciousness that one engages

---

[3] Much arguably depends on what precisely we mean when talking of something being an object. The phenomenologists typically define an object as something that appears in a specific manner. More specifically, for x to be an object is for x to appear as something that stands in opposition to or over against the subjective experience of it (compare the German term *Gegenstand*). Galen Strawson, by contrast, who vigorously defends the claim that the self is an object, opts for a rather different definition. He writes, 'to be an object (if objects exist) is simply to be a "strong unity"' (Strawson 2009: 298).

in when one is appraising how one is perceived by others. The former kind of self-awareness might be necessary for the latter, but it is certainly not sufficient. Likewise, although there is certainly more to being a human self than being an experiential self, the claim being made is that the first-personal character of consciousness is a necessary precondition for something like self-conscious thinking and first-person self-reference (see Zahavi 1999; Grünbaum and Zahavi 2013).

Ultimately, however, and this will become increasingly clear as we progress, I don't think we should make do with the thin notion of an experiential self. This notion, although fundamental, has some clear limitations, and it must be supplemented by thicker notions that do justice to other important aspects of self. More specifically, our account of human selfhood will remain inadequate as long as we fail to consider the self that forms plans, makes promises, and accepts responsibilities, the self that is defined and shaped by its values, ideals, goals, convictions, and decisions. Consider as a case in point the issue of emotional investment; consider that we respond emotionally to that which matters to us, to that which we care about, to that towards which we are not indifferent. In that sense, one might argue that emotions involve appraisals of what has importance, significance, value, and relevance to oneself. Consider the extent to which emotions like shame, guilt, pride, hope, and repentance help to constitute our sense of being a temporally extended self. Consider in this context also the role of boundaries and limits. Your limits express the norms and rules you abide by; they express what you can accept and what you cannot accept. They constitute your integrity. To ask others to respect your boundaries is to ask them to take you seriously as a person. A violation of, or infringement upon, these boundaries is felt as invasive and in some cases as humiliating. When it comes to these facets of self, I consequently think (and this is something I shall elaborate further in Part III) that boundaries, values, and emotions are highly significant, but I don't think an emphasis on boundaries has much to do with the endorsement of an enduring soul-substance that remains the same from birth to death. And I don't see why opposition to the latter should necessitate a rejection of the former as well. In the former case, we are dealing with a culturally, socially, and linguistically embedded self that is under constant construction. But is this a reason for declaring the self in question illusory? I don't see why, unless, that is, one's prior metaphysical commitments dictate it.

In recent years, quite a number of people have stressed the existence of convergent ideas in Western phenomenology and Buddhism. It has been claimed that both traditions represent serious efforts to nurture a disciplined first-person approach to consciousness (Varela and Shear 1999), and some have even started to speak of a Buddhist phenomenology (Lusthaus 2002). I am not denying that there might be some truth to this, but when appraising Buddhist views of the nature and status of self, one should not overlook that they are also driven and motivated by strong metaphysical and soteriological concerns, and that this occasionally leads to claims and conclusions that are quite far removed from phenomenology. As an example, consider the Abhidharmic view that billions of distinct mind-moments occur in the span of a blink of the eye (Bodhi 1993: 156).

Dennett (1992) and Metzinger (2003) both deny the reality of the self, and part of their reason for doing this, part of the reason why they think the self is fictitious, is that a truly fundamental account of reality on their view can dispense with the self. Many Buddhist metaphysicians would share this view owing to their endorsement of a thoroughgoing *mereological reductionism*, according to which no composite entity is ultimately real (MacKenzie 2008; Siderits 2011). Although I have sympathy for the idea that we shouldn't multiply entities beyond necessity, I think the view in question is far too austere. By the same token, one would have to declare the world we live in and know and care about (including everyday objects and events like chairs, operas, marriage ceremonies, and civil rights) illusory. Such a view would be quite different from any phenomenological attempt to rehabilitate our life-world.

4.2 Normativity and narrativity

Let me now turn to the other version of the criticism, that is, the one that, like me, embraces realism about self and which would deny the austere metaphysics of the Buddhist critics, but which emphasizes the normative rather than experiential basis of selfhood.

In *Self-Constitution: Agency, Identity, and Integrity*, Korsgaard argues that human beings, qua rational beings, have a distinct form of identity, a norm-governed form of identity for which we are ourselves responsible (Korsgaard 2009, p. xii). Importantly, she doesn't deny self-consciousness to non-human animals. As she readily admits, self-consciousness comes in degrees and takes many forms. When a tiger stands downwind of her intended prey, she is locating herself with respect to her prey in physical space, and this constitutes a rudimentary form of self-consciousness. Likewise, an animal that makes gestures of submission when a more dominant animal enters the scene is locating himself in social space, and this too is a form of self-consciousness. But, for Korsgaard, human beings are capable of being self-conscious in a very particular way, a way that might even be considered the distinguishing mark of rationality. We can be aware not only that we desire or fear certain things, but also that we are inclined to act in certain ways on the basis of these desires or fears. That is, we can be conscious of the potential grounds of our actions, the principles on which our actions are based (Korsgaard 2009: 115). Moreover, we can subject our beliefs and actions (and emotional reactions) to critical assessment. Korsgaard argues that the result of this form of self-consciousness is a liberation from the control of instincts. Instincts still operate within us, in the sense that they are the source of many of our incentives. But instincts no longer *determine* how we respond to those incentives, that is, what we do in the face of them. They *propose* responses, but we may or may not act in the way they propose. To that extent, self-consciousness opens up a space between the incentive and the response, a space Korsgaard calls 'reflective distance' (Korsgaard 2009: 116). Korsgaard even talks of this reflective self-consciousness as involving a self-division, in that it separates the perceptions from their automatic normative force (Korsgaard 2009: 213). Indeed, if we are to subject our different beliefs and desires to a critical, normative evaluation, it is not sufficient simply to have immediate first-personal access to the states in question. Rather, when we reflect, we step back from our ongoing mental activities and, as Richard Moran has pointed out, this stepping back is a metaphor of distancing and separation, but also one of observation and confrontation. The reflective distancing is what allows us to relate critically to our mental states and put them into question (Moran 2001: 142–3). Korsgaard now links this analysis to the issue of self-identity by claiming that it is when I act in accordance with normative principles, it is when I allow them to govern my will, when I endorse, embrace, and affirm them, that I make them my own and thereby decide who to be (Korsgaard 2009: 43). The self-identity in question is consequently quite literally a process of self-constitution; it is an identity that is constituted by our choices and actions (Korsgaard 2009: 19). Korsgaard furthermore speaks of this process as involving the selection of certain social roles, and of fulfilling such roles with integrity and dedication. It also involves the task of integrating such roles into a single identity, into a coherent life (Korsgaard 2009: 25).

Like Korsgaard, Harry Frankfurt is not out to deny the subjectivity of experience. In fact, he readily accepts that consciousness entails a basic form of self-consciousness. Moreover, he does so without endorsing some version of a higher-order theory of consciousness. He writes:

the self-consciousness in question is a sort of *immanent reflexivity* by virtue of which every instance of being conscious grasps not only that of which it is an awareness but also the awareness of it. It is like a source of light which, in addition to illuminating whatever other things fall within its scope, renders itself visible as well. (Frankfurt 1988: 162)

According to Frankfurt, however, this fact shouldn't make us overlook a significant difference, namely, the one existing between experiences that, so to speak, are mere happenings in the history of my mental life and experiences that are my own in a much more profound sense. In other words, even if it could be argued that an experience, that is, a conscious thought, perception, desire, emotion, etc., cannot occur without an experiencer, since every experience is necessarily an experience for someone, this truism masks crucial distinctions. Consider, for instance, thoughts that willy-nilly run through our heads, thoughts that strike us out of the blue; consider passions and desires that are felt, from the first-person perspective, as intrusive—as when somebody says that when he was possessed by anger, he was not in possession of himself; or take experiences that are induced in us through hypnosis or drugs, and compare these cases with experiences, thoughts, and desires that we welcome or accept at the time of their occurrence. As Frankfurt argues, although the former class might indeed be conscious events that occur in us, although they are events in the history of a person's mind, they are not that person's experience, thought, or desire

(Frankfurt 1988: 59–61). They only become so in so far as the person endorses them. A person is consequently not simply to be identified with whatever goes on in his mind. To disapprove of or reject felt passions or desires means to withdraw or distance oneself from them. To accept passions or desires, to see them as having a natural place in one's experience, means to identify with them (Frankfurt 1988: 68). Frankfurt concedes that it is difficult to articulate the notion of identification at stake in a satisfactory manner, but ultimately he suggests that when a person decides something without reservations,

the decision determines what the person really wants by making the desire on which he decides fully his own. To this extent the person, in making a decision by which he identifies with a desire, *constitutes himself.* The pertinent desire is no longer in any way external to him. It is not a desire that he 'has' merely as a subject in whose history it happens to occur, as a person may 'have' an involuntary spasm that happens to occur in the history of his body. It comes to be a desire that is incorporated into him by virtue of the fact that he has it *by his own will.* . . . even if the person is not responsible for the fact that the desire *occurs,* there is an important sense in which he takes responsibility for the fact of having the desire—the fact that the desire is in the fullest sense his, that it constitutes what he really wants—when he identifies himself with it. (Frankfurt 1988: 170)

Frankfurt's basic point is consequently that the identification in question amounts to a specific form of ownership that is constitutive of self. Or rather, and importantly, arguably his emphasis is on *authorship* rather than mere *ownership.* This point tallies rather well with Albahari's focus on personal ownership, and also with her suggestion that the constitution of a sense of self is closely linked to the issue of emotional investment (though, of course, there is nothing to suggest that Frankfurt would agree with Albahari's metaphysical conclusion, that is, her scepticism about the self) (Albahari 2006: 171, 178–9). They also share the view that the mere subjectivity of experience is insufficient for selfhood. On their view, we need to distinguish between being merely conscious or sentient, and being a self. The requirements that must be met to qualify for the latter are higher.

How precisely should we understand the idea that being a self is an achievement rather than a given, more a question of an act than of a fact? Let me examine in some detail a currently rather influential attempt to underscore the normatively constructed character of selfhood, namely, the so-called *narrative account of self.* By comparing and contrasting the narrative account with the minimalist account I am proposing, we shall get a better idea of what is distinctive about the latter.

Why should it be natural for us to think of the self in terms of narrative structures? A standard answer is that selves, fundamentally speaking, are agents, and that our actions gain intelligibility by having a place in a narrative sequence. If we are to make sense of the idea that somebody is acting for reasons, we need to appeal to narratives, since they are what allows us to make sense of the current situation by situating it in a meaningful temporal context (Rudd 2012: 178). It is within the framework of such narratives that we can ask the central who-questions: 'Who is this?' 'Who did this?' 'Who is responsible?' To ask for the identity of the one who is responsible is, consequently, to ask for his narrative identity. When confronted with the question 'Who am I?' we will typically tell a certain life story, a story that emphasizes certain aspects that we deem to be of special significance, to be that which constitutes the leitmotif in our life, to be that which defines who we are, that which we present to others for recognition and approval (Ricœur 1988: 246). This is why it has been claimed that any attempt to elucidate the notions of selfhood or personal identity independently of and in isolation from notions such as narrativity, intelligibility, and accountability is bound to fail (MacIntyre 1985: 218).

Consider that self-comprehension and self-knowledge is not something that is given once and for all; rather, it is something that has to be acquired and which can be obtained with varying degrees of success. As long as life goes on, there is no final self-understanding. The same, however, might also be said of what it means to be a self. This is why being a self is quite different from being slim, 46 years old, or increasingly grey-haired. Who I am is not something given, but something evolving, something that is realized through my projects. There is no such thing as who (in contrast to what) I am independently of how I understand and interpret myself. In short, no account of who one is can afford to ignore the issue of one's self-interpretation, since the former is (at least partially) constituted by the latter.

It is important to understand that the emphasis on narratives is not merely to be understood as an epistemological thesis. I attain insight into who I am by situating my character traits, the values and ideals I endorse, the goals I pursue, etc. within a life story that traces their origin and development; a life story that tells where I am coming from and where I am heading. In a similar manner, I get to know who you are by learning your life story. But the reason why narratives constitute a privileged way to obtain knowledge about the self is, according to the proposal currently under consideration, precisely because they constitute it. As Bruner puts it, 'A self is probably the most impressive work of art we ever produce, surely the most intricate' (Bruner 2003: 14). Thus, for most narrativists, narratives do not merely capture aspects of an already existing self, since there is no such thing as a pre-existing self, one that just awaits being portrayed in words. To believe in such a prelinguistic given is quite literally to have been misled by stories.[4]

The narrative account is quite explicit in emphasizing both the *temporal* and the *social dimension* of selfhood. Narration is a social process that starts in early childhood and continues for the rest of our lives. Who one is depends on the values,

---

[4] Peter Goldie is one of the exceptions. He specifically distinguishes a narrative self and a narrative sense of self, and while he concedes that there is a distinctive narrative way of thinking of oneself, he finds the notion of a distinct narrative self otiose (Goldie 2012: 117–21). One limitation with this more modest proposal, however, is that it risks ignoring the extent to which our self-interpretation and self-understanding affect our self-identity, that is, who we are.

ideals, and goals one has; it is a question of what has significance and meaning for one, and this, of course, is conditioned by the community of which one is part. The concepts I use to express the salient features of who I take myself to be are concepts derived from tradition and theory and will vary widely from one historical period to the next and across social class and culture. As Bruner points out, our self-making stories are not made up from scratch; they pattern themselves on conventional genres. When talking about myself, my selfhood becomes part of the public domain, and its shape and nature is guided by cultural models of what selfhood should and shouldn't be (Bruner 2003: 65). Furthermore, others are not only called upon to hear and to accept the narrative accounts we give of our actions and experiences. Who we take ourselves to be is also influenced by how we are perceived and understood by others. We come to think of ourselves as others think of us. Our very identity is affected by our adaptation, incorporation, and retelling of the stories that others tell about us. This is so even if we explicitly reject or resist these stories.

When I interpret myself in terms of a life story, I might be both the narrator and the main character, but I am not the sole author. The beginning of my own story has always already been made for me by others, and the way the story unfolds is only in part determined by my own choices and decisions. Thus, as has often been claimed, one cannot be a self on ones own, but only together with others. To that extent selfhood is something that constitutively depends on others. To come to know oneself as a person with a particular life history and particular character traits is, consequently, both more complicated than knowing one's immediate beliefs and desires, and less private than it might initially seem (Jopling 2000: 137). In fact, the story of any individual life is not only interwoven with the stories of others (parents, siblings, friends, etc.), it is also embedded in a larger historical and communal meaning-giving structure (MacIntyre 1985: 221). I am the inheritor and continuer of a tradition, or, to quote Dilthey and Husserl:

The historical world is always there, and the individual does not merely contemplate it from without but is intertwined with it.... We are historical beings before we are observers of history, and only because we are the former do we become the latter. (Dilthey 2002: 297)

That which I have constituted originally (primally instituted) is mine. But I am a 'child of the times'; I am a member of a we-community in the broadest sense—a community that has its tradition and that, for its part, is connected in a novel manner with the generative subjects, the closest and the most distant ancestors. And these have 'influenced' me: I am what I am as an heir. What is really and originally my own? To what extent am I really primally instituting (urstiftend)? I am it on the basis of the 'tradition'; everything of my own is founded, in part through the tradition of my ancestors, in part through the tradition of my contemporaries. (Husserl 1973b: 223)

The narratives we tell influence the way we relate to our remembered past and anticipated futures. They are consequently not merely of relevance when it comes to what has happened, but are also evoked in order to make sense of the future direction and unfolding of our lives. According to the narrative account of selfhood, it is precisely narratives that allow for a synthesis of the diverse and heterogeneous aspects of life; they allow us to link temporally dispersed episodes in such a way as to make sense of them. They allow for a coordination of past, present, and future, and establish a web of semantic relations that unite events across time into a meaningful whole (Atkins 2004: 347, 350). Indeed, according to the narrative approach, we weave stories of our lives, we organize and unify our experiences and actions according to narrative structures, and the claim has precisely been that this is what constitutes us as persisting selves. As MacIntyre puts it, the unity of the self 'resides in the unity of a narrative which links birth to life to death as narrative beginning to middle to end' (MacIntyre 1985: 205). When engaged in a self-constituting narrative, what happens to me is interpreted not as an isolated incident, but as part of an ongoing self-involving story. Whether or not a particular action, experience, or characteristic counts as mine, in the emphatic sense of the term, is consequently a question of whether or not it is included in my self-narrative (Schechtman 2007: 162). Thus, and this is another way of emphasizing the active accomplishment involved, rather than merely being a question of having a history, being a self is a question of leading a life in the sense of understanding that life as a narrative (Schechtman 2011: 395). Indeed, as Schechtman argues, to make past experiences ours, to affirm the identity of the past self and the present self, it is not sufficient simply to remember these past experiences from the first-person perspective. The existence of psychological connection and continuity is insufficient. Rather, we must identify with the temporally removed experience; we must care about and feel an affective connection to it. It must be something that matters to us. The more strongly we appropriate it by weaving it into our narrative, the more fully and completely it is our own (Schechtman 2007: 167, 171, 174, 175).[5] In fact, episodic memories are altogether not as essential for a narrative sense of self as might initially have been assumed. Based on the testimonies of others, I can construct a narrative of, and thereby forge links to, a past that I no longer recollect from the first-person perspective. I might consequently integrate episodes and events that I have forgotten about into my self-narrative (Goldie 2012: 126).

As should be clear by now, the narrative approach is mainly concerned with the issue of long-term diachronic identity and persistency, and insists that the experience of a self as unified across a lifetime relies upon one's ability to situate one's memories, personality traits, goals, and values within a coherent narrative structure. Ricœur has occasionally presented his own notion of narrative identity as a solution to the traditional dilemma of having to choose between the Cartesian notion of the self as a principle of identity that remains the same throughout the diversity of its different states and the positions of Hume and Nietzsche, who held an identical subject to be

---

[5] In a paper published in 2001, Schechtman specifically labels the kind of affective connection that she deems essential for diachronic identity *empathic access*. As will become clear in Part II, I think this is a rather unfortunate use of the notion 'empathy'.

nothing but a substantialist illusion (Ricœur 1988: 246). Ricœur suggests that we can avoid this dilemma if we replace the notion of identity that they respectively defend and reject with the concept of narrative identity. The identity of the narrative(ly extended) self rests upon narrative configurations. Unlike the abstract identity of the same, the narrative identity can include changes and mutations within the cohesion of a lifetime. The story of a life continues to be reconfigured by all the truthful or fictive stories a subject tells about him- or herself. It is this constant reconfiguration that makes 'life itself a cloth woven of stories told' (Ricœur 1988: 246). Similar claims can be found in Schechtman, who has argued that narratives constitute the phenomenological unity of consciousness over time (2007: 167), and in Atkins, who claims that the narrative model does justice to the importance that a person attaches to being the same experiential subject over time. It secures the continuation of one's concrete first-person perspective (Atkins 2004: 342). When faced with this kind of claim, it is striking, however, how much weight Atkins puts on the reflective stance. Indeed, she even explicitly defines the first-person perspective as a *reflective* structure of human consciousness. This is also a tendency we find in other advocates of a narrative account of self.

How should we assess the narrative account? It very much targets what it takes to be specific to human self-identity, and considers self-persistence an achievement rather than a given. It is something we can succeed in, but also something we can fail at. It is a constructed identity and one where historical and narrated time plays a significant role. Rather than seeing temporality as an obstacle or challenge to self-identity, it would be more correct to consider it a crucial prerequisite.

Like most interesting accounts, however, the narrative approach faces some problems. One initial difficulty concerns the very notion of narrative. When it is being claimed that the self is a product of a narratively structured life, that it is constructed in and through narration, the claim cannot be that selfhood requires the actual composition of an autobiography. We consequently need to distinguish deliberately constructed narratives from the narratives that supposedly characterize our ongoing lives. The former is merely the expression of the kind of narrative self-interpretation that we allegedly continuously engage in. For my self-interpretation to count as narrative is, as Schechtman puts it, simply for me to understand the different life episodes in terms of their place in an unfolding story (Schechtman 1996: 97). It is a question of organizing my experiences and actions in a way that presupposes an implicit understanding of me as an evolving and thoroughly temporal protagonist, though Schechtman also argues that we at least occasionally have to be able to explicitly narrate and articulate some portion of our lives (Schechtman 2011: 407). Making such a distinction between an explicit and an implicit narrative is crucial if one wants to avoid an objection that has frequently been raised against the narrative account, the objection, namely, that although self-narratives might capture something about who we are, our selfhood cannot be reduced to that which is narrated, and that we consequently shouldn't make the mistake of confusing the reflective, narrative grasp of a life with the pre-reflective experiences that make up that life prior to the experiences being organized into a narrative (Drummond 2004: 119). To tell an explicit story about one's own life is after all not simply a recounting of the brute facts; rather, it is, as Bruner admits, an interpretative feat (Bruner 2003: 12–13). Stories are not simply records of what happened; they are essentially constructive and reconstructive phenomena that involve deletions, abridgements, and reorderings. Since our lives are far too complex and multifaceted to fit into one single narrative, a storyteller will consequently impose more coherence, integrity, fullness, and closure on the life events than they possessed while simply being lived. To that extent, the storytelling necessarily involves an element of confabulation (Gallagher 2003).

To distinguish a lived implicit narrative from an articulated and explicit narrative can alleviate some of these problems. However, making this move also makes it urgent to spell out precisely what such lived narratives amount to. Some authors have suggested that it is the very beginning–middle–end structure of our life events that is important, and that this proto- or micro-narrative structure should be seen as an extension of certain temporal configurations already found in experience and action (Carr 1991: 162). The problem with this type of retort, however, is that, by severing the link between language and narrative, it threatens to make the latter notion too inclusive and consequently too diluted. Moreover, and this is a point that has been made by Menary, if one opts for such a deflationary definition of narratives, one runs the risk of jettisoning some of the core features of the narrative approach (Menary 2008: 71). Not only is the importance of the fundamental public role of narratives, the fact that narratives are told by people to other people, suddenly downplayed, but apparently narratives are also turned into something given and innate rather than something that is actively produced and accomplished.

In short, one problem facing the narrative account is to find the right balance between a too rich and a too impoverished notion of narrative. Another obvious question to ask is whether Atkins is right when she insists that the narrative account gives a 'central and irreducible role to the first-person perspective' (Atkins 2004: 341). Does it really do justice to the first-person character of our experiential life, or does its focus on the self as a reflective construction ignore a necessary presupposition, namely, our pre-reflective experiential subjectivity? Self-narratives may capture something important about who we are, but is the narrative model capable of delivering an exhaustive account of what it means to be a self? Is *the* self merely a narrative construction? Are narratives the primary access to self? These are the kinds of radical claim that one can find among many of the defenders of the narrative account. Dennett has claimed that the self has no reality, since it is merely the fictional centre of narrative gravity. It is the abstract point where various stories intersect (Dennett 1991: 418; 1992). A similar view can also be found in Wilhelm Schapp's classical work *In Geschichten verstrickt*. Human life is a life that is caught up in stories; it is nothing apart from these stories, and such stories provide the only possible access to oneself and to others (Schapp 2004: 123, 126, 136, 160).

In its dominant version, the narrative approach combines an epistemological and an ontological thesis. Per se, I don't have a problem with either thesis, nor with their conjunction. I do think the stories we tell about ourselves reflect how we view ourselves, and that these stories come to shape our self-understanding and thereby also who we are. Thus, I would readily concede that narratives play a role in the constitution of a certain dimension or aspect of selfhood. However, I would oppose the exclusivity claim, that is, the claim that *the* self is a narratively constructed entity and that *every* access to oneself and to the selves of others is mediated by narratives. I consequently don't think the narrative approach (or any other normatively oriented approach to selfhood) can stand alone. Whereas narratives might be important tools for self-reflection, for making sense of ourselves, we shouldn't overlook the role of passivity and facticity. Who I am isn't exclusively a question of how I understand myself and how this is expressed in the story I tell about myself. It is also a question of who I am quite independently of what I decide. Indeed, as Menary points out, it is close to incoherent to claim that the subject of the experiences that the story is about is the story itself (Menary 2008: 72). The narrative account also has to be supplemented by an account that specifically targets the first-person character of our experiential life. In order to tell stories about one's own experiences and actions, one must already be in possession of a first-person perspective. To that extent, experiential ownership is a prelinguistic presupposition for any narrative practice, rather than the outcome of active storytelling.[6]

A consideration of pathology can illuminate the issue further. In *Making Stories*, Bruner admits that certain features of selfhood are innate and that we need to recognize the existence of a primitive, pre-conceptual self, but at the same time he maintains that dysnarrativia (which we encounter, for instance, in Korsakoff's syndrome and Alzheimer's disease) is deadly for selfhood and that there would be nothing like selfhood if we lacked narrative capacities (Bruner 2003: 86, 119; see also Young and Saver 2001: 78). Apart from wondering why Bruner doesn't make the obvious move and concede that it is necessary to operate with different complementary notions of the self, one might also ask whether his allusion to neuropathology is really to the point. Alzheimer's disease is a progressive, degenerative brain disorder that results in profound memory loss and changes in behaviour, thinking, and reasoning, as well as a significant decline in overall functioning. The person suffering from Alzheimer's disease will consequently have a wide range of cognitive impairments; the comprehension and expression of speech (and narratives) will only be one of the areas affected. So even *if* no self remains in the advanced stages of Alzheimer's disease, one cannot without further ado conclude that dysnarrativia was the cause of

---

[6] To claim that an experience only becomes owned the moment I tell a story about it is incidentally also challenged by many of the classical analyses of self-reference by means of the first-person pronoun, which showed that 'I' ('me', 'mine') cannot without loss be replaced by definite descriptions, and that one might refer successfully to oneself even when suffering from complete amnesia (see Zahavi 1999).

its death. (If one were on the lookout for a disorder that specifically targeted narrative capacities, global aphasia might be a better choice—but then again, who would want to claim that those struck by global aphasia cease to be selves?) Furthermore, there is a big if. It is by no means obvious that Alzheimer's disease brings about destruction of the first-person perspective, or complete annihilation of the dimension of mine-ness, or that someone who has been deprived of autobiographical memory and narrative identity would also lack perspectival ownership and no longer be affectively self-involved in any felt pain and discomfort.

In a number of studies, Stan Klein has investigated the effects of various losses of episodic memory on self-experience and self-knowledge. His patients have included not only people with advanced stages of Alzheimer's disease, but also people with severe forms of amnesia. Klein concludes that although there has been a tendency to charac-terize late-stage Alzheimer's patients as lacking a sense of self, empirical findings suggest that such individuals retain a first-person identity. Even in those extreme cases where their memory-based personal narratives have succumbed to the devastations of amnesia, and where consciousness has become partitioned into time-slices of one second's duration, a sense of self-unity and continuity is reportedly felt (Klein and Nichols 2012). The patients clearly maintain a subjective sense of themselves as experiencing entities, albeit one beset by confusion and concern. They are worried, fearful, and troubled by the 'holes' in their mental life, and behave exactly as one would expect a conscious subject to react to the cognitive chaos and experiential changes wrought by the disease (Klein 2012: 482). But if this is true, and if Alzheimer's disease does in fact constitute a severe case of dysnarrativia, we should draw exactly the opposite conclusion from Bruner. We would be forced to concede that there must be more to being a self than what is addressed by the narrative account. This is also the conclusion drawn by Damasio, who explicitly argues that neuropathology provides empirical evidence in support of a distinction between core self and autobiographical self, and also reveals that whereas core consciousness can remain intact even when extended consciousness is severely impaired or completely absent, a loss of core consciousness will cause extended consciousness to collapse as well (Damasio 1999: 17, 115–19).

When it comes to the relation between selfhood and experiential subjectivity, it is now urgent to distinguish a variety of different options. The most dismissive attitude can be found in Charles Taylor. In his view, the self is a kind of being that can only exist within a normative space. To be a self is to stand in an interpretative and evaluative relation to oneself, and people must possess enough 'depth and complex-ity' to count as full-blown persons in order to qualify as a self (Taylor 1989: 32). Taylor consequently claims that any attempt to define selfhood through some minimal or formal form of self-awareness must fail, since such a self is either non-existent or insignificant (Taylor 1989: 49). Thus, on Taylor's account experiential subjectivity has no relevance for, and can safely be ignored by, a theory of the self. However, considerably more conciliatory options are also to be found and have recently been proposed by Schechtman and Rudd (Schechtman 2011; Rudd 2012).

Rudd explicitly questions whether a narrative account really has to reject the idea of a core sense of self which is prior to narrative selfhood and which is necessary in order to make sense of the latter. In fact, he argues that as a narrativist he can accept, as a purely conceptual point, that the experiential self constitutes a minimal specification of what is necessary (though not sufficient) for selfhood, so that a narrative self is necessarily an experiential self, but also more than that (Rudd 2012: 195).[7] Furthermore, he could also accept the claim that the experiential self is more basic than the narrative self if this claim is taken simply in a developmental sense:

Infants do not have a narrative sense of self, but they do presumably have some sort of basic experiential selfhood; they are at least mental subjects. But it is not as if this basic infantile non-narrative subjectivity persists into adulthood, alongside the developed narrative sense. Rather, as the child grows and starts to develop self-consciousness, his or her basic subjectivity develops into narrative selfhood. (Rudd 2012: 195)

Rudd consequently denies that we need to posit an experiential core self existing alongside or underneath the narrative self. More specifically, he insists that for any normal adult human being, the first-personal character of experience takes a specifically narrative form. The sense in which I experience my experiential life as mine is temporal, and the structure of that temporal experience is a narrative one (Rudd 2012: 195). A very similar proposal is made by Schechtman, who urges us to consider the possibility that

the kind of phenomenological self-consciousness that makes a self is a qualitatively different *kind* of consciousness than the brute first-personal awareness we presumably share with many animals, and that this different kind of consciousness requires narrative. The idea would be that the character (and not just the content) of first-personal experience is different for self-narrators than for non-narrators. (Schechtman 2011: 410)

Rudd's and Schechtman's considerations raise at least two pressing issues. The first concerns the significance of the first-personal character of experience, that is, the formal for-me-ness or subjectivity of experience. Is it merely an indispensable and necessary prerequisite for selfhood, so that there could be no self without it (for which reason it is something that any plausible theory of self must consider and account for), or does it actually in and of itself constitute a minimal form of selfhood? The second issue is whether this first-personal character remains invariant through development, or whether it is necessarily changed and altered through language acquisition and socialization.

When it comes to the first question, Rudd's own view isn't entirely clear to me. On the one hand, he writes that he could accept the idea that infants do have some sort of basic experiential selfhood prior to acquiring a narrative self. But if so, the former ought to constitute not only a necessary but also a sufficient condition for selfhood.

---

[7] A version of this view has earlier been defended by David Carr, who grants that experiences and actions must already be given as mine if I am to worry about how they hang together or make up a coherent life story, but who then claims that such unity is merely a necessary and not a sufficient condition for selfhood (Carr 1986b: 97).

But Rudd also writes that there 'is no more basic level of selfhood at which experiences are had before being interpreted in narrative terms' (Rudd 2012: 196). At times, however, he distinguishes being a subject from being a self, and also employs the term 'subjecthood'. It is likely that he would claim that whereas experiential for-me-ness is necessary and sufficient for basic subjecthood, it is only necessary but not sufficient for selfhood.

At this point, however, the dispute seems to be terminological, and to be a question of whether it is better to distinguish between subjecthood and selfhood than between different levels or aspects of selfhood. My preference is for the latter, but nothing really important seems to hang on this as long as both parties agree that our experiential life is as such and from the beginning characterized by pre-reflective self-consciousness and by first-personal character and for-me-ness.

But what then about the second issue that was brought up by Rudd and Schechtman? Does experiential selfhood remain invariant from infancy into adulthood, or is it necessarily changed and transformed in the developmental process? Is narrative selfhood a layer on top of a pre-existing structure, or does the former radically transform the latter, just as dye mixed with water leaves no water uncoloured? Let us grant that concepts and language pervasively shape our experience; let us grant that we experience the world and ourselves differently because of the conceptual capacities we have. If we grant this, would it then be misguided to search for a common core, a commonality, between the experiential life of language-using adults and the sentient life of infants and non-human animals? We should not make the mistake of overlooking the difference between the *what* and the *how* of experience, between the *content* and the *mode* or *manner* of presentation. *What* we experience might well be different, but that doesn't show or imply that the basic first-personal character of experience is also different. Indeed, if the argument presented in Chapter 2 to the effect that pre-reflective self-consciousness is an integral and constitutive feature of phenomenal consciousness is correct, then it is difficult to see why that shouldn't hold true for experiences that are narratively structured as well. It is difficult to see how language acquisition should change and transform the very basic structure of pre-reflective self-consciousness. It is consequently important not to lose sight of how formal a notion of selfhood the minimal notion is. To stick to the dye and water analogy, the fact that the water becomes coloured shouldn't make us overlook the fact that the coloured water remains water and retains its liquid properties.[8]

---

[8] Were one to maintain that there is no commonality between the proto-subjectivity of animals and infants and the full-fledged subjectivity of those humans who have been initiated into a language (neither when it comes to the content, nor when it comes to the mode or form), were one to maintain that there is no commonality between the self-disclosing character of experience and our conceptualized self-consciousness, one would have to explain how infants can be transformed into full-fledged subjectivities. How is this transformation possible and how does it happen? One ought to avoid a two-tiered account that leaves us with an unbridgeable dualism between the non-conceptual sentience of the infant and the conceptualized mind of the adult; that is, one must allow for some measure of developmental continuity; one must be able to account for the difference between the two that does not make their developmental connection completely unintelligible.

5

Self and Diachronic Unity

A traditional way of defending the existence of self has been by arguing that our mental life would collapse into unstructured chaos if it were not buttressed by the organizing and unifying function of an ego. Consider the claim that experiences never occur in isolation, and that the stream of consciousness is an ensemble of experiences that is unified both at a given moment and over time, both synchronically and diachronically. On a classical view, we need to appeal to a self in order to account for this diachronic and synchronic unity. To think of a simultaneous or temporally dispersed plurality of experiences is to think of myself as being conscious of this plurality, and as the argument goes this requires an undivided, invariable, unchanging me. The self is a principle of identity. It is that which persists and resists temporal change. On some accounts, the unity of the self is consequently taken to be something with explanatory power rather than something that itself is in need of an explanation. This is also why the self has occasionally been ascribed a certain supratemporal or atemporal character.

As I have already made clear, experiential selfhood is not a product of social interaction or the result of a higher cognitive accomplishment, but a basic and indispensable experiential feature. So far, however, my focus has primarily been on synchronic unity and on the question of what properties something must have in order to count as a self. What we now need to consider is the relation between the experiential self and temporality. Does the experiential self have any diachronic persistence, or is it minimal in the sense of being temporally non-extended?

Consider for a moment an argument made by Georges Dreyfus. According to Dreyfus, what is experientially present is an ever changing stream of consciousness. Interestingly, and in opposition to some of the bundle theorists, Dreyfus denies that experiences are fundamentally impersonal and that the attribution of first-personal character to our experiential life is a post hoc fabrication. Rather, on his view, our experiences are from the very start intrinsically self-specified (Dreyfus 2011: 120). But although Dreyfus by implication is prepared to accept the reality of subjectivity, he insists that distortion arises the moment we interpret this subjectivity as a persisting self (Dreyfus 2011: 123). In short, the undeniable presence of a transient flow of self-aware experiences doesn't entail the existence of an enduring self-entity; rather, the latter is, on Dreyfus's view, an illusory reification. More specifically, whereas Dreyfus wants to retain perspectival ownership and synchronic unity—and claims that both features are guaranteed by subjectivity—he denies that there is a diachronically unified self. There is no temporally extended and persisting self (Dreyfus 2011: 131). But is this position really viable?

Consider the phenomenological claim that we all experience change and persistence. We can hear an enduring tone or a melody, just as we can see the flight of a bird. Its smooth, continuous movement is something we see; it is not something we merely infer. This phenomenological finding must be accounted for, and as a distinguished line of thinkers has argued, a mere succession of isolated momentary points of experience cannot explain and account for our experience of duration. To perceive an object as enduring over time, consciousness must itself be experientially unified. One possibility, which we find developed in Husserl, is to insist on the *width of presence*. According to Husserl, the basic unit of temporality is not a 'knife-edge' present, but a 'duration-block', that is, a temporal field that comprises all three temporal modes of present, past, and future. Husserl employs three technical terms to describe the temporal structure of consciousness. There is (1) a 'primal impression' narrowly directed towards the strictly circumscribed now-slice of the object. The primal impression never appears in isolation and is an abstract component that by itself cannot provide us with a perception of a temporal object. The primal impression is accompanied by (2) a 'retention', or retentional aspect, which provides us with a consciousness of the just-elapsed slice of the object, thereby furnishing the primal impression with a past-directed temporal context, and by (3) a 'protention', or protentional aspect, which in a more or less indefinite way intends the slice of the object about to occur, thereby providing a future-oriented temporal context for the primal impression (Husserl 1962: 202). According to Husserl, the concrete and full structure of all lived experience is consequently *protention–primal impression–retention*. Although the specific experiential contents of this structure change progressively from moment to moment, at any one given moment this threefold structure of inner time-consciousness is present as a unified field of experiencing or manifestation.

In investigating the structure of time-consciousness, Husserl was interested in the question not merely of how we can be aware of objects with temporal extension, but also of how we can be aware of our own ongoing stream of experiences. Husserl's investigation was consequently supposed to explain not merely how we can be aware of temporally extended units, but also how consciousness unifies itself across time. According to his model, however, the retention of, say, past notes of a melody is accomplished, not by a literal re-presentation of the notes (as if I were hearing them a second time and simultaneously with the current note), but by a retention of my just-past *experience* of the melody. In short, each actual phase of consciousness retains not only the just-past tones, but also the previous phase of consciousness. The retentional process consequently not only enables us to experience an enduring temporal object; it does not merely enable the constitution of the identity of an object in a manifold of temporal phases; it also provides us with a non-observational, pre-reflective, temporally extended self-consciousness. This is why Husserl's account of the structure of inner time-consciousness (protention–primal impression–retention) must be understood as an analysis of the (micro-)structure of first-personal givenness (see Zahavi 1999):

The flow of the consciousness that constitutes immanent time not only *exists* but is so remarkably and yet intelligibly fashioned that a self-appearance of the flow necessarily exists in it, and therefore the flow itself must necessarily be apprehensible in the flowing. The self-appearance of the flow does not require a second flow; on the contrary, it constitutes itself as a phenomenon in itself. (Husserl 1966a: 83)

Given such considerations, how then would Husserl view the relation between self and time? Does he explain the diachronic unity of consciousness by an appeal to some underlying, undivided, invariable, unchanging, trans-temporal entity? In his early work *Logische Untersuchungen*, Husserl explicitly denied that the unity intrinsic to our experiential life was conditioned or guaranteed by any ego. He argued that whatever synthesizing contribution the ego could have made would be superfluous since the unification had already taken place in accordance with intra-experiential laws. Thus, on Husserl's early view, the stream of consciousness is self-unifying, and since the ego, properly speaking, is the result of this unification, it cannot be something that precedes or conditions it (Husserl 1984a: 364).[1] Although, Husserl's general view on the ego was to change, he continued to hold onto some of the claims originally made in *Logische Untersuchungen*. If we look, for instance, in the *Vorlesungen zur Phänomenologie des inneren Zeitbewusstseins*, we will find no reference to the ego as the ultimate unifying or synthesizing agent. Rather, the unity in question is established or woven through the interplay between primal impression, retention, and protention, that is, through the structures of inner time-consciousness. Does this make Husserl some kind of reductionist? After all, if one holds the view that the unity of the stream of consciousness comes about as the result of a process of temporal self-unification rather than through the unifying powers of a separate and enduring ego, it might be tempting to conclude that the diachronic unity and identity of consciousness is then ultimately explainable by and reducible to certain (causal and functional) relations that obtain between the different experiences. This, however, is not Husserl's view. Rather, Husserl repeatedly insists on the importance of not conflating or collapsing an analysis of consciousness that targets different intentional acts, say, acts of perception, imagination, or judgement, into an analysis of the structure of inner

---

[1] A very similar view was later defended by Sartre. As Sartre points out at the beginning of the essay *La Transcendance de l'Égo*, many philosophers have considered the ego a formal principle of unification. Many have argued that our consciousness is unified because the 'I think' might accompany each of my thoughts (Sartre 1957: 34, 37). But is this really true, or is it rather the 'I think' which is made possible by the synthetic unity of our thoughts? In other words, is the ego an expression rather than a condition of unified consciousness? Sartre's own view is clear. On his account, the nature of the stream of consciousness does not need an exterior principle of individuation, since it is per se individuated. Nor is consciousness in need of any transcendent principle of unification, since it is, as such, a flowing unity (Sartre 1957: 38–40).

time-consciousness. In insisting on this difference and on the difference between our transitory experiences and the abiding dimension of experiencing, that is, between *die Erlebnisse* and *das Erleben* (Husserl 1980: 326; compare Husserl 1973b: 46), Husserl is making the same claim as I have repeatedly done when stressing the need for a distinction between the plurality of changing experiences and the ubiquitous first-personal character of consciousness. If we take three different intentional experiences, say, a visual perception of an armadillo, an anticipation of a forthcoming anniversary, and a rejection of the claim that Pluto is a planet in our solar system, these three experiences obviously have different intentional structures. The very manifestation of the three experiences, however, does not in each case have a different structure; rather, what we find is always the same basic structure of inner time-consciousness. Moreover, while from a first-person perspective it certainly makes sense to say that I had an experience of joy or was perceiving a flower, and that these experiences, although once present to me, have now ceased and become absent and past, the very field of experiencing, with its threefold structure of protention–primal impression–retention that allows for experiential presence, cannot itself become past and absent *for me*. To claim that the field of experiencing must be distinguished from the specific experiences that arise, endure, and become past in it, and that it is in no way reducible to either some specific experiential content or some relation that might obtain between the individual experiences, is not, of course, to claim that it has a distinct and independent existence, as if there could first be a pure or empty field of experiencing upon which the concrete experiences would subsequently make their entry; rather, the experiencing simply is the invariant dimension of pre-reflective self-manifestation possessed by each and every experience.

An examination of Husserl's laborious attempt to spell out the microstructure of lived subjective presence ought to make those who claim that the subjectivity of experience is trivial and banal in the sense that it doesn't call for further examination and clarification reconsider their claim. As just mentioned, Husserl's analysis of the interplay between protention, primal impression, and retention is an attempt to understand better the relationship between selfhood, self-experience, and temporality. Thus, on Husserl's account it is not enough simply to pay attention to the first-person perspective. Rather, the temporality of this perspective has to be investigated. Ricœur's work *Temps et récit* has occasionally been read as containing a fundamental criticism of Husserl's phenomenological investigation of time. But even if Ricœur is right in pointing to the limitations of a phenomenological investigation of inner time-consciousness (there is more to the temporality of human existence than what is thought of in Husserl's investigations), this does not make Husserl's investigation superfluous. On the contrary, it remains pertinent for an understanding of the temporality of experiential life. Moreover, it targets a dimension of selfhood that is pretty much ignored by Ricœur in his focus on narrative identity.

This is not the right place to delve further into the intricacies of Husserl's exceedingly complex account of temporality (see, however, Zahavi 1999, 2003, 2007a, 2010a), but two important insights can be gathered from his analysis. The first is that one might deny that the diachronic and synchronic unity of consciousness is conditioned by a distinct self without questioning or denying the reality of the self. Secondly, even the analysis of something as synchronic as a present experience must include a consideration of temporality, since every experience is a temporally extended lived presence. For that very reason, we should reject the attempt to make a clear-cut distinction between synchronic unity and diachronic unity. You cannot have synchronic unity without some amount of diachronic unity (even if short-lived). To claim otherwise is to miss the fundamentally temporal character of consciousness.

All very well, the sceptic might retort, but even if one were to go along with this, it would hardly commit one to accept also the existence of a temporally extended and diachronically unified self. Or would it?

In his book *Stream of Consciousness: Unity and Continuity in Conscious Experience*, Barry Dainton defends a model of consciousness that he calls the simple conception of experience (Dainton 2000: 57). According to this view, and in contrast to various higher-order representationalist accounts, the synchronic and diachronic unity of consciousness is best understood as a product of primitive inter-experiential relationships. Moreover, experiential processes are intrinsically conscious and hence self-revealing. Given that phenomenal unity is an experienced relationship between conscious states, we do not have to look at anything above, beyond, or external to experience itself in order to understand the unity we find within experience; rather, experiences are self-unifying both at a time and over time (Dainton 2000: 48, 73). As Dainton puts it, consciousness does not consist of a stream running beneath a spot of light, nor of a spot of light running along a stream. Consciousness is the stream itself, and the light extends through its entire length (Dainton 2000: 236–7).

In his book *The Phenomenal Self*, Dainton develops this view further, and explicitly defends an experiential approach to self. Initially, he argues for a distinction between what he calls *psychological continuity*, which might involve persisting personality traits, beliefs, endorsed values, etc., and *experiential continuity* (Dainton 2008, p. xii). Using various thought experiments, he argues that the two forms of continuity can be dissociated, and suggests that a consideration of such cases shows experiential continuity to be the most important. One of the guiding intuitions he appeals to is the absurdity of the idea that an unbroken stream of consciousness might start off as yours and end up as somebody else's (Dainton 2008: 18). Likewise, he considers it absurd to suggest that your stream of consciousness can flow on in an ordinary straightforward manner with the same subjective character but fail to take you along with it—even if the concrete psychological states are altered or replaced during the process (Dainton 2008: 26). He consequently argues that the persistence of self is guaranteed by experiential continuity (Dainton 2008: 22).[2] His position is thus strongly opposed to the Buddhist idea that just as we cannot keep track of waves in such a way as to give a determinate answer to the question whether it is the same wave as before or a new wave, we cannot, when faced with a new experience, give a determinate answer to the question whether or not it belongs to the same experiencer as the just-elapsed experience (see Ganeri 2012: 10, 199).

Given his approach, Dainton is, however, faced with a problem, which he spends considerable effort (in fact most of his book) trying to solve, namely, the so-called bridge problem. Experiences in a single uninterrupted stream of consciousness may be linked by phenomenal continuity and belong to the same subject, but what about experiences in distinct streams (interrupted by gaps of unconsciousness)? On what basis do we assign two experiences that are separated by dreamless sleep to a common owner (Dainton 2008, p. xx)? The bridge problem might not be a problem for people favouring a brain-based account, since causal and physical relations can span losses of consciousness. But it is, according to Dainton, very much a problem for people adopting an experience-based approach to self (Dainton 2008: 75).

Dainton's solution to the problem is to reject what he calls the Essentially Conscious Self (ECS) thesis, that is, the thesis that a self is essentially a conscious entity, one that cannot lose consciousness and continue to exist, in favour of the Potentially Conscious Self (PCS) thesis, which claims that a self is an entity that is capable of being conscious. On the latter view, a self can lose consciousness and continue to exist provided it retains the capacity to be conscious (Dainton 2008: 79).

According to Dainton, defenders of the ECS thesis basically have two options. They can deny that there are interruptions in the stream of consciousness and opt for the view that we never truly lose consciousness during the normal course of our lives, or they might accept that there are indeed interruptions in the stream of

---

[2] As we saw earlier, Dainton denies that we need *mineness*, understood as some primitive ownership quality, to explain whether an experience is experienced as mine (Dainton 2008: 242–3). Given the one-level simple conception of experience that Dainton endorses, we do not need to posit such a quality to explain why we are always aware of our own experiences; rather, experiences are intrinsically conscious items, and as such do not need any further assistance to enter our awareness. He takes this to constitute an objection to my own view, but since I wholeheartedly agree with these latter claims, part of the disagreement must be terminological. Something similar seems to be the case when it comes to Dainton's answer to the objection that one might remain in existence (with a very low level of experiential capabilities) without being a self. As he says, if by 'self' we simply mean 'subject of consciousness', that is, if we operate with a minimal notion of self, the proposal is nonsensical. But as Dainton then remarks, there are those who equate selves with beings who are capable of being aware of themselves as selves, and although he concedes that self-awareness comes in different forms, he also thinks that anyone who is reduced to a minimal level of sentience will be incapable of self-awareness in any interesting sense (Dainton 2004: 388). I don't see why one should accept this. One might equally well dispute that the minimal notion of self is a self in any interesting sense whatsoever—and this is, of course, what many have done. In short, as I see it, the minimal notion of self goes hand in hand with a minimal sense of self-awareness, and if one accepts the former there is no reason to reject the latter, especially if, like Dainton, one defends the view that experiences are self-revealing. In fact, given his endorsement of the latter view, it is hard to understand why he is so opposed to the idea that experience is characterized by a minimal and non-reflective self-consciousness (Dainton 2008: 242).

consciousness and then opt for one of the two following possibilities. Either they can try to explain how the self can somehow retain its unity across such interruptions, or they can bite the bullet and defend the view that the self only exists as long as we remain awake, and that a new self is born each time we wake up from dreamless sleep (Dainton 2004: 380–1; 2008: 77–9). Dainton finds all these options untenable and consequently chooses to defend the PCS thesis.

Although, or perhaps precisely because, I have much sympathy for an experiential approach to the self, I have qualms about this solution. One worry I have is that the PCS thesis simply departs too radically from the experiential approach. Consider that Dainton himself admits that the PCS thesis makes actual experience lose its central role (Dainton 2008: 112). He writes that the persistency conditions of a conscious subject must be the same as those of an unconscious subject (Dainton 2008: 76), and that the difference between being conscious and being unconscious is comparatively minor when seen from the perspective of the PCS thesis (Dainton 2008: 80). To put it differently, I fear that the solution proposed by Dainton ends up jettisoning most of the core insights of the experiential approach. Moreover, I think the ECS thesis has some resources that Dainton fails to consider. But before addressing those, let me first consider Galen Strawson's view.

As already mentioned, Strawson has argued that if we wish to answer the meta-physical question concerning whether or not the self is real, we will first need to know what a self is supposed to be. In order to establish that, our best chance is to look at self-experience, since self-experience is what gives rise to the question in the first place by giving us a vivid sense that there is something like a self. Thus, as Strawson readily concedes, the metaphysical investigation of the self is subordinate to the phenomenological investigation. The latter places constraints on the former: nothing can count as a self unless it possesses those properties attributed to the self by some genuine form of self-experience (Strawson 2000: 40). More specifically, Strawson has argued that the phenomenological investigation can proceed in several ways. One possibility is to investigate what ordinary human self-experience involves; another is to investigate the minimal form of self-experience. What is the least you can make do with and still call a(n experience of) self?

Strawson is mainly interested in the latter question. His conclusion, which he at one point calls the *pearl view*, is that self-experience is at the very least a sesmet-experience; that to have self-experience is at the very least to experience oneself as a sesmet—as a subject of experience that is a single *mental thing*. By contrast, he considers issues like personality, agency, and long-term diachronic persistency to be inessential features. They may be important when it comes to human self-experience, but something can lack them and still be a genuine self(-experience) (Strawson 2009: 172). As for the metaphysical question, Strawson not only takes his view to be perfectly compatible with a materialist outlook. He also considers the self to be real if by self we mean a thin self, a sesmet. When it comes to the more enduring kind of personal self, he is considerably more sceptical (Strawson 2000: 44–8).

What more is there to say about the thin self that Strawson is focusing on? He basically defends the view that any experience involves an experiencer, that is, a subject of experience. Experience is necessarily experience-for. Experience necessarily involves what-it-is-likeness, and experiential what-it-is-likeness is necessarily what-it-is-likeness for someone (Strawson 2009: 271). Or to take a formulation from his conclusion: if experience exists, subjectivity exists, and that entails that subject-of-experience-hood exists (Strawson 2009: 419). In short, as long as there is experience, there is also necessarily a subject of experience. Experience is experiencing and experiencing involves a subject, just as a branch-bending involves a branch (Strawson 2011: 260). Importantly, Strawson doesn't simply take this to be a conceptual and metaphysical claim. It is also an experiential or phenomenological claim: the subject of experience is something that is essentially present and alive in conscious experience (Strawson 2009: 362). Moreover, we are dealing with a quite minimal notion. A subject of experience isn't something grand. It is minimal in the sense that it is what is left when everything else except the being of experience is stripped away (Strawson 2011: 254). It is thin in the sense that it lacks ontic depth; it cannot on its own be, say, a morally responsible agent. In fact, it is something of such a kind that it is true to say that there must be a subject of experience wherever there is experience, even in the case of mice or spiders, or sea snails—simply because selves just are subjects of experience and experience is essentially experience-for (Strawson 2009: 276, 401). On this account, of course, there is no thin self during experienceless episodes. The thin self does not and cannot exist in the absence of experience. It is necessarily experiential and cannot merely have dispositional being (Strawson 2011: 260). I would agree with all of this. And it is interesting that Strawson then levels a criticism against Dainton that resembles my own. Strawson writes:

> my position stands in stark contrast to Dainton's position in his book *The Phenomenal Self*, for he defines the self or subject of experience wholly dispositionally, as a collection of potentialities. His view accords with the idea that an entity that was a subject of experience could exist without ever actually having any experience. My focus on the thin conception of the subject leads me to say (less naturally to most present-day philosophical ears) that no actual subject of experience ever exists in a universe in which millions of Daintonian subjects of experience exist but never have any experience. (Strawson 2009: 370)

What about the issue of temporality? As Strawson repeatedly emphasizes, any sort of self must be extended in time since no experience can be instantaneous, if an instant is defined as something with no temporal duration at all. Every thin subject consequently does have a synchronic unity with some temporal extension (Strawson 2009: 256, 388). However, Strawson also argues that each distinct experience has its own experiencer (Strawson 2009: 276). He concedes that there is nothing per se in the definition of a thin subject that necessitates that thin subjects are short-lived or transient entities. But given that, as a matter of fact, there are many temporal breaks in the human stream of consciousness, thin subjects are short-lived in the human case. How short-lived? Perhaps two to three seconds.[3] Thus, Strawson ultimately defends what might be called the *transience view* of the self (Strawson 2009: 9). During the ordinary lifetime of a human being, one and the same organism might be said to be inhabited by a vast multitude of ontologically distinct short-lived selves.

In some respects, I take Strawson's thin self and my own experiential self to be remarkably similar. Both of us defend an experiential notion of self which some would undoubtedly take to be a very deflationary notion of self. Both of us defend the relevance of phenomenology when it comes to this notion of self, and both of us concede (and this is something I shall return to *in extenso* later in the book) that there are limits to what this notion can accomplish, a limit that is nicely captured by Strawson's reference to its lack of ontic depth. So what are the differences? If we disregard a number of minor ones, some of which are terminological, there is arguably one substantial difference, which concerns the question of persistency and transience.

According to Strawson, the so-called stream of consciousness is, in reality, a series of isolated short-term experiential episodes. Each of these has its own ontologically distinct subject (Strawson 2009: 399). Thus, a thin subject cannot survive a break in experience, since it cannot exist at any moment unless there is an experience for it to be the subject of. In short, every time there is a new experience, there is also a new subject or thin self. Although there is an I or self at any given moment, there is no self that endures for long; rather, as Strawson puts it, I am continually completely new (Strawson 2009: 247).

As Strawson points out, it is not obvious that this conclusion, which defends the reality of self, will satisfy the pro-selfers. After all, the self that he is committed to is not one that he takes Buddhism to reject:

The pro-selfers will say that the selves I claim to exist don't really deserve the name, and that by using 'self' in this way I'm obscuring the fact that there are other things that do deserve the name. The anti-selfers will agree with the pro-selfers that the selves I claim to exist don't deserve the name, and say that by using 'self' in this way I'm obscuring the fact that nothing deserves the name. Does this matter? Not much, I think. (Strawson 2009: 5)

One question, which I unfortunately cannot pursue here, is whether Strawson's position offers us a convincing account of temporal experience, including our experience of temporally persisting and enduring objects. But let me instead focus on the issue of diachronicity. Must an experiential approach to the self choose between Dainton's recourse to potentiality and Strawson's plurality of transient selves, or is another more appealing alternative available?

---

[3] Strawson ultimately thinks the precise extension is an open question, and that other possibilities to be considered are $1/1.855 \times 10^{-43}$ seconds (Planck time), 1 ms, 25 ms, 500 ms, a lifetime, or sempiternity (Strawson 2009: 398).

Strawson distinguishes three candidates for selfhood. There is the thick whole creature (for instance, the human being), there is the traditional inner entity (that is, the subject conceived as some sort of persisting inner entity that can exist in the absence of any experience), and finally there is the sesmet, the short-lived subject that cannot exist in the absence of any experience (Strawson 2009: 374). I would suggest that the notion of an experiential self developed in the preceding offers us a fourth option, situated somewhere between Strawson's sesmet and the traditional inner entity. After all, the experiential self is not a separately existing entity, one that can exist in the absence of experience, nor is it simply reducible to a specific experience; rather, it can be identified with the ubiquitous dimension of first-personal character that must be distinguished from but can be shared by a multitude of changing experiences.

On the view I am defending, there is indeed no experiential self, no self as defined from the first-person perspective, when we are non-conscious. But this does not necessarily imply that the diachronic identity and unity of the experiential self is threatened by alleged interruptions of the stream of consciousness (such as dreamless sleep or coma), since the identity of this self isn't based on or dependent upon uninterrupted experiential continuity. Whether the same experiential self is present in two temporally distinct experiences depends on whether the two experiences in question partake in the same dimension of mineness or for-me-ness. If they do, they can jointly constitute an instance of temporally dispersed self-consciousness. Thus, I don't see why one should accept the claim that phenomenal unity does not 'obtain between experiences that are separated by significant temporal intervals' (Bayne 2013: 202). What is decisive here is not the objective temporal distance between the two experiences, but whether, say, the past experiential episode is first-personally accessible to the present act of recollection. In the latter case, both episodes are part of the same stream of consciousness; there is no breach of the unity of consciousness, and no breach of the unity of the experiential self.

Now, some might object that such a proposal confers some rather weird persistency conditions on selfhood. How can the experiential self pop in and out of existence in such a fashion? How can it, so to speak, survive a period of non-existence? I am not sure these questions are well posed, however. They assume that the proper way to approach the question regarding experiential diachronicity is from a third-person perspective. They think of the stream of consciousness in analogy with a cord, and compare the dreamless sleep with a cutting of the cord. From such a perspective, one can then view 'the' stream of consciousness as consisting of a sequence of discrete episodes (Dainton even speaks of a sequence of distinct streams of consciousness) interrupted by periods of unconsciousness.[4] Given such a setup, we

---

[4] Compare, by contrast, Bergson's claim in *Essai sur les données immédiates de la conscience* that any attempt to conceive of the stream of consciousness as a line or series of distinct conscious states ranged alongside one another presupposes a view from above, a view that, so to speak tries to take it all in at once.

would then be faced with the problem of how to link these discrete units. And as Stokes has pointed out, the only real option available to Dainton is that it happens inferentially; that is, whereas I can experience that S2 at t_2 is identical to S1 at t_1 as long as t_2 and t_1 are not separated by periods of unconsciousness, my conviction the following day that *I* went to bed last night is purely inferential and is no long grounded experientially (Stokes 2014). But if we instead adopt a first-person perspective, which supposedly is the perspective an experience-based approach should adopt, the situation looks rather different. From the first-person perspective, it is not as if one has to reach back and establish a connection to a separate stream of consciousness. Although there is certainly something it is like to fall asleep and to wake up, there is in dreamless sleep no first-personal absence of a first-person perspective (for a similar line of argument, see Klawonn 1990b: 103–4). There are no extended periods of unconsciousness, and linking up with an experience you had yesterday, say, an acute experience of shame or embarrassment, is no different from linking up with an experience you had earlier this morning. In both cases, we are faced with a diachronically unified consciousness. It is hard to see why an analysis of the former recollection should motivate us to move away from a focus on real experience to a focus on experiential powers and the capacity to produce experience.

Let me emphasize that I remain quite non-committal on the question whether or not diachronic self-consciousness can count as evidence for the existence of an underlying persisting non-experiential (brain-)substrate. The self I am defending is the experiential self, the self as defined from the first-person perspective—neither more nor less.

Ah, some might say, but that must mean that our experience of diachronic unity is after all 'merely' phenomenological and consequently devoid of any metaphysical impact. But to think that one can counter the phenomenological experience of unity over time with the claim that such an experienced unity can never reveal anything about the true metaphysical nature of consciousness is to make use of the appearance–reality distinction outside its proper domain of application. This is especially so given that the reality in question, rather than being defined in terms of some spurious mind-independence, should be understood in terms of experiential reality. For comparison, consider the case of phenomenal consciousness. Who would deny that pain experience is sufficient for the reality of pain? As Peacocke has recently put it, we should 'avoid a double standard that accords to subjects a treatment that it does not apply to consciousness' (Peacocke 2012: 92).

To argue that the diachronic unity of consciousness would be illusory if it weren't supported by a matching unity on the subpersonal level is to misunderstand the task at hand. As Strawson points out, even if you became convinced that your mental life depended for its existence on the successive existence of a series of numerically

---

For Bergson such an approach, with its reliance on spatial notions and categories, does violence to the lived time that is unique to and distinctive of consciousness (Bergson 1910: 91, 98–9).

distinct brains or neuronal entities, this would not annihilate your sense of the self as a diachronically persisting entity (Strawson 2009: 81). I agree, but I would add that our experience of the temporally extended and unified stream of consciousness is *eo ipso* an experience of the real (and not merely illusory) diachronicity of the experiential self. Were one after all to insist that, say, a minute-long experiential sequence really contains twenty to thirty metaphysically distinct (but qualitatively similar) short-term selves, one would inevitably be confronted with the question regarding their relationship. I do not see any real alternative to the following proposal: metaphysically speaking, we are dealing with selves that, although they might stand in a unique causal relationship to one another, are still as different from each other as I am from you. And I must admit that I find that proposal absurd. But even if similarity doesn't amount to identity, surely, some might object, we need to distinguish an account claiming that the stream of consciousness involves some form of experiential unity from an account claiming that it somehow involves diachronic self-identity. My response, however, would be to question the relevance and significance of that distinction in the present context. In my view, the unity provided by the first-personal character is sufficient for the kind of experiential self-identity that I am eager to preserve. If you find this insufficient (did anybody mention Kant's billiard balls?), I think you are looking for the wrong kind of identity.[5] Thus, when discussing the relation between the experiential self and the issue of diachronic unity, one should recall the guiding idea, that experiential selfhood should be defined in terms of self-experience rather than vice versa.

Saying this admittedly leaves a number of questions pertaining to the nature of personal identity unanswered. Some have argued that episodic memory presupposes personal identity and merely provides evidence for one's own continued existence: as Reid writes, my memory testifies not only that this was done, but that it was done by me, who now remembers it. If it was done by me, I must have existed at that time, and continued to exist from that time to the present (Reid 1863: 345). Locke's radical idea, by contrast, was that personal identity was constituted subjectively through inner consciousness and that questions regarding personal identity consequently had to be distinguished sharply from questions pertaining to the identity of the human being or the identity of the underlying substance. This is why he could claim that 'whether we are the same thinking thing; *i.e.* the same substance or no' is a question which 'concerns not *personal identity* at all' (Locke 1975: 336). Indeed, as Locke continued,

---

[5] For comparison, consider a remark made by Husserl in a text dating from 1921, where he argues that the ego apprehends its own duration in acts of recollection; it apprehends that it was also the subject of the past experience. But as Husserl then adds, the identity and persistence of the ego is fundamentally different from the identity of an ordinary persisting entity. Consider a tone. The identity of the tone is linked to the fact that it endures from one moment to the next; it has, so to speak, a temporal stretch. If there is an interruption, a moment of silence, the numerical identity of the tone will sunder, and we will instead have two qualitatively identical tones. Husserl explicitly denies that the same holds true for the ego (Husserl 1973b: 42–3).

it is by the consciousness it has of its present Thoughts and Actions, that it is *self* to it *self* now, and so will be the same *self* as far as the same consciousness can extend to Actions past or to come; and would be by distance of Time, or change of Substance, no more two *persons* than a Man be two Men, by wearing other Cloaths to Day than he did Yesterday, with a long or short sleep between: The same consciousness uniting those distant Actions into the same *Person*, whatever Substances contributed to their Production. (Locke 1975: 336)

The radicalism of Locke's proposal is admirable, but it is a view that many have found unpersuasive. It has, for instance, been argued that consciousness can neither be necessary for personal identity (since I remain accountable for deeds that I did in the past even if I am no longer able to remember them) nor sufficient (since I will not be the same person as Socrates even if I seem to remember from the inside actions actually done by Socrates).[6] Regardless of whether one opts for Reid's or Locke's account, or perhaps rather the contemporary refinements of each, one must also consider the challenges presented by various cases of memory disorders, including amnesia and false memories.

Consider the case of somebody who in 2013 claims to be Napoleon and sincerely insists that he has vivid memories of participating in the battle of Waterloo. Wouldn't it be absurd to take the presence of such memories as evidence for the long-term diachronic persistency of the self? Obviously, our memories can be distorted. This is why many psychologists and cognitive scientists have urged us to abandon the myth that memories are passive or literal recordings of reality. They are, as Daniel Schacter puts it, not like 'a series of family pictures stored in the photo album of the mind' (Schacter 1996: 5). One prevalent source of error is known as impaired source memory. You might have read about something and now remember it as something you personally lived through, or you might remember an experience as your own although it actually happened to someone else who told you about it. You might, in short, be right in remembering having seen or heard or experienced a certain event before, but you are wrong about the source of your recollection (Lindsay and Johnson 1991; Schacter 1996). It is likely that the person who is claiming to have a first-person recollection of Napoleon's defeat must have acquired information about the battle of Waterloo previously. The presence of his episodic memories does testify to his persisting, that is, temporally extended, existence; he existed at the time when he acquired the information he is now remembering. But, of course, that time is in all likelihood much later than 18 June 1815. Mistakes like these are not only possible: they are also less rare than one might think. However, far more dramatic forms of mistake also exist, including what is known as spontaneous confabulation and delusional memory (Kopelman 1999). Thus, people might have apparent memories; they might sincerely believe that they are remembering events in their own lives,

---

[6] For an extensive discussion, see Thiel (2011).

events that they have never previously experienced or thought about and which, in fact, never happened to themselves or anyone else.

Episodic memory is not infallible, but contrary to what Dreyfus is claiming (2011: 132), I do not think that there is necessarily any mistake or distortion involved in remembering an experience as mine. However, to deny that there is an experiential self during experienceless episodes is obviously to concede that the persistency conditions of such a self cannot be the same as that of an organism. Now, some might take this concession as a blatant admission of defeat. After all, what we arguably need is an account that can accommodate the fact that the subject who is currently having experiences was once an experienceless foetus and might at some point in the future end up in a persistent vegetative state. However, this alleged defeat could also be interpreted as a distinct virtue of the proposed model, since a notion of selfhood that is tailored to be equally applicable to all three cases (like certain biological or animalist notions) could well be accused of missing something absolutely crucial in its focus on the (lowest) common denominator, namely, the role of experience. In short, I wouldn't recommend settling for and making do with a notion of selfhood that is also applicable and ascribable to a philosophical zombie (who, although it lacks experiences, is presumably still a living organism).

In a number of writings, the Danish philosopher Erich Klawonn has offered a sustained defence of the idea that the first-personal givenness of experience, or what Klawonn also calls the I-dimension or the dimension of primary presence, is of paramount importance for a proper (non-reductionist) theory of personal identity (Klawonn 1987, 1990a,b, 1991, 1998). Klawonn initially points out that we must distinguish my field of experience from whatever transitory experiential contents it contains, and then argues that the experiences can change entirely in content without ceasing to be given as mine and without me ceasing to be who I am, as long as they remain exposed in the experiential field in question, that is, as long as they retain their specific first-personal form of being. In fact, Klawonn explicitly argues that the subjective or first-personal givenness of an experience is the necessary and sufficient condition for the selfhood of that experience, and that the self can be defined as—and the unity of consciousness explained by means of—the invariable first-personal givenness of a system of changing experiences (Klawonn 1998: 60; see also 1991: 136). Using this framework, Klawonn then engages critically with the reductionist (especially Parfitian) discussion of personal identity, and argues that the field of presence-to-me constitutes a 'further fact' that can explain strict self-identity through time (1990a: 44, 57; 1990b: 101). Although Klawonn is prepared to accept that there are cases where no introspective scrutiny can settle whether I am identical with some past person or not (1990b: 100), he still argues that my diachronic self-identity extends as far as the field of primary presence. Even if I am de facto unable to settle whether I am identical with the infant that was born in 1967 and dubbed Dan Zahavi, this doesn't change what the identity would amount to and consist in, if it obtained, namely, the strict numerical identity of the field of primary presence, that is, the dimension of first-personal experiencing (Klawonn 1991: 229, 232; compare Fasching 2009, 2011; Hart 2009).

I have sympathy with this line of thinking, though one might wonder whether it isn't going beyond what a strictly experiential approach to selfhood can deliver, in so far as it maintains that the experiential self of a present conscious episode can be identical to the experiential self of a past episode even when the past episode is no longer first-personally retrievable or accessible. Although I don't think it makes sense to talk of a distinct problem of personal identity (in contrast to physical identity) unless there is, at least occasionally, a subject of experience, I am consequently less confident that the notion of an experiential self in and of itself will allow us to address or solve all relevant questions concerning diachronic persistency. At any rate, my current aim is more modest than Klawonn's, since I have no intention of engaging with the complex discussion of personal identity. Whereas in previous chapters I have defended the view that there is a tight link between experiential selfhood and pre-reflective (synchronic) self-consciousness, my primary objective in this chapter has been to focus on diachronic unity in order to show that although the experiential self might be minimal, it is not atemporal or temporally non-extended. So even if one of the motivations for introducing the notion of a narratively extended self was to address the issue of diachronic unity, it would be a mistake to think that the latter would be entirely off limits to the experiential account I am favouring. Indeed, it would be quite misguided to claim that we only come to enjoy temporally structured self-experiences after we have acquired narrative capacities. The experiential self has some temporal extension, and our pre-reflective self-consciousness includes some awareness of diachronicity.

6

Pure and Poor

If anyone should be in doubt at this point, my proposal is influenced by Husserl. In the following let me engage in a more exegetically oriented excavation in order to throw some light on Husserl's own position, since this will pave the way for some of the topics to be discussed in Part II.

6.1 Privacy and anonymity

My point of departure will not be Husserl, however, but Merleau-Ponty. Let me start by considering an account defended by Merleau-Ponty in *Les Relations avec autrui chez l'enfant*. This is a lecture course on child psychology that he gave at the Sorbonne, but, contrary to what the title might indicate, Merleau-Ponty isn't primarily interested in various empirical findings pertaining to early forms of social interaction. Rather, he is raising and attempting to answer substantial philosophical questions concerning the relation between self and other. Indeed, his point of departure is precisely the alleged incapacity of classical psychology to provide a satisfactory solution to the problem of how we relate to others, an incapacity that, according to Merleau-Ponty, is due to the fact that classical psychology bases its entire approach on certain unquestioned and unwarranted philosophical prejudices. First and foremost among these is the fundamental assumption that experiential life is directly accessible to one person only, namely, the individual who owns it (Merleau-Ponty 1964a: 114), and that the only access one has to the psyche of another is indirect and mediated by his or her bodily appearance. I can *see* your facial expressions, gestures, and actions, and on the basis of that I can then make more or less educated guesses about what you think, feel, or intend (Merleau-Ponty 1964a: 113–14). Classical psychology has routinely explained the move from the visible exteriority to the invisible interiority by way of an argument from analogy, but Merleau-Ponty is quick to point to a number of difficulties inherent in this strategy. The objections he raises are very similar to the ones raised by Scheler years earlier, in *Wesen und Formen der Sympathie*, objections I shall return to in Part II. For now, suffice it to say that Merleau-Ponty concludes his criticism by rejecting the idea that my experiential life is a sequence of internal states that are inaccessible to anyone but me. Rather, on his view, our experiential life is above all a relation to the world, and it is in this comportment towards the world that I shall also be able to discover the consciousness of the other. He writes, 'The perspective on the other is opened to me from the moment I define him and myself as "conducts" at work in the world, as ways of "grasping" the natural and cultural world surrounding us' (Merleau-Ponty 1964a: 117). Being a world-directed consciousness myself, I can encounter others who act, and their actions are meaningful to me because they are also my possible actions. Merleau-Ponty consequently argues that we need to redefine our notion of psyche, as well as revise our understanding of the body. If it is my bodily experience that can appropriate and understand the conduct of others, the former must be defined, not as a sum of sensations, but as a postural or corporeal schema (Merleau-Ponty 1964a: 117). Here is what Merleau-Ponty writes:

the other who is to be perceived is himself not a 'psyche' closed in on himself, but rather a conduct, a system of behavior that aims at the world, he offers himself to my motor intentions and to that 'intentional transgression' (Husserl) by which I animate and pervade him. Husserl said that the perception of others is like a 'phenomenon of coupling'. The term is anything but a metaphor. In perceiving the other, my body and his are coupled, resulting in a sort of action which pairs them. This conduct which I am able only to see, I live somehow from a distance. I make it mine; I recover it or comprehend it. Reciprocally I know that the gestures I make myself can be the objects of another's intention. It is this transfer of my intentions to the other's body and of his intentions to my own, my alienation of the other and his alienation of me, that makes possible the perception of others. (Merleau-Ponty 1964a: 118)

There is much that one could dwell on in this passage. It illustrates Merleau-Ponty's substantial agreement with at least part of Husserl's account, and one crucial challenge is to explain why the transference in question is not a form of projection—but more about this in Part II. However, here I want to focus on a different issue, namely, something Merleau-Ponty writes in direct continuation of the quotation just given. He observes that this account will remain unavailable if one presupposes that the ego and the other are in possession of an absolute consciousness of themselves, as if each were absolutely original vis-à-vis the other (Merleau-Ponty 1964a: 119). This is, of course, an idea that we also encounter elsewhere in Merleau-Ponty's writings, for instance, in a famous passage in *Phénoménologie de la perception*, where he declares that 'Others can be evident because I am not transparent for myself, and because my subjectivity draws its body along behind itself' (Merleau-Ponty 2012: 368). However, in the present text, Merleau-Ponty is more interested in the second part of the claim. He goes on to write that the perception of others becomes comprehensible if one assumes that there is an initial state of undifferentiation, and that the beginning of psychogenesis is precisely a state where the child is unaware of himself and the other as different beings. At this initial stage, we cannot say that there is any genuine communication: communication presupposes a distinction between the one who communicates and the one with whom he communicates. But referring to Scheler, Merleau-Ponty goes on to say that there is a state of pre-communication, where the other's intentions somehow play across my body while my intentions play across his

(Merleau-Ponty 1964a: 119). In this first phase there is consequently, on Merleau-Ponty's view, not one individual over against another, but rather an anonymous collectivity, an undifferentiated group life (Merleau-Ponty 1964a: 119). As he would later formulate it in *Signes*:

The solitude from which we emerge to intersubjective life is not that of the monad. It is only the haze of an anonymous life that separates us from being; and the barrier between us and others is impalpable. If there is a break, it is not between me and the other person; it is between a primordial generality we are intermingled in and the precise system, myself–the others. What 'precedes' intersubjective life cannot be numerically distinguished from it, precisely because at this level there is neither individuation nor numerical distinction. (Merleau-Ponty 1964b: 174)

In *Les Relations avec autrui chez l'enfant* Merleau-Ponty describes how the initial anonymous life gradually becomes differentiated. He describes how the child becomes aware of his own body as distinct from the bodies of others, and in particular he highlights the importance of the child's confrontation with his own specular image (and this is something I shall return to in Part III). Through this mirror-mediated self-objectification the child becomes aware of his own insularity and separation, and correlatively aware of that of others (Merleau-Ponty 1964a: 119). Merleau-Ponty argues not only that this view can be defended on phenomenological grounds, but that similar insights have been reached by gestalt psychology and psychoanalysis. He refers to the work of Henri Wallon, for instance, who argued that there is an initial confusion between me and the other, and that the differentiation of the two is crucially dependent upon the subsequent objectification of the body (Merleau-Ponty 1964a: 120).

When Merleau-Ponty says that the child is initially entirely unaware both of himself and of others, and that consciousness of oneself and of others as unique individuals only comes later, there is an ambiguity in the claim that makes it difficult to assess. Is Merleau-Ponty simply claiming that the child only becomes explicitly aware of the difference between himself and others at a relatively late stage (a late realization that is perfectly compatible with there being a differentiation between self and other from the start), or is he defending the more radical claim that the very distinction between self and other is derived and rooted in a common anonymity?

There are passages in both the Sorbonne lectures and *Signes* that support the latter, more radical view.

6.2 The personal I, the pure I, and the primal I

If we now turn to Husserl, we find him arguing that it holds a priori that 'self-consciousness and consciousness of others are inseparable' (Husserl 1954: 256 [253]), or as he puts it a bit later in the same text, 'Experiencing—in general, living as an ego (thinking, valuing, acting)—I am necessarily an "I" that has its "thou," its "we," its "you"—the "I" of the personal pronouns' (Husserl 1954: 270 [335–6]). More generally speaking, Husserl ascribes a *relative mode of being* to the personal I (Husserl 1952: 319). As he puts it on several occasions, if there were no you, there would also be no I in contrast to it; that is, the I is only constituted as I in contrast to the you (Husserl 1973a: 6, 247). Indeed, as Husserl writes in a famous quotation that Merleau-Ponty was later to discuss in detail, 'subjectivity is what it is—an ego functioning constitutively—only within intersubjectivity' (Husserl 1954: 175 [172]).

Husserl consequently holds that the personal I has its origin in social life. Persons have abilities, dispositions, habits, interests, character traits, and convictions, but persons do not exist in a social vacuum. To exist as a person is to exist socialized into a communal horizon, where one's bearing to oneself is appropriated from the others:

The origin of personality is found in empathy and in the further *social acts* that grow out of it. For personality, it is not enough that the subject becomes aware of itself as the center of its acts; rather, personality is constituted only as the subject enters into social relations with others. (Husserl 1973b: 175)

My being as a person is consequently not my own achievement; rather, for Husserl it is a result of my 'communicative intertwinement' with others (Husserl 1973c: 603; see also 1973c: 50).

At first glance, it seems as if there is quite some agreement between Husserl's position and Merleau-Ponty's. In fact, it wouldn't be unreasonable to say that on Husserl's account as well, the I and the you constitute a common system. As Husserl puts it in *Ideen II*, 'According to our presentation, the concepts I and we are relative: the I requires the thou, the we, and the "other." And, furthermore, the Ego (the Ego as person) requires a relation to a world which engages it. Therefore, I, we and world belong together' (Husserl 1952: 288). Rather than saying that the I is prior, or that the I and the you are simply equiprimordial, on some occasions Husserl even seems to assign priority to the other, for instance, in the following well-known quotation from *Zur Phänomenologie der Intersubjektivität II*, where he says, 'The other is the first human being, not I' (Husserl 1973b: 418).

There is, however, a slight catch to this way of presenting matters. Husserl operates with several complementary notions of I, and what I have been discussing so far is not the most fundamental notion. When Husserl writes that the I is transformed into a personal I through the I–thou relation (Husserl 1973b: 171), and when he writes that what distinguish human beings from animals is that although the latter have an I-structure, only human beings have a personal I (Husserl 1973c: 177), he is clearly indicating that the personal I is a founded I. But what then constitutes the deeper and more fundamental dimension of I, according to Husserl, and what is the relation between this dimension of I and others?

Let us consider for a moment the analysis he offers in *Ideen II*. There Husserl highlights the absolute individuation of consciousness. He writes, 'The pure Ego of any given *cogitatio* already has absolute individuation, and the *cogitatio* itself is something absolutely individual in itself.... The lived experiences in the flux of consciousness have an essence that is absolutely their own; they bear their individuation in themselves' (Husserl 1952: 299–300; see also Husserl 2006: 386). The pure ego that Husserl refers to here is, as he writes, not something secret or mysterious, but just another name for the subject of experience (Husserl 1952: 97). The stream of consciousness is not a mere bundle of experiences; rather, all experiencing is the experiencing of a subject that doesn't stream like its experiences (Husserl 1952: 103, 277). But although the pure ego must be distinguished from the experiences in which it lives and functions, since the former preserves its identity, whereas the latter arise and perish in the stream of consciousness, replacing each other in a permanent flux (Husserl 1952: 98–9; 1974: 363), it cannot in any way exist independently of them, or be thought in separation from them (and vice versa). It is a transcendence, but in Husserl's famous phrase, *a transcendence in the immanence* (Husserl 1976: 123–4).

It is consequently imperative not to conflate the pure ego with the personal ego.[1] Not only is the personal ego, in contrast to the pure ego, intersubjectively constituted, but it is also characterized by a different type of historicity and individuality. As we have already seen, for Husserl, to exist as a person entails an appropriation of the others' attitudes towards oneself. However, while writing that the development of a person is determined by the influence of others, by the influence of their thoughts, their feelings, and commandments, regardless of whether or not the person in question realizes this or not, Husserl also argues, in a quite Frankfurtian manner, that in so far as I do not merely yield passively to the influence of others, but instead, through an active position-taking (*Stellungnahme*), appropriate or annex their opinions, they become my own in a more substantial sense. In fact, not only is it precisely in taking ownership of one's convictions and by following self-imposed guidelines that Husserl sees the possibility for rational self-responsibility and thereby for a certain autonomy of reason (Husserl 1952: 269; compare Moran 2001: 51), but he also argues that my decisions come to form and shape who I am, and that my individuality is expressed in the pervading and concordant style of my thinking and deciding and in the unity of my behaviour (Husserl 1952: 270; 1973b: 196). Finally, Husserl also speaks of how the pure ego develops into a personal ego with a history in so far as sedimentations accrue and enduring habits are established (Husserl 1952: 151, 265). To rephrase, whereas the pure ego possesses a purely formal kind of individuation, a more concrete kind of individuality is constituted in and through my personal history, by my moral and intellectual decisions and convictions, and by my

---

[1] One must also distinguish Husserl's notions of pure ego and transcendental ego, although some interpreters use the notions interchangeably. Not only is it possible to discuss and endorse what Husserl calls the pure ego without adopting or embracing a transcendental philosophical perspective, but a full consideration of the transcendental ego, that is, a full consideration of the subject qua constitutive dimension, would also have to include far more than the pure ego.

identification with and participation in various social groups. I am, in short, not merely a pure and formal subject of experience, but also a person with abilities, dispositions, habits, interests, character traits, and convictions, and to focus exclusively on the former is to engage in an abstraction (Husserl 1962: 210). In order to know who I am qua human personality, I need to look at the *Unendlichkeit der Erfahrung*. Persons are, as Husserl puts it, unities that in principle are capable of infinite development (Husserl 1973b: 204); they are constituted by and continuously enriched in the interplay between self-experience and other-experience (Husserl 1973a: 432; 1971: 112). Obtaining that kind of self-knowledge is, in short, an unending quest. By contrast, in order to know what the pure ego is, an ego with no dispositions, traits, or preferences, one single *cogito* can be sufficient. This might all sound strange, and has in fact made Ricœur criticize Husserl for failing to acknowledge what Ricœur calls the 'wounded *cogito*' (quoted in Kearney 1984: 27). But rather than reading Husserl's assertion as attesting to his failure to recognize the richness and complexity of human life, it is much more reasonable to read the statement, and Husserl's subsequent emphasis on the fact that the pure ego contains no hidden inner richness, as an accentuation of the formality and emptiness of the pure ego. It is, to some extent, a very thin and deflationary notion. As Edith Stein puts it at one point, 'the pure "I" has no depth' (Stein 2008: 110). It is pure but also poor. It is pure in the sense of being formal, and consequently poor in terms of content (Husserl 1976: 179). But this should not make us deny its existence or importance.

In a few places, including *Die Krisis* and *Zur Phänomenologie der Intersubjektivität III*, Husserl introduces yet another term for the most fundamental dimension of I, namely, *Ur-Ich*, or *primal I*. Let us take a look at a few passages that explicitly target this dimension of I:

it was wrong, methodically, to jump immediately into transcendental intersubjectivity and to leap over the primal 'I,' the ego of my epoché, which can never lose its uniqueness and personal indeclinability. (Husserl 1954: 188 [185])

I am not *an* ego, who still has his *you*, his *we*, his total community of cosubjects in natural validity. (Husserl 1954: 188 [184])

The 'I' that I attain in the epoché ... is actually called 'I' only by equivocation. (Husserl 1954: 188 [184])

Two issues are highlighted in these quotations. First, the I in question differs from our ordinary notion of I. Secondly, this I isn't dependent upon or relative to others in the same way as the personal I. Whereas in regard to the latter, as we have seen, Husserl writes that if there were no you, there would also be no I, since the I is only an I in contrast to a you (Husserl 1973a: 6, 247), in regard to the former he writes that the absolute I is unique in a way that rules out multiplication as meaningless, for which reason it cannot be *an* ego (among many) (Husserl 1973c: 589–90).

The obvious question we are now faced with is what precisely this primal I amounts to. Can the notion be defended, and is Husserl right in insisting upon its uniqueness and indeclinability? A comprehensive answer to these questions would have to discuss the precise relation between the pure ego and the primal I, and would in particular have to consider the transcendental philosophical context of Husserl's analysis. I shall bracket these exegetical concerns, however, and instead home in on a specific aspect that I take to be of more immediate relevance for the specific focus of my investigation.

When Husserl speaks of the radical singularity of the primal I, and denies that it can be pluralized, he is not talking about the substantial or metaphysical uniqueness and indeclinability of the primal I, but rather referring to the unique first-personal character of consciousness. This interpretation can, for instance, be supported by one of Husserl's unpublished research manuscripts, where he argues that 'I' does not admit of any plural as long as the word is used in its original sense. Others do experience themselves as I, but I can only experience myself, and not them, as I (Husserl 1932: 127a). Thus, I do not have a second exemplar alongside myself of which I could say, 'das bin Ich'. Accordingly, I cannot speak of *an* I when 'I' means precisely *I*. This I is absolutely unique and individual (Husserl 1932: 138a).[2] But, as Husserl also makes clear, this focus on the uniqueness of the primal I in no way rules out a multiplicity of similarly unique primal I's. He writes, 'The unique I—the transcendental. In its uniqueness it posits "other" unique transcendental I's—as "others" who themselves posit others in uniqueness once again' (Husserl 1932: 138b).

As I understand Husserl, his emphasis on the primal I is an attempt to do justice to the first-personal character of consciousness; it is an attempt to point to the intrinsic and 'absolute individuation' of consciousness (compare Husserl 1952: 97), an individuation that the subject does precisely *not* first acquire through a confrontation and interaction with others. In short, according to Husserl, it is perfectly legitimate to conduct a formal analysis of the relation between selfhood, pre-reflective self-consciousness, and the structures of the stream of consciousness without introducing others into the analysis. When it comes to the peculiar mineness (*Meinheit*) of experiential life, this is an aspect that can be characterized without any contrasting others (Husserl 1973c: 351). But as Husserl also points out, even though our experiential life is inherently individuated, we must realize that it is a formal and empty kind of individuation, one that equally characterizes every other possible subject (Husserl 1973b: 23).

---

[2] In a text dating from 1907, Lipps makes a somewhat similar point. He writes, 'I only know immediately of myself. I say "myself" rather than "my self". If I speak of "my" self I presuppose other selves. Thus, the self that I originally know of, prior to knowing about others, is not "my" self. Nor it is "a" self or "this" self. For "a" self is a self among many selves, and "this" self is an individual self in contrast to other individual selves. The self of which I originally know is simply "I"; the "I" not as a substantive, but as a personal pronoun. This then becomes my I, this I, an I, in short, an individual I, when other I's stand before me' (Lipps 1907a: 694). Consider also the fact that it seems less awkward to speak of a self or the self (notwithstanding Kenny's well-known criticism; Kenny 1988: 4) than to speak of selves. If one wants to pluralize the notion, it is more natural to speak of self and others.

The advantage of this interpretation is that it allows us to connect Husserl's late and rather infrequent talk of the primal I with his persisting preoccupation with the issue of self-consciousness. As already mentioned, Husserl emphasized the ubiquitous presence of self-consciousness in experiential life, and on repeated occasions equated the first-personal character of consciousness, a primitive form of self-consciousness, and a certain basic sense of selfhood. Interpreting the notion of the primal I in this way also allows one to establish a link to Husserl's earlier notion of *Urbewusstsein*, or 'primal consciousness'.[3] The notion of primal consciousness, which Husserl had already used in his early lecture course *Einleitung in die Logik und Erkenntnistheorie* from 1906–7, doesn't refer to a particular intentional experience. Rather, the term designates the pervasive dimension of pre-reflective and non-objectifying self-consciousness that is part and parcel of any occurring experience (Husserl 1984b: 245–7). Indeed, although it would lead us too far to explore this angle in further detail, it is surely no coincidence that the term 'primal consciousness' occurs at central places in Husserl's lectures on the phenomenology of inner time-consciousness (Husserl 1966a: 89, 118–20).

One important methodological issue that is highlighted in Husserl's discussion of the primal I concerns the potentially misleading character of ordinary language when it comes to describing this dimension. As Husserl wrote in the central passage that I quoted in part earlier:

> The 'I' that I attain in the epoché . . . is actually called 'I' only by equivocation—though it is an essential equivocation since, when I name it in reflection, I can say nothing other than: it is I who practice the epoché. (Husserl 1954: 188 [184])

What Husserl is stressing here is that the notion of the primal I obviously departs from the ordinary everyday concept of I, and that the labelling of the primal I as 'I' can lead to misunderstandings if the usual connotations are retained. At the same time, however, he also emphasizes that the continuing use of the term 'I' is necessary and unavoidable. Not only do we lack a better term, but Husserl obviously also wishes to retain the experiential meaning of the term. He is pointing to something that all of us are thoroughly familiar with, namely, the fundamental first-personal character of consciousness, although in ordinary life we frequently fail to understand its proper significance.

Husserl's reflections regarding the equivocation of the term 'I' when used to designate the basic level of self-experience can a fortiori be transferred to notions such as mineness and first-personal character. Not surprisingly, some have objected to my own use of the term 'mineness', claiming that the primary meaning of 'mine' developmentally speaking is 'not yours'. And similarly, it has been argued that it makes little sense to speak of a first-personal character or of a first-person perspective unless in contrast to a second- and third-person perspective. Thus, on this line of

---

[3] This connection seems to be missing in Taguchi's otherwise excellent treatment (Taguchi 2006).

reasoning, both terms are contrastive terms whose meaning is provided by second-personal social space (Hutto 2008: 15). But just like Husserl, I have been using the terms to refer to the basic individuation and self-presentational character of experience. I can see why the terms might generate confusion, but I don't see any obvious alternatives.

6.3 The solipsism of lived experience

As I pointed out earlier, there is an ambiguity in Merleau-Ponty's position on the self–other relation as it is articulated in his Sorbonne lectures. When he says that the child is initially entirely unaware both of himself and of others, and that consciousness of oneself and of others as unique individuals only comes later, is Merleau-Ponty simply claiming that the child only becomes explicitly aware of the difference between himself and others at a relatively late stage, or is he defending the more radical claim that the very distinction between self and other is derived and rooted in a common anonymity? There are passages that can be interpreted in support of the latter view. If this is indeed Merleau-Ponty's position, we are dealing with a noticeable and marked departure from Husserl's view.

However, let me briefly consider another central text by Merleau-Ponty, namely, the chapter 'Others and the Human World' in *Phénoménologie de la perception*. He writes there that the perception of other people is problematic only for adults. The infant has no awareness of himself or of others as private subjectivities. Merleau-Ponty continues by saying that this infantile experience must remain as an indispensable acquisition even in later life if something like an intersubjective world is to be possible. Prior to any struggle for recognition, prior to any understanding of the alien presence of the other, there must be a common ground. We must all remain, at some level, mindful of our peaceful coexistence in the world of childhood (Merleau-Ponty 2012: 372). But, Merleau-Ponty then asks, will this model really work? Isn't it basically an attempt to solve the problem of intersubjectivity by doing away with the individuality of perspectives, by doing away with both ego and alter ego? If the perceiving subject is anonymous, so is the perceived other, and to try to reintroduce a plurality of subjects into this anonymous collectivity is hopeless. Even if I perceive the grief or the anger of the other in his conduct, in his face or hands, even if I understand the other without recourse to any 'inner' experience of suffering or anger, the grief and anger of the other will never quite have the same significance for me as they have for him. For me these situations are appresented; for him they are lived through (Merleau-Ponty 2012: 372). Merleau-Ponty then goes on to talk of an insurmountable solipsism that is rooted in lived experience (Merleau-Ponty 2012: 374). Although I am outrun on all sides by my own acts, and submerged in generality, the fact remains that I am the one by whom they are experienced. In the end, he even refers to 'the indeclinable "I"' (Merleau-Ponty 2012: 375). This brings his position far closer to Husserl's. It could, of course, be objected that the Sorbonne lectures are later, and that they might represent Merleau-Ponty's more developed view. But, interestingly enough, in those very lectures we also find passages where Merleau-Ponty claims that Scheler, in order to make the experience of others possible, ended up defending a kind of panpsychism that led to a denial of the individuation of consciousness and thereby also to the destruction of the very distinction between I and other (Merleau-Ponty 2010: 32). This is a result that Merleau-Ponty finds unacceptable. As will become clear in Part II, this criticism is probably based on a misinterpretation of Scheler, but the criticism indicates that Merleau-Ponty, even in those later lectures, favoured the less radical view, or at least remained undecided or simply unclear about how far he wanted to go.

7

A Multidimensional Account

Let me try to take stock. Over the previous chapters, I have presented and defended the idea that a minimal form of selfhood is a built-in feature of experiential life. I started by considering the views of some ardent anti-realists, and argued that the contemporary discussion and conceptualization of selfhood is considerably more complex and sophisticated than the sceptics seem to realize. The notion of the self that they are out to deny is not a notion that is widely endorsed. I then went on to argue that it is both possible and desirable to operate with a more minimalist notion of selfhood, and that one can consequently be a realist about the self without committing oneself to the existence of the kind of unchanging soul-substance that is being rejected by the self-sceptics. More specifically, I defended the view that phenomenal consciousness involves self-consciousness in the weak sense that there is necessarily something it is like for the subject to have or live through the experiences. Experiences necessarily involve an experiential perspective or point of view, they come with perspectival ownership, and rather than speaking simply of phenomenal what-it-is-likeness, it is more accurate to speak of what-it-is-like-for-me-ness. Importantly, this for-me-ness of experience doesn't denote some special kind of I-qualia; rather, it refers to the first-personal character or presence of experience, to the fact that we have a different pre-reflective acquaintance with our own ongoing experiential life than we have with the experiential life of others and vice versa. My central claim was then that this feature of experience amounts to and can be identified with experiential selfhood.

Having presented the core of the proposal, I next considered a variety of objections. According to a first line of attack, experiential life lacks for-me-ness and first-personal character either frequently, or entirely, or in some special cases, for which reason selfhood cannot be a pervasive feature of experiential life. According to one version of the objection, experiential ownership is the outcome of a meta-cognitive operation that involves conceptual and linguistic resources. I argued that such a view, rather than really constituting a relevant objection, is trading on ambiguities in the employed notions of subjectivity and self-consciousness, and ultimately targets a position that differs from my own. According to another version of the objection, phenomenal consciousness is strictly and exclusively world-presenting. I argued that such a proposal overlooks the distinction between the phenomenal character of the experienced object and the phenomenal character of the intentional act, and that it also has difficulties accounting for the difference between a non-conscious and a conscious intentional episode. I finally considered the claim that pathology presents us with relevant exceptions to the view that self and consciousness are tightly interwoven, and I argued that this only holds true if one forgoes a minimalist construal and defines for-me-ness and self-consciousness in a more robust and inflated way than I do.

Having responded to this first line of objections, I went on to consider a different kind of challenge, according to which subjectivity and selfhood must be distinguished and their difference preserved. As one version of this objection has it, experiences might indeed be characterized by self-consciousness and perspectival ownership, but this in no way warrants the positing of a unified self. As I pointed out, however, the problem with this criticism is that without further ado it opts for a rather specific definition of selfhood, one that in important ways differs from the one I am defending. Not surprisingly, this kind of reply immediately led to another version of the objection, according to which the minimalist definition of selfhood that I am defending is just too minimalist and deflationary. Having considered in some detail the suggestion that our self-identity, rather than simply being equated with a specific experiential dimension, is constituted by our normative commitments and endorsements, I argued that whatever merits the latter view might have, it cannot stand on its own. It necessarily presupposes the first-personal features that are targeted by the experiential approach. Ultimately, however, we shouldn't lose sight of the principal point: that experiential life is as such and from the beginning characterized by first-personal character and presence, by pre-reflective self-consciousness and for-me-ness. As long as that is recognized, the question of whether one ought to distinguish a minimalist level of selfhood from a more complex one, or rather differentiate subjecthood from selfhood proper, is of less importance. Nothing really decisive hangs on this terminological choice. Not surprisingly, however, my own preference is for the former option. I do not merely think that this option is systematically defensible and historically precedented (as pointed out in Chapter 6). I also think the continuing reference to a level of experiential selfhood will help to remind us of the proper significance of the experiential features in question.

Perhaps it might at this stage be objected that my definition of minimal selfhood ends up being so formal that, despite my repeated claims to the contrary, it ceases to be experiential. In short, is my own proposal not vulnerable to the very objection that I directed against Dainton's PCS thesis? I don't think so. The minimal self might be intertwined with and contextualized by the intentional acts it structures, by memories, expressive behaviour, and social interaction, by passively acquired habits, inclinations, associations, etc. To that extent, a narrow focus on the minimal self will indeed involve an abstraction. But that is not to say that the minimal self is itself a mere abstraction. There is no reason to question its experiential reality; it is not a mere potentiality.

In the course of my discussion, I have contrasted two different approaches to self: a narrative approach, which highlights the importance of authorship, commitment, and normativity, and an experiential approach, which puts more emphasis on ownership, pre-reflective self-consciousness, and phenomenality.[1] By emphasizing this contrast, I have, I hope, succeeded in highlighting what is distinctive about the notion of an experiential self. The question to ask is then whether we can make do with just one of them, or whether we need both accounts? Although I take the experiential approach to be the more fundamental of the two, I am happy to concede that the narrative approach, which I have treated as an example of a more normatively oriented account, captures something important, something that might be specific to human selfhood. Rather than simply being a brute fact, rather than simply being something waiting to be discovered, who we are is also a question of our self-interpretation, of who we take ourselves to be. To avoid misunderstandings, however, let me emphasize that although I do think the narrative account of the self captures aspects of what it means to be a self that isn't captured by the experiential account, including aspects that might be uniquely human, I am not saying that one isn't a proper human self if, like Strawson's episodic individuals, one has no sense of one's own life as a well-ordered cohesive narrative (Strawson 2004). I would, however, insist that there is more to human selfhood than merely the experiential component. There is also an eliminable normative dimension (linked to notions such as commitment, decision, responsibility, reflection), even if it doesn't necessarily take a narrative form. The important point, though, is to recognize the need for a multidimensional account. We shouldn't accept being forced to choose between viewing selfhood as either a socially constructed achievement or an innate and culturally invariant given. Who we are is as much made as found. This is why I favour a multifaceted and multi-layered model of self that is ultimately more impure or hybrid than the one defended by Dainton (Dainton 2008: 76), but probably more in line with what Strawson would say, especially after he has explicitly acknowledged that the thin notion of self doesn't exclude other notions even if the thin notion possesses a certain metaphysical primacy (Strawson 2011: 262).

To complicate matters, however, we shouldn't make the mistake of assuming that the two notions of self just outlined jointly present us with an exhaustive account of the self. Consider, for instance, the dimension of self that Neisser targets in his discussion of the *interpersonal self*. Neisser argues that this sense of the self grows out of the infant's interactions and reciprocations with others, and he specifically links it to a special kind of self-experience, the experience of self-in-relation-to-others (Neisser 1988: 43). Although I haven't really explored this aspect so far, it will be very much the focus of my investigation in Part III.

---

[1] The contrast is not supposed to entail that the narrative self is non-experiential. But on most accounts it is the result of an accomplishment and not an intrinsic feature of our experiential life.

For now, let me just emphasize that the multidimensional model I am proposing allows for a reconciliation of various positions that at first sight might seem incompatible. Why is there no incompatibility or straightforward contradiction involved in embracing both views? Obviously, because they target different aspects or levels of selfhood, and the minimalist notion of an experiential self is fully compatible with a more complex notion of a socially and normatively embedded self. Take, for instance, the case of Mead. He was earlier listed as a defender of a social constructivist approach to the self. On his view, we are selves not by individual right, but in virtue of our relation to one another. He writes, 'When a self does appear it always involves an experience of another; there could not be an experience of a self simply by itself' (Mead 1962: 195). However, in *Mind, Self and Society*, Mead also concedes that one could talk of a single self if one identified the self with a certain feeling-consciousness, and that previous thinkers such as William James had sought to find the basis of self in reflexive affective experiences, that is, in experiences involving self-feeling. Mead even writes that there is a certain element of truth in this, but then denies that it is the whole story (Mead 1962: 164, 169, 173). For Mead, the problem of selfhood is fundamentally the problem of how an individual can get experientially outside himself in such a way as to become an object to himself. Thus, for Mead, to be a self is ultimately more a question of becoming an object than of being a subject. In his view, one can only become an object to oneself in an indirect manner, namely, by adopting the perspectives of others on oneself, and this is something that can only happen within a social environment (Mead 1962: 138). In short, it 'is the social process of influencing others in a social act and then taking the attitude of the others aroused by the stimulus, and then reacting in turn to this response, which constitutes a self' (Mead 1962: 171).

What at first sight looked like a substantial disagreement might in the end be more of a terminological dispute regarding the appropriate use of the term 'self', a dispute that can be resolved the moment we discard the ambition of operating with only one notion of selfhood. Having said this, it would be naive to imagine that every disagreement will automatically dissolve the moment one recognizes the need for a distinction between different levels or aspects of selfhood. Disagreement obviously persists with anti-selfers and ego-phobes like Metzinger, who insist that rigorous philosophical analyses of, and scientific research on, the self and self-consciousness must be protected from the degenerated debates found in philosophical phenomenology (Metzinger 2011: 294). Moreover, there are still forms of social constructivism that remain incompatible with the current proposal. To show why, let us move forward in time. Given my introductory remarks, one might have received the impression that the attempt to argue for the socially constructed character of selfhood was primarily a thing of the nineteenth and twentieth centuries. But this is, of course, incorrect, since one can also find constructivist tendencies in contemporary cognitive science.

In an article from 2003, for instance, Wolfgang Prinz argued that the 'social construction of subjectivity and selfhood relies on, and is maintained in, various discourses on subjectivity' (Prinz 2003: 515). Prinz consequently distances himself from the naturalist idea that a self is a natural entity and instead holds the view that it depends on the social and cultural resources on which and from which it is built (Prinz 2012: 35, 182). Indeed, on his account, selves are socio-cultural constructs rather than natural givens. They are constituted within culturally standardized frameworks that control the socialization of individuals. What is remarkable about Prinz's proposal is that he explicitly defines the notion of self in terms of 'me-ness' (Prinz 2003: 517); that is, the notion of self that he considers to be a social construct is very akin to the kind of experiential self that I have been articulating here. As a consequence, the position defended by Prinz is quite radical. The radicalism is not primarily to be found in his claim that the unity and consistency of the self, rather than being a natural fact, is a cultural norm, but in his endorsement of the view that human beings who have been denied all socially mediated attributions of self—like, say, the famous case of Kaspar Hauser—would be 'completely self-less and thus without consciousness' and therefore remain 'unconscious zombies' (Prinz 2003: 526).

As far as I can see, Prinz endorses a version of the higher-order theory of consciousness and assumes that phenomenal consciousness is conditioned by second-order representations. The point he then makes is that the relevant second-order representations are socially mediated. It is by appropriating the mental organization that others impute to oneself that one acquires subjective experiences (for a comparable view, see Gergely 2007). But although one can understand this line of reasoning if one accepts a higher-order account, it becomes quite implausible if one rejects such an account, as I think one should.

Whereas some of the social constructivists mentioned earlier were referring to other aspects of the self when discussing its socially mediated character, Prinz is very much focusing on the same aspect of selfhood as I, and this is also why his social constructivism remains incompatible with my own position. Prinz is right to insist that a thorough social constructivism regarding selfhood must also defend the socially constructed character of phenomenal consciousness, and he clearly shows the (absurd) implications of such a view.

PART II
Empathic Understanding

8

Subjectivity and Intersubjectivity

In Part I, I have outlined and defended an experiential notion of self. In doing so, one of my targets of criticism has been the kind of social constructivism that argues that the self is constructed and negotiated through social interaction and that all self-experience is intersubjectively mediated. I am not disputing that we de facto live together with others in a public world from the very start, but I would deny that the very mineness or for-me-ness of experience is constitutively dependent upon social interaction. In short, I am not disputing the de facto coexistence of (minimal) selfhood and intersubjectivity, I am denying their constitutive interdependence. As was made clear in Chapter 6, the position I have been defending is in many ways indebted to a Husserlian outlook. On closer consideration, however, shouldn't this make us pause? Isn't phenomenology and in particular Husserlian phenomenology faced with notorious problems when it comes to the issue of intersubjectivity? Isn't it, precisely because of its unremitting commitment to subjectivity, infamous for being incapable of handling the problem of the other in a satisfactory manner (see Habermas 1984)?

Over the years, the notion of an experiential self has encountered some resistance. I think one reason for this opposition has been the worry that if one takes the reflexivity that constitutes basic selfhood to be a built-in feature of the individual mind, one that is not constitutively dependent upon one's relation to others, then one either directly or in a more oblique manner commits oneself to a form of Cartesianism, where the essence of selfhood is taken to be a kind of self-enclosed solitary interiority (see Maclaren 2008). As far as I can judge, it is precisely this kind of suspicion that has led many to reject outright the notion of an experiential self, and made them opt for a more robust and socially mediated notion, one that either stresses the co-constitution of self and other, or argues that one only obtains the reflexive self-relation constitutive of selfhood by being socialized into a publicly shared space of normativity (Rousse 2013).

To some extent, it is easy to deflate the worry. As I have repeatedly made clear, the experiential self is defined as the very subjectivity of experience and is not something that exists independently of the experiential flow. On this reading, there is no pure, experience-independent, experiential self. Whether or not this self is then isolated, worldless, and disembodied will depend entirely upon one's more general account of experience. In previous publications, I have defended an embodied and embedded account of experience. But I hope my current proposal is so formal (and neutral) that it might also appeal to people with divergent views on the nature of experience, including those who favour more internalist neurocentric accounts. However, there is as such nothing in the notion of experiential self that makes it incompatible or in tension with a strong emphasis on the fundamental intentionality or being-in-the-world of consciousness. For that reason, it is a simple fallacy to insist that the 'notion of a real, central, yet wafer-thin self is a profound mistake' since the latter notion disregards 'the roles of context, culture, environment, and technology in the constitution of individual human persons' and fails to recognize 'the inextricable intimacy of self, mind, and world' (Clark 2003: 139). It is no coincidence that most phenomenological accounts of experience have precisely emphasized the unity of world-awareness and self-experience. This is, for instance, why Merleau-Ponty could write that at the root of all our experiences and all our reflections we find a being who immediately knows itself, not by observation, not by inference, but through direct contact with its own existence (Merleau-Ponty 2012: 390), while at the same stating that 'there is no "inner man," man is in and toward the world, and it is in the world that he knows himself' (Merleau-Ponty 2012, p. lxxiv).

As I have repeatedly pointed out, I favour a multidimensional account of self. Whereas I have already defended what I take to be a presocial form of self(-experience), that is, one that isn't socially constituted, I shall explore in Part III what I take to be a socially mediated and constituted form of self(-experience). The aim of Part II will be to say something about how in the first place we relate to and come to understand others. Contrary to what has been suggested by some, I don't think an appreciation of the significance of phenomenal consciousness and a recognition of the fact that we enjoy a first-personal acquaintance with our own experiential states should go hand in hand with the view that the experiential lives of others are not manifest or present or given in any straightforward sense to us, and that second- and third-person ascriptions of mental states is consequently a highly indirect, highly inferential endeavour. To put my worry in more general terms, I think it would be quite unfortunate if the long-overdue recognition of the importance of subjectivity and the first-personal character of consciousness went hand in hand with a commitment to an inferentialist account of intersubjectivity, according to which our ascription of a mental life to others is based on an inference to best explanation. To suggest, as Searle has done, that the indirect means of verifying claims about black holes or subatomic particles might 'give us a model for verifying hypotheses in the area of the study of human and animal subjectivity' (Searle 1999: 2074) is to make a move in the wrong direction. Not only shall I show in the following that there is no conflict between defending the notion of an experiential self and arguing that we can be experientially acquainted with the subjectivity of others. I shall also defend the view that the notion of an experiential self, rather than preventing a satisfactory solution to the problem of other minds, is in fact a precondition for a reasonable account of intersubjectivity.

Incidentally, the history of the very notion of intersubjectivity suggests a similar conclusion. The German term *Intersubjektivität* made its first sporadic appearance in 1885 in a work by Johannes Volkelt and was then picked up by James Ward and first used in English in 1896. Initially, the concept was used to describe something with universal validity, something that was valid for everybody, something that was valid independently of every subject. This sporadic use of the term subsequently found its way into philosophy of science. The first systematic and extensive philosophical discussion and treatment of the notion of intersubjectivity can, however, be found in the work of none other than Husserl. Although Husserl remained deeply interested in the link between intersubjectivity and objectivity, he ultimately used the former term to designate a plurality of subjects and the relation that exists between them (Husserl 1973a,b,c). This understanding of the term, which was subsequently taken up by later phenomenologists and which then (through the work of Schutz) found its way into sociology and social theory, places the term alongside related terms such as sociality, social cognition, and interpersonal understanding.

Before commencing my investigation, however, I need to make one caveat. In *L'Être et le néant* Sartre remarks that if we are to escape solipsism it will be crucial to realize that the relation between self and other, rather than merely being a relation of knowledge, is a relation of being (Sartre 2003: 268). One important concern highlighted by this remark is whether an account of intersubjectivity and sociality that only attends to the epistemic or cognitive relation between subjects might miss something quite significant. At the same time, Sartre's remark suggests that the truly distinctive contribution of a phenomenology of intersubjectivity, far from being located in its investigation of how we come to know others, is to be found in its exploration of the ontological (and affective and normative) intertwinement of self and other.

There is some truth to this. In the following, however, my main focus will nevertheless be on the question of how and to what extent we can experience and understand others. There are several reasons for this choice. First of all, I wish to show that an insistence on the inherent and essential first-personal character of experiential life in no way prevents or prohibits one from recognizing and respecting the distinctiveness of other-experience. Secondly, this emphasis on other-experience will allow me eventually to introduce and discuss a special kind of socially mediated self(-experience), one that is enabled by such other-experience and which involves a certain internalization of the other's perspective on oneself. An added benefit of this focus is that it intersects with parallel discussions in philosophy of mind and cognitive science, thereby allowing for a constructive exchange between phenomenology and contemporary discussions of social cognition. Let me finally add that when in the following I refer to social cognition, I shall be using the term 'cognition' in a broad sense, one in which cognition, rather than being restricted to propositional knowledge and contrasted with perceptual and emotional experiences, covers and includes the latter.

Whereas part of my criticism in Part I was directed against social constructivist accounts that proceed from others to self and argue that the latter is constituted through some process of introjection, my critical target in Part II will primarily be projectivist accounts that proceed from self to others and claim that social cognition and interpersonal understanding crucially depends upon the ability to project one's own psychical states into others. My more positive thesis will be that although interpersonal understanding comes in many shapes and forms, we also ought to recognize that the more complex forms rely on and presuppose empathy understood as a perceptually based and theoretically unmediated experience of the other.

9

Empathy and Projection

How do we get to know and understand others? Is social cognition perceptual or inferential in nature? Is our understanding of others in principle like our understanding of trees, rocks, and clouds, or does it differ in fundamental ways from our understanding of inanimate objects? Do we understand others in analogy to ourselves, that is, does self-understanding have primacy over the understanding of others, or is the understanding of self and other equally primordial, basically employing the same cognitive mechanisms?

In recent decades, much of the discussion of social cognition has taken place within the framework of the so-called theory of mind debate. The term 'theory of mind' was originally introduced by Premack and Woodruff in a seminal paper on intentionality in primates:

In saying that an individual has a theory of mind, we mean that the individual imputes mental states to himself and to others (either to conspecifics or to other species as well). A system of inferences of this kind is properly viewed as a theory, first, because such states are not directly observable, and second, because the system can be used to make predictions, specifically about the behavior of other organisms. (Premack and Woodruff 1978: 515)

The expression 'theory of mind' has since been used to refer to our ability to attribute mental states to self and others and to interpret, predict, and explain behaviour in terms of mental states such as intentions, beliefs, and desires. The claim has been that we ascribe mental states to others because such ascriptions facilitate predictions and explanations. It was originally assumed that it was the possession and use of a *theory* that provided an individual with the capacity to make this attribution. Becoming aware of someone else's (or even one's own) mental state was consequently typically taken to be a question of inferring from a piece of observable behaviour to the mental state that had caused it via a suitable psychological theory. The coinage of the term 'theory of mind' was consequently neither neutral nor innocent.[1] Early on, however,

---

[1] Something similar can be said about another frequently used term for the same capacity, namely 'mind-reading.' Although that term doesn't per se entail that the capacity is theoretical in nature, it still suggests that we come to identify mental states on the basis of bodily behaviour in a manner analogous to the way in which we grasp meaning on the basis of written inscriptions (cf. Apperly 2011: 4). The potentially tendentious presupposition is obviously that mind-reading is a skill we need to acquire just as we need to learn how to read texts. For the infant, written words and sentences have no semantic meaning. Are the

the debate became split on this specific issue and was for a while considered to be a dispute between two views. On one side, one would find the *theory-theory of mind* and on the other, the *simulation theory of mind*. According to the theory-theory, mental states are theoretical entities that we attribute to others on the basis of a folk-psychological theory of mind. Theory-theorists were, however, split on the issue of whether the theory in question was implicit and the result of the maturation of innate mind-reading 'modules' (Baron-Cohen 1995), or whether it was explicit and acquired in the same manner as ordinary scientific theories (Gopnik and Wellman 1995). Simulation theorists, on the other hand, would deny that our understanding of others was primarily theoretical in nature, and maintain that we use our own mind as a model when understanding the minds of others. Some would claim that the simulation in question involved the exercise of conscious imagination and delibera-tive inference (Goldman 1995), some would insist that the simulation, although explicit, was non-inferential in nature (Gordon 1986), and finally there were those who would argue that the simulation, rather than being explicit and conscious, was implicit and sub-personal (Gallese 2009).

For a while theory-theory and simulation theory were supposed to be mutually exclusive theoretical paradigms, and there was widespread agreement that they were the only two games in town (Stich and Nichols 1995). Since the mid-1990s, however, things have become more complicated. Many participants in the debate went on to advocate hybrid approaches that incorporate elements of both theory-theory and simulation theory. Alvin Goldman became a prominent defender of this strategy (Goldman 2006), and so did Shaun Nichols and Stephen Stich. Consider the follow-ing quotation from their book *Mindreading*:

many writers, ourselves included, began to characterize debates over the plausibility of these new accounts as part of a *two-sided* battle in which either simulation theory or the 'theory theory'... would 'win'. Though understandable enough in the context of those early debates, this proved to be a very unfortunate way of characterizing the theoretical landscape, since it ignored the possibility that the correct account of mindreading might be provided by a *hybrid* theory. (Nichols and Stich 2003: 132)

Nichols and Stich further argued that a hybrid theory might be needed because mindreading, rather than being simply one thing, is in fact a variety of different processes. Some of these might then be explained by off-line simulation, some by what Nichols and Stich called 'information-rich processes' (invoking either modules or a theory-like information base), and some by processes which, as they put it, did not fit comfortably into either of those two categories.

---

actions and expressions of others equally meaningless to the infant prior to its acquisition of mind-reading skills? Given these reservations, I will in the following only use the term 'mind-reading' if I am either describing the positions of those who do employ the term, or if I am explicitly referring to forms of social understanding that are based on inferential theorizing or imaginative projection.

Many neuroscientists and psychologists reached similar conclusions. The first wave of social neuroscience was characterized by attempts to dissociate two distinct neural systems, one involving low-level neural resonance mechanisms and shared circuits, the other connected to more elaborate forms of mental state attribution. The fact that these two neurobiological systems were dissociable, and that this could be demonstrated in experiments targeting 'highly simplified "pieces" of social informa-tion processing' (Zaki and Ochsner 2012: 212) and involving tasks with simplified and non-naturalistic stimuli, did not imply, however, that the two systems were in fact dissociated in most ecologically valid social contexts—a fact that the second wave of social neuroscience was eager to highlight:

> studies employing naturalistic methods suggest that the demands of most social situations would engage these systems—and the processes they underlie—simultaneously. This probabil-ity motivates a shift away from an either/or argument...and toward a 'when and how' approach to better discriminating the situations likely to engage one or both of these systems. (Zaki and Ochsner 2012: 214)

It is by now increasingly recognized that social understanding, rather than being one single cognitive process, is a collection of different abilities that interact in various ways, and that we need multiple complementary accounts in order to cover the variety of abilities, skills, and strategies that we draw on and employ in order to understand and make sense of others. At the same time, however, fundamental disagreements persist concerning the nature of social cognition. One nice illustration of this can be found in the study of empathy.

Although in recent years there has been something of an upsurge of interest in and work on empathy, there is still no clear consensus about what precisely it is, and how it is related to and different from emotional contagion, motor mimicry, emotional sharing, imaginative projection, perspective taking, empathic distress, and empathic concern. Is empathy a question of sharing another's feelings, or caring about another, or being emotionally affected by another's experiences though not necessarily experiencing the same experiences? Is it a question of imagining oneself in another's situation, or of imagining being another in that other's situation, or simply of making inferences about another's mental states? Does empathy necessarily entail that an observer *feels* the same emotion that she detects in another person? Does empathy preserve or abolish the difference between self and other? People disagree about the role of sharing, and caring, and imagination in empathy, just as they disagree about the relation between empathy and social cognition in general.

For some, the most rudimentary forms of empathy are motor mimicry and emotional contagion. Thus, whereas Eisenberg has argued that empathy and emo-tional contagion is a question of simply feeling the same emotion as the other in a way that is neither highly self-involved nor other-directed in orientation (Eisenberg 1986: 31), Darwall has claimed that emotional contagion constitutes the most primitive form of empathy, and that mimicry is one of its central mechanisms

(Darwall 1998: 264–6). Likewise, Gordon has defined 'facial empathy' as a process in which, by replicating the facial expressions of others, we tend to catch their emotions (Gordon 1995: 729; see also Hodges and Wegner 1997; Hatfield et al. 2009). For others, by contrast, it has been urgent to opt for a more narrow definition of empathy that allows one to preserve the distinctions between empathy, on the one hand, and emotional contagion, on the other (Decety et al. 2008; de Vignemont and Singer 2006). It has been argued, for instance, that emotional contagion is 'self-centered', whereas empathy is essentially 'other-centered' (de Vignemont 2009).

Given this lack of consensus, it shouldn't be surprising that there is also quite a bit of disagreement about the role empathy plays in social cognition. Gallese has insisted that empathy 'is relevant when accounting for all aspects of behaviour enabling us to establish a meaningful link between others and ourselves' (Gallese 2001: 43), and has argued that it provides us with a direct experiential understanding of others. Likewise, Hoffman has argued that empathy is 'the glue that makes social life possible' (Hoffman 2001: 3). Peter Goldie, by contrast, has defended a far more complex model of empathy. On his view, it is correct to speak of empathy only when a person reaches an understanding of another's mental state by way of a simulative process of imagining what it is like *for that other person* to be in the situation she is in (Goldie 2000). More specifically, Goldie argues that

Empathy is a process or procedure by which a person *centrally imagines the narrative* (the thoughts, feelings, and emotions) of another person. There are three necessary conditions for empathy.... First, it is necessary for empathy that I be aware of the other as a centre of consciousness distinct from myself. Secondly, it is necessary for empathy that the other should be someone of whom I have a *substantial characterization*. Thirdly, it is necessary that I have a grasp of the narrative which I can imaginatively enact, with the other as narrator. (Goldie 2000: 195)

One implication of this view is that empathy would have a far more modest role to play in social understanding than many philosophers and psychologists have believed. Indeed, given that empathy, on Goldie's account, presupposes that I am aware of the other as a centre of consciousness distinct from myself, empathy obviously cannot be what in the first instance provides that kind of awareness. It consequently cannot play any foundational role in our understanding of others.

Not only are conflicting definitions currently being proposed with diverging implications for the contribution that empathy can supposedly make to interpersonal understanding, but there is also no agreement on whether empathy is a natural kind or rather a multidimensional construct. Defenders of the latter view include Frédérique de Vignemont, who distinguishes *mirror empathy* and *reconstructive empathy* (de Vignemont 2010), and Karsten Stueber, who distinguishes *basic empathy*, which he defines as a mechanism of inner imitation that underlies our theoretically unmediated quasi-perceptual ability to recognize other creatures directly as minded creatures, from *re-enactive empathy*, which he defines as involving the use of our cognitive and deliberative capacities to re-enact or imitate the thought processes of others (Stueber 2006: 20–1). Such proposals are not unique to philosophers. Atkinson, for instance, has distinguished a perceptually mediated empathy from a more cognitive form of empathy (Atkinson 2007), whereas Jean Decety and colleagues have defended a multifactorial account and argued that empathy relies on dissociable components, and that a variety of structural dysfunctions is consequently possible. In short, what we find in psychopathy, autism, narcissistic personality disorder, etc. is not one single empathy deficit (Decety et al. 2007: 251).

Sometimes it can be illuminating and clarifying to consider the historical origin of contested notions. The notion of empathy doesn't have a long history. The German term *Einfühlung* was first used in 1873 in the domain of aesthetics by the philosopher Robert Vischer, but was then taken over by Theodor Lipps, who introduced it into the field of social cognition and used it to designate our basic capacity for understanding others as minded creatures. It was Lipps's notion that Edward Titchener, the American psychologist, had in mind when he translated *Einfühlung* as 'empathy' (Titchener 1909).[2]

The concept of empathy has a distinct philosophical origin, but it was soon adopted and co-opted by psychologists. In 1910 the Fourth Congress for Experimental Psychology took place in Innsbruck. During that meeting the phenomenologist Moritz Geiger presented a paper entitled 'Über das Wesen und die Bedeutung der Einfühlung', in which he very carefully surveyed and discussed how the concept of empathy had been employed by Lipps and by contemporaneous psychologists and philosophers like Siebeck, Volkelt, Witasek, and Groos. During the ensuing discussion, however, he was criticized by a member of the audience, a Fräulein Martin, who made the following remark:

When I arrived, I expected to hear something about experiments in the field of empathy. But what have I heard except plenty of old theories. I have heard nothing about experimental results. But this is no philosophical association. I believe the time is ripe for those who want to present these kinds of theories to show us whether or not they can be confirmed by experiments. (quoted in Geiger 1911: 66)

Such impatience with philosophy is, of course, not unique to Martin. Could it be that one reason why fundamental issues continue to remain unresolved and contested in the debate on empathy is the predominance of philosophical rumination and the lack of proper science? I am somewhat doubtful that matters would improve if philosophy

[2] Interestingly, the notion of sympathy is older. It was used by both Hume and Adam Smith to designate what many today would term empathy. In fact, the difference between Hume's and Smith's conception also mirror contemporary disagreements. Whereas Hume seems to have thought of sympathy as a natural and automatic process of affective resonance that allows us to receive the inclinations and sentiments of others (Hume 2000: 236), Smith took it to involve some kind of imaginative perspective taking, where we place ourselves in the other's situation (Smith 2002: 11). These two accounts anticipate later discussions of low-level vs. high-level empathy. Incidentally, Lipps might have been influenced by Hume's account since it was Lipps who translated Hume's *A Treatise of Human Nature* into German.

were pushed to the side, but what needs to be considered is the historical origin and context of the notion of empathy, and the extent to which traditional philosophical assumptions and positions continue to shape and influence the scientific debate for good and for ill.

A natural starting point is Lipps's classical contribution. According to Lipps, there are three distinct domains of knowledge—knowledge of external objects, self-knowledge, and knowledge of others—and he takes these domains to have three distinct cognitive sources, namely, perception, introspection, and empathy (Lipps 1909: 222). Lipps is consequently quite adamant that empathy must count as a modality of knowledge *sui generis*. It is something novel that can in no way be explained by or reduced to some kind of analogical inference (Lipps 1907a: 697–8, 710). In fact, Lipps devotes a considerable amount of effort to criticizing the argument from analogy, and many of his objections would later resurface in the writings of phenomenologists such as Scheler and Merleau-Ponty.

But what exactly does Lipps understand by empathy, which he takes to be a psychological (and sociological) core concept? How does he define it? One perhaps initially slightly surprising claim of his is that empathy involves self-objectification (Lipps 1909: 222). We shouldn't forget, however, the aesthetic origin of the notion. If I experience trees or mountains as animated or besouled, if I hear the wind and experience it as having a melancholy sound, or see a cloud and experience it as threatening, the source of such psychological content is in fact myself (Lipps 1907b: 355). What is really happening is that I am projecting part of myself into these external objects (Lipps 1909: 225, 237), and this is for Lipps what empathy more generally is all about. To feel empathy is to experience a part of one's own psychological life as belonging to or in an external object; it is to penetrate and suffuse that object with one's own life (Lipps 1909: 224).

Let us consider the case of social cognition. Lipps emphasizes throughout the role of expressions, and argues that gestures and expressions manifest our emotional states, and that the relation between the expression and what is expressed is special and unique, and quite different from, say, the way smoke represents fire (Lipps 1907a: 704–5). I might come to experience that smoke and fire often go together, but regardless of how frequently they co-occur, their relationship will always be different from that which exists between the expression and the emotion. The smoke does not manifest or express the fire. The fire is not present in the smoke in the way anger is present in the facial expression. When we perceive the facial expressions of others, we immediately co-apprehend the expressed emotions, say, the joy or fear. This does not, however, mean that we actually perceive the joy or fear. According to Lipps, joy and fear cannot be perceived, since they are not to be found in the external world. We only know directly of these emotions through self-experience, or to put it differently, the only emotions we have experiential access to are our own. So although we apprehend the joyful or fearful face as a unified phenomenon, analysis will show that the perceived gestalt and the co-apprehended emotion arise from two different sources. The visual gestalt comes to me from the external world, whereas the felt emotion is drawn from myself. The perceived face consequently comes to possess psychological meaning for me because I am projecting myself into it (Lipps 1907a: 714). But how is this supposed to happen?

Lipps refers to something he calls the *instinct of empathy*, and more specifically argues that it involves two components, a drive directed towards imitation and a drive directed towards expression (Lipps 1907a: 713). In the past I have been joyful. Back then I experienced an instinctual tendency to express the joy. The expression wasn't experienced as something next to or on top of the joy but as an integral part of the feeling. When I now see the expression elsewhere, I have an instinctual tendency to imitate or reproduce it, and this tendency will then evoke the same feeling that in the past was intimately connected to it (Lipps 1909: 229–30; 1907a: 719). When I experience the feeling anew, it will be linked to the expression I am currently perceiving and will be projected into it (Lipps 1907b: 359). In short, when I see a joyful face, I will reproduce the expression of joy, this will evoke a feeling of joy in me, and this felt joy, which is co-given with the currently perceived facial expression, will then be attributed to the other, thereby allowing for a form of interpersonal under-standing (Lipps 1907a: 717–19).

Importantly, we don't merely project psychological meaning into the expressions we see. We also tend to believe that they really do contain mental life, and that this isn't merely something that has been added by us. That this is so is, according to Lipps, a fact that cannot be explained any further; it simply has to be taken for granted as a given (Lipps 1907a: 710, 721).

One implication of Lipps's model is that there are rather strict limitations to what I can come to understand empathically of the other. The imitated expression can only evoke an affective state in myself that resembles the affective state of the other if I myself have had the affective state in question in the past (Lipps 1907a: 718–19). Therefore, I can only empathically understand those of the other's experiences that I have already enjoyed myself, or to put it differently, Lipps's account of empathy doesn't allow me to recognize anything in the other that is new, anything that I am not already familiar with, anything that I haven't put there myself. Consequently, it shouldn't really come as a surprise that Lipps repeatedly speaks of other individuals as multiplications of one's own ego, that is, as products of empathic self-objectifica-tion (1907b: 360). A particular striking articulation of this view can be found in his book *Die ethischen Grundfragen*, where Lipps writes:

The other psychological individual is consequently made by myself out of myself. His inner being is taken from mine. The other individual or ego is the product of a projection, a reflection, a radiation of myself—or of what I experience in myself, through the sense perception of an outside physical phenomenon—into this very sensory phenomenon, a peculiar kind of reduplication of myself. (Lipps 1905: 17)

Lipps's position is by no means of mere historical interest. It has remained influential and has a number of modern heirs. Not surprisingly, it is in particular within the simulationist camp that the notion of empathy has resurfaced as a central category. Indeed, it has even been argued that simulationists are today's equivalents of empathy theorists (Stueber 2006, p. ix). In his book *Simulating Minds*, Goldman explicitly equates *empathy theory* with *simulation theory* (Goldman 2006: 11), and states that mind-reading is an extended form of empathy (Goldman 2006: 4). Indeed, according to simulation theory, a necessary condition for mind-reading 'is that the state ascribed to the target is ascribed as a result of the attributor's instantiating, undergoing, or experiencing, that very state' (Goldman and Sripada 2005: 208).

In making their case, simulationists have frequently appealed to certain by now well-known examples (Goldman 1992; Gallese and Goldman 1998). Let me briefly describe two of them. Consider first the case of Mr Crane and Mr Tees, who were scheduled to leave the airport on different flights at the same time. They travelled from town in the same limousine, which was caught in a traffic jam, and arrived at the airport thirty minutes after the scheduled departure time of their flights. Mr Crane is told that his flight left on time. Mr Tees is told that his flight was delayed and left just five minutes ago. Who do you think is more upset? The vast majority (96 per cent) of people who were asked this question would say that it was Mr Tees who was more upset (Kahneman and Tversky 1982). How did they arrive at this conclusion? Did they, as suggested by some theory-theorists, possess and apply a folk-psychological theory to Crane's and Tees's respective situations, one that would allow them to infer their relative degree of upsetness? Or is it not more likely that they simply employed a kind of imaginative projection? They imaginatively projected themselves into the shoes of Crane and Tees, allowing each situation to play itself out in their own minds. Pretending to be in Tees's situation generated greater upset than pretending to be in Crane's situation, so people attributed greater frustration to Mr Tees (Goldman 1992: 20).

Consider another example. You are engaged in a game of chess. If you wish to predict your opponent's next move, how do you go about doing that? Rather than relying on some general theory about how chess players act in certain specific situations, one plausible suggestion is that you can gain information about the minds of others by pretending to be in their 'mental shoes'. You can use your own mind as a model, use it to 'mirror' or 'mimic' the minds of others. In the case in question, you can simply imagine yourself being in your opponent's position, and having decided what you would choose to do, you then predict that he would do the same (Gallese and Goldman 1998: 496).

Of course, nobody is claiming that simulation is a foolproof method, and there might be various confounding factors, including what is known as egocentric biases. If you happen to be a chess master and your opponent is a novice, it wouldn't make much sense to ascribe your preferred move to him. Thus, if the simulation routine is to succeed, the attributor must quarantine his own idiosyncratic desires and beliefs

(Goldman 2006: 29). If he fails to do so, he will not reach an understanding of the other, but will merely come to understand how he himself would have acted under different circumstances. But even granted this complication, both examples have been taken by many to support the simulationist approach rather than the theory-theory approach. In fact, Goldman has argued that the rampant existence of quarantine failures and egocentric biases supports simulation theory since such afflictions are precisely likely to happen if mind-reading proceeds by simulation (Goldman 2012).

On closer consideration, however, there is something rather unsatisfactory about both examples. It should be obvious that our understanding of others comes in many shapes and forms. Even if no single model can do justice to the whole variety, any account that aspires to be the core account, the default model, should at the very least be able to capture prototypical everyday situations. But how representative is the kind of interpersonal understanding we encounter in the two examples? In the example with Mr Crane and Mr Tees, you are being told a certain story, and then asked to predict the outcome. But consider the following version, where we replace a detached fictionalized scenario with a real-life encounter. You are working at the check-in counter in an airport when you suddenly see two people rush in and run towards the counter. When they reach the counter, it becomes clear that they are Mr Crane and Mr Tees and that both have missed their respective planes. Whereas Crane is calm and relaxed, Tees seems very tense, and when you inform him that he only missed his flight by five minutes, he starts to abuse you verbally. If at this point you were asked to assess whether Crane or Tees was most upset, you would undoubtedly say Tees. But how plausible is it to suggest that you reached this conclusion on the basis of an elaborate simulation?

The chess example can easily be changed in a similar manner. While facing your opponent and being absorbed in trying to figure out what his next move is going to be, he startles you by suddenly removing all the pieces from the board with a sweep of his hand while screaming, 'Cheat!' How plausible is it to claim that you need to put yourself in his shoes imaginatively in order to determine that he is frustrated and angry rather than, say, blissfully happy?

Many of the classical examples and experiments sought to test subjects' predictions of how protagonists in stories would react (Mar 2011). They rarely considered ecologically valid real-life situations. But any convincing theory of social cognition should be able to account for our face-to-face encounters with others. But does pretence and imaginative projection really play a crucial role on this basic level? As Wittgenstein once remarked, 'Do you look into *yourself* in order to recognize the fury in *his* face?' (Wittgenstein 1980: §927).

In his more recent work, Goldman concedes that an account of mind-reading should be able to cover the whole range of mental states, including sensations, feelings, and emotions. It shouldn't just address the issue of belief ascription (Goldman 2006: 20). This is precisely why Goldman now distinguishes what he calls *low-level mind-reading* from *high-level mind-reading* (Goldman 2006: 43), and argues that we need to recognize the existence of a simple, primitive, and automatic ability to attribute basic emotions such as fear, anger, and disgust to others on the basis of their facial expressions (Goldman and Sripada 2005).

How can we explain this kind of basic 'mind-reading', that is, our ability to recognize someone's face as expressive of a certain emotion? One model considered by Goldman is the so-called *reverse simulation model*. Some empirical research suggests that the expression of a number of so-called basic emotions, including anger, disgust, and fear, are cross-cultural and universal, though there are, of course, culturally specific rules about how to manage expressions in public (Ekman 2003: 4, 10, 58). The fact that even congenitally blind individuals normally exhibit such facial expressions (Matsumoto and Willingham 2009) supports the conclusion that these basic emotional expressions are innate. Furthermore, it has been discovered that we involuntarily mimic the other's facial, vocal, and postural expression. Even presentations of pictures of facial expressions produce covert and subtle activation of the observer's own facial musculature, which mimics the presented faces. Finally, there is substantial evidence suggesting that changes in a person's facial musculature, be they voluntary or involuntary, can produce the corresponding emotional state (Niedenthal 2007; Laird 2007).

Given these pieces of evidence, the following model suggests itself: When seeing a target's expressive face, an observer involuntarily imitates the observed facial expressions. The resulting changes in the observer's own facial musculature activate afferent neural pathways that produce the corresponding emotion. This emotion is then classified according to its emotion-type and finally attributed to the target whose face is being observed (Goldman 2006: 127).

When compared to Lipps's model, this proposal has one distinct advantage. It doesn't rely on or draw on your own past experiences; rather, the coupling is hardwired. In principle, observing the facial expressions of others might give rise to new emotions in yourself, emotions you haven't felt before. But the proposal is faced with other difficulties. One obvious problem concerns the transition from step one to step two. How do you get from experiencing and classifying your own emotion to attributing the same kind of emotion to another? I shall return to these questions later, but it should already be clear that there are reasons to doubt that face-based emotion recognition can be explained by reverse simulation, since the latter certainly doesn't seem sufficient for the former. Is it necessary? That has been called into question as well, since some individuals with Möbius syndrome—a congenital syndrome whose most prominent symptom is complete facial paralysis—are able to recognize others' emotional expressions (Calder et al. 2000; Bate et al. 2013). This finding, which incidentally also presents a problem for Lipps, obviously counts against the proposal that emotion recognition is conditioned and enabled by facial mimicry (Atkinson 2007; Goldman 2006: 208).

Given this difficulty, Goldman ultimately opts for a different model, which he labels the *unmediated resonance model* (Goldman 2006: 132). This model appeals to interpersonal mirroring mechanisms and to findings suggesting that the same neural substrate is activated both when we experience an emotion ourselves and when we recognize the emotion in others. It then proposes that the perception of a target's emotional expression directly triggers activation of the neural substrate of the same type of emotion in oneself, thereby making the process a kind of unmediated matching, one that bypasses the need for and feedback from facial mimicry (Goldman 2006: 128; see also Iacoboni 2009: 111).[3] The existence of paired deficits, that is, neuropathological cases where impairment in the experience of a specific emotion is paired with a selective deficit in recognizing that same emotion in others, has been taken to provide further support for the idea that emotion attribution requires emotion experience (Goldman 2006: 110; Keysers 2011: 44).[4] However, some caution might be necessary. Even though damage to a specific brain area might impede attributions of emotions to both self and other, the fact that these impairments are paired, the fact that the very same brain area is involved in both processes, doesn't prove that simulation is involved, or that there is a direct causal link between first-person emotion experience and third-person emotion ascription. Another possibility is that they are both enabled by a causally prior set of processes (Atkinson 2007: 366). There is a crucial difference between claiming that my ascription of a certain emotion to you requires me to experience the very same kind of emotion immediately prior to ascribing it to you and claiming that the same neural substrate subserves both the first-person experience of an emotion and the third-person ascription of the same kind of emotion to others. The latter claim is considerably weaker.[5]

I shall return to and discuss further the issue of interpersonal mirroring mechanisms later, but one question to consider now is why such low-level mirroring should count as a form of simulation. For one, it doesn't involve any pretend states. But on

---

[3] It is incidentally not obvious that Goldman's clear-cut distinction between reverse simulation and unmediated resonance would be accepted by all mirror neuron theorists. According to Keysers, for instance, mirror neurons are shaped, formed and changed through social interaction. On his construal, the child only develops a shared circuit for facial expressions because her parents imitate the child's own facial expressions (Keysers 2011: 68).

[4] Interestingly, the patients in question didn't lack theoretical understanding of the relevant emotion. They could provide entirely normal descriptions of scenarios that would induce the emotion. But although they didn't lack this intellectual knowledge, they were quite deficient in their ability to recognize the facial (and postural) expression of the emotion or sensation (Goldman 2006: 128–9, 133).

[5] Consider for comparison, the case of cerebral achromatopsia. Damage to the ventral occipital cortex can lead to a complete loss of colour vision and make the patients see the world in shades of grey. In a famous case discussed by Sacks, this loss of colour vision also affected the patient's visual imagery (Sacks 1995: 5). There was consequently a paired deficit. The patient could neither see nor imagine colour. But what should we conclude from this? It seems more reasonable to suggest that the perception and imagination of colour is enabled by the same neural mechanism, than to propose that colour perception presupposes colour imagination, and that it is the colour generated internally in the mind which is then projected outwards and onto the worldly objects.

Goldman's view, pretend states are *not* essential to simulation; rather, they are only to be found in high-level forms of mind-reading. In his view, a process P can be called a simulation of another process P* as long as P duplicates, replicates, or resembles P* in some significant respects (Goldman 2006: 36). Given that basically everything resembles everything else in some respect, it is obviously important to specify what is meant by 'significant'. On one reading, it is the existence of matching emotions in target and attributer that makes the process one of simulation (Goldman and Sripada 2005: 208). More specifically, Goldman suggests that the observation of another's emotional expression automatically triggers the experience of that emotion in myself, and that this first-personal experience then serves as the basis for my third-person ascription of the emotion to the other. As he writes, in the context of discussing disgust expressions, 'the evidence points toward the use of one's disgust experience as the causal basis for third-person disgust attributions' (Goldman 2006: 137). It is consequently no coincidence that Goldman considers a more apt name for the whole process to be simulation-plus-projection (Goldman 2006: 40), thereby affirming the structural similarity between his own account and the one we found in Lipps. When considering Goldman's explicit definition of projection as 'the act of assigning a state of one's own to someone else' (Goldman 2006: 40), and when reading Lipps's assertion that 'Psychologically considered, "other human beings" are multiplications of myself' (Lipps 1900: 418), one might wonder whether, according to simulation-ism, we ultimately remain stuck in some kind of egocentric predicament that prevents us from truly understanding others.

Goldman is by no means the only one to favour an account similar to Lipps's. The same holds true for Iacoboni and Gallese, who both refer to and endorse Lipps's idea that empathy involves a form of inner imitation (Gallese 2003a: 519; Iacoboni 2007: 314).

One noteworthy difference between Goldman's and Gallese's discussion of empathy, however, is that the latter is far more interested in the historical origins of the notion. On Goldman's construal the debate goes back roughly fifty years to Ryle and Wittgenstein, though Goldman does acknowledge that simulationist themes can be found scattered in earlier theorists, such as Lipps and Dilthey (Goldman 2006: 18). What is conspicuously absent from Goldman's overview, however, is any reference to the discussion of empathy found in phenomenology. I am thinking here not merely of the significant and substantial contributions found in Husserl and Merleau-Ponty, but also of more specific works such as Edith Stein's *Zum Problem der Einfühlung*, Gurwitsch's *Die mitmenschlichen Begegnungen in der Milieuwelt*, Scheler's *Wesen und Formen der Sympathie*, and Schutz's *Der sinnhafte Aufbau der sozialen Welt*. Gallese, by contrast, refers favourably not only to Lipps's discussion of inner imitation, but also to Stein's account of empathy, and to Husserl's and Merleau-Ponty's understanding of intersubjectivity (Gallese 2001). Indeed, Gallese is quite explicit (and more on this later) about considering his own notion of embodied simulation to be akin to, and a further development of, the phenomenological proposal (Gallese et al. 2004: 397; see also Iacoboni 2007).

In a footnote added in a late Polish translation of his dissertation from 1918 on Bergson, which was supervised by Husserl, Roman Ingarden made the following observation:

At the time when this treatise was written, extensive discussions took place regarding so-called 'empathy', a notion that had been proposed by the psychologizing German aestheticians such as, for instance, Theodor Lipps. A number of phenomenologists such as M. Geiger, Max Scheler, Edith Stein and later also Husserl participated in this discussion and it became increasingly clear that the classical theory of 'empathy' which considered it a kind of projection of one's own psychical states into foreign bodies had to be abandoned and replaced by a theory of a special kind of perception of the psychical states as they are manifest in bodily expression. (Ingarden 1994: 170–1)

This passage from Ingarden highlights the need for a distinction between Lipps's definition of empathy in terms of inner imitation, and the subsequent analyses found in phenomenology. Whereas Lipps's criticism of the argument from analogy found approval among later phenomenologists, they were by and large quite critical of his own positive account. As we shall see, the phenomenologists offer a distinct and multilayered analysis of the intentional structure of empathy, one that differs rather markedly from recent attempts to explain empathy in terms of mirroring, mimicry, imitation, emotional contagion, imaginative projection, or inferential attribution. In fact, contrary to Dennett's repeated characterization of classical phenomenology as an *autophenomenology*, that is, as a phenomenology with no interest in the mental life of others (Dennett 1987: 153–4), classical phenomenology did very much engage in *heterophenomenology*. Indeed, one reason why the phenomenological analysis will be of particular interest is precisely because, while remaining firmly committed to the first-personal character of consciousness, it highlights and respects what is distinctive about the givenness of others.

10

Phenomenology of Empathy

10.1 Phenomenological misgivings

In his habilitation thesis *Die mitmenschlichen Begegnungen in der Milieuwelt* from 1931, Gurwitsch argues that despite its explicit criticism of the argument from analogy, Lipps's theory of empathy belongs to the same family of theories (Gurwitsch 1979: 20). It still accepts the basic but questionable assumption that, strictly speaking, all we can be said to perceive is physical qualities and their changes, such as the distortion of facial muscles, and that this perceptual input is psychologically meaningless. According to Lipps, it is only by animating what is perceptually given with what we know from our own case that we can come to know that we are encountering another minded creature. It is only by drawing on our own inner experience that we are able to move from the input to the actual ascription to others of mental states, such as joy or happiness.

But is this really plausible, or ought we not to consider and ultimately endorse the view that the perceptually given, namely, the expressive phenomena in question, already provide us with some kind of access to the mental life of others (Gurwitsch 1979: 32, 56)? Gurwitsch further observes that Lipps's appeal to instinct is unsatisfactory in that it sets aside the job of analysis (Gurwitsch 1979: 20). A similar criticism can be found in Stein and Husserl, who in turn claim that Lipps's reliance on instinct amounts to the 'bankruptcy of scientific investigation' (Stein 2008: 41) and constitutes a 'refuge of phenomenological ignorance' (Husserl 1973a: 24). Their most systematic criticism, however, is directed at Lipps's claim that (inner) imitation constitutes the basis of empathy.

First of all, such a theory doesn't explain what it is supposed to explain. Let us assume that an observed expression arouses in me the impulse to imitate it, and that as a result of the close link between expression and experience, I come to experience the associated emotion myself. This might explain why a certain experience occurs in me, but it doesn't offer an explanation of how I come to understand the other. To be happy oneself and to believe that another is happy are two quite different things (Gurwitsch 1979: 24–5). The former state does not per se entail either knowledge about the origin of the feeling or knowledge about the similarity between one's own feeling and that of the other. The other's affective state might be the cause of my own, but it also needs to be its intentional object if we are to speak of any kind of social comprehension (Stein 2008: 22–4). Rather than explaining empathy, that is, empathy understood as an experience of the minded life of others, Lipps's account is consequently better geared to handle something like 'motor mimicry' or 'emotional contagion'.[1] There is therefore, as Stein puts it, a discrepancy between the phenomenon to be explained and the phenomenon actually explained (Stein 2008: 24).

Of course, Lipps did argue that empathy involves two steps: imitation and projection. My perception of the other's expression will, in a rather mediated way, evoke a feeling in myself, and this feeling is then attributed to the other through projection. However, rather than solving the problems, the appeal to projection merely aggravates them, since Lipps never manages to justify the epistemic legitimacy of the projection. Lipps himself pointed to the similarity between the projection found in empathy and the projection found in animism, and, as Scheler observes, Lipps's theory remains incapable of accounting for the difference between a warranted and an unwarranted projection (Scheler 2008: 241). As this latter criticism suggests, the aim of Scheler's investigation isn't merely descriptive. It isn't merely a question of describing how we de facto seem to experience others. Scheler is also interested in the epistemological question of whether our understanding of others can be justified experientially. I shall return to this point later.

Ultimately, the phenomenologists do not merely dismiss the proposal that imitation is sufficient for empathic understanding; they also question whether it is necessary. Why should the mind become like its object in order to grasp it? On Lipps's account, I can only ascribe pain or happiness to another if I undergo the same experiences myself. Indeed, if the imitation is to serve any explanatory purpose, my own felt pain or joy must precede rather than follow my conscious recognition of the pain or joy in the other. But, as Scheler writes, we might understand from the wagging tail of a dog that he is happy to see us, but this hardly requires us to imitate the expression ourselves (Scheler 2008: 11). Indeed, aren't we able to understand expressions that we are unable to imitate, say, if we suffer from facial paralysis? Moreover, how plausible is it to claim that I have to be scared myself in order to understand that my child is scared, or that I need to become furious myself if I am to recognize the fury in the face of my assailant (Husserl 1973a: 188)? We might encounter a furious stranger and become furious ourselves, but our empathic understanding of the stranger's emotion might also elicit the reverse response, namely, a feeling of fear. In either case, however, our emotional reaction is exactly that: a reaction. Now, it might well be that the emotions we perceive in others induce emotional resonances and action tendencies in our own bodies, and that these responses then feed into and influence the way we apprehend the other, but

---

[1] Stein is also known for criticizing Lipps for conflating empathy (*Einfühlung*) with emotional identification (*Einsfühlung*), that is, for taking empathy to involve a complete identification of observer and observed (Stein 2008: 16). More recently, however, Stueber has argued that this specific criticism of Stein is based on too uncharitable an interpretation of Lipps (Stueber 2006: 8).

there is a decisive difference between acknowledging this and defending the view that our understanding of the other's emotion requires us to have that very emotion ourselves.

Before I move on to a more extensive discussion of the different positive accounts of empathy offered by the phenomenologists, first a word about terminology, since not all of them were equally happy about the term.

According to Scheler, we enjoy a basic and direct experiential access to others (I shall say more about what this amounts to in a moment), but unfortunately he doesn't stick to a single term when referring to this basic form of understanding. Rather, he uses terms such as *Nachfühlen* (reproduction of feeling), *Nachleben* (reproduction of experience), *Nacherleben* (visualizing of experience), or *Fremd-wahrnehmung* (perception of other minds) (Scheler 2008: 9, 238). In these cases, the standard English translation might be less than ideal, but Scheler himself must also be blamed for the inevitable confusion. How can *Nachfühlen* and *Fremdwahr-nehmung* refer to one and the same phenomenon? As we shall see, Scheler rejects the view that our understanding of the emotional experience of others is based on an imitation or reproduction of the emotion in question, but if so, why then does he himself use a term like *Nachfühlen*? The fact remains, however, that Scheler is quite unequivocal in his rejection of the view that our understanding of the emotional experiences of others requires us to have the same emotion ourselves (Scheler 2008: 9–10). For want of a better term, I have decided to use 'empathy' as the best way of capturing what Scheler was referring to when he spoke of our basic experience of others. Now, it so happens that he himself uses the German term *Einfühlung* rather sparingly, and frequently rather dismissively as part of his criticism of Lipps. However, Scheler's reservation is due mainly to his categorical rejection of the projective theory of empathy (2008, p. xlviii), and it is telling that other contemporary phenomenologists referred to his own theory as a theory of empathy (Husserl 1950: 173).

As for Husserl, he frequently uses the term *Einfühlung*, though his preferred term, especially in his later writings, is simply *Fremderfahrung*. On some occasions, moreover, he openly expresses reservations regarding the term *Einfühlung*. In a manuscript from 1914–15 he calls it 'a false expression', since in his view it remains unclear whether the term is meant to designate the projection of one's own self into another body or rather the actual encounter with another embodied self (Husserl 1973a: 335–9). Thus, one reason why many have been wary of the term is obviously because it seems to commit one to a projectivist account.

Finally, if we turn to Stein, she defines empathy as a form of other-directed intentionality, and specifically asks us to disregard any other traditional connotation the term might have (Stein 2008: 14). It is for this reason, Stein writes, that Scheler's polemic against empathy is not directed against what she calls empathy (Stein 2008: 30).

I shall follow Stein's recommendation, and when in the following I refer to the account of empathy found in Scheler, Husserl, Stein, and Schutz, I shall be referring to their respective accounts of how we experience others.

10.2 Scheler

Scheler's work *Wesen und Formen der Sympathie* (1923) is frequently listed as an example of a phenomenological investigation of emotional life. But in addition to presenting us with detailed analyses of various emotional phenomena, the work must be considered a significant contribution to the phenomenology of intersubjectivity and social cognition. It is no coincidence that at the outset Scheler states that the problem of how we understand other minds is a foundational problem for the human sciences. It is one that must be resolved if we are to determine the scientific status of history, psychology, sociology, etc. with any degree of adequacy (Scheler 2008, pp. xlviii–xlix).[2]

For Scheler, social understanding is not primarily a theoretical matter. His account seeks to highlight its experiential and emotional character. Let us look at some of the cases discussed by him.

Consider first the situation in which you see the face of a crying child, but rather than seeing it as expressing discomfort or distress, you merely see a certain distortion of the facial muscles, that is, you don't see it as emotionally expressive. Compare this (pathological) case with the situation in which you see the same face as emotionally expressive, but without feeling any concern or compassion, that is, while remaining indifferent. And finally consider the situation in which you respond emotionally, for instance, by feeling compassion for the child. For Scheler, the last situation counts as a case of sympathy (*Mitgefühl*). But in order to feel sympathy, in order to feel concern for, say, somebody who is suffering, you first need to realize or recognize that the other is indeed suffering. So it is not through pity or sympathy that I first learn of someone being in pain; rather, the latter's suffering must already be given in some form to me, must already be understood by me, if I am to feel sympathy for him (Scheler 2008: 8). This prior cognitive understanding is provided by something that Scheler designates using various terms, including *Nachfühlen*, and which in the following I shall render as 'empathy'. Whereas empathy has to do with a basic perceptually based understanding of others, sympathy adds an emotional response.

Now, apart from stressing the difference between empathy and sympathy, the point of Scheler's examples is also to remind us that it is possible to empathize with somebody while being indifferent to his plight (Scheler 2008: 8–9, 14; see also Darwall 1998: 261). There is on Scheler's view no contradiction involved in saying

---

[2] The book was initially published in 1913 under the title *Zur Phänomenologie und Theorie der Sympathiegefühle und von Liebe und Hass*, but Scheler changed the name of the second edition, which was substantially reworked and doubled in size.

that A empathizes with B, in the sense of understanding what B is living through, without A feeling any pity or compassion for B (Scheler 2008: 8). Just think of the person who feels *Schadenfreude*, the skilled interrogator, or the sadist. A high degree of empathic sensitivity might come in handy if one wants to manipulate and exploit people.[3] It is also a precondition for cruelty, since cruelty requires an awareness of the pain and suffering of the other, and must be sharply distinguished from a pathological insensitivity to the pain of others (2008: 14). Furthermore, and to complicate matters, Scheler also argues that sympathy doesn't necessarily have a positive moral value. It depends on the situation and the character of the emotional response. If I feel sorrow over your joy, or gloat over your misery, or rejoice in your pleasure over somebody else's suffering, I do not remain indifferent: I am responding emotionally, but in a way that is of negative moral value (2008: 5–6, 133).

It could be objected that there is something rather artificial about Scheler's distinction between empathy and sympathy. Is it really true that the most basic form of social cognition is emotionally neutral, and that any emotional response is only added in a secondary step? Would it not be more correct to insist that all normal interpersonal understanding involves emotional responsivity, and that flat affect is only to be found in certain pathological cases? I think there is some truth to this objection, but I also think Scheler can be interpreted in a way that makes his view compatible with such an observation. Although our empathic understanding of others might very rarely leave us unaffected, although it might even be the case that when seeing the distress of the other, we have a natural tendency to attend to and care for the other—a tendency that, however, can be suppressed and overridden—the question to ask is whether our very capacity to recognize and understand the expressions of others is enabled and conditioned by this emotional response. This is what Scheler would deny.

Consider, now, a second group of cases. You might enter a bar and be swept away by the jolly atmosphere, or you might encounter a funeral procession and your mood might drop. A distinctive feature of what is known as 'emotional contagion' (*Gefühlsansteckung*) is that you literally catch the emotion in question (Scheler 2008: 15). It is transferred to you. It becomes your own emotion. In emotional contagion the feeling you are infected by is phenomenally given not as belonging to another, but as your own. It is only its causal origin that points to the other (2008: 37). Indeed, when infected by the panic or jolly mood of others, you might not even be aware of them as distinct individuals. But all of this is precisely what makes emotional contagion different from empathy and sympathy. For Scheler, both of the latter presuppose not only self-consciousness, but also a felt separation between self and

---

[3] Anthropological research on empathy reports that people in different parts of the world (including the Indo-Pacific, Latin America, and northern Canada) try to mask their face, that is, not express their feelings or thoughts, because of a widespread fear that their enemies might exploit empathy to detect their vulnerabilities and cause harm (Hollan 2012).

other (2008: 23, 64). In both sympathy and empathy, the focus is on the other, on his thoughts and feelings, and the distance between self and other is preserved and upheld.[4] To feel sorry for another person is to be sorry for the other as other. To suggest that sympathy involves some kind of fusion with the other is to transform it into egoism. This is also why Scheler rejects not only the suggestion that sympathy requires the sympathizer to have the corresponding emotion herself (2008: 42), and the proposal that sympathy necessarily involves imagination and requires me to imagine what it would be like for me to be in the other's shoes (2008: 39), but also metaphysical theories of the kind found, for instance, in Schopenhauer according to which the existence of sympathy and compassion ultimately testifies to the metaphysical unity of all individuals (2008: 51, 54).

One can be infected by the feelings of others, by their joy or fear, not only without knowing anything about the other individuals, but also without knowing anything about their intentional objects. This is one of the reasons why emotional contagion shouldn't be conflated with what Scheler terms 'emotional sharing' (*Mitfühlen*). Think of a situation in which a couple is enjoying a movie together. Not only do both perceive and enjoy the movie, but they also empathically experience that the other is jointly attending to and enjoying the movie, which is something that affects the structure and quality of their own enjoyment. Although A doesn't see the movie through B's eyes, its being seen and enjoyed by B is part of the experience that A has of the movie (and vice versa). In short, what the individuals experience when they share an emotion is not independent of the relation they have to each other. We are dealing with experiences that, rather than being independent of each other, are constitutively interdependent, experiences that the subjects could only have in virtue of their reciprocal relation to each other. In short, emotional sharing requires and involves not only similarity, but also a preservation of difference, as well as an amount of mutual understanding. Emotional sharing is consequently not simply different from emotional contagion, it is also something over and above empathy. It adds, as the name indicates, reciprocal sharing and co-regulation to the understanding that is provided by empathy. Contrast this with the situation in which a mutual friend interacts with the couple. He might perceive their enjoyment without being joyful himself (perhaps because he finds the movie silly or because he is in a bad mood). In this case, the friend would be empathically directed at their enjoyment

---

[4] Scheler also introduces the notion of emotional identification (*Einsfühlung*), which he considers a limiting case of emotional contagion. Here it is not merely a concrete feeling of another that is unconsciously and involuntarily taken as one's own; rather, the other ego is identified with one's own self (2008: 18). Although Scheler repeatedly and unequivocally asserts that empathy and sympathy differ radically from this emotional identification, in changes made in the 1923 edition of his work he also claims that emotional identification (*Einsfühlung*) is a precondition for empathy (*Nachfühlung*) (2008: 96). To insist that empathy must be distinguished from various processes involving contagion, imitation, and mimicry is, of course, not to rule out that the former might in some way rely on and depend upon the latter. But even if that were the case, the argument would still be that the latter remain unable to account for the distinctive features of the former.

without experiencing the joy as his own. Indeed, their joy and his empathic understanding of it would clearly be qualitatively different and distinct (Scheler 2008: 12–13, 37).

Now, on Scheler's view, empathy isn't simply a question of intellectually judging that somebody else is undergoing a certain experience; it is not the mere thought that this is the case; rather, Scheler defends the view that we are empathically able to experience other minds (Scheler 2008: 10). It is no coincidence that Scheler repeatedly speaks of 'the perception of others' (*Fremdwahrnehmung*), and even entitles his own theory 'a perceptual theory of other minds' (2008: 220). He writes in what must count as a *locus classicus*:

> For we certainly believe ourselves to be directly acquainted with another person's joy in his laughter, with his sorrow and pain in his tears, with his shame in his blushing, with his entreaty in his outstretched hands, with his love in his look of affection, with his rage in the gnashing of his teeth, with his threats in the clenching of his fist, and with the tenor of his thoughts in the sound of his words. If anyone tells me that this is not 'perception', for it cannot be so, in view of the fact that a perception is simply a 'complex of physical sensations', and that there is certainly no sensation of another person's mind nor any stimulus from such a source, I would beg him to turn aside from such questionable theories and address himself to the phenomenological facts. (2008: 260)

For Scheler, empathy is what allows me to experience other subjects. It neither entails that the other's experience is literally transmitted to me, nor does it entail that I undergo the experience I perceive in the other. Rather, to experience empathically, say, the emotion of another necessarily differs from the way you would experience the emotion if it were your own. Scheler consequently rejects the proposal that empathy should be based on a direct association between cues coming from others and one's own similar past experiences, as if one's ability to empathize with, say, parents who have lost their only child or a drowning man fighting for his life would not only be conditional upon one having gone through such an ordeal oneself, but would even entail an actual reproduction of that past experience. What is overlooked by this proposal, on his view, is the extent to which we are able to grasp another person's state of mind directly in the available expressive phenomena. Even if you have no children yourself, being with a couple who are grieving the loss of their son can give you an understanding of what that is like. Moreover, not only is such a reproduction unnecessary, but if it was a requirement, it would be a source of error rather than a basis for insight, since it would lead to personal distress and egoistic drift (2008: 46–7).[5]

---

[5] The belief that having experienced a life event oneself will give one more insight into another person's similar life experience is widespread, but might be unwarranted. Empirical research suggests that people with similar life experiences, such as childbirth and parental divorce, are not always more accurate at determining how another feels in the same situation compared to those without such experience (Hodges 2005).

Scheler also dismisses the suggestion that the empathizer must at the very least have been first-personally acquainted with some of the basic elements of the empathized experience. As he points out, not only does such a proposal mistakenly think that an experience is composed of atomistic mental particles, but it also leaves it entirely unclear how we should subsequently go about reconstructing the experience to be understood on the basis of such elements. What could guide this combination if not a prior understanding of the end result (Scheler 2008: 47)? Scheler's criticism highlights one of the challenges facing any account arguing that empathy requires a significant similarity between the empathizer and the target. The obvious question to ask is how specific the match must be in order to count as significantly similar. To claim that I can empathize with someone who is distressed because of the death of her 2-year-old Airedale terrier, or with someone who is suffering from an attack of biliary colic, only if I have been distressed over the loss of the same kind of dog or undergone a similar attack with the same kind of intensity in the past is hardly convincing. By contrast, to claim that I can only empathize with a minded creature if I have a mind myself seems eminently plausible, but also rather trivial. If an imitation-based account of empathy is to say something plausible yet non-trivial, it must position itself somewhere in between these two extremes. The question is where. Must the empathizer feel (or have felt, or in principle be able to feel) exactly the same kind of emotion or sensation, say, mortification or nausea? Is it enough if the empathizer is first-personally acquainted with a member of the same family of emotions, or might it be sufficient if the empathizer has simply had (or is in principle able to have) an emotion with the same kind of valence? The less specific the demand is, the more plausible the account might be. But obviously, this increase in plausibility goes hand in hand with a decrease in explanatory power.

For Scheler the matter is in any case clear. Although at one point he remarks that the scope of our comprehension might be restricted by the range of experiences we are intrinsically capable of (Scheler 2008: 46), he flatly denies that we can only understand experiences in others that we have ourselves undergone in the past.[6] For him, such a claim has as little merit as the claim that we can never come to understand something new, but only that which we have already experienced before. In fact, one problem with the projective theory of empathy is precisely that it imprisons us within our own mind. It fails to do justice to the genuine and true self-transcendence that we find in empathy; to the fact that empathic understanding can expand our life and lead us beyond the limitations of our own actual experience (2008: 46, 49).

Despite Scheler's emphasis on the visibility and perceptual accessibility of other minds, it is important to realize that he isn't claiming that all aspects of the

---

[6] Consider the example of a 4-year-old boy who, upon hearing about the death of his friend's mother, said solemnly: 'You know, when Bonnie grows up, people will ask her who was her mother, and she will have to say "I don't know". You know, it makes tears come in my eyes' (Radke-Yarrow et al. 1983: 493).

experiential life of an individual is equally accessible to others. Whereas in some cases we can intuit the other's experiences, there are also, on Scheler's account, some important limitations.

Bodily sensations constitute one of these limitations (Scheler 2008: 255). I can have the same *kind* of headache or kidney pain as someone else, but I cannot literally perceive his or her specific pain or, say, gustatory sensations. This is an important clarification, since it immunizes Scheler from an obvious objection. If I observe a man enjoying his dinner or a woman in labour, what I am directly acquainted with, on Scheler's model, is not the specific taste of, say, smoked salmon, or the specificity of the pain sensation, but rather the general state of enjoyment or suffering. Thus, Scheler even concedes that the only way to understand the specific sensations that another person (or animal) is living through is through reproduction. In short, whereas I might see that a child or a bat is exhausted, if I want to know what it is like for someone to taste papaya juice, I have to taste the juice myself (2008: 48).

Whereas we can learn something about the other from his automatic and involuntary expressions, Scheler also insists that there is a limit to how far this will get us, especially since there are dimensions of the mind that aren't tied to bodily expressions. If we wish to grasp what he calls the 'spiritual being of the other', that is, the essence of his personhood, we need to rely on communication. More specifically, Scheler claims that the distinct cognitive activities of the other person, his or her thoughts, will remain concealed and hidden until the other decides to reveal and communicate them (Scheler 2008: 102, 225). This is why language proves so essential for higher forms of social understanding. Yet, even then, there will remain something ineffable in the other. There is, according to Scheler, an absolute intimate sphere of personhood that even the act of free communicative intention cannot fully disclose (2008: 66, 219).[7]

Scheler's investigation and analysis of the difference between emotional contagion, empathy, sympathy, and emotional sharing is restricted to the personal level. He is not concerned with the various sub-personal mechanisms that might be involved in social cognition. His main objection against competing theories seems to be that they are phenomenologically inadequate and that they fail to do justice to our actual experience. On this basis, it might be natural to conclude that his project is exclusively descriptive. It seeks to describe how we experience other minds, but it doesn't address the epistemological question concerning whether such experiences are trustworthy. But this is a mistake. Not only does Scheler provide a more systematic

---

[7] On some occasions, though, Scheler suggests that love is what can bring us closest to the essence of the other's individuality. As he would say, our instincts make us blind, love makes us see (2008: 157). One way to understand this claim is to consider the unsubstitutability and irreplaceability of the loved one. If you love somebody, you don't merely love a certain collection of attributes that happens to be found and instantiated in the loved one. Rather, for it to count as real love, you would supposedly continue to love that person even if his or her attributes changed. Likewise, your love wouldn't be satisfied by simply encountering the same collection of attributes in someone else.

criticism of the argument from analogy, but ultimately he also seeks to provide an account of the nature of expression and experience that would make it comprehensible how expressions can be said to manifest our experiential lives; how, by perceiving the expressions of others, we can be said to experience their psychological states; and thereby also how our understanding of others can be experientially justified.

What kind of problem is the argument from analogy supposed to solve? It is supposed to solve the problem of other minds. Why should there be a problem to start with? Because the only mind I allegedly have direct access to is my own mind. My access to the mind of another, by contrast, is always mediated by his or her bodily behaviour. And how could the perception of another person's body provide me with information about his mind? The proposed solution is as follows: In my own case, I can observe that I have experiences when my body is causally influenced, just as I can observe that these experiences frequently bring about certain actions. I can observe that other bodies are influenced and act in similar manners, and I therefore infer by analogy that the behaviour of other bodies is associated with experiences similar to those I have myself. In my own case, being scalded by hot water gives rise to a feeling of intense pain; this experience then leads to the quite distinct behaviour of screaming. When I observe other bodies being scalded by hot water and screaming, I assume that in all likelihood they are also feeling pain. Thus, the argument from analogy can be interpreted as an inference to the best explanation, one that brings us from observed public behaviour to a hidden mental cause. Although this inference does not provide me with indubitable knowledge about others, and although it does not allow me actually to experience other minds, at least it gives me more reason to believe in their existence than to deny it.

By arguing that our understanding of others is inferential in nature, according to Scheler the argument from analogy opts for a cognitively too demanding account. From very early on, infants are sensitive and responsive to facial expressions. But to suggest that the child compares the visual presentation of, say, the other's smile with the facial movements he himself makes when happy, and that the infant then projects his own felt happiness into the invisible interiority of the other's body, is psychologically implausible. Moreover, the argument assumes that the way in which my own body is given to me is similar to the way in which the body of the other is given to me. However, my own body, as it is interoceptively and proprioceptively felt by me, does not correspond point by point to the other's body as it is visually presented to me. Indeed, if I am to detect a similarity between, say, my laughing or screaming and the laughing or screaming of somebody else, I need to adopt a more global perspective. I need to grasp the bodily gestures as expressive phenomena, as manifestations of joy or pain, and not simply as physical movements. But if such an understanding is required for the argument from analogy to succeed, the argument obviously presupposes what it is supposed to establish (Scheler 2008: 240; see also Gurwitsch 1979: 14, 18; Merleau-Ponty 2012: 368).

Scheler also questions two of the presuppositions that are at work in the classical argument from analogy. First, it assumes that my point of departure is my own consciousness. This is what is at first given to me in a quite direct and unmediated fashion, and it is this purely mental self-experience that is then taken to precede and make possible the recognition of others. One is at home in oneself and one then projects into the other, whom one does not know, what one already finds in oneself. Incidentally, this implies, as I have already pointed out, that one is only able to understand those psychological states in others that one has already experienced in oneself. Secondly, the argument also assumes that we never have direct access to another person's mind. We can never *experience* her thoughts or feelings. We can only infer that they must exist based on what is actually given to us, namely, her bodily behaviour. Although both these assumptions might seem perfectly obvious, Scheler rejects both. As he points out, we ought to pay attention to what is actually given, rather than letting some theory dictate what can be given (Scheler 2008: 244). On his view, the argument from analogy underestimates the difficulties involved in self-experience and overestimates the difficulties involved in the experience of others (2008: 244–6). We should not ignore what can be directly perceived about others, and we should not fail to acknowledge the embodied and embedded nature of our own self-experience. Scheler consequently denies that our initial self-acquaintance is of a purely mental and solitary nature, as if it anteceded our experience of our own expressive movements and actions, and as if it took place in isolation from others. He considers such an initial self-acquaintance a mere fiction (2008: 252). In addition, he argues that there is something highly problematic about claiming that intersubjective understanding is a two-stage process of which the first stage is the perception of meaningless behaviour and the second an intellectually based attribution of psychological meaning. Rather, in the face-to-face encounter, we are confronted neither with a mere body, nor with a pure soul, but with the unity of an embodied mind. Scheler speaks of an 'expressive unity' (*Ausdruckseinheit*), and claims that *behaviour* is a psychophysically undifferentiated notion. It is only subsequently, through a process of abstraction, that this unity is divided and our interest then proceeds 'inwards' or 'outwards' (2008: 218, 261).

Foreshadowing something that both Sartre and Levinas would later discuss in more detail, Scheler writes that I experience, say, the hostility or love in the expression of another's gaze long before I can specify the colour of his eyes (Scheler 2008: 244). Indeed, on Scheler's account, our primary knowledge of nature is knowledge of expressive phenomena, and the most fundamental form of perception is the perception of the psychophysically undifferentiated expression. He finds this claim corroborated by newborns' preferential interest in expressive faces and human voices. This knowledge of a living world is taken to precede our knowledge of a dead and mechanical world. So, for Scheler, it is not the case that we first see inanimate objects and then animate them through a subsequent addition of mental components. Rather, at first we see everything as expressive, and we then go through a process of de-animation. Learning is, as he puts it, a question of 'de-souling' (*Entseelung*) rather than of 'ensouling' (*Beseelung*) (2008: 239). Scheler even postulates the existence of what he calls a universal grammar of expression, one that enables us to understand, to some extent at least, the expressions of other species, be it the gasping fish or the bird with the broken wing (2008: 11, 82).

When defending a perceptual theory of other minds, and when rejecting the proposal that our access to the minds of others is always inferentially mediated, Scheler is consequently not simply making a psychological point. He isn't merely claiming that it seems psychologically as if we have immediate access to the minds of others, an observation that without further ado is compatible with the claim that this psychological immediacy is enabled and subserved by various unconscious inferences. No, Scheler is also making an epistemological claim. He is opposing the view according to which our encounter with others is first and foremost an encounter with bodily and behavioural exteriorities devoid of any psychological properties. According to such a view, which has been defended by behaviourists and Cartesians alike, behaviour, considered in itself, is neither expressive nor significant. All that is given is physical qualities and their changes. Seeing a radiant face means seeing certain characteristic distortions of the facial muscles. But, as Scheler insists, this account presents us with a distorted picture, not only of behaviour but also of the mind. It is no coincidence that we use psychological terms to describe behaviour and that we would be hard-pressed to describe the latter in terms of bare movements. In the majority of cases, it will be quite hard (and artificial) to divide a phenomenon neatly into its psychological and behavioural aspects: think merely of a groan of pain, a laugh, a handshake, an embrace. In his view, affective and emotional states are not simply qualities of subjective experience; rather, when expressed, they become visible to others. In fact, only thereby do they gain full visibility for ourselves as well, since repression of the emotional expression will necessarily lead to a reduction of the felt quality of the emotion. The fact that I need to express my own emotions in order to feel them fully is another reason why we shouldn't exaggerate the difference between self- and other-experience (Scheler 2008: 251).

Instead of attempting to secure access to the minded life of others through technical detours, Scheler consequently argues that we need a new understanding of the given. If the realm of expressive phenomena is accepted as the primary datum or primitive stratum of perception, access to the minds of others will no longer present us the same kind of problem.

10.3 Husserl and Stein

10.3.1 The preoccupation of a lifetime

Edith Stein arrived in Göttingen in 1913 in order to study with Husserl. He eventually became her doctoral supervisor, and it was Husserl who suggested that she should work on the topic of empathy. In 1916 Stein submitted her dissertation *Zum Problem der Einfühlung*, which to this day stands as one of the most succinct presentations of a phenomenological analysis of empathy. There are many points of overlap between Stein's analysis and Husserl's own account, but the former has an attractive conciseness.

Husserl's investigation of empathy, by contrast, is not restricted to a few select publications, say, *Ideen II* or *Cartesianische Meditationen*. Rather, the most thorough treatment is to be found in the research manuscripts contained in Husserliana 13–15, that is, in the three volumes on phenomenology of intersubjectivity. The timespan of these manuscripts, covering the period from 1905 to 1937, makes it clear that empathy was a topic that Husserl worked on during most of his philosophical career. It is therefore also not surprising that many of his other works contain remarks and reflections on empathy. This includes not only works such as *Krisis*, *Formale und transzendentale Logik*, *Phänomenologische Psychologie*, or more recently published Husserliana volumes such as *Einleitung in die Philosophie*, *Einleitung in die Ethik*, *Transzendentaler Idealismus*, or *Die Lebenswelt*, but also, and perhaps slightly more surprisingly, even works such as *Logische Untersuchungen* and *Ideen I*.

That Husserl remained preoccupied with the issue and considered it to be of particular importance is indicated by the fact that he chose to dwell on it in his very last lecture course, which he gave in the winter semester of 1928–9, and which carried the title *Phänomenologie der Einfühlung in Vorlesungen und Übungen*. But, of course, the fact that he kept returning to the issue also suggests that it continued to remain a problem for him, and that he was unable to reach a definite and (in his own mind) fully satisfying solution. For this reason, the aim and scope of my own discussion will necessarily have to be limited. It is impossible in a single chapter to give an exhaustive analysis of Husserl's theory of empathy. In fact, there might not even be one single coherent theory, since over the years Husserl pursued different directions. In the following, I shall focus mainly on ideas and themes that I take to be particularly prominent or promising.

This is the first preliminary point I need to make. The second concerns an additional restriction. As I have argued elsewhere, Husserl's main interest in inter-subjectivity was motivated by transcendental philosophical concerns (Zahavi 1996). It is important to keep in mind that this transcendental preoccupation also manifests itself in his analysis of empathy. This is why in §62 of *Cartesianische Meditationen* Husserl criticizes Scheler for having overlooked the truly transcendental dimension of the problem, namely, the fact that intersubjectivity is involved in the very consti-tution of objectivity. Or, as he puts it, only constitutive phenomenology will be able properly to formulate, address, and solve the problem of empathy (Husserl 1950: 173). A theory of empathy consequently has greater implications than one might expect. It has ramifications for a transcendental account of reality (Husserl 1973c: 5). But important as this dimension of the problem might be, it is one that by and large I shall ignore in the following. My focus will be on the narrower question of how we come to experience others. Although Stein acknowledges the transcendental aspect of the issue, her main focus in *Zum Problem der Einfühlung* is similarly restricted.

10.3.2 Empathy and perception

In *Phänomenologische Psychologie* Husserl wrote as follows: 'The intentionality in one's own ego that leads into the foreign (*fremde*) ego is the so-called empathy' (Husserl 1962: 321; translation modified). This is also the view of Stein, who repeatedly argues that empathy, rather than being a distinct and specific emotion (like embarrassment, shame, or pride), is the name for a *sui generis* form of intentionality directed at other experiencing subjects (Stein 2008: 4, 68). Thus, for Stein, empathy is quite generally the term of choice for the experience of another consciousness (Stein 2008: 10). It is the basic cognitive source for our comprehension of other subjects and their experiences, and it is what more complex kinds of social cognition rely on and presuppose (Stein 2008: pp. v, 4).

One of the recurrent questions that kept preoccupying both Husserl and Stein was how to understand the intentional structure of empathy. On Husserl's standard model, we have to distinguish between *signitive, pictorial,* and *perceptual* ways of intending an object: I can talk about Mount Fuji although I have never seen it; I can see a detailed drawing of Mount Fuji; or I can perceive Mount Fuji myself. Similarly, I can talk about how fantastic it must be to fly in a hot-air balloon; I can see a television programme about it; or I can try it myself. For Husserl, these different ways of intending an object are not unrelated. On the contrary, there is a strict hierarchical relation between them, in the sense that the modes can be ranked according to their ability to give us the object as directly, originally, and optimally as possible. The object can be experienced more or less directly, that is, it can be more or less present. The lowest and most empty way in which the object can be intended is in the signitive act. These (linguistic) acts certainly have a reference, but apart from that, the object is not given in any fleshed-out manner. The pictorial acts have a certain intuitive content but, like signitive acts, they intend the object indirectly. Whereas signitive acts intend the object via a contingent representation (a linguistic sign), pictorial acts intend the object via a representation (picture) which bears a certain resemblance to the object as seen from a certain perspective. It is only the actual perception, however, that gives us the object directly. This is the only type of intention that presents us with the object itself in its bodily presence (*leibhaftig*), or, as Husserl says, *in propria persona*. The tricky question is then where to place empathy within this classification. The answer provided by Husserl is remarkably consistent throughout his career, though it is an answer that remains characterized by an important vacillation. Already in *Logische Untersuchungen* he had written that common speech credits us with percepts of other people's inner experiences: we, so to speak, *see* their anger or pain. As he then goes on to say, such talk is to some extent correct. When a hearer perceives a speaker give voice to certain inner experiences, he also perceives these experiences themselves but, as Husserl then adds, the hearer doesn't have an inner but only an outer perception of them (Husserl 1984a: 41). So, on the one hand, Husserl argues that my experience of others has a quasi-perceptual character in the sense that it grasps the other him- or herself (Husserl 1973a: 24). On the other hand, he also says that although the body of the other is intuitively given to me *in propria persona*, this is not the case with the other's experiences. They can never be given to me in the same original fashion as my own experiences; they are not accessible to me through inner consciousness. Rather, they are appresented through a special form of apperception or, to use a different terminology, they are co-intended and character-ized by a certain co-presence (Husserl 1952: 198; 1973a: 27; 2002b: 107).

Like Husserl, Stein compares and contrasts empathy with perception. Empathy is unlike perception in that it doesn't give us its object, the empathized experience, originally. There will always, and by necessity, remain a difference in givenness between that which I am aware of when I empathize with the other, and that which the other is experiencing. To experience, say, the emotion of the other consequently differs from the way you would experience the emotion if it were your own. This is also why Stein rejects the proposal that empathy should make us undergo the emotion we perceive in the other. It doesn't literally involve the transmission of the other's experience into one's own mind. Rather, what is distinct-ive about empathy is precisely that the empathized experience is located in the other and not in oneself. However, although empathy differs from perception by not giving us the object originally, it does resemble perception in so far as its object, say, the empathized pain or distress, is given directly, unmediated, and non-inferentially as present here and now (Stein 2008: 5). To exemplify, consider a situation in which a friend tells me that he has lost his mother, and I become aware of his distress. What kind of awareness is this? I don't see the distress the same way I see the colour of his shirt; rather, I see the distress 'in' his pained countenance (2008: 5). On Stein's account, this more complex act, which allows for a co-apprehension of that which is expressed in the expression, still deserves to be called a form of perception. Why? Because although I lack a first-person experience of the distress—it is not given as *my* distress—it is nevertheless the case that I experience rather than imagine or infer my friend's distress. Stein consequently contrasts empathy with a more cognitive com-prehension of the other's experience that intends this experience without grasping it directly. This could happen, for instance, if somebody wrote to me and informed me that he was sad. On the basis of this information I could then grasp his state of mind, but his sadness would not be given to me perceptually (2008: 92). In such a case, we would be dealing with an indirect comprehension of the other, one that is derivative and that refers back to empathy understood as a more basic experiential grasp of the other's experience (2008: 20, 26). It is precisely the possibility of such an experiential givenness that on Stein's view is ignored by those favouring the argu-ment from analogy. Now, Stein is by no means denying that we occasionally employ a kind of inferential reasoning, but on her view it never provides us with an *experience* of other minds, but only with a more or less probable knowledge of others' mental states (2008: 29).[8]

What should we conclude? Does empathy allow for a direct experience of the other, or is empathy necessarily indirect and mediated? These are the questions that Husserl, in particular, kept struggling with. In some places Husserl is rather unequivocal. He writes that empathy is a distinct and direct kind of empirical experience, one that allows the empathizing ego to experience the consciousness of the other (Husserl 1973a: 187). As it is formulated in *Ideen II*: 'Empathy is not a mediate experience in the sense that the other would be experienced as a psycho-physical annex to his corporeal body, but is instead an immediate experience of the other' (Husserl 1952: 375; translation modified). Husserl also claims that empathy is what allows the other to be present to me—perceptually present (Husserl 1973c: 514)—and that the other is given to me originally in empathy; for what I see is not a sign, not a mere analogue, but rather *the other* (Husserl 1973b: 385; 1993: 182; 1950: 153; 1973c: 506). Along similar lines, Husserl speaks of how the other is given in his being-for-me (*Für-mich-sein*) in empathy, and how that counts as a form of perception (Husserl 1973c: 641). If I talk with another, if we see one another with our own eyes, there is an immediate contact, an immediately experienced personal relationship. We 'see' the other qua person, and not merely as body (Husserl 1952: 375). Indeed, speaking of foreign subjectivity, Husserl writes that

It would be countersensical to say that it is inferred and not experienced when given in this original form of empathic presentation. For every hypothesis concerning a foreign subject already presupposes the 'perception' of this subject as foreign, and empathy is precisely this perception. (Husserl 1973b: 352)

In *Ideen II* and elsewhere Husserl distinguishes two different attitudes that we can take towards the other, a *naturalistic* and a *personalistic*. In the naturalistic attitude, the other is given in a twofold step as a composite entity. First, the other's body is given to us as a material unity, and functionally dependent upon and located in this material object; the other's experiential life is then posited as a founded stratum.

---

[8] A comparable criticism of the argument from analogy can be found in Cassirer's *Philosophie der symbolischen Formen*: 'If our certainty of the "other ego" were based on nothing more than a chain of empirical observations and inductive inferences—if it were based on the supposition that the same expressive movements as we perceive in our body or similar ones appeared also in other physical bodies, and that the same cause must always correspond to the same effects—it would be hard to conceive of a conclusion with so little foundation. Both as a whole and in its details this inference proves on closer investigation to be thoroughly vulnerable. For one thing, it is a well known logical principle that although we can infer like effects from like causes, we cannot conversely infer like causes from like effects, since one and the same effect can be produced by very different causes. But even apart from this objection, an inference of this kind could at best provide the basis for a provisional assumption, a mere probability.... The certainty that the reality of life is not limited to the sphere of one's own existence would itself be a purely discursive cognition and moreover one of highly questionable origin and value' (Cassirer 1957: 82–3).

Husserl then contrasts this attitude, which is prevalent in the sciences, with the personalistic attitude, which is the attitude of our daily life, and which is the one he takes to be the more fundamental. In this attitude, the other is from the beginning given in a unified manner as a person, rather than as a composite of two externally intertwined or causally related entities (Husserl 1952: 228). When encountering the other in the personalistic attitude, when I see the other dance, laugh, or discuss something, I don't see a conjunction of two realities, but one expressive unity. I don't see a mere body; nor do I through the body intend an annexed mind. I see a human being. More specifically, Husserl speaks of how the mindedness of the other, his thinking, feeling, desiring, is intuitively present in the gestures, the intonation, and the facial expressions. Indeed, the expressivity of the other is imbued with psychological meaning from the start (1952: 235), and according to Husserl, it is precisely empathy that allows us to understand and grasp this psychological meaning (1952: 244). Husserl is consequently rather clear in his rejection of the idea that empathic apprehension should involve a two-step procedure, one where the other is first perceived as an ordinary physical object, and then only in a second step, through some kind of projection, as endowed with a mind or psyche (1952: 240).

To strengthen the claim concerning the perceptual or intuitive character of empathy, Husserl occasionally compares the kind of interplay between presentation and appresentation that we find in empathy with the mixture of presentation and appresentation that we find in ordinary object perception. When I perceive an object, say, a sofa, the object is never given in its totality but always incompletely, in a certain restricted profile or adumbration. It is consequently never the entire sofa, including its front, back, underside, and inside, that is given intuitively, not even in the most perfect perception. Despite this, the object of my perception is exactly the sofa and not the visually appearing profile. Our perceptual consciousness is consequently characterized by the fact that we persistently transcend the intuitively given profile in order to grasp the object itself. That is, perception furnishes us with a full object-consciousness, even though only part of the perceived object is intuitively given (Husserl 1973d: 49–50). Husserl's explanation for why we can be said to see more than what is given, for why perception involves a presence-in-absence, is well known. He argues that our intuitive consciousness of the present profile of the object is accompanied by an intentional consciousness of the object's horizon of absent profiles. The meaning of the presented profile, in short, is dependent upon its relation to the absent profiles of the object, and no perceptual awareness of the object would be possible if our awareness were restricted to the intuitively given:

The improperly appearing objective determinations are co-apprehended, but they are not 'sensibilized,' not presented through what is sensible, i.e., through the material of sensation. It is evident that they are co-apprehended, for otherwise we would have no objects at all before our eyes, not even a side, since this can indeed be a side only through the object. (Husserl 1973d: 55)

According to its own meaning, it [the perception] is anticipatory—the anticipation (*Vorgriff*) concerns something co-intended—and in such a radical fashion that even in the content of that which is perceptually given as itself, there is, on closer inspection, an element of anticipation. In fact, nothing in perception is purely and adequately perceived. (Husserl 1959: 45)

In other words, in order for a perception to be a perception-of-an-object, we have to transcend that which is intuitively given and co-intend the absent profiles, bringing them to a certain appresentation, which is why every perception entails a *Hinaus-deutung*, to use Husserl's word, that is, an element of interpretation (Husserl 1962: 183; 1966b: 19). Importantly, however, although object perception involves such a mixture of presentation and appresentation, we still say that it is the object itself rather than merely the intuitively appearing front that we perceive (Husserl 1973a: 26; 1950: 151). Moreover, what is presented and what is appresented are not given in separation and are not united by means of some inference. The same arguably holds true for our experience of others (Husserl 1973b: 332). In short, it is important for Husserl to stress that even ordinary perception involves apperception. The fact that empathy also involves apperception is consequently, in and of itself, no argument against its experiential and intuitive character.

This is not to say, of course, that there are not also important differences between empathy and object perception. According to Husserl, not only do I, in the face-to-face encounter, grasp the other and what he or she is living through much more vividly than the back of an object, which I don't see (Husserl 1973b: 486). But more importantly, whereas the absent, and merely appresented, profiles of the object can in turn become originally present to me, namely, if the requisite movements are carried out, this can never happen with the other's experiences (Husserl 1950: 139). This is an important qualification, which points to the limits of any comparison of other-perception and object perception. Empathy is what allows us to know the experiential life of others, or as Husserl puts it in a text from 1909: 'All the difficulty disappears if empathy counts as the mode of presentation of foreign consciousness' (Husserl 1973a: 20). But while occasionally arguing that empathy does amount to perception of the other (Husserl 1973a: 343), Husserl also insists that even the most perfect perception of the psychical life of another lacks the originality of self-perception. It cannot give us the empathized experience itself in its original presence (Husserl 1973a: 347, 440; 1974: 389; 1952: 199–200; 1950: 139). On occasions, Husserl even claims that the psychical life of another is in principle inaccessible to direct perception (Husserl 1966b: 240).

As should be clear by now, there is a certain tension, or uncertainty, in Husserl's account. I think, however, that it is possible to reconcile Husserl's different claims by means of some slight reformulations. His occasional insistence on the indirect nature of empathy is clearly motivated by his worry that any claim concerning a direct experiential understanding of others would amount to the claim that we have the same kind of first-personal acquaintance with other people's consciousness that we have with our own, that is, that the only way in which the mental states of another could be directly given to us would be for us to be in those states. Were that the case, however, the experiences of others would have become our own and no longer remain that of others (Husserl 1973c: 12). But this worry is, I think, ultimately misguided. It assumes that there is a single gold standard of what directness amounts to, and that direct access to one's own mental life constitutes the standard against which everything else has to be measured. In other contexts, however, Husserl is careful to point out that it is unacceptable to transfer the demands we put on evidence in one domain to other domains where these demands are in principle incapable of being realized. He claims that it is countersensical to treat what must count as the essential characteristic of a certain mode of givenness and cognition as deficiencies (Husserl 1976: 176, 321). And there are even places where he emphasizes that it would be a mistake to measure empathy against the standards of either self-perception or external object perception. Empathy has its own kind of originality, its own kind of fulfilment and corroboration, and its own criteria of success and failure (Husserl 1954: 189; 2003: 65, 122; 1973b: 352, 385; 1973a: 225).

Employing that insight, one could respect the difference between first-person and third-person acquaintance with psychological states without making the mistake of restricting and equating experiential acquaintance with first-person acquaintance. Why not argue that it is possible to experience minds in more than one way? Arguably, there is no more direct way of knowing that another is in pain than seeing him writhe in pain. Husserl is not as clear and consistent on this issue as one could have wished for, but as the following couple of quotations from *Erste Philosophie II* might illustrate, I don't think such a proposal would be disagreeable to his way of thinking:

The perception of the foreign lived body is rather, as we must say, according to its own essence a perception through original interpretation.... The spatial-objectual perception and inter-pretative regard that attaches to the grasping of a foreign lived body, as expressive under-standing, is, compared to simple external perception and the already founded perception of one's own lived body, its own basic form of experience, which is still rightly to be designated as perception. (Husserl 1959: 63)

Just as what is past can be originally given as past only through memory, and what is to come in the future can as such only be originally given through expectation, the foreign can only be originally given as foreign through empathy. Original givenness in this sense is the same as experience. (Husserl 1959: 176)

Furthermore, as Husserl repeatedly stresses, the fact that my experiential acquaint-ance with the mind of the other differs from my first-person acquaintance with my own mind (and from the other's experiential acquaintance with his or her own mind) is not an imperfection or shortcoming. On the contrary, it is a difference that is constitutional. It is precisely because of this difference, precisely because of this asymmetry, that we can claim that the minds we experience are *other* minds. As

Husserl points out, had I had the same access to the consciousness of the other as I have to my own, the other would cease being an other and would instead become a part of me (Husserl 1950: 139). In addition, although I do not have access to the first-personal character of the other's experience, although I don't experience it as it is experienced by the other, the fact that there is more to the other's experience than what I am grasping is salient to me, as Husserl repeatedly emphasizes (Husserl 1950: 144; 1973c: 631). To demand more, to claim that I would only have a real experience of the other if I experienced her feelings or thoughts in the same way as she herself does, is nonsensical, and fails to respect what is distinct and unique about the givenness of the other.

How should one compare and assess the relation between Scheler's view and that of Husserl and Stein? Both of the latter would strongly object to the former's claim that we can experience not only our own experiences, but also those of another, through a kind of inner experience or intuition (Scheler 2008: 242; Stein 2008: 30–2; Husserl 1984a: 41). Their worry is obviously that Scheler, by making such a claim, downplays what they take to be an essential difference between self-experience and other-experience, thereby leading to fusion and confusion. I think, however, that this specific controversy is more apparent than real. First of all, Scheler specifically defines inner intuition as an act that grasps the psychical, regardless of whether it is my own or that of the other (Scheler 2008: 249). In and of itself, this definition does not involve or entail a disregard of the difference between one's own experiences and those of the other. And in fact, Stein concedes that the definition itself is compatible with her own account of empathy. Secondly, although Scheler does indeed highlight the visibility and perceivability of some of the other's psychological states, he also, as already mentioned, repeatedly emphasizes that there are dimensions of the other that are absolutely inaccessible to others. But what about the following passage from *Wesen und Formen der Sympathie*, where Scheler speaks of

an immediate flow of experiences, *undifferentiated as between mine and thine*, which actually contains both our own and others' experiences intermingled and without distinction from one another. Within this flow there is a gradual formation of ever more stable vortices, which slowly attract further elements of the stream into their orbits and thereby become successively and very gradually identified with distinct individuals. (Scheler 2008: 246)

This quotation suggests that the differentiation between self and other is derivative and founded, and that it might be based on some kind of undifferentiated stratum of experience. If this were a correct interpretation, it would present strong evidence against the proposal that the controversy between Scheler on one side and Husserl and Stein on the other is more apparent than real. Consider, however, the direct continuation of the quotation:

But the essential links in the process are simply the facts: (1) that every experience belongs *in general to a self*, so that wherever an experience is given a self is also given, in a general sense;

(2) that this self is necessarily an *individual self*, present throughout every experience (in so far as such experiences are adequately given), and not therefore primarily constituted by the interconnection between them; (3) that *there is an 'I' and a 'Thou' in a general sense*. But which individual self it may be, that owns a given experience, whether it is our own or another's, is something that is not necessarily apparent in the experience as immediately presented. (Scheler 2008: 246)

This passage hardly supports the claim that Scheler should defend the view that there is a fundamental stratum of pre-individuated experiencing. This, of course, still leaves it a somewhat open question how precisely to interpret Scheler's reference to an undifferentiated flow of experience. One possibility, which I cannot pursue any further here but which at least should be mentioned, is to employ the distinction between authorship and ownership, and argue that although an experience for essential reasons always remained owned, it might have no clear author.[9]

10.3.3 Coupling and analogical transference

Claiming that in empathy we enjoy a direct, experiential understanding of others is not to say that we should take empathy as a primitive and unanalysable *factum brutum*, as Husserl accuses Scheler of doing (Husserl 1973b: 335). In other words, and to paraphrase A. D. Smith, Husserl is not trying to explain our awareness of others by appeal to empathy; rather, the term is a label for an accomplishment, and the task Husserl sets himself is to explain how empathy is possible as an intentional achievement (Smith 2003: 213). As we shall see, Husserl's investigation eventually made him highlight the role of the empathizing subject's own bodily self-experience.

As we have already seen, one of Husserl's recurrent ideas is that our empathic understanding of another subjectivity involves an element of apperception or interpretation, though he is also adamant that the apperception in question is neither an act of thinking, nor some kind of inference (Husserl 1973c: 15; 1950: 141). Occasionally he speaks of the process as involving what he calls analogical transference, and it is in this context that the central notion of *coupling*, or *pairing* (*Paarung*), is introduced (Husserl 1973c: 15).

What is coupling? According to Husserl's general account of intentionality, patterns of understanding are gradually established through a process of sedimentation and they thereby come to influence subsequent experiences (Husserl 1966b: 186). What I have learnt in the past does not leave me untouched. It shapes my understanding and interpretation of new objects by reminding me (in a completely tacit manner) of what I have experienced before. My current understanding of *x* will, in short, be aided by my previous experience of something analogous (Husserl 1973a: 345), and ultimately all apperceptive connections, all interpretations, might be said to rely on such analogical links to past experiences (Husserl 1950: 141). To exemplify,

---

[9] Such an interpretation might also fit Scheler's observation that we often reproduce thoughts of others that we have read or heard about as our own (Scheler 2008: 245).

after first having learned the function of a pair of scissors, the next time a child sees a pair of scissors she will immediately apprehend its functionality. She will do so without performing any inference and without explicitly having to think of or recall the first pair of scissors. According to Husserl, the apprehension of the new pair of scissors as a pair of scissors contains an associative reference to the original pair of scissors that is established passively (Husserl 1950: 141). Similarly, assume that you see and touch a guava for the first time. Next time you see one, your prior familiarity with its tactile qualities will infuse your experience of the new fruit. If you then happen also to taste the new exemplar, this new experience will in turn affect your apprehension and recollection of the first fruit. The relevance of these examples for empathy is seemingly straightforward. When I encounter another, my self-experience will serve as a reservoir of meaning that is transferred onto the other in a purely passive manner. As a result of this, a phenomenal unity is established. We are apprehended as a pair, as being alike and as belonging together, while still being separate and different (Husserl 1985: 225); that is, the coupling or pairing entails no fusion. Husserl writes:

Closely connected with the first peculiarity is the circumstance that *ego* and *alter ego* are always and necessarily given *in an original 'pairing'*.... First of all, let us elucidate the essential nature of any 'pairing' (or any forming of a plurality). Pairing is a *primal form of that passive synthesis* which we designate as '*association*', in contrast to passive synthesis of 'identification'. In a *pairing association* the characteristic feature is that, in the most primitive case, two data are given intuitionally, and with prominence, in the unity of a consciousness and that, on this basis—essentially, already in pure passivity (regardless therefore of whether they are noticed or unnoticed)—, as data appearing with mutual distinctness, they *found phenomenologically a unity of similarity* and thus are always constituted precisely as a pair. (Husserl 1950: 142)

Alter ego refers to ego—and vice versa (Husserl 1973b: 530). The latter point is crucial. The transfer of meaning occurring through the process of coupling is not unidirectional. We are dealing with a reciprocal transference (Husserl 1973c: 252), or as Husserl puts it in *Cartesianische Meditationen*, there is a 'mutual transfer of sense' (Husserl 1950: 142; compare Merleau-Ponty 1964a: 118).[10] In coming to understand the other, I draw on what I know from my own case, but through my encounter with the other, my own self-experience is also modified. In fact, not only that but Husserl even speaks of 'a mutual awakening' where both are overlaid with the 'sense of the other' (Husserl 1950: 142), thereby suggesting that the reciprocal transfer happens simultaneously. Thus, Husserl is quite explicit in emphasizing that since every coupling is reciprocal, my understanding of the other also 'uncovers my own psychic life in its similarity and difference' (Husserl 1950: 149). The fact that the transfer of meaning is bidirectional, the fact that as a result of the coupling I come to possess experiences I would have been incapable of on my own, speaks against the suggestion

---

[10] See also Theunissen's more critical reading (1977: 62), as well as Yamaguchi's reply (1982: 87).

that we should be dealing with a simple form of projection, where I ultimately find in the other only what I have put there myself. The latter implication would also go against Husserl's repeated insistence that empathy allows us to encounter true transcendence, and that our consciousness in empathy transcends itself and is confronted with, as he puts it, otherness of a completely new kind (Husserl 1973b: 8–9, 442). To that extent, empathy might indeed be said to be more a question of appreciating difference than of achieving similarity (Ratcliffe 2014).

Husserl's insistence on this latter point occasionally makes him question whether analogy really plays as fundamental a role as he is wont to claim. After all, as he admits, a process of analogizing doesn't lead to the apprehension of anything truly new (Husserl 1952: 168). In a text from 1914–15 he even writes, 'Actually, no empathy[11] occurs ... Nor does any kind of analogizing occur, no analogical inference, no transference by analogy ... Rather, the "apperception" of the foreign psychic life takes place without further ado' (Husserl 1973a: 338–9). Criticizing what might count as a version of simulation theory, Husserl also insists that it is nonsense to claim that in order to understand that the other is angry, I must experience anger myself, and that my own anger should somehow function as an analogue for the other's anger. Empathy is precisely not a kind of reproduction or reduplication of oneself (Husserl 1973a: 188; 1973b: 525). To experience the other is not like experiencing a transformation of oneself, as might happen in imagination. Such imaginative transformation wouldn't provide for an encounter with the other, but would only confront me with myself as different (Husserl 1973c: 314). Furthermore, although it is true that we sometimes imagine what it must be like for the other, what the other must be going through, it is simply unconvincing to claim that every act of empathy involves such imagination. When we empathically understand the other, we do so immediately and often without any imaginative depiction, and in those circumstances where we do depict the other's experience imaginatively, we precisely consider that an exception (Husserl 1973a: 188).

Despite these occasional misgivings, Husserl normally stresses the importance of analogy. When I apperceive another body as a lived body, for instance, I am, on his account, dealing with an analogical apperception that draws on and involves a re-presentation of my own self-experience (Husserl 1973a: 251). Indeed, in so far as the apprehension of the other involves re-presentation, the latter necessarily points back to a proper presentation, which is constituted by my own immediate self-experience (Husserl 1973a: 288). As Husserl puts it in various texts, subjectivity is primordially present to me in virtue of my self-experience and is only then apperceptively carried over to the other (Husserl 1962: 242; 1950: 140; 1959: 62; 1973b: 295). To that extent bodily self-experience constitutes a foundation for the perception of embodied others (1973a: 333), though Husserl also points out that the

---

[11] From the text, it is clear that Husserl is using the term 'empathy' here to designate a kind of imaginative transposition.

self-experience in question doesn't have to be temporally antecedent (Husserl 1950: 150). Moreover, the self-experience that needs to be in play is a *Durchgangserfahrung* and not a terminating experience (Husserl 1973b: 468). It is not a question of actively comparing the two of us, nor does my body first have to be an object of attention, but there must be some form of self-givenness, otherwise no transfer of meaning could occur (Husserl 1973a: 336).

At this stage, however, Husserl voices a concern. Even if it is true that I always enjoy bodily self-experience, the only thing that could motivate an analogizing apprehension or apperceptive transfer of sense would presumably be a perceived similarity between the body over there and my own body (Husserl 1950: 140). But it is hardly true that I originally observe my own body in the same way I perceive the body of others. Originally, my bodily subjectivity is given to me as that through which I experience the world; I don't perceive my own lived body as a spatial object. But isn't this what is required (Husserl 1973a: 344; 1973c: 661)? Moreover, occasionally Husserl seems to claim that I only learn of the identity between my own lived body and my externally appearing body through the other, that is, by adopting the other's perspective on my own body (Husserl 1973a: 420). As he puts it in a text dating from 1921, the apprehension of my own body as an object and as a physical thing is a mediated and secondary experience. It is one I only acquire through the other (Husserl 1973b: 61; see also 1973b: 63, 238, 322). But if this is correct, his argumentation would seem to involve a vicious circle and consequently fail.

Husserl himself does, however, suggest a few possible ways out. One idea that he primarily pursues in *Cartesianische Meditationen* is that the appearance of the other body reminds me of the possible appearance of my own body, reminds me of what my own body would look like if it appeared over there (Husserl 1950: 146). On occasions, however, he also seems to realize that this account, with its reliance on me having to imagine what my own body would look like, is unsatisfactory (Husserl 1973b: 522; compare Overgaard 2003). A more promising approach is the insight that although a thorough objectification of the body might be something intersubjectively mediated, my lived body is also, and already from the very start, continuously externalizing itself, and that this exteriority is co-given as an integral part of my own bodily self-experience (Husserl 1973b: 491). One of the issues frequently emphasized in Husserl's phenomenological analysis of the body is consequently its peculiar two-sidedness. My body is given to me as an interiority, as a volitional structure, and as a dimension of sensing, but it is also given as a visually and tactually appearing exteriority. And the latter experience, the fact that my own self-experience is characterized by this remarkable interplay between *ipseity* and *alterity*, is, according to Husserl, precisely one of the elements that must be in place if empathy is to be possible (Husserl 1952: 165–6; 1973c: 652; 1959: 62; 1973b: 457; 1973a: 263). Along similar lines, Stein writes that a fusion between inner and outer bodily perception already takes place in my own case.[12] When I move my own limbs, I am not merely kinaesthetically aware of them; I can also have an exteroceptive and tactile perception of the movements. In short, it is because my own body is simultaneously given as a physical body and as a lived body that it is possible for me to empathize sensuously with other bodies that are similarly constituted. A pure I with no lived body of its own could consequently not perceive and understand other animated living bodies (Stein 2008: 99). Thus, just as Merleau-Ponty would later argue, both Husserl and Stein take a proper account of embodiment to be crucial if we are to make it comprehensible how we can come to understand others. Moreover, when speaking of the resemblance between one's own body and the body of another, we shouldn't forget that the other body also behaves similarly; it moves and acts in similar ways (Husserl 1973b: 280; 1973a: 289), and my continuous experience of it as another subjective body is precisely conditional upon my experience of its continuous and harmonious behaviour (Husserl 1950: 144). More important for the coupling than the presence of similar visual appearances might consequently be the reciprocity between and complementarity of my own intentional behaviour and expressive movements and those of the other. As A. D. Smith also points out in his analysis of *Cartesianische Meditationen*, what might lie at the root of empathy is a basic attunement to the responsiveness of the other. The other responds to you and your actions in a way that inanimate objects do not (Smith 2003: 243, 248).

How should we reconcile Husserl's various statements? On the one hand, he emphasizes the involved transfer of sense and the role of analogy; on the other, he questions its relevance, rejects outright the centrality of projection, and repeatedly accentuates the transcendence of the other.

One way to square Husserl's thoughts on this issue, at least to some extent, is as follows. When Husserl insists that the original givenness of my own lived body, the *Urleib*, or primal body, constitutes the reference point and anchor point for any experience of other bodies, and when he claims that every apperception has an origin which prescribes a certain norm or standard of meaning, and that this *Urnorm* is the foundation of every experience of others (Husserl 1973a: 57; 1973b: 125–6), one might understand the notion of *Urnorm* in two rather different ways. Either one can understand it as a kind of matrix that I rely and draw on when understanding others. On this reading, Husserl would claim that the subject interprets others in terms of a sense of mentality that it has first grasped *in foro interno* and which it then projects and imposes more or less successfully onto others. Another possibility, however, which I find considerably more promising, is to see the self-experience in question as a necessary foil on the basis of which others can be experienced as others. The other

---

[12] This is an idea that would later be further developed by Merleau-Ponty. As he writes at one point, 'I do not translate the "givens of touch" into "language of vision," nor *vice versa*; I do not assemble the parts of my body one by one. Rather, this translation and this assemblage are completed once and for all in me: they are my body itself ' (Merleau-Ponty 2012: 151; see also 2012: 368).

might be a self in his or her own right, but the other can only appear as other for me in relation to and in contrast to my own self-experience. But in this case, my self-experience doesn't constitute the model or matrix; rather, it is simply that against which the other's difference and transcendence can reveal itself. To put it differently, although Husserl would insist that (bodily) self-experience is a precondition for other-experience, there is a decisive difference between arguing that the former is a necessary condition (and that there would be no other-experience in its absence) and claiming that self-experience somehow serves as a model for other-experience, as if empathy is basically a question of projecting oneself into the other. As already pointed out, I do not think Husserl holds the latter view.

10.3.4 The objects and levels of empathy

So far, the analysis seems to suggest that empathy is a unitary concept for both Husserl and Stein, and that its object is the other subject. Both assumptions must be modified.

In the course of her investigation, Stein distinguishes different levels of accomplishment (*Vollzugsstufen*) (Stein 2008: 19). At first, I might be confronted with the doubt or elation in the other's face, and I might have a vague and relatively empty comprehension of the other's experience. But if I then try to understand it better, if I try to explicate its character, I will no longer face the other's experiential state as an object. Rather, its intentionality will pull me along, and I will turn towards its intentional object. It is only after I have successfully accomplished this clarification that I will again face the other's experience as an object, but this time with an increased comprehension. To exemplify, consider a situation in which you come across a crying child. Empathy will allow you to discern the child's distress even before you know why the child is upset. But if your empathy goes deeper, it will seek to understand what it is that has upset the child. Finally, having grasped the object of the emotion, you will again turn towards the child, but this time with a better (and more fulfilled) understanding of her distress. Even when I follow the intentional pull of the child's distress and turn towards, say, the absent mother, the distress is given to me in a quite peculiar manner. It is not felt as my own distress, nor as a remembered distress, let alone simply as an imagined distress. No, it is throughout given to me as the other's distress, as a distress lived through by the other (Stein 2008: 10). This is precisely what is peculiar and distinct about empathy, and this is why Stein continues to label empathy a *sui generis* kind of experience (Stein 2008: 10).

In some places, Stein also articulates what ultimately amounts to a somewhat different account of the different levels or stages of empathy. First, I perceive the other's expression of joy. In a subsequent move, I put myself in the other's place, carry out the experience that was already co-given to me emptily together with his countenance, and then experience that which comes to expression (Stein 2008: 93). She further argues that the extent to which I am able to bring the other's experience to empathic fulfilment depends upon my own experiential life. Those experiences of the other that can be derived from my own personal structure can be fulfilled, even if de facto they are experiences I haven't yet had. When there is a greater divergence between our respective constitutions, it might be impossible for me to fulfil the empathically intended but emptily given experience. I can certainly empathize with humans of other age groups and gender than myself, and I can also empathize with some non-human animals. But the further I deviate from the type human being, the emptier and more lacking in fulfilment the empathy will be (Stein 2008: 66; compare Scheler 2008: 48). As Stein then makes clear, however, this reliance on the concrete content of my own experiential life only concerns the extent or degree of fulfilment. It isn't required in order to obtain a more empty presentation of the other's experiences (Stein 2008: 128–9). More importantly, at no point does Stein suggest that it is the imaginative enactment that provides empathy with its distinctive other-directed attitude; that is, at no point does she suggest that empathy can be reduced to or explained by imagination. At any rate, somebody who empathizes with another does not necessarily go through all these different stages, since he might often remain satisfied with one of the lower levels (Stein 2008: 10).

If we move on to Husserl, we also find him distinguishing different levels of empathy. The most fundamental form of empathy is the one that allows us to apprehend the perceptually given body as a lived body, that is, most fundamentally as a sensing body (Husserl 1973a: 66, 70, 435–6). This form of sensual empathy (to use a term from Stein 2008: 65), which Husserl also calls animal apperception or experience of animality, happens passively and associatively (Husserl 1973a: 455, 475–6). Husserl then contrasts this most basic and fundamental kind of empathy with a more active form that targets the understanding of that which is expressed in bodily expressions, namely, beliefs, decisions, attitudes (Husserl 1973a: 435).[13] In a manuscript from 1931–2, Husserl operates with even more levels. The first level of empathy is the appresentation of the other lived body as sensing and perceiving. The second level is the appresentation of the other as physically acting, say, moving, pushing, or carrying something. The third level goes beyond this and attends to the purposefulness of the action and grasps, say, the running of the other as flight (Husserl 1973c: 435). On a few occasions, Husserl goes even further and also speaks of the kind of empathy involved in appropriating foreign traditions (Husserl 1973c: 436; 2006: 372–3).

In other words, although Husserl would claim that a first level of empathy is constituted by coupling, by a passive and involuntary associative bonding of self and

---

[13] Texts written around 1920 are characterized by some indecision on this specific issue. In these texts, Husserl at times designates the most basic form of empathy as an improper (*uneigentliche*) form of empathy and contrasts it with empathy proper (*eigentliche Einfühlung*), which is the more active kind (Husserl 1973a: 438, 457). But on some occasions he also wonders whether it might be better to reserve the name empathy for empathy proper and instead characterize the more basic form of animal apperception as a constitutive level that precedes empathy (Husserl 1973a: 475). Given Husserl's subsequent account of coupling, I think one must conclude that he ultimately opted for the first alternative.

other on the basis of their bodily similarity, he would maintain that this is only the first, primitive level and would never agree with the claim that it amounts to the full range of interpersonal understanding. The latter only reaches its culmination in acts of communication. Thus, we shouldn't overlook that expressions can also be voluntary and serve communicative purposes. When I assert a proposition, I also express a belief and thereby show my state of mind. As Husserl remarks in a well-known passage:

Leibniz said that the monads have no windows. But I think that every psychic monad has infinitely many windows—namely, every truly comprehending perception of a foreign lived body is such a window. And each time I say, 'please, dear friend,' and my friend responds to me with understanding, then through our open windows, an I-act of my I is passed over into the I of my friend and vice versa; a reciprocal motivation has established a real unity between us— yes, has actually established a real unity. (Husserl 1973a: 473)

As for the question regarding the proper object of empathy, Husserl denies that I normally thematize the other as an object when empathizing.[14] Rather, when empathically understanding the other, I so to speak go along with his or her experiences, and attend to their object (Husserl 2003: 617; 1973c, 427, 513).[15] It is consequently important to emphasize that the other, rather than being given to me simply as a nucleus of experiences, is given as a centre of orientation, as a perspective on the world. The other is consequently not given in isolation or purity for me; rather, the other is given as intentional, as directed at the same world as I, and the other's world, and the objects that are there for him, are given along with the other (Husserl 1973b: 140, 287; 1973a: 411; 1952: 168; 1950: 154; compare Stein 2008: 69). This is, of course, one reason why our perception of others is so unlike our ordinary perception of objects. As soon as the other appears on the scene, my relation to the world will change, since the other will always be given to me in a situation or meaningful context that points back to the other as a new centre of reference. The meaning the world has for the other affects the meaning it has for me. The foreign world-perspective that is co-given along with my apprehension of the other

---

[14] By contrast, according to Husserl the primary object in sympathy, care, and pity (*Mitleid*) is the other him- or herself and not the object of the other's distress. Thus, the intentional object of my sympathy and the intentional object of the other's distress differ. To use Husserl's own example, if the other is sad over the fact that his mother had died, I am also sad about this, and sad about the fact that he is sad. But it is his sadness that is my primary object; it is only subsequently and conditional upon that that the death of his mother is also something that saddens me (Husserl 1973b: 189–90; compare Snow 2000: 66). More generally speaking, Husserl emphasizes the distinction between empathy and sympathy (just as he distinguishes both of these from emotional contagion). Whereas empathy is a form of understanding, sympathy involves care and concern (Husserl 2004: 194).

[15] If this is so, it would qualify a claim by De Preester. In a paper from 2008, she argues for the following significant difference between Merleau-Ponty's and Husserl's accounts of coupling: whereas the mediating term between ego and alter ego for Husserl is bodily similarity, it is for Merleau-Ponty the intended object of action to which ego and alter ego are equally directed. De Preester consequently claims that only Merleau-Ponty holds the view that it is by having the same intentional object and by trying to accomplish the same goal that I come to understand the other's actions (De Preester 2008: 136–7).

obviously varies according to how I apprehend the other. If the other is blind, I won't co-apprehend the other's visual perspective on the world, unless, that is, my empathy is led astray by egocentric bias (Stein 2008: 70, 72–3). In general, however, my own perspective on the world will be enriched through my empathic understanding of the other. Both Stein and Husserl consequently emphasize the interrelation between the experience of others and the constitution of a shared world, or to rephrase it using a concept from developmental psychology, for both of them empathy and social referencing are closely linked.

For Husserl, the experience of another necessarily involves accepting the validity of some of the other's experiences. If nothing else, my experience of the lived body of another necessarily presupposes that the very same body I perceive externally is also lived through by the other (Husserl 1973c: 158–9; 1973a: 252; 1973b: 83), which is why Husserl characterizes the body of the other as the first intersubjective datum, as the first object that is accessed by a plurality of subjects (Husserl 1973b: 110). As he puts it in *Zur Phänomenologie der Intersubjektivität II*:

> For in the validity of my experience of others, through which the others are there for me as existing, the co-validity of their experiences for me is already included. That his lived body is not only the physical body I directly perceive it to be, but is a lived body, already includes the co-acceptance of the perception that the other has of his lived body as the same body that I perceive, and likewise for his surrounding world as materially the same as the surrounding world that I experience. I cannot posit others without co-positing, along with their experiencing life, that which they experience—i.e. without positing, in co-acceptance, what I presentify them as experiencing, positing this in the same way as I accept what I experience more originally on my own. (Husserl 1973b: 388; compare Merleau-Ponty 2012: 369)

This is an idea that Husserl would also draw upon in his account of the constitution of objectivity, since he there defends the view that my experience of the significance and validity of objects changes the moment I realize that others experience the same objects as I (see Zahavi 1996).

At the same time, however, and this is of particular importance in this context, both Husserl and Stein recognize that I can be part of what the other intends. So again, when I experience others, I do not merely experience them as psychophysical objects in the world; rather, I experience them as subjects who experience worldly objects, myself included (Husserl 1973c: 4–5; 1952: 169; 1950: 158). In fact, through my experience of others I can precisely come to attain a new experience of myself. Stein writes that through a process of iterative or reflexive empathy, in which I empathically comprehend empathic acts that are directed at myself, I can come to adopt an alienating attitude towards myself and thereby come to see myself as others see me. To that extent, empathy can function as an important source of self-knowledge (Stein 2008: 130; see also Husserl 1950: 149). Likewise, Husserl refers to cases in which my self-experience and my experience of an empathized subject who empathizes with me coincide as cases of higher-order empathy (Husserl 1973b: 315).

He claims that it is through this process of mediated self-experience, by indirectly experiencing myself as one viewed by others, that I come to experience myself as human (Husserl 1952: 167–9; 1973c: 13, 665). Why is this important? Because, as Husserl proceeds to point out, I am not what I am for myself, independently of the other; nor is the other independent of me. Everybody is for himself and at the same time for the other in an inseparable being-for-one-another. On occasion, Husserl does speak of empathy as involving a situation in which one ego mirrors itself directly in the other (Husserl 1973c: 7; 1973b: 300). But on the basis of further analysis (and this is also, of course, in line with his account of coupling), he ultimately concludes, in manuscripts from the 1930s, that we are not dealing with an ineffective mirroring (*kraftlose Spiegelung*), but that the being of self and other is a being-for-one-another, that is, that they are constitutively intertwined (Husserl 1973c: 191, 194). These are topics that I shall explore further in Part III.

10.4 Schutz

The phenomenological analysis of intersubjectivity and sociality obviously didn't come to an end with the contributions of Husserl and Stein. It would at this point be too much of a diversion if I were to discuss the rich analyses to be found in Heidegger, Sartre, Merleau-Ponty, or Levinas (but see Zahavi 1996, 2001, 2002, 2007b). Rather, in the following I shall focus on a slightly less well-known figure, whose contribution to an analysis of interpersonal understanding has been unjustly neglected in recent years, namely, Schutz. What is particularly interesting about Schutz's account is that while he recognizes the fundamental and irreducible character of the face-to-face encounter, at the same time he emphasizes the heterogeneity of interpersonal understanding. Interpersonal understanding comes in many shapes and forms, and if we wish to do justice to this variety and complexity we have to go beyond what empathy can deliver.

In his book *Der sinnhafte Aufbau der sozialen Welt*, published in 1932, Schutz rejects what he considers to be the two extreme positions of Scheler and Carnap. Whereas the former, on Schutz's reading, argues that I have as direct an access to the lived experiences of others as I have to my own, the latter supposedly argues that we never have any experience of other minds at all, but only of physical objects (Schutz 1967: 20–1). By contrast, Schutz defends the view that we are experientially acquainted with the psychological life of others, while denying that the experiences of others are intuitively given to us in their full self-presence. In Schutz's view, the body of the other is no mere physical object, but a field of expression that reveals the experiential life of the other (Schutz 1967: 22). However, he continues, to speak simply of the body as a field of expression remains too imprecise a way of talking. It may refer to the fact that the external behaviour of the other person indicates his subjective experiences, or it may refer to the fact that the subject 'is deliberately seeking to express something' by acting in a certain way. And as Schutz points out, many things that are expressions in the first sense—reddening with anger, for instance—are hardly expressions in the second. It would consequently be incorrect to say that, say, a woodsman by the act of chopping is deliberately expressing his desire to cut down trees, since one can only speak of an expression in this second sense if that which is expressed is intended as a message to a recipient (Schutz 1967: 22–3). On the basis of his distinction between these two types of expression (which Schutz adopts from Husserl's *I. Logische Untersuchung*; see Husserl 1984a: 31–2), Schutz further insists that we have to distinguish what he calls 'expressive movements' (which lack any communicative intent) from what he calls 'expressive acts' (which include it) (Schutz 1967: 116), and he faults Scheler for having exclusively focused on expressive movements when providing examples of our supposedly direct access to the experiences of others.[16] If we again take the woodcutter at work as our example, Schutz concedes that to a certain extent we might be said to perceive the woodcutter's experience of effort as he wields his axe, but ridicules the suggestion that we should also be able to intuit directly *why* he is acting the way he does (Schutz 1967: 23–4). Similarly, although on Schutz's view it is permissible to say that certain aspects of the other's consciousness, such as his joy, sorrow, pain, shame, pleading, love, or rage, are given to us directly and non-inferentially, he denies that it follows from the fact that we can intuit these surface attitudes that we are also directly acquainted with the why of such feelings. But when we speak of understanding (the psychological life of) others, what we mean is precisely that we understand what others are up to, why they are doing what they are doing, and what that means to them. In short, interpersonal understanding crucially involves an understanding of the actions of others, of their whys, meanings, and motives. And in order to uncover these aspects, it is not sufficient simply to observe expressive movements and actions; we also have to rely on interpretation; we also have to draw on a highly structured context of meaning (Schutz 1967: 23–4).

Schutz admits that in some cases we rely on imagination, memory, or theoretical knowledge when attempting to understand others. We can, for instance, attempt to identify the goal of their actions and then imagine how we would seek to accomplish it and what experiences we would be living through. Or we might rely on memory and remember what we went through when in the past we sought to realize a similar goal (Schutz 1967: 114). Finally, we can also make use of our general knowledge

---

[16] For more on Schutz appraisal of Scheler's theory of intersubjectivity, see Schutz (1962: 150–79). As for Schutz's appraisal of Husserl's account, it changed over time. Husserl famously took the problem of intersubjectivity to call for a transcendental analysis. Initially, Schutz followed him in this, but he subsequently changed his mind. For a vivid illustration of this shift, consider the following two statements. In a letter to Husserl dated 26 April 1932 Schutz writes, 'Thus I found in your development of the problem of transcendental intersubjectivity the key to almost all sociological problems that have beset me for so many years' (Husserl 1994: 482). In a later, and much discussed, article from 1957, however, Schutz writes as follows: 'It can, however, be said with certainty that only such an ontology of the life-world, not a transcendental constitutional analysis, can clarify that essential relationship of intersubjectivity which is the basis of all social science' (Schutz 1975: 82). For further discussions of this issue, see Zahavi (1996).

regarding the kind of action in question and then seek to infer its causes and motives (Schutz 1967: 175). As Schutz emphasizes, however, the strategies just outlined are ones we primarily employ after the fact, that is, in situations where the person we seek to understand isn't one with whom we are directly perceiving and interacting. In the latter case, that is, in the face-to-face encounter, there is, according to Schutz, a concrete *we-relationship*, a shared motivational context in which our respective streams of consciousness are interlocked, immediately affecting each other, and in such situations there is a form of other-understanding that isn't exclusively based on theory, imagination, or past experiences (Schutz 1967: 115, 157, 172–5). When it comes to understanding the why of the other's actions, when seeking to understand the reasons and motives of the other, we shouldn't overlook that our perception of the other person, as another agent, is never of an entity existing outside a specific situation, but of an agent within a pragmatic context that throws light on the intentions of that agent. If, on a football field, I see you running towards a football, my understanding of your intentions is obviously facilitated by the fact that I can also see the football and the football field, and the actions that they afford. Moreover, there is a temporal dimension to the face-to-face encounter: we grow old together, as Schutz puts it (Schutz 1967: 163, 172); and the fact that we experience what comes before and after a certain expressive movement or act obviously also aids our understanding. It is precisely within such common, and mainly pragmatic, situations that expressive phenomena occur. When I work or converse with my partner, she might shake her head or wrinkle her brow. But these facial expressions and bodily gestures are not unambiguous. They do not reveal psychological states simply or uniformly. Each person has different facial expressions and habits. But this is rarely a problem, since we do not encounter expressions in isolation. They always occur in a given context, and our understanding of the context, of what comes before and after, helps us to understand the expression (Gurwitsch 1979: 114; Sartre 2003: 371). Finally, as Schutz points out, when interacting directly with somebody, I have the unique possibility of having my assumptions about his experiences confirmed or disconfirmed by direct questions (Schutz 1967: 140, 174). If somebody is acting in a puzzling way, the easiest way to gain further information is not by engaging in detached theorizing or internal simulation; it is to employ one's conversational skills and ask the person for an explanation.

To understand fully Schutz's line of reasoning, which accentuates the extent to which concrete other-understanding relies on practical engagement and involvement, we need to take a closer look at some of his technical terms and distinctions. Adopting and modifying a central Husserlian idea, Schutz speaks of a 'general thesis of the other self', thereby denoting our fundamental conviction that the other exists, endures, and consciously undergoes subjective experiences (Schutz 1967: 145). He also speaks of this attitude in terms of 'other-orientation' (*Fremdeinstellung*). An especially significant case of other-orientation is what Schutz labels 'thou-orientation' (*Dueinstellung*) (Schutz 1967: 146, 163). This is a form of intentionality where the other is bodily co-present and immediately given as a psychophysical unity. Moreover, the thou-orientation is directed at the living reality of the other; it doesn't involve any awareness of the other's character traits, beliefs, or occurrent experiences. Thus, in the pure thou-orientation I grasp the *Dasein* rather than the *Sosein* of the other. That is, the thou-orientation provides me with an awareness of the presence of the other, but not with any specific awareness of what is going on in the other's mind.[17] Schutz stresses that a pure thou-orientation is a limit concept. In real life, we always experience real people with their own personal characteristics and traits. The thou-orientation of our daily life is consequently not a pure thou-orientation but an actualized and determinate thou-orientation. It is always coloured by knowledge regarding the other (Schutz 1967: 162–4).

The thou-orientation can be reciprocal or one-sided. It is one-sided if it exists without any reciprocation on the part of the other, say, if I am secretly observing somebody. However, when two people are reciprocally oriented towards each other, or, to adopt the first-person perspective, when I ascertain that the other towards whom I am thou-oriented is also thou-oriented towards me, we get what Schutz calls a *we-relationship* or a *living social relationship* (Schutz 1967: 157). Again, in its purity the we-relationship is a formal limit concept. In daily life, the we-relationship is always concretized and contextualized (Schutz 167: 164), and can take many different forms. The partner can, for instance, be experienced with different degrees of intimacy and intensity.

One important aspect of Schutz's theory that I haven't addressed so far concerns his claim regarding the heterogeneity of the social world; it is structured in multiple ways. Correlatively speaking, interpersonal understanding is not a unitary phenomenon. It differs in character depending on whether the other in question is bodily present, or, rather, removed from us in space or time. It depends, in short, on whether the other belongs to the world of our associates, contemporaries, predecessors, or successors, or to use Schutz's original terms, whether the other belongs to our *Umwelt*, *Mitwelt*, *Vorwelt*, or *Folgewelt* (Schutz 1967: 14). So far the focus has exclusively been on social relationships that take place within our *Umwelt*, but this focus is too narrow and limited; it only covers a small, though admittedly central and fundamental, part of the social world. But we shouldn't forget that I am also able to understand and interact with those whom I have previously encountered face to face but who now live abroad, or those of whose existence I know, not as concrete individuals, but as points in social space defined by certain roles and functions, say, tax officials or railway guards, just as I can rely on and relate to those who produced the artefacts I am currently using, or those who existed before I myself did, that is, the

---

[17] For an interesting convergence, consider Honneth, who writes that the foundation of intersubjectivity is a form of existential recognition that lies below the threshold of and provides the foundation for all those more substantial forms of recognition where the other person's specific characteristics are affirmed (Honneth 2008: 51, 90).

members of the *Vorwelt*, who can continue to influence me although I am in no position to influence them (Schutz 1967: 142–3). Thus, Schutz repeatedly stresses the multilayered character of the social world, and argues that one of the important tasks of a phenomenological sociology is to conduct a careful analysis of these different strata.

Let us take a closer look at the way we engage with our contemporaries, that is, those whom I could experience directly since we coexist in time, but whom as a matter of fact I do not since they are not present in my immediate surroundings. Whereas the face-to-face relationship involves a direct experience of the other, even if it can be very casual, say, a chance meeting with a stranger on a train, my understanding of my contemporaries is by definition indirect, inferential, and impersonal, though it can otherwise differ widely in character (Schutz 1967: 177, 181). Compare, for instance, my relation to and understanding of a close friend of mine who has just moved outside the range of direct experience, with my relation to and understanding of the postman or the anonymous producer of the pencil I am currently using. Although they all belong to my *Mitwelt*, my understanding of them obviously differs dramatically. Nevertheless, although I might have a very intimate knowledge regarding my friend, my understanding of him qua contemporary will still lack the directness and pre-predicative character of the face-to-face encounter (Schutz 1967: 178, 183); it will always be based on interpretative judgements that draw on my general knowledge of the social world.

To illustrate the shift of orientation in my attitude when I understand and interact with my contemporaries, Schutz introduces the term *they-orientation* (Schutz 1967: 183). In contrast to thou-orientation, in which I am directly aware of the living presence of the other's consciousness as it is manifested in expressive movements or expressive acts, my understanding of my contemporaries is always general in form, is always shaped and framed by structures of typicality (Schutz 1967: 181, 184). When I understand a contemporary, I don't consider him as a unique person; rather, I conceive of him as an instantiation of a type, and leave individual characteristics and changes out of account. This even holds true for close friends of mine, since my dealings with them are conducted under the assumption that they remain homogeneous and stay the same (Schutz 1967: 182, 184). Schutz next distinguishes *characterological* ideal types from *habitual* ideal types. Characterological ideal types typify the other in terms of character and temperament—people like N behave in such and such a way when faced with such and such a situation—and are precisely the types that are prevalent in my dealing with contemporaries with whom I have had direct experience in the past. By contrast, habitual ideal types typify the other in terms of social functions and roles and are of a more anonymous kind (Schutz 1967: 196). Consider, for instance, the kind of social understanding that occurs when I post a letter. When doing so, my action is guided by assumptions I make regarding some of my contemporaries, namely, the postmen. I assume that they will read the address and send the letter to its recipient. I don't know them personally and I don't think of them as particular individuals, but by behaving the way I do, I relate to them as ideal types, as bearers of certain functions. As Schutz puts it, when I am they-oriented I have 'types' for partners (Schutz 1967: 185). And, of course, for this social process to work, the postmen have to relate to me as well, not as a particular individual, but as a typical customer. Taking up a mutual they-orientation, we think of each other as *one of them* (Schutz 1967: 202). Typification (and stereotyping) consequently facilitates everyday predictability.

In ordinary life we move between *Umwelt* and *Mitwelt* constantly, and, as Schutz points out, the change from one to the other presents no problem. This is so because we always interpret our own behaviour and that of the other within contexts of meaning that transcend the here and now. In that sense, a narrow concern with the question of whether our relationship is direct or indirect is a somewhat academic exercise (Schutz 1967: 178). This is even more so, given that the use of ideal types is not limited to the world of contemporaries (or the world of our predecessors or successors). The ideal types we acquire become part of our stock of knowledge, and start to influence our face-to-face interactions as well; that is, they come to serve as interpretative schemes even in the world of direct social experience (Schutz 1967: 185).

Schutz considers the face-to-face encounter to be basic in the sense that all other forms of interpersonal understanding presuppose it (Schutz 1967: 162). Thus, Schutz would insist that the experience of the bodily presence of others is prior to and more fundamental than any understanding of others that draws on imaginative projection, memory, or theoretical knowledge. We only start to employ the latter strategies when we are already convinced that we are facing minded creatures, but are simply unsure about precisely how we are to interpret the expressive phenomena in question. We would not start to enquire into the meaning of another's actions, we would not attempt to predict or explain them, were we not already convinced that the other was a minded, experiencing subject. But although Schutz takes the face-to-face encounter to be fundamental, he also keeps emphasizing that it has some clear limitations. If we wish to develop a proper social relationship, if we wish to reach a deeper level of interpersonal understanding, we have to go beyond what is directly available (Schutz 1967: 168). Ordinarily, we always bring a whole stock of knowledge to the encounter with the other, both knowledge of a more general sort, but frequently also knowledge regarding the particular person in question, knowledge of his habits, interests, etc. (Schutz 1967: 169). Indeed, it is crucial to realize that our understanding of others never takes place in a vacuum; it doesn't have the format of a snapshot.

10.5 The phenomenological proposal

As I pointed out in Chapter 9, there is currently little consensus about what empathy is. Rather, what one finds in the contemporary debate is a multitude of competing definitions. One rather useful way of mapping some of the central options has been provided by Battaly (2011). According to her reconstruction, the three main positions are as follows:

1. Some conceive of empathy as a sharing of mental states, where sharing is taken to mean that the empathizer and the target must have roughly the same type of mental state.[18] On this account, empathy does not involve knowledge about the other; it doesn't require knowing that the other has the mental state in question. Various forms of contagion and mimicry consequently count as prime examples of empathy.

2. Others argue that empathy requires both sharing and knowing. Thus, it is not enough that there is a match between the mental state of the empathizer and the target; the empathizer must also cognitively assign or ascribe the mental state to the target. In so far as empathy on this account requires some cognitive grasp and some self–other differentiation, low-level simulation like mimicry and contagion are excluded.

3. Finally, there are those who emphasize the cognitive dimension, and argue that empathy doesn't require sharing, but that it simply refers to any process by means of which one comes to know the other's mental state, regardless of how theoretical or inferential the process might be.

If empathy is the label for a distinctive accomplishment, if it is supposed to constitute a distinct kind of social understanding rather than simply collapse into either emotional contagion or inferential mind-reading, it seems advisable to stay clear of both 1 and 3. But should we adopt 2?

Let us take a closer look at a sophisticated attempt to cash out this second option, namely, an account that has been defended by de Vignemont, Singer, and Jacob in various publications. On their view, empathy requires isomorphic affective (emotional or sensory) states in empathizer and target. That is, an interpersonal similarity constraint holds true in the case of empathy. In addition, they stipulate a number of other conditions that must be met if empathy is to obtain. There are a handful of slightly different definitions in circulation, but let me focus on a recent one, which is due to Jacob (2011):

(i) *Affectivity condition*: both target and empathizer must experience some affective state or other.

(ii) *Interpersonal similarity relation condition*: the target's experience s and the empathizer's experience s^* must stand in some similarity relation (e.g., both must experience some kind of pain or fear).

(iii) *Causal path condition*: the empathizer's being in affective state s^* is caused by the target's being in affective state s.

---

[18] As I shall argue later, this is ultimately quite a problematic use of the term 'sharing'.

(iv) *Ascription condition*: there could not be empathetic understanding unless the empathizer ascribed the appropriate affective state to the target.

(v) *Caring condition*: the empathizer must care about the target's affective life. (Jacob 2011: 523)[19]

In contrast to various other proposals, there is on this account no attempt to distinguish different kinds or levels of empathy, nor is there any mentioning of the direct or non-inferential character of empathy. Rather, the focus is squarely on the affective nature of empathy. In fact, de Vignemont and Jacob explicitly argue that the affectivity condition is what allows one to distinguish empathy, which they also label affective mind-reading, from standard mind-reading (de Vignemont and Jacob 2012: 305). So not only is it on this account impossible to empathize with another person's intentions or beliefs, but if one understands what the other is feeling without feeling it oneself, one is also not empathizing with the other. The second condition is supposed to distinguish empathy from sympathy, while the function of the third condition is to allow for a distinction between empathy and cases where two unrelated individuals by coincidence happen to fulfil conditions (i) and (ii). Satisfaction of the fourth condition distinguishes empathy from a vicarious experience generated by a contagious process. The fifth condition might be slightly puzzling; after all, to define empathy in terms of care seems to blur the distinction between empathy and sympathy. But Jacob argues that the addition of the caring condition is necessary in order to capture the fact that empathy, rather than being the default response to one's awareness of another's experience, is on the contrary subject to top-down modulation by contextual factors (Jacob 2011: 8). De Vignemont and Jacob further propose that the five conditions allow for a systematic account of the distinction between empathy, sympathy, emotional contagion, and standard mind-reading (De Vignemont and Jacob 2012: 307).

Let us consider the proposed distinction between empathy and sympathy. Suppose someone sees that his friend is afraid and feels sad for him. On the present scheme, this should be a case of sympathy rather than empathy, and indeed this seems the most natural way to describe it. However, it is questionable whether the reason why it should be classified in this way is that the two people are in different affective states. For what if someone sees that her friend is sad and feels sad for him? Now the interpersonal similarity relation condition is met, and it is likely that the other conditions are met as well, and so, according to the proposal, it cannot any longer be a case of sympathy, but must instead be a case of empathy. But that does seem a bit odd. Allegedly the two cases are similar in that someone is feeling sadness and concern directed at another person's plight. And is it really plausible to suggest

---

[19] Slightly different versions of the account can be found in de Vignemont and Singer (2006) and de Vignemont and Jacob (2012).

that what would otherwise have been a clear case of sympathetic concern becomes a case of empathizing instead, merely because we change the target subject's emotion?

A quite common phenomenon is that one person expresses a certain emotion (say, anger) and another person sees this and reacts with a different type of emotion (say, fear). But this sort of case has no straightforward place in the proposed classificatory scheme. In not meeting the interpersonal similarity requirement, this case can count neither as a case of empathy nor as a case of emotional contagion. Nor can it count as sympathy: the frightened person will typically not feel concern for the person expressing anger. So the only available option is to classify it as a case of cold mind-reading or cognitive perspective taking on a par with, say, me inferring from the fact that somebody is asking for aspirin that the person is in pain. In other words, if I react with fear to someone else's anger, this is a case of cognitive perspective taking; but if I react with anger, I am, if the other conditions are met, empathizing. But is this really convincing?

Over the years, Jacob has modified his position slightly. In the paper published in 2011, Jacob exemplified the similarity condition by writing that both individuals must experience some kind of pain or fear. In a paper from 2012, by contrast, de Vignemont and Jacob are more specific and now argue that the similarity condition entails that the character *and* content of the affective states must be similar (2012: 305). If a similarity of content is required for the similarity condition to be fulfilled, the previously mentioned objection is clearly beside the point. If X is angry with Y, and Y as a result is angry with X, the two individuals might be in similar affective states, but given that the respective objects of their anger are very different, the similarity requirement is not met, and we are not faced with a (counter-intuitive) case of empathy (Dullstein 2012).

Is this modification (or clarification) enough to salvage the proposal? One initial concern is that it implies that it would be impossible for, say, a parent to empathize with her child's grief, fear, anger, or joy if the mother didn't know what the child was grieving for, fearing, or feeling angry or joyful about. Is that really plausible? Another concern is that de Vignemont and Jacob's classificatory scheme apparently forces them to blur the distinction between basic cases of emotion recognition and more sophisticated cases of belief ascription, and to categorize both as instances of standard mind-reading. Moreover, they explicitly take empathy to be a special kind of third-person mind-reading (de Vignemont and Jacob 2012: 310), which is more complex and less direct than standard mind-reading (de Vignemont 2010: 292; de Vignemont and Singer 2006: 439). After all, whereas empathy must meet five requirements, the simpler and presumably more widespread standard mind-reading only has to meet one requirement: that of attributing a mental state to another (de Vignemont and Jacob 2012: 307). Thus, and this is obviously quite significant, on their proposal, empathy is not what establishes an awareness of the other person's mental state in the first place. Rather, empathy requires a prior understanding of the other's mental life in order to get off the ground, and is then supposed to allow for an enhanced understanding of the other's feeling. Now, over the years, empathy has been defined in various ways, and if de Vignemont and Jacob want to reserve the term for a rather narrow class of phenomena, primarily exemplified by the case of empathic pain, they can of course choose to do so, but, as should be clear by now, such a use differs dramatically from the way the term was introduced and used by early empathy theorists. In fact, it is obvious that the account of empathy just outlined and the phenomenological account discussed earlier have little in common except the name. We are not dealing with two competing accounts of the same phenomenon, but with accounts of two quite distinct phenomena.

It is certainly not as if Scheler, Stein, Husserl, and Schutz are agreeing on everything, but there is still, I think, a sufficient amount of overlap between their respective theories to warrant talking about a distinct phenomenological account of empathy. The phenomenologists are united in their rejection of the claim that empathy involves a simulation-plus-projection routine. They all deny that empathy is a projective process that centrally involves either the imaginative adaptation of another person's point of view or at least some form of inner imitation (compare Goldman 2006: 40; Stueber 2006: 15, 28). If presented with Goldman's view, they would have argued that such an account conflates empathy with other kinds of interpersonal understanding, and ultimately, owing to a misbegotten Cartesian heritage, disregards the fact that we can and do experience other minds. More specifically, what we find in the phenomenological tradition is arguably a fourth option that isn't included in Battaly's listing. For the phenomenologists, empathy is certainly not a question of abstractly ascribing a certain mental state to another. Just as we ought to respect the difference between thinking about a lion, imagining a lion, and seeing a lion, we ought also to respect the difference between thinking about Adam's distress or embarrassment, imagining what it must be like for him to be distressed or embarrassed, and being empathically acquainted with his distress and embarrassment in the direct face-to-face encounter. In the latter case, our acquaintance with Adam's experiential life has a directness and immediacy to it that is not shared by whatever beliefs I might have about him in his absence. Moreover, this empathic acquaintance doesn't presuppose or entail sharing in any straightforward sense of the term. To empathically understand that your friend loves his wife is quite different from loving his wife yourself. It doesn't require you to share his love for his wife. Likewise, you might empathically grasp your colleague's joy when he receives notice of his promotion even though you are personally chagrined by this piece of news. The fact that you don't share his joy, the fact that you are feeling a very different emotion, doesn't make it any less a case of empathy, doesn't make your awareness of his joy merely inferential or imaginative in character. Furthermore, empathy is frequently one-sided; it certainly doesn't have to be reciprocal. But that is arguably a clear requirement for sharing proper (which is also why the notion of experiential sharing might be far more relevant in the context of a discussion of we-intentionality; see Chapter 15). To claim that I am (aware of) sharing one of your experiences, while denying that you are (aware of) sharing one of mine, doesn't seem to make very much sense.

None of the phenomenologists would accept the claim that one can only empathize with affective states; rather, they would take empathy to refer to our general ability to access the life of the mind of others in their expressions, expressive behaviour, and meaningful actions. On their account, it is possible to empathize with the cognitive, affective, and conative experiences of the other, that is, with his or her beliefs, perceptions, feelings, passions, volitions, desires, intentions, etc. Empathy is the experience of the embodied mind of the other, an experience which, rather than eliminating the difference between self-experience and other-experience, takes the asymmetry to be a necessary and persisting existential fact. Whereas the experience of empathizing is first-personally given, the empathized experience is not given first-personally to the empathizer. To insist that it is, is to miss what is distinctive about empathy, namely, the fact that it is a distinct form of other-directed intentionality, which allows the other's experiences to disclose themselves as other rather than as our own (Husserl 1959: 176). Consequently, one cannot empathize with unowned experiences. The empathized experiences are given as belonging to another; they are given as lived through first-personally by that other. To that extent, the phenomenological analysis of empathy is in perfect accord with that tradition's focus on and respect for the first-personal character of consciousness. In fact, there might be some affinity between the phenomenological account of empathy and what Robbins and Jack have called adopting the 'phenomenal stance', where this involves regarding the other as a locus of phenomenal experience (and not simply as a system of intentional states) and having some felt appreciation of the qualitative and hedonic character of the other's phenomenal states (Robbins and Jack 2006: 69–70). Furthermore, according to the phenomenological proposal, empathy takes different forms, it has different stages or levels, and amounts to a special kind of experiential understanding, one that, to use Husserlian terminology, provides intuitive fulfilment, confirmation, or satisfaction to more indirect or signitive ways of intending or judging about other people's mental lives. We might phrase this by saying that empathy provides a special kind of knowledge by acquaintance. It is not the standard first-person acquaintance, but rather a distinct other-acquaintance. Importantly, however, when saying that empathy can provide a special kind of understanding, this is not meant to suggest that empathy provides an especially profound or deep kind of understanding. In order to obtain that, theoretical inferences and imaginative simulations might very well be needed. No, the specificity of the access is due to the fact that it is basic and intuitive; that is, the empathized experience is given directly as existing here and now.

One implication (and limitation) of the phenomenological proposal is that by highlighting and emphasizing the intuitive character of empathy, it also restricts it to face-to-face-based forms of interpersonal encounter. Importantly, this doesn't mean that empathy is necessarily restricted to dyadic relationships. It might very well be possible to empathize with a group, say, a mourning family. However, on many other accounts, and this is also reflected in colloquial speech, it makes perfect sense to say that we can also empathize with individuals or groups of people not present, and even with fictional literary figures. For the phenomenologists such uses of the term must at the very least be considered derivative. Moreover, any claim to the effect that, say, people in Copenhagen felt empathy with those affected by the earthquake and tsunami in Tōhoku in 2011 might be problematic in that it blurs the distinction not only between empathy and sympathy, but also between empathy understood as a perception-based direct acquaintance with the minds of others and some kind of imaginative projection or theoretical inference. Thus, one obviously should also not overlook that the present proposal doesn't support or accord with the idea that empathy is per se morally significant and basically equivalent with compassion.

In the contemporary debate on empathy, one can encounter distinctions between mirror empathy, motor empathy, affective empathy, perceptually mediated empathy, re-enactive empathy, and cognitive empathy, to mention just a few of the options available. As should have become clear by now, one reason why it continues to be so difficult to reach a commonly accepted definition of empathy is because people have been using the notion to designate quite different phenomena. For the same reason, it is not obvious that it makes very much sense to try to determine once and for all what empathy really is. Although one might make the case that one ought to stick to the traditional use of the term (as already mentioned, it was introduced by Lipps as a general term for our understanding of others) instead of identifying it with, say, prosocial behaviour or a very special kind of imaginative perspective taking, it is not evident that such a strategy would be particularly productive or illuminating. Thus, rather than promoting the phenomenological account of empathy as the right account, I think a more reasonable verdict is that the phenomenological analyses of empathy contain various important insights that contemporary debates on social cognition and interpersonal understanding ought to incorporate. In fact, given the polysemic character of the notion of empathy (and also the fact that not all phenomenologists were equally happy about using the term), one might even wonder whether it would not be best simply to drop it and instead present the findings as contributions to the more general field of social cognition. Although one could certainly do so, here is one reason for resisting such a move. I think Lipps, Husserl, and many others got it right when they urged us to respect the irreducible difference between our knowledge of external objects, our self-knowledge, and our knowledge of others. Continuing to use and employ the notion of empathy (rather than the notion of, say, social perception) might help us to keep that point in mind.

11

Empathy and Social Cognition

Of late, a number of people have suggested that theory-theory and simulation theory share a number of crucial but questionable assumptions that ultimately impede a correct understanding of central forms of social interaction, including basic face-to-face engagement, and that we need to consider different alternatives altogether. Many of the philosophical arguments and objections being launched against the mainstream accounts have a phenomenological heritage (Thompson 2001; Gallagher 2005; Zahavi 2005; Gallagher 2007; Overgaard 2007; Ratcliffe 2007; Gallagher and Zahavi 2008; Zahavi 2008; Fuchs and De Jaegher 2009). Though these critical perspectives differ in their details, a persistent claim is that the extensive investigations of intersubjectivity found in thinkers such as Husserl, Heidegger, Merleau-Ponty, Stein, and Scheler contain highly perspicacious insights concerning the nature of social cognition that directly challenge core assumptions of both theory-theory and simulation theory. Within the last few years, this claim has been met with various objections by authors such as Currie (2008), Herschbach (2008), Spaulding (2010), Jacob (2011), and Lavelle (2012). When taking a bird's-eye perspective on the debate, however, it is difficult to avoid the impression that the parties involved are to some extent talking at cross-purposes. Part of the disagreement is clearly based on the fact that people are using and understanding the terms involved differently. Moreover, it is also far from clear that the different theories are all addressing the same explanandum. In what follows, my aim will not be to engage in a more general discussion of the nature of social cognition that assesses the merits and demerits of the different accounts; rather, I shall focus on some of the recent discussions of, and objections to, a phenomenological account of empathy. In this way, I hope to clarify further what precisely the phenomenological proposal entails.

11.1 Mirror neurons and embodied simulation

As I mentioned in Chapter 8, in recent years there has been a growing emphasis on the fact that a theory of social cognition should be able to cover the whole range of mental states, including sensations and emotions, and not simply address the issue of belief ascription (Goldman 2006: 20). This has made some simulationists argue that we need to distinguish two kinds of empathy. Thus, as previously mentioned, Stueber distinguishes *re-enactive empathy*, which he defines as involving the use of our cognitive and deliberative capacities to re-enact or imitate the thought processes of others, from a more *basic empathy*, which he defines as a mechanism of inner imitation that underlies our theoretically unmediated quasi-perceptual ability to recognize other creatures directly as minded creatures (Stueber 2006: 20–1). A related division can also be found if we turn to social neuroscience, where the discovery of so-called *mirror neurons* has been interpreted as lending support to the existence of a low-level form of empathy (Gallese et al. 2004; Goldman 2006). Let us take a look at these empirical findings.

In order to survive and prosper in a complex society, we need to be able to recognize, understand, and respond to others. But how do we accomplish that? According to one model, mental states attributed to other people are conceived of as unobservable, theoretical posits invoked to explain and predict behaviour in the same fashion that physicists appeal to electrons and quarks to predict and explain observable phenomena. According to Gallese, however, recent findings in neurobiol-ogy suggest that our capacity to understand others as intentional agents might draw on more primitive sources than various linguistic and mentalistic abilities, namely, those involving mirror neurons (Gallese and Goldman 1998; Gallese 2001: 34; 2009: 522). It has consequently been proposed that social understanding, rather than relying on abstract thinking and propositional rules, is facilitated by and ultimately rooted in the 'machinery of motor control' (Keysers 2011: 17).

At the beginning of the 1990s Rizzolatti, Gallese, and Fogassi discovered that a group of neurons in the premotor cortex of the macaque monkey fired not only when the monkey performed a certain action, say, grasping an object with the hand, but also when it observed other individuals, be it other monkeys or humans, performing the same goal-directed action (Gallese 2001: 35). Subsequent research has shown that the mirror neurons fire regardless of whether the relevant activities are seen or heard. They even fire if the motor activity required for achieving the goal involves non-standard sequences of movements, thereby establishing that the activity of the mirror neurons is not simply a response to specific movements. The existence of mirror neurons has since been confirmed by fMRI (functional magnetic resonance imaging) and TMS (transcranial magnetic stimulation) studies and by single-cell recordings. There is now also good evidence for the existence of mirror neuron systems in human brains (Rizzolatti and Craighero 2004).

Given these findings, Gallese and his colleagues proposed that action observation, and in particular action understanding, implies action simulation (Gallese 2001: 37). When we observe an action, our motor system becomes active as if we were executing the very same action that we are observing, that is, we simulate the action. And our ability to understand observed behaviour as intentional, as mind-driven, is precisely dependent upon this link between observer and observed. In order to understand the action, the presence of the visual information is insufficient. Rather, the motor schema of the observer has to be involved. That is, the observer must rely on his or her own internal motor knowledge (provided by the mirror neurons) in order to translate the observed movement, 'in principle, devoid of meaning for the observer— into something that the observer is able to understand' (Gallese 2009: 520-1). I understand the action of the other because it is an action I could perform myself. If, by contrast, the observed behaviour of the other cannot be matched onto the observer's own motor repertoire, the goal cannot be detected and understood (Gallese 2001: 36).

Gallese isn't merely arguing that action understanding relies on mirror-resonance mechanisms. He ultimately claims that interpersonal relations of all kinds, including action understanding, the attribution of intentions, and the recognition of emotions and sensations, rely on automatic and unconscious embodied simulation routines (Gallese 2003a: 517). The very same neural substrate that is endogenously activated when we execute actions or subjectively experience emotions and sensations is exogenously activated when we observe somebody else act or experience emotions and sensations. Our recognition of emotions and sensations in others consequently activates the same brain regions that we would use ourselves when experiencing those very states. Observing another person in pain activates many of the same regions involved in the subjective experience of pain, including the rostral anterior cingulate cortex and cerebellum (Singer et al. 2004). Observing others experience disgust activates regions involved in the subjective feeling of disgust, such as the insula (Wicker et al. 2003). And observing others experience fear activates regions such as the amygdala (Whalen et al. 2001), a region also involved in the subjective experience of fear. So when we encounter somebody and observe their actions or their displayed emotions or sensations, we don't just see them. In addition to the sensory information we receive from the other, internal representations of the body states associated with the other's actions, emotions, and sensations are evoked in us, and it is as if we were doing a similar action or experiencing a similar emotion or sensation. One might consequently speak of a kind of neural simulation, since the subject's brain replicates the brain activity of the target, thereby building a kind of bridge between the two. Rather than locating the mirror neurons exclusively in the premotor cortex, and rather than defining them as premotor neurons that merely respond to observation and execution of the same action, these recent findings have made it customary to adopt a broader definition and to speak of a 'mirror neuron system', or of far more widespread and dispersed 'shared circuits' or 'neuronal reson- ance mechanisms', that allow us to share vicariously the actions and emotions of others. The mirroring takes place spontaneously and doesn't require any kind of effortful perspective taking. It is automatic, non-predicative, and non-inferential, which is why Gallese argues that it allows for a direct experiential understanding of others, one that doesn't rely on cognitive operations or conceptual reasoning (Gallese et al. 2004: 396).

As already mentioned, Gallese has been interested in the early discussions of empathy, and he refers favourably not only to Lipps's discussion of inner imitation (Gallese 2003a: 519), but also to Stein's account, and to Husserl's and Merleau- Ponty's understanding of intersubjectivity (Gallese 2001: 43–4). Indeed, Gallese is quite explicit in arguing that his own notion of embodied simulation is akin to, and a further development of, the phenomenological proposal (Gallese et al. 2004: 397; see also Iacoboni 2009). More specifically, Gallese makes use of Merleau-Ponty's notion of *intercorporeity*, which he takes to refer to the mutual resonance of intentionally meaningful sensorimotor behaviours (Gallese 2009: 523). However, he also refers to Husserl's discussion of empathy in *Ideen II* and *Cartesianische Meditationen*, and employs Husserl's notion of coupling, seeing it as exemplifying the idea that 'the self–other identity at the level of the body enables an intersubjective transfer of meaning to occur' (Gallese 2003b: 175; compare Gallese 2005: 39; 2008: 774; Iacoboni 2009: 265).

Like Gallese, Iacoboni has argued that mirror neuron activity links self and other in a way that questions traditional Cartesian as well as more recent cognitivist assumptions about how social understanding comes about. We do not have to draw complex inferences or run complicated algorithms in order to understand others; rather, the work is already accomplished by the mirror neurons (Iacoboni 2009: 7). Understanding others is consequently far easier than has frequently been thought. Without resorting to magic tricks of any kind, our brains are capable of accessing other minds by means of the simple physiological properties of the mirror neurons, that is, by using neural mechanisms of mirroring and simulation (Iacoboni 2009: 264). But as Iacoboni also points out, the functioning of mirror neurons only makes sense if we are dealing with agents who interact with other people in a shared environment, where the classical dichotomies (such as action–perception, subject–world, or inner–outer) have dissolved. This view, according to Iacoboni, is reminiscent of themes found in existential phenomenology, which is why he has labelled his own project 'existential neuroscience' or 'neurophysiologic phenomenology' (Iacoboni 2007: 319; 2009: 17). Indeed, for Iacoboni, not only has the discovery of mirror neurons for the first time in history provided a plausible neurophysiological explanation for complex forms of social cognition and interaction (Iacoboni 2009: 5); mirror neurons also seem to explain why, as he puts it, 'existential phenomenologists were correct all along' (Iacoboni 2009: 262).[1]

To sum up, according to embodied simulation, social cognition typically involves an attempt to replicate, imitate, or simulate the mental life of the other. But in contrast to the standard account of simulation theory as it has been developed by Goldman, embodied simulationists primarily want to characterize simulation as automatic, unconscious, prelinguistic, and non-meta-representational. On their view, intercorporeity is more fundamental than any explicit attribution of propositional

---

[1] One significant claim that shouldn't be overlooked is that mirror neurons on Iacoboni's account are not ready-made from the start; rather, they are shaped, formed, and changed by the interaction between self and other (Iacoboni 2009: 134). This might seem puzzling, if mirror neurons are what are supposed to allow for a meaningful interaction between self and other in the first place, but Iacoboni also claims that some mirror neurons are already present at birth (Iacoboni 2009: 155). So presumably, these innate mirror neurons constitute the basis for the subsequent development.

attitudes to others, and remains the main source of knowledge we directly gather about others (Gallese 2009: 524).

How should we assess such claims? Is the notion of embodied simulation in line with the phenomenological accounts of empathy? Can the former be said to constitute a further development and perhaps even a scientific vindication of the latter? This has in fact been the conclusion reached by a number of authors:

- Though warning against any facile empirical confirmation of phenomenology, Jean-Luc Petit, in an early article from 1999, claims that the discovery of mirror neurons amply justifies Husserl's view 'that our empathic experience of the other is an internal imitation of the movement accomplished by the other' (Petit 1999: 241).
- In a paper published in 2001 Evan Thompson suggests that 'the mirror neuron findings support Husserl's position that our empathic experience of another depends on one's "coupling" or "pairing" with the other' (Thompson 2001: 9), rather than on various inferential processes.
- In an article from 2006, Dieter Lohmar argues that 'the neurological discovery of mirror neurons is of eminent importance for the phenomenological theory of intersubjectivity' (Lohmar 2006: 5).
- Finally, to just mention one further example, in a paper from 2008, Helena De Preester writes that it is easy to translate the core of the mirror neuron hypothesis into Husserlian terminology: 'the visual perception of the body of the other is mapped onto our own kinaesthetic representation, or the *Körper* is mapped onto the *Leib* (and receives the latter's status). Thanks to this identification, an understanding of the other arises' (De Preester 2008: 139).

I would be more cautious. The fact that Gallese and Iacoboni refer rather indiscriminately to Lipps and the phenomenologists should make us pause. Lipps does indeed talk frequently of empathy in terms of an inner imitation, but as should be clear by now, his account was one from which all the phenomenologists to varying degrees distanced themselves. Ultimately, however, the question of whether embodied simulation is in line with the phenomenological proposal is too complex a question to allow a simple yes or no answer.

On the one hand, there do indeed seem to be some striking similarities. For Husserl, the most basic form of empathy is one involving the coupling of self and other. The coupling in question takes place between acting and expressive bodies, it draws on a capacity for cross-modal matching, and it is passive in the sense of not being initiated voluntarily or coming about as a result of deliberation or reflection. As Thompson correctly points out, this 'phenomenological conception of the bodily basis of empathy can be linked to mind science by referring to the growing body of psychological and neurophysiological evidence for coupling mechanisms linking self and other at sensorimotor and affective levels' (Thompson 2007: 393). In fact, both Husserl and Stein write that when I perceive the movements of the other body, it is as if I were over there, as if I were moving my limbs (Husserl 1973c: 642; 1952: 164; Stein 2008: 65). My own kinaesthetic system is affected by my perception of the other's moving body and by my anticipation of the other's future movements (Husserl 1973b: 527; 1973c: 642). But as Husserl is also careful to add, this doesn't entail that I project what I experience in myself into the other (Husserl 1973a: 311). Likewise, Stein stresses that although, through a process of motor empathy, I might come to feel the movements and sensations of the other, these sensations and movements are given as belonging to the other, and are precisely brought into relief as such in contrast with my own sensations (Stein 2008: 65).

Similarities can also be found if we briefly move on to Merleau-Ponty, who insists that we must rehabilitate the experience of others that has been distorted by intellectualist analyses (Merleau-Ponty 2012: 191). Although Merleau-Ponty would claim that in perceiving an angry gesture, we are perceiving the anger itself and not merely psychologically meaningless behaviour, he denies that the meaning of the gesture is perceived in the same way as the colour of the carpet. The other's gestures point to an intentional object, and I understand the meaning of those gestures, not by looking behind them, but by attending to the part of the world that they highlight (Merleau-Ponty 2012: 191–2). In order to understand the expressive behaviour, the behaviour must be possible for the observer, or as Merleau-Ponty puts it, the 'understanding of gestures is achieved through the reciprocity between my intentions and the other person's gestures, and between my gestures and the intentions which can be read in the other person's behaviour. Everything happens as if the other person's intention inhabited my body, or as if my intentions inhabited his body' (Merleau-Ponty 2012: 190–1). I experience my own body as a capacity to act in the world, and I perceive the other's body as a familiar way of dealing with the same world. Ultimately, Merleau-Ponty, like Husserl, would argue that a proper account of embodiment is crucial if we are to make it comprehensible how we can come to understand others, and that the problem of other minds ceases to be so much of a problem the moment we understand consciousness as both embodied, and embedded in the world (Merleau-Ponty 1964b: 175; 2012: 366–7).

On the other hand, however, one shouldn't overlook what might ultimately amount to some important differences between the phenomenological account of empathy and the theory of embodied simulation.

First, as we have seen, Husserl is very explicit about the need for distinguishing various levels of empathy (and interpersonal understanding). And although he would claim that the first level is constituted by a passive and involuntary associative bonding of self and other on the basis of their bodily similarity, he would never agree with the claim that this amounts to the full range of interpersonal understanding. If we turn to the defenders of embodied simulation, we will, however, find slightly conflicting views regarding its explanatory scope. How much can mirror-resonance mechanisms explain? Will they, as Ramachandran predicts, do for psychology what the discovery of DNA did for biology (Ramachandran 2000)? Can they more or less explain every aspect of social cognition, from an understanding of the movements and actions of others to an understanding of their emotions, sensations, and intentions, or do they merely target the foundations of interpersonal understanding?

It is informative here to consider a criticism that Emma Borg and Pierre Jacob have directed against what they take to be the inflated claim made by some proponents of embodied simulation. Borg (2007) and Jacob (2008) both argue that although mirror neurons might help us to decode another agent's motor intentions, they cannot help us to determine his or her prior intentions. Although they might help us to understand that the perceived movement is a goal-directed act of, say, grasping, they can't tell us why it happened.[2] In response to this kind of criticism, Gallese has defended a deflationary take on what it means to determine the intention of others, and argued that determining why a given act is executed can be equivalent to detecting the goal of the still-not-executed but impending subsequent act (Gallese 2007a: 661–2). But even if one accepts this, and a fortiori the claim that mirror neurons are involved in the detection of intentions, there is obviously much more that needs to be in place before we can be said to understand fully the actions of others, that is, what others are up to, why others are doing what they are doing, and what that means to them. Furthermore, even if it were true that my understanding of another's actions or emotional expressions are subserved by a perception–action matching system, there are obviously many instances in which I speculate about the mental states of another in that person's absence. I might try to anticipate the mood of my lover before proposing to her, or speculate about how others assessed my performance long after they have left the lecture hall, or consider which birthday present might be most heartening to an ill colleague, or realize upon reflection that in my previous conversation with my diving instructor I misunderstood his intentions, etc. In such cases, where there are no perceptual cues available, where there is no access to the facial expressions, vocal tone, movements, and posture of the other, it is doubtful whether the mirror neurons can be of much help. The plausibility of the mirror neuron hypothesis consequently increases in reverse proportion to its alleged explanatory scope. It might not only be wiser to opt for a more modest claim—and in fact, in some places Gallese explicitly concedes that an emphasis on the importance of embodied simulation in no way rules out that more sophisticated cognitive mentalizing skills might also be needed, and that the two are not mutually exclusive (Gallese 2007b: 10)—but doing so might also increase the compatibility between this proposal and the phenomenological account.

---

[2] Recent work by Cristina Becchio has incidentally challenged this claim. According to Becchio, different intentions affect the kinematic patterns of the movement; for example, the specific way one reaches for and grasps an apple depends on what one subsequently intends to do with it (say, eat it, throw it at someone, or hand it to someone). Furthermore, observers are sensitive to such differences in the visual kinematics and are able to anticipate the agent's subsequent actions simply on the basis of these differences (Becchio et al. 2012).

Secondly, Gallese is quite explicit in arguing that the mirror neuron system allows for a direct experiential understanding of others (Gallese 2007b: 9). At the same time, however, he explicitly and repeatedly aligns himself with simulation theory and, like Lipps, considers empathy a form of inner imitation (Gallese 2003a: 519). But isn't there a tension here? Isn't the reliance on and reference to inner imitation precisely premissed on the assumption that we are not experientially acquainted with the psychological life of others? Wasn't it precisely because he took other people's mental states to be unobservable and inherently invisible that Lipps insisted that we must rely on internal simulations in order to make the leap from the perceptual input, which is psychologically meaningless, to the output, which is the ascription of mental states to the other? In short, wasn't the assumption precisely that we need internal simulation in order to supplement the input with information coming from ourselves in order to generate the required output? This also seems to be Gallese's view, for, as he writes, the observer must rely on his or her own internal motor knowledge (provided by the mirror neurons) in order to translate the observed movement— 'in principle, devoid of meaning for the observer—into something that the observer is able to understand' (Gallese 2009: 520–1). One finds similar claims in other mirror neuron theorists as well. Keysers, for instance, has argued that what we see acquires meaning by being linked to our own actions: 'Once I link the sight of someone grasping a piece of chocolate and bringing it to his mouth with my own ability to do so, what I see stops being an abstract impression, devoid of meaning' (Keysers 2011: 10). One wonders why it is necessary to make such a strong claim. There is an important difference between saying that the actions of others remain meaningless for me unless I can draw on my own motor repertoire to interpret them and saying that a detection of similarity and like-me familiarity facilitates the understanding by making it faster and less effortful. Likewise, there is a significant difference between arguing that the psychological meaning of a gesture or facial expression cannot simply be picked up by any visual system and that more is needed than simple perceptual acuity and arguing that the seen receives its psychological meaning from the spectator through a process of projection. Interestingly, whereas Merleau-Ponty in *Phénoménologie de la perception* seems to have emphasized mainly the direction from self to other, he highlights the reverse direction in the text *Les Relations avec autrui chez l'enfant* and speaks of how, through the other's conduct, I discover themes of possible activity for my own body (Merleau-Ponty 1964a: 117). Thus, although at times it might sound as if Merleau-Ponty is emphasizing the importance of mirroring and matching, in other places he is clearly highlighting the significance of complementarity. This is the case, for instance, when he refers to the internal relation that obtains between my own body and that of the other, and claims that the other appears as the completion of the system and that 'the other's body and my own are a single whole, two sides of a single phenomenon' (Merleau-Ponty 2012: 370). Thus, to speak, as Merleau-Ponty does, of self and other as 'collaborators in perfect reciprocity' (2012: 370) suggests an approach to social cognition where the encounter with the other's actions, rather than simply occasioning a mere replication or simulation of those actions, elicits a dynamic response that takes those actions as affordances for further complementary actions (see Gallagher and Miyahara 2012). In order to capture what Merleau-Ponty has in mind, it might consequently be better to liken social understanding to dancing than to mirroring. In any case, in so far as the embodied simulation approach wishes to emphasize its link to the classical phenomenological account of empathy, it ought to distance itself more clearly from the Lippsian model of projective empathy.

Thirdly, and in direct continuation of this, what we find in Husserl is a recurrent emphasis on and respect for the otherness and alterity of the other.[3] This is also part of the reason why Husserl distances himself from the idea that the best way to conceive of the relation between self and other is in terms of mirroring. As we have also seen, however, another reason is that he takes mirroring to be too static a concept. It doesn't capture the dynamic and dialectical intertwinement between self and other. Husserl's view on this seems in obvious tension with the persistent emphasis by mirror neuron theorists on the importance of mirroring, though it should be noted that Gallese in a recent publication has admitted that the mirror metaphor itself might be misleading, since it suggests the presence of an exact match between object and observer, thereby disregarding individual differences (Gallese 2009: 531). Nevertheless, in so far as the mirror neuron theorists frequently highlight the centrality of imitation and sharing, and also argue that mirror neurons are critical for the 'simple forms of empathic resonance that are observed in emotional contagion' (Iacoboni 2011: 46), one might wonder whether there is sufficient focus on the other-centred character of empathy. Such a focus certainly seems absent in the account provided by Keysers, who argues that the mirroring of mirror neurons makes 'others become part of us' (Keysers 2011: 6), that the classical divide between self and other 'becomes fuzzy and permeable in this process' (Keysers 2011: 16), and that the mirror system, by projecting the observer's own experience into the things he observes, 'certainly doesn't help us realize that other organisms might be different from us' (Keysers 2011: 55). Gallese, by contrast, explicitly concedes that imitation and self–other identity do not really do the trick of accounting for interpersonal understanding, since, in contrast to what is required in the case of emotional contagion, there has to be difference as well; that is, the other must preserve his or her character of otherness (Gallese 2007b: 11; 2009: 527).

Fourthly, and most importantly, any comparison of the phenomenological account of empathy with the attempt to explain empathy in terms of mirror-resonance mechanisms shouldn't forget that we are dealing with accounts targeting a personal and a sub-personal level respectively (although mirror neuron theorists occasionally ignore this distinction and characterize embodied simulation as both

---

[3] For more on this topic, see Derrida (1967); Waldenfels (1989); Zahavi (1999).

unconscious and automatic as well as pre-reflective and experience-based; Gallese 2003a: 521; 2007b: 10), and as long as one is not so naive as to believe in straightforward isomorphism, it is not at all obvious that such accounts can be compared in any direct fashion. For the same reason, it might be best to avoid the claim that the discovery of the mirror neurons has confirmed the phenomenological account or that the latter supports the mirror neuron hypothesis. A more prudent and more cautious claim would be that work on mirror neurons, as well as other neuroscientific findings, can complement the phenomenological description by clarifying some of the mechanisms that might underlie empathic coupling and show how the latter 'need not be something mysterious or even impossible' (Ratcliffe 2006: 336).

A final observation: Even if one went further than I have done and ultimately concluded that there are remarkable similarities between the phenomenological proposal and the mirror-resonance hypothesis, this would still leave various questions unanswered. Would the presence of such similarities, for instance, demonstrate that Husserl's phenomenological account—contrary to the claim made by some of his defenders—is really a version of simulation theory, or would the right conclusion to draw be the opposite, namely, to deny that Gallese's notion of embodied simulation is really a form of simulationism at all? In an article dating from 1997, Stich and Nichols wrote that the term 'simulation' ought to be retired since 'the diversity among the theories, processes and mechanisms to which advocates of simulation theory have attached the label "simulation" is so great that the term itself has become quite useless' (Stich and Nichols 1997: 299). Since then that verdict has only gained in plausibility. When considering the varieties of simulation theory currently on offer, and this includes proposals by figures like Gallese, Iacoboni, Goldman, Tomasello, Heal, Mitchell, and Gordon, it is difficult to detect a really unified research programme. In fact, at times the main commonality seems to be a shared rejection of the claim that what lies at the root of our mentalizing abilities is a sort of theory. To put it differently, one reason why simulation theory is something of an umbrella term, a label for a variety of rather different positions, is presumably that many initially accepted the claim that the theory-theory and the simulation theory constituted the only two options. So if you weren't a theory-theorist, you had to align yourself with simulation theory. The moment this forced choice is rejected as a false choice, the moment it is realized that other alternatives might be viable, it might be necessary to reconsider some of the original divisions, and even reclassify some of the positions initially labelled as simulationist, including embodied simulationism.[4]

As this last comment ought to remind us, our theoretical models and the way we conceive of, say, intersubjectivity obviously influence our interpretation of the empirical findings. This is something we should not forget when discussing the relation between empathy and mirror neurons, and between phenomenology

---

[4] This might already be happening. In a paper from 2012, Lavelle classifies Gallese as an advocate of the direct perception approach to social cognition (Lavelle 2012: 214).

and neuroscience, and when we assess the question that has been lurking in the background, namely, the feasibility and desirability of a naturalized phenomenology (Gallagher 1997; Zahavi 2004b, 2010b; Ratcliffe 2006; Gallagher and Zahavi 2008).

11.2 The role of context

The suggestion that empathy provides us with some kind of 'direct experiential understanding' of others has been met with the objection that empathy is influenced by contextual factors, and that it is susceptible to top-down modulation, and can be moderated and influenced by prior knowledge and experience. Given all of this, it must count as an indirect process (de Vignemont and Singer 2006: 437). To illustrate, just take something as apparently simple as face-based emotion recognition. We shouldn't forget that emotions are intentional. They are about something, and in order to understand them, it is not enough simply to pay attention to their expressions; we also need to look at the context in order to determine what they are about. Moreover, outside psychology labs we very rarely encounter expressions in isolation. When we encounter others, we encounter them in a shared world, and our understanding of each other takes place in a specific context and situation. It is precisely within such common, and mainly pragmatic, situations that expressive phenomena occur (Gurwitsch 1979: 114; Sartre 2003: 371). When working or conversing with my partner, he might shake his head or wrinkle his brow. But these facial expressions and bodily gestures are not unambiguous. They do not reveal psychological states simply or uniformly. The 'same' expression can take on different meanings in different situations. One might, for instance, blush in anger, in shame, or from exertion. However, this rarely poses a problem, since we do not encounter expressions in isolation (Gurwitsch 1979: 35–6, 95, 106; Barrett et al. 2011). Expressions occur in a given context, and our understanding of the context, of what comes before and after, helps us to understand whether a blush means shame or anger, or is the result of physical exertion. But if this is so, if we really need to consider contextual cues in order to discriminate different emotional expressions, we ought to reconsider the claim that empathic understanding is a form of direct and theoretically unmediated acquaintance (Jacob 2011: 538).

But is it really impossible for something to be given directly and contextually at the same time? Arguably it all depends on what we mean by 'direct'. Consider the case of vision. Vision usually counts as the paradigm of direct experience. I can read about Angel Falls in the Canaima National Park in Venezuela, I can inspect a photograph of it, and I can see and experience it in its splendour. On most accounts, the latter acquaintance is of a more direct kind than the two former. But—and this is an old insight found, for instance, in the work of many gestalt psychologists—whenever we perceive an object, we perceive it in a perceptual field. We are conscious of it in a particular setting, and the way it is given to us is influenced by contextual cues, by what is co-given with it. But does that contradict the claim that the perceptual object is directly given, or might it be possible for something to be given directly and contextually at the same time? Consider another case. You are sitting enjoying a glass of 1982 Château Margaux. Owing to your acquired and honed skills as a wine connoisseur, you are able to detect and discern flavours and aromas imperceptible to a novice. Does that make your access to the wine in question indirect? Consider, finally, the case of a utensil, say, a trocar. To see something as a trocar, a lot of background knowledge is required. A whole network of equipmental contexture, to use a Heideggerian phrasing, must be in place. But does this turn the trocar into an inherently unobservable and theoretically postulated construct? Does it entail that you literally cannot be said to perceive a trocar? Does it make your access to it indirect in the same way as our positing of, say, black holes or subatomic particles? Or should we rather say that our possession of the relevant background knowledge is what allows us to *see* the trocar the way we do?[5]

Perhaps one could admit that context is involved in even the most basic aspects of object perception and concede that this doesn't jeopardize the direct character of perceptual intentionality, while still objecting that since somebody can have perfect vision and still not see the trocar as a trocar, this proves that whatever it is that allows others actually to understand the trocar as a trocar must be something over and above perceptual acuity. Or what about the case of prosopagnosia? Surely that is a neurological rather than an ophthalmological defect. I cannot engage here with the complex discussion found in the field of philosophy of perception, but let me suggest that we should avoid an overly restrictive reading of perception, one that basically equates perception with the passive intake of sensory information. Given such a reading, it is questionable whether we could ever be said to perceive unified objects at all, let alone temporally extended objects (see Chapter 10.3.2).

In any case, when making the claim that there is a fundamental form of social cognition that is direct, few, if any, phenomenologists would deny that the social understanding in question is influenced and enriched by background knowledge, contextual cues, and past experiences. Critics might argue that this just proves that social cognition is indirect, and that any insistence on its direct character simply involves a misuse of the term 'direct'. In reply, let me first point out that if this were correct, it would entail that the dispute is largely terminological. And it should be obvious that one cannot simply reject the phenomenological proposal by making the case that our ordinary understanding of others is contextual, since this is not being disputed. Secondly, however, I think one should acknowledge that there simply isn't any established view on what 'direct' means. Rather than seeing 'direct' and 'contextual' as the relevant contrast, I find it far more relevant to focus instead on the difference between 'direct' and 'indirect', or 'mediated'. An example of an indirect act

---

[5] For the uninitiated, a trocar is a surgical instrument with a sharply pointed and often three-sided end that is used within a cannula, and designed to be inserted into a vein, an artery, bone marrow, or a body cavity.

would be the case in which one is aware of the Matterhorn in virtue of perceiving a photograph of it. By contrast, in some (not all, but some) cases, my apprehension of the other's psychological state can be said to be direct in the sense that that state is my primary intentional object. There is, so to speak, nothing that gets in the way, and it is not as if, first, I am directed at an intermediary, something different from the state, and only then, in a secondary step, I target it. Moreover, and importantly, the state is experienced as actually present to me, thereby making the experience in question very different from, say, reasoning that the other is upset because the letter she received has been torn up, or inferring that the other is drunk because he is surrounded by a dozen empty beer bottles, or concluding that the other must be furious because I would be furious if I had been subjected to the same treatment as he. I take all these cases to constitute indirect forms of social cognition, and to insist that my recognition of, say, the other's joy or fear in her facial expression is also indirect simply blurs important distinctions.

One recurrent objection to the claim that we can be directly acquainted with others' mental states is that such a claim is simply absurd, since it overlooks the fact that we do not have the same kind of access to the minds of others that we have to our own (de Vignemont 2010: 284). To phrase it differently, any convincing account of our understanding of others must respect the asymmetry between self-experience and other-experience. It must respect the fact that, whereas I am first-personally acquainted with my own experiential life, I do not have first-personal access to the minds of others. The problem though, as already pointed out in Chapter 10.3.2, is that this objection construes direct access to another's mental state on the model of direct access to one's own mental state, as if the latter constitutes the gold standard of what directness amounts to. But it only makes sense to speak of indirect knowledge where this can be contrasted with a more direct form of knowledge, and arguably there is no more direct way of knowing that another is in pain than seeing him writhe in pain. By contrast, noticing a bottle of painkillers next to his bedside together with an empty glass of water and concluding that he has been in pain is an example of knowing indirectly or by way of inference (Bennett and Hacker 2003: 89, 93).

One reason why the problem of other minds seems so persistent is that we have conflicting intuitions about the accessibility of the mental life of others. On the one hand, there is something right about the claim that the feelings and thoughts of others are manifest in their expressions and actions. In many situations, we do have a direct, pragmatic understanding of the minds of others. We empathically grasp the anger, joy, nervousness, or resoluteness of the other; we do not have to infer their existence. On the other hand, there also seems to be something right in the Cartesian idea that the mental life of another is, in some respect, inaccessible. There are situations in which we have no reason to doubt that the other is distracted, upset, or just plain bored. There are other situations in which we have no clue to their precise state of mind. It seems wrong to claim that the mental life of others is essentially inaccessible, but it also seems wrong to claim that everything is open to view. As Søren Overgaard puts it, the challenge is to reconcile the two intuitions, rather than letting one of them go (Overgaard 2005). As I see it, it is exactly this challenge that the phenomenologists are trying to meet.

When I claim that I am able to *experience* others, and as a consequence do not exclusively have to rely on and employ inferences, imitations, or projections, this is not meant to entail that I can experience the other in precisely the same way as she herself does. Third-person acquaintance with psychological states does differ from first-person acquaintance. But we shouldn't make the mistake of restricting and equating experiential acquaintance with first-person acquaintance. It is possible to experience minds in more than one way. As Wittgenstein once put it, 'My thoughts are not hidden from [the other], but are just open to him in a different *way* than they are to me' (Wittgenstein 1992: 34–5). Nor should we make the mistake of confusing different kinds of access with different degrees of certainty. As Wittgenstein also pointed out, even if I had no uncertainty with regard to the mental state of another (say, in the case where I observe the victim of a car accident writhe in pain), that would not make it *my* state (Wittgenstein 1982: §963). Furthermore, we should recognize that each type of acquaintance has its own strengths and weaknesses, and that second- and third-person acquaintance only 'falls short' of first-person acquaintance if it is assumed that the latter is privileged and that it is the internal aspiration of the former to approximate the latter as closely as possible (Moran 2001: 157). The fact that my experiential access to and acquaintance with the minds of others differs from my first-person acquaintance with my own mind is precisely not an imperfection or shortcoming. On the contrary, it is a difference that is constitutional. It is precisely because of this difference, precisely because of this asymmetry, that we can claim that the minds we experience are *other* minds. Indeed, a more precise way of capturing what is at stake is by saying that we experience bodily and behavioural expressions as expressive of an experiential life that transcends the expressions. There is, so to speak, necessarily more to the mind of the other than what we are grasping, but this doesn't make our understanding non-experiential.

Some might consider this a mere terminological fix to a serious philosophical challenge. By simply stipulating that we ought to operate with a deflated notion of direct access in the domain of social cognition, one that entitles us to say that we are directly acquainted with another's psychological state whenever we intuit it in the other's intentional and expressive behaviour, phenomenologists mistakenly think they can solve the problem of other minds. I don't think this objection is justified, but my main concern for now is merely to emphasize that the phenomenological claim concerning the possibility of a direct experiential acquaintance with another's psychological state is not in tension with the important point that we do not have access to other people's states 'as if they were our own'. We must, of course, respect the difference between self-ascription and other-ascription, between a first-person perspective and a third-person perspective, but we should avoid doing so in a manner that gives rise to the mistaken view that only my own experiences are given to me and that the behaviour of the other shields his experiences from me and makes their very existence hypothetical (Avramides 2001: 187).

When I empathically grasp the trepidation in the other's voice, or the concentration and effort in her actions, I am *experiencing* another subjectivity, and not merely imagining it, simulating it, or theorizing about it. That we can have an actual experience of the psychological life of others, and do not have to make do with mere inferences or imaginative projections, is, however, not to say that everything is open to view. As Husserl points out, the perception of others is always partial and is always open to correction (Husserl 1973a: 225). In fact, there will always be an indeterminate horizon of not expressed interiority (Husserl 2005: 70), and a complete knowledge of the other will for ever remain impossible.[6] Experiential directness doesn't entail infallibility or exhaustiveness. Another person's mind is never exposed in such a way that we immediately, effortlessly, and infallibly have complete access to its innermost thoughts and feelings. But, of course, that is not what is being claimed. Furthermore, our direct acquaintance with other minds might be quite limited. I might directly intuit that my partner is in a bad mood, but still be unsure whether she is tired, uneasy, or depressed. Indeed, I may completely fail to discover the precise nature of the emotion, though I might notice that 'something is wrong' and be motivated to explore it further. Sometimes, indeed, our direct acquaintance with others might be limited to the bare recognition of their existence. We immediately perceive the presence of mind, but fail to discern anything further with regard to it (Duddington 1918: 168). Deception is obviously also a possibility. The other's expressions can deceive us, but this possibility certainly doesn't warrant the claim that we are precluded from seeing, say, pleasure in the other's face when in fact the facial display is sincere (Green 2007: 126).

It might at this point be helpful to consider a threefold distinction that can be unearthed from several of the phenomenological analyses. On the one hand, we should distinguish our ability to grasp empathically the mindedness of the other, that is, our coming to experience that another has a mind in the first place, from our ability to determine another's specific state of mind. On the other hand, we should distinguish our ability to determine the current experiential episode of another from our ability to reason about that person's past and future mental states and behaviours. Let me label these different achievements the grasping of the *that*, the *what*, and the *why*. Consider, to start with, that in daily life we often wonder whether others like us or not, find us trustworthy or not, or attractive or not. We wonder whether others are being truthful or deceptive, and whether others are motivated by greed or generosity. We very rarely wonder whether others are minded in the first place.

---

[6] Such knowledge would, for one, require me to possess full insight into the other's individual historicity, and this is something I can only ever disclose in part; just as, for that matter, I can only disclose part of my own, which is why my own self-knowledge will also always remain partial (Husserl 1973c: 631–2).

In fact, this is something that is not only taken for granted when starting to enquire into the meaning of another's action; it is also something the certitude of which is of a quite different magnitude from whatever certitude we might have regarding the ascription of specific mental states to others. Even if there is much about the other that is not readily accessible, although we might be uncertain about the specific beliefs and intentions of others, this uncertainty does *not* make us question their very mindedness. As Gurwitsch wrote at one point, in ordinary life we are never faced with the choice of whether or not we wish to take the people we are meeting in the street or conversing with as real people or mere automatons. And, he then asks, where does this deep-rooted certainty, which far exceeds our confidence in well-confirmed scientific hypotheses, come from (Gurwitsch 1979: 10–11)? Furthermore, consider the distinction between the what and the why question. It is one thing to determine what a person is experiencing or doing; say, being sad or angry or reaching for a cup. But even if empathy might allow us to grasp directly (part of) what a person is experiencing or doing, this will not as such provide us with an understanding of *why* somebody is sad or angry or performing the action in question. According to the phenomenological proposal, empathy amounts to experiential acquaintance with other minds. But although we should recognize its importance, we also need to recognize is limitations. There is a limit to how far empathy (plus sensitivity to the immediate context) can get us. Our everyday understanding of others draws on other resources as well. If we wish to unearth *why* somebody is feeling the way he does or *why* he is acting the way he does, we might have to consider the larger social, cultural, and historical context and thereby go beyond the offerings of empathy.

Consider, to take a quite mundane example, a game of peekaboo. When the parent removes his hands from his face and pops back into view, the child might squeal in delight. But whereas we might have to draw on our imaginative powers or our theoretical knowledge regarding the child's cognitive and emotional repertoire in order really to understand why she reacts so intensely, why she finds such a simple game so interesting and fascinating (Bruner and Sherwood 1976), it is less obvious that our sensitivity to the mindedness of the child, or our comprehension of her enjoyment, is to the same extent dependent upon theorizing and/or simulation.

What these distinctions should make clear is that the phenomenologists, in addition to being interested in some of the same questions as simulationists and theory-theorists, namely, how we determine the other's specific state of mind and come to understand its relation to the person's past and future mental states and behaviours, are also interested in a somewhat different question, namely, the question of how we come to understand that another has a mind in the first place. As Merleau-Ponty observes at one point, if direct perception fails, I might resort to analogical reasoning in my attempt to know others, but the latter will 'not teach me about the existence of others' (Merleau-Ponty 2012: 368). A stated ambition of many of the phenomenologists has been precisely to show that traditional attempts to solve the problem of other minds, including various forms of analogical inference, fail

(Gurwitsch 1979: 1–33), and to argue that the very problem, and the scepticism it has often given rise to, are premissed on a flawed conception of mentality (Merleau-Ponty 1964a: 114).

Interestingly, and perhaps also slightly confusingly, phenomenologists have taken empathy to play a role when it comes to addressing both types of concern. What was brought out by my analysis of Husserl's and Stein's investigations was that they both took empathy to work along a continuum. At one end of the scale, empathy is understood as a basic sensitivity to the mindedness of others. It can also, however, provide us with a direct acquaintance and grasp of the more specific character of the other's psychological life.[7]

Interpersonal understanding comes in many shapes and forms, and a single model cannot do justice to the whole variety. We should consequently be wary of any theory that claimed that our understanding of others is solely a question of, say, direct empathic understanding, imaginative projection, analogical reasoning, or inference to best explanation. We need multiple complementary accounts in order to cover the variety of abilities, skills, and strategies that we draw on and employ in order to understand and make sense of others. We might understand others in terms of their individual history or personality trait, we might employ stereotyping, we might predict from inductive generalization, or if we know little about the others in question, we might simply predict from self, expecting them to act as we would (Andrews 2009). The phenomenological authors I have been discussing are not claiming that all forms of social cognition can be explained by empathy. They are not denying that, in some cases, we rely on imagination, memory, or theoretical knowledge when attempting to understand others. In fact, they readily concede that if we really want to understand the full psychological life of others, if we really want to understand what others are up to, why they are doing what they are doing, and what that means to them, then we have to go beyond a narrow focus on face-to-face interaction and embodied engagement. In short, none of them are disputing that we have to go beyond what is directly available if we wish to attain deeper levels of interpersonal understanding. If one accepts this view, the question remains where precisely to draw the line. In what cases and how frequently do we draw on forms of mind-reading based on imagination and inference, and when are more direct forms of social understanding sufficient? But more important than this adjudication is the

---

[7] The tripartite distinction just made has bearings on the claim that empathy is susceptible to top-down modulation and can be moderated and influenced by prior knowledge, experience, and context. Is such a claim targeting the that, the what, or the why aspect? According to one study, participants were significantly more sensitive to the pain of individuals who had contracted AIDS as a result of a blood transfusion as compared to individuals who had contracted AIDS as a result of their drug addiction (Decety et al. 2010). Another study found that men (but not women) showed an absence of empathic activity in the anterior cingulate cortex and anterior insula when they were observing a player in pain who had previously treated them unfairly in a sequence of Prisoner's Dilemma games (Singer et al. 2006). Both these studies seem primarily to address the issue of whether and to what extent one is affected by the suffering of the other. As far as I can see, they don't have any bearing on our capacity to grasp *that* the other is conscious.

question of whether the latter is a precondition for the former, that is, whether theory- or simulation-based mind-reading necessarily presuppose a more direct form of social understanding in order to get off the ground. This is what the phenomeno-logical account of empathy is claiming, and this is the view I am defending. The foundation of interpersonal understanding is to be found not in detached belief ascriptions but in a far more fundamental sensitivity to animacy, agency, and emotional expressivity.

11.3 The invisibility claim

Let us grant that others are given to us as minded, and that we often come to be aware of their mental states without having to invest any conscious effort in the process. It could then be objected, however, that although such a description might capture how things seem to normal subjects, it ultimately remains unenlightening, since it is compatible with radically different models of the mechanisms that cause our aware-ness of others' mental states (McNeill 2012). To put it differently, it could be claimed that any direct understanding of others on the experiential level is made possible by various cognitive processes going on at the sub-personal level. Whereas phenomen-ology concerns itself with how things seem, cognitive science deals with the real underlying mechanisms, and as long as one is not so naive as to believe in a straightforward isomorphism between the personal and the sub-personal level, there is no reason to think that the former descriptions should be of any relevance for the latter explorations. This seems to be the view espoused by Spaulding, who writes: 'The debate in mindreading between the Theory Theory and the Simulation Theory is a debate about the architecture and sub-personal processes responsible for social cognition. Neither account is committed to any view on what phenomenology tells us is going on in our ordinary interactions' (Spaulding 2010: 131). A somewhat similar objection has been raised by Jacob, who has argued that the so-called 'simple phenomenological argument' is unsuccessful and ultimately relies on too naive a trust in the ability to unearth and disclose non-conscious processes introspectively (Jacob 2011: 526).[8]

What is the simple phenomenological argument? It basically runs as follows: If simulation or theorizing is explicit (that is, a conscious process), and the default way in which we understand others, and therefore pervasive in our everyday social cognition, then one ought to have some awareness of the different steps that one goes through as one consciously simulates or theorizes about the other's mental

---

[8] The primary contribution of phenomenological philosophy to the field of social cognition has incidentally never been the careful compilation of introspective data. It is no coincidence that all the major figures in the phenomenological tradition have openly and unequivocally denied that the method they employ is a method of introspection (see Gurwitsch 1966: 89–106; Husserl 1952: 38; 1984b: 201–16; Heidegger 1993: 11–17; Merleau-Ponty 2012: 59; Zahavi 2007c).

states. Certainly, when trying to understand why somebody is acting or reacting in a certain way, we might explicitly try to put ourselves in the target's mental shoes or engage in theory-based inference, but to claim that we engage in either (or both) whenever we understand others as minded creatures isn't supported by experiential evidence (Gallagher 2007). Now, in response Jacob remarks that he finds the argument unconvincing since it involves a misleading use of the implicit–explicit distinction. According to Jacob, the distinction between implicit and explicit as it is used in the theory of mind debate applies to cognitive tasks that can be carried out either explicitly via the use of language or implicitly without using language. And in both cases, we are dealing with cognitive heuristics whose states, operations, and computations are meant to be beyond the scope of conscious awareness.

Not all theory-theorists and simulationists would, however, agree with Spaulding's and Jacob's assessment. Goldman's appeal to available introspective evidence as a prima facie argument in support of simulation theory would hardly make sense unless he was referring to a process that was consciously available and accessible (Goldman 1995: 82; 2006: 147). The same holds true for claims made by Waytz and Mitchell, who argue that simulation 'involves a vicarious response in which a perceiver experiences the same current mental state as that of another person' (Waytz and Mitchell 2011: 197). Consider also the following definition of implicit and explicit simulation provided by two of Jacob's colleagues and collaborators:

Simulation can be conceived as the explicit, conscious imaginary enactment of the mental states and processes of others. It can be considered as a subpersonal process unfolding automatically and without conscious control. Or it can be thought of as a hybrid of implicit and explicit simulation.... We... believe that simulation is the root form of interpersonal mentalization and that it is best conceived as a hybrid of explicit and implicit processes, with subpersonal neural simulation serving as a basis for explicit mental simulation. (Jeannerod and Pacherie 2004: 128–9)

Thus, some simulationists obviously do have conscious processes in mind when they talk of simulation. The same holds true for the way some theory-theorists talk about theory. At least, this would be the natural way to understand Alison Gopnik when she argues that the same cognitive processes are responsible for both scientific progress and the development of the child's understanding of the mind, and that there is a striking similarity between the acquisition of scientific knowledge and the child's ability to interpret behaviour in terms of an agent's mental state (Gopnik 1996: 169).

But there is a more fundamental problem with the view espoused by Spaulding. The sub-personal mechanisms investigated by theory-theory and simulation theory are mechanisms supposed to explain something. What is the explanandum? Ultimately, the full diversity of personal-level social cognition and interaction. If we mischaracterize the explanandum, if we don't possess careful descriptions of its different facets—which is arguably one of the things that phenomenology can offer—it will be rather difficult to locate and identify the relevant sub-personal mechanisms. This is presumably also why many defenders of simulation theory and theory-theory have opted for exactly the opposite conclusion. They do not argue that the phenomenological descriptions are irrelevant to cognitive science, but rather that their own preferred theory is precisely capable of doing justice to the phenomenological findings.

Thus, in recent years one can find simulationists and theory-theorists who are willing to accept the direct accessibility and visibility of mental states, but who would simply maintain that this can be handled by their own position. Currie, for instance, has argued that there is no inconsistency in holding the view that empathy is simulation-based and still insisting that we literally see the emotions of others. On his account, simulation provides information which feeds directly into the visual system, thereby contributing to a visual experience in which various properties are made manifest. And as he then emphasizes, these properties 'are given to me in visual experience itself ' (Currie 2011: 90).

A related reply has been proposed by Jane Lavelle in her defence of theory-theory. Lavelle initially argues that the mere detection of properties of light by the visual system, although necessary, isn't sufficient for epistemic seeing. In order for someone to have a perceptual experience of, say, a car, it is not enough that her visual system picks up light information; additional knowledge has to be added, and the addition in question, which takes place non-consciously, is an inferential process (Lavelle 2012: 222). On this account, any kind of epistemic perception, any perception of something *as* something, requires and is enabled by theory. In a second step, Lavelle then points out that theoretical knowledge might not only influence the content of one's perception (seeing a blur on the X-ray picture versus seeing cancer); it might even make what was initially unobservable accessible to observation. Drawing on debates found in philosophy of science regarding the relation between theory and observation, Lavelle consequently argues that it is crucial not to commit the fallacy of thinking that theoretical entities are necessarily unobservable and invisible. Some theoretical entities, such as neutrinos, are in fact unobservable. We cannot observe neutrinos; we can only infer their existence on the basis of their observable effects. Other theoretical entities, such as shingles, are in fact observable. We can only grasp the meaning of the term 'shingles' by understanding its role within a broader network of beliefs about viruses, and their effects and causes. To that extent, shingles is a theoretical term, but it is also something that can be observed on the skin of the afflicted if we possess the proper theory. Thus, theoretical entities need not be unobservable, although—and this, of course, is crucial—they will be to those who lack the theory. The central question, according to Lavelle, is then whether 'mental states are theoretical entities in the same way that shingles are, or whether they are more akin to neutrinos' (Lavelle 2012: 228). If the former was the case, we could indeed be said to see someone's intentions or emotions when our observation of their movements and facial expressions was informed by the relevant theory of mind. If the latter was the case, we could only see movements and expressions, and we would need to employ inferences in order to get from these visible effects to the unobserv-able mental states that are their underlying causes. In either case, however, our understanding of mental state concepts is supposed to depend on our knowledge of the positions that these concepts occupy within the theory. Thus, the concepts are taken to receive their sense from the theory in which they are embedded, rather than from some form of direct acquaintance.

Although Lavelle is right in insisting that theoretical entities are not necessarily unobservable, and although both she and Currie might be right when they claim that simulation theory and theory-theory are not necessarily committed to the invisibility claim, that is, to the claim that the mental states of others are unobservable, it is undeniable that prominent defenders of both theory-theory and simulation theory have for a long time routinely assumed that other minds are in fact characterized by a fundamental invisibility. They remain concealed and hidden, and it is precisely because we are not directly acquainted with the mental states of others—which are frequently described as 'inherently unobservable constructs' (Mitchell 2008)—that we need to rely on and employ either theoretical inferences or internal simulations. Without a commitment to a view like this, the constant appeal to internal imitations and projections and abductive inferences would make little sense. Indeed, as Epley and Waytz repeatedly state in their survey chapter on mind perception in *The Handbook of Social Psychology*, others' mental states are unobservable and inherently invisible, and it is precisely because people lack direct information about others' mental states that they must base their inferences on whatever information about others they do have access to. They must make a leap from the observable behaviour to the unobservable mental states, a leap employing either simulation or theoretical inference (Epley and Waytz 2009: 499, 505, 518). In short, theory-theory and simulation theory have frequently shared a fundamental background assumption, namely, that the minds of others are hidden, which is why they have considered one of the main challenges facing a theory of social cognition to be the question of how and why we start ascribing such hidden mental entities or processes to certain publicly observable bodies.

It is easy to illustrate the prevalence of this idea. Here are a few quotations:

One of the most important powers of the human mind is to conceive of and think about itself and other minds. Because the mental states of others (and indeed of ourselves) are completely hidden from the senses, they can only ever be inferred. (Leslie 1987: 139)

Normal humans everywhere not only 'paint' their world with color, they also 'paint' beliefs, intentions, feelings, hopes, desires, and pretenses onto agents in their social world. They do this despite the fact that no human has ever seen a thought, a belief, or an intention. (Tooby and Cosmides 1995, p. xvii)

Mental states, and the minds that possess them, are necessarily unobservable constructs that must be inferred by observers rather than perceived directly. (Johnson 2000: 22)

Often the invisibility thesis is asserted without any argument right at the beginning of the analysis and apparently serves to motivate the ensuing approach. This can be illustrated by three further quotations. Rebecca Saxe and colleagues start their article by writing:

Unlike behaviorists, normal adults attribute to one another (and to themselves) unobservable internal mental states, such as goals, thoughts, and feelings, and use these to explain and predict behavior. This human capacity for reasoning about the mental causes of action is called a theory of mind. (Saxe et al. 2004: 87)

Likewise, at the beginning of *Mindreading*, Nichols and Stich state that a

motivation for studying the development of mindreading derives from the fact that the central concepts implicated in mindreading, for example, *belief, desire, intention*, are remarkably sophisticated concepts referring to unobservable states. (Nichols and Stich 2003: 4)

On the very first page of Ian Apperly's *Mindreaders*, he writes:

mindreading is mysterious because there are genuine conceptual puzzles about how it is even possible to know the minds of others. Most obviously, we do not have direct access to what other people know, want, intend or believe, but must infer these mental states on the basis of what they do and say. (Apperly 2011: 1)

As I read these statements, the claim is not merely that propositional attitudes are invisible, but that this holds true for our psychological life as such, that is, for all our mental states including our desires, feelings, and intentions. They are all hidden from view. In fact, it has even been claimed that the inaccessibility of other minds makes the question of whether a given creature possesses a mind at all unanswerable (Gray and Schein 2012: 407). But is this assumption really sound? Is it really true that mental states (whether all of them or only those belonging to others) are invisible constructs, and that our engagement with others as minded creatures is initially (or even exclusively) a question of attributing such hidden states to them? Is it really the case that all I can see is the other's perspiration, his flushed face, wrinkled forehead, his jerky motion of the arms, the hunched lips, the clenched fists, and the trembling, but not his fear, embarrassment, desire, and frustration? Is it really the case that when faced with a weeping person, I first perceive drops of liquid rolling from her eyes, distortions of her facial muscles, and broken sounds, and only then in a subsequent move come to realize that the person is grieving? This is obviously an assumption that the phenomenological account of empathy is calling into question.

Although Lavelle might be right in arguing that the theory-theory is not necessarily committed to such a view and can in fact endorse the visibility of mental states as long as it is enabled by theory, such a move would constitute a rather marked departure from the original tenet of theory-theory. It is no coincidence that Premack and Woodruff in their seminal paper stressed that the imputation of mental states to self and other required a system of inferences, that is, what they called a theory of mind, precisely because such states are not directly observable (Premack and Woodruff 1978: 515).

Compare the following three accounts. One account denies that we can ever be directly and immediately acquainted with the mental states of others; all we have access to is mere behaviour, and any ascription of mental states to others will involve an inference to best explanation that fundamentally transcends the experientially given by positing unobservable entities. A second account argues that we need background knowledge in order to be able to grasp and discern that which is directly available. A third account argues that our direct acquaintance with another's mental states is made possible by various sub-personal inferential processes. Rather than emphasizing the affinity between these accounts, I think one ought to recognize their crucial differences (which is not to deny that the latter account is compatible with both of the former). It is primarily the first of the three accounts that the phenomenological proposal is opposing and objecting to (see Zahavi 2005).

Even on Lavelle's account, however, the observability of mental states presupposes the acquisition of the proper theory. There is still an epistemological gap between the input and the output, a gap that must be closed by theoretical knowledge. Over time we become experts on reading other minds. Having achieved this expertise, we tend to see things at once, even though what we see is actually the result of a complex theoretical process. We draw on accumulated theoretical knowledge, but our expertise makes us unaware of the inferential processes and makes us believe that our understanding is immediate and non-inferential (Gopnik 1993). It is unquestionable that we do indeed come to understand some expressions and some forms of expressive behaviour as the result of a learning process (though one might have doubts about whether the latter ought to be described in terms of theory acquisition). Coming to understand a foreign language or a highly idiosyncratic or codified form of expression are obvious candidates. The question, though, is whether we necessarily pass through a developmental phase in which the theory and the expertise haven't yet been acquired and in which all the mental states of others are consequently unobservable and indecipherable to us. Consider again by comparison our comprehension of language. Before we have acquired the necessary skills, written words and sentences are literally meaningless. After we have acquired those skills, words and sentences are perceived as meaningful. But is a similar development really to be found in our interaction with others—which seems to be an implication of Lavelle's account?

On many readings, possessing a theory of mind and being able to attribute mental states to others is a question of having beliefs about others' (and one's own) mental states, and consequently something that involves meta-representations and second-order intentionality. For a while, the ability to ascribe false beliefs to others was considered a crucial milestone in the acquisition of a theory of mind. The reasoning went roughly as follows: In order to ascribe false beliefs to others (and to himself), the child must be able to understand that beliefs might differ from, and thus be distinct from, real-world events and situations. The child's understanding that a person had a false belief consequently provides compelling evidence that the child is able to appreciate the distinction between world and mind, between reality and beliefs about reality, and thereby is in possession of a theory of mind. Not surprisingly, it was then also claimed that individuals who were unable to pass the standard false-belief tasks, and consequently lacking a theory of mind, were also mind-blind and unable to experience others as minded creatures (Carruthers 1996b: 262; Frith and Happé 1999: 1, 7; Baron-Cohen 1989).[9]

Today, however, it is widely recognized that even if the ability to pass false-belief tasks might constitute an important milestone, it is quite doubtful whether such tasks, which target our ability to make detached and reflective predictions about other people's behaviour, are particularly good at measuring the kind of psychological ability that underpins ordinary social understanding (Gallagher 2005). In short, although the ability to attribute false beliefs to others certainly does play a role in social understanding, it is quite unlikely to be what underpins our basic capacity to experience others as minded. As subsequent research has shown, there are not only a number of other belief tasks that can be solved by children much earlier than the standard false-belief tasks, but there is also ample evidence that children have some understanding of other people's perceptions, attentions, desires, intentions, and emotions before they are able to understand (false) beliefs. Indeed, long before the child starts to wonder about your specific belief content, she has interacted with and treated you as a social partner.

Consider, for instance, findings discussed by Csibra. In a paper from 2010, Csibra argues that infants are able to recognize that they are being addressed by someone else's communicative intentions long before they are able to specify what those intentions are, that is, that they are sensitive to the presence of communicative intentions before they are able to access the content of those intentions (Csibra 2010: 143). He takes this innate ability to be one of the crucial sources for the development of communicative skills, and then highlights three stimuli that are discriminable even by newborns and which specify that the infant is the addressee of the communicative act: eye gaze, 'motherese', and turn-taking contingency (Csibra 2010: 144). Already neonates show a preference for looking at faces that make eye contact with them (rather than at faces with closed eyes or averted eyes). Just like eye contact, the prosody of 'motherese' indicates to the infant that he is the addressee of the utterances and it elicits preferential orientation to, and positive affect towards, the source of such stimuli (Csibra 2010: 148). Most important, however, might be

---

[9] It is important to remember that many theory-theorists explicitly argue that we come to know our own beliefs and occurrent mental states in the same way that we come to know the beliefs and experiences of others. In both cases, the same cognitive mechanisms, the same process of mind-reading, is in use (Gopnik 1993; Carruthers and Smith 1996). For a criticism of this view, see Nichols and Stich (2003) and Zahavi (2005).

the interactive responsivity and complementarity that we find in turn-taking contingency. As Murray and Trevarthen showed in their famous study from 1985, young infants are quite sensitive to the contingent structure of the ongoing inter-action itself. In their experimental setup, mothers and their 6- to 8-week-old infants were placed in separate rooms but kept in contact via double closed-circuit television. Thus, each partner saw and heard a full-face, life-size video image of the other. As long as the video presentation was 'live', the interaction proceeded normally. How-ever, the first minute of interaction was videotaped, and the tape of the mother was then rewound and replayed on the infant's screen. Although the infants saw the same mother, the same gestures, and the same displays of affection as they had seen a moment ago, the reaction of the infants changed dramatically. Whereas the infants had been happy and actively engaged during the initial, real-time interaction, they now exhibited signs of distress, turning away from the mother's image, frowning, grimacing, etc. The infants' distress during the replay was evidently produced by some kind of mismatch between their mothers' responses and their own; that is, not only were the infants able to detect that the interactions were out of tune, but they also preferred the contingent structure of these interactions to random stimulation (Murray and Trevarthen 1985).

From very early on, infants are able to discriminate animate and inanimate objects and distinguish biological movement from non-biological movement (Reid and Striano 2007). Eye contact and facial expressions are also of paramount importance to the young infant. In an article surveying and summarizing research on socio-cognitive development in infancy, Philippe Rochat and Tricia Striano conclude that infants manifest an essentially innate sensitivity to social stimuli, that there is already an early form of intersubjectivity at play from around 2 months of age, where the infant has a sense of shared experience and reciprocity with others (Rochat and Striano 1999: 4), and that the 'echoing of affects, feelings and emotions that takes place in reciprocal interaction between young infants and their caretakers' is a 'necessary element to the development of more advanced social cognition, including theory of mind' (Rochat and Striano 1999: 8). Except for some forms of pathology, there is no initial phase in which the infant is confronted with meaningless behav-iour; rather, the infant comes equipped with an innate, automatic, and pre-reflective ability to tune in to and respond to the expressive behaviour of others. A young infant is certainly not yet able to appreciate that his mother has a mind with its own first-personal character, but in so far as the infant is aware of his mother, he is aware of her as being different from his pacifier and pillow. It will no doubt take the child a long time before he understands what precisely the difference consists in, but unless he is aware that they differ, he wouldn't behave towards his mother the way he does.

Prima facie such findings are hard to reconcile with the claim that social cognition is through and through theory-mediated. But one way a theory-theorist can bypass this challenge is obviously by opting for a different account of theory. Rather than arguing that the theory of mind is acquired in the same way as scientific theories, and that the child is a little scientist who is actively constructing and revising theories in the light of incoming experientially derived data,[10] it could argue that the core of folk-psychological theory is hardwired and innately given as part of our evolutionary heritage, and that it operates on a sub-personal level.

This move, however, is not without its own difficulties. First, do sub-personal mechanisms really involve routines that merit the name of theorizing? It is crucial to avoid the fallacy of simply assuming that personal-level theorizing and sub-personal-level theorizing are isomorphic processes whose main difference is their respective relation to conscious experience.[11] Whereas it is relatively easy to understand what is meant by theorizing as long as the term denotes personal-level processes, the use of the term to denote sub-personal processes might increase the plausibility of the claim that they are ubiquitous, but at the cost of making the meaning of the term much less clear.

Secondly, we have already seen how Lavelle argued that any epistemic seeing, any seeing of something *as* something, requires theory. The obvious problem with such a claim is that it becomes quite hard to avoid what is known as the *promiscuity objection* (Blackburn 1995). Almost everything turns out to be theoretical and theory-mediated, including seeing a pancake as a pancake or a door handle as a door handle. Thus, any amount of background knowledge, regardless of how unsystematic and unstructured, is taken to amount to a theory (Jackson 1999: 93), and as a result the notion of theory ends up being so diluted that it is quite vacuous.[12] One might well ask whether this isn't simply a sign of bankruptcy, but even if it weren't, it obviously has the implication that gaining access to other minds is no longer dramatically more challenging than getting access to objects in the environment (Dretske 1973). Our grasp of the intentions and emotions of others would be just as (in)direct as our perception of lemons and screwdrivers. Whatever the merits of such

[10] Gopnik and Wellman compare the transition that occurs between a 3-year-old and a 4-year-old child's understanding of mind to the transition between Copernicus' *De Revolutionibus* and Kepler's discovery of elliptical orbits (Gopnik and Wellman 1995: 242).

[11] A somewhat similar objection can be made vis-à-vis the use of the term 'simulation' as a label for sub-personal mirroring processes. Consider the often asserted claim that since our recognition of specific emotions in others activates the same brain regions that are active when we ourselves experience the very same kind of emotions, third-person emotion attribution involves matching emotions in target and attributer. Does it really make sense to apply personal-level terms such as anger, happiness, sadness, fear, and disgust to non-conscious, sub-personal mechanisms, and to claim that the presence of a specific neural activity—even in the absence of the characteristic experiential and behavioural manifestation—is sufficient to constitute a token of the emotion in question? If, by contrast, the presence of a specific non-conscious process is merely a necessary and enabling condition, rather than a sufficient condition, it will no longer be legitimate to speak of matching emotions in target and attributer simply because the neural activity matches, and will therefore no longer be natural to speak of simulation.

[12] This is also why some theory-theorists have simply bitten the bullet and accepted a much stronger definition of theory. Botterill, for instance, has argued that every theory necessarily involves explanatory and predictive power along with counterfactual projection. He also mentions the introduction of unobservable entities and the implicit definition of concepts as a recurrent element. He concludes by arguing that theories are characterized by producing cognitive economy through the integration of information within a small number of general principles (Botterill 1996: 107–9).

a proposal, it ought again to be clear that we have moved rather far from the initial formulation of the problem that the theory of mind was supposed to provide a solution to. Why was it initially proposed that social cognition involves theoretical inferences? The explanation was typically that we needed such processes in order to account for a certain cognitive achievement, namely, the move from the input, which was taken to be psychologically meaningless—such as the perception of physical qualities and their changes, say, a distortion of facial muscles—to the output, namely, the ascription of mental states, say, joy or sadness, to the other. In short, the processes were needed in order to supplement the input with information coming from elsewhere in order to generate the required output. Depending on whether one opted for a personal-level or a sub-personal-level version of the account in question, opinions differed regarding the status of the cognitive step, but in all cases there was agreement about the explanandum. If, by contrast, we concede that there is no move from the perception of mere behaviour to the attribution of hidden mental states, but rather that we perceive the behaviour as minded from the start, not only have we departed from what is usually considered the standard view of the theory of mind positions, we have also changed the explanandum. To suggest that the explanatory power of the mechanisms favoured by theory-theory can remain unaffected by this change is to endorse a rather unusual view of the relation between explanandum and explanans. If phenomenological analysis tells us that the perceptually observed expressive phenomenon is already saturated with psychological meaning and that this is part of the explanandum, we might want to reconsider postulating mechanisms supposed to bridge a non-existent gap, that is, processes that involve either inferring mental states from the perception of mindless bodies or the projection of one's own experiences upon such mindless bodies.

To claim that the empathic understanding of another's facial expression of disgust is just as theoretical as the perceptual understanding of something as a garden chair (and vice versa), and that both perceptions are enabled and underpinned by various sub-personal cognitive processes involving, say, rule-based manipulations of symbolic representations, not only changes the character of what is at stake in the theory of mind debate. To construe the existence of such sub-personal cognitive processes as an objection to the phenomenological idea of direct empathic understanding is also to misunderstand the nature of the latter claim. The phenomenological account of empathy is not committed to a rejection of the view that empathy is enabled by various sub-personal mechanisms or non-conscious processes (just as direct realism in the philosophy of perception is not necessarily opposed to the existence of causal intermediaries). To speak of empathy as involving direct access to the minds of others is to make a claim about the intentional object and about the more general structure of intentionality. As already pointed out, it is a mistake to consider directness and contextuality as excluding alternatives. One can concede that our typical understanding of others is contextual without endorsing the view that our engagement with others as minded creatures is primarily and fundamentally a question of attributing hidden mental states to them. Likewise, it is a mistake to consider directness as necessarily opposed to complexity. Saying that we can be directly acquainted with certain mental states of others is consequently not to argue that the process that allows for this direct apprehension must necessarily be simple.[13] The crucial point, and this is what the term 'direct' is supposed to capture, is that the object of my apprehension, the mental state of the other, is my primary intentional object. It is the state itself that I am facing, there is nothing that gets in the way, and the state is experienced as actually present to me. This is precisely what distinguishes empathy from other, more indirect forms of social cognition.

In a way that is reminiscent of Husserl's considerations in *Logische Untersuchungen*, Dretske has pointed out that colloquial speech does suggest that another person's fear, anger, frustration, and embarrassment are visible. After all, we frequently say that we can see anger in the other's eyes, see his mounting fear or frustration, or his embarrassment (Dretske 1973: 36). According to Dretske, however, it is important to distinguish the claim that we can see *that* somebody is happy, or interested, or irritated, or bored from the claim that we can see somebody else's happiness, interest, irritation, or boredom. After all, although the feelings and thoughts might not themselves be visible, they can modify those parts of the person that we can see in characteristic ways, thereby making the presence of the former easily identifiable. We consequently have to distinguish the claim that we can directly see that something is the case (say, that Mary is happy) by seeing the object itself (Mary's happiness) from the claim that we can see that something is the case without seeing the object itself, but by seeing something else (say the colour of Mary's face, the shape of her mouth, etc.). According to Dretske, we should endorse the latter claim and reject the former. But although Dretske's account does make it permissible to say that we can *see* that others are angry, depressed, nervous, or distracted, his proposal ultimately remains committed to the invisibility claim by assuming 'without further argument that the elements that constitute a person's mind, whatever their exact ontological status (states, episodes, processes, events), are elements that others cannot see' (Dretske 1973: 37).

11.4 The spectre of behaviourism

At this point, it could be objected that although one's understanding of another's intentions or emotions can be informed and influenced by one's observation of the other's goal-directed and expressive behaviour, we need to distinguish the effects and the causes. The expressive behaviour is caused by the underlying mental states, and the former doesn't constitute the latter (Jacob 2011: 531). In short, one can only be

---

[13] One illustration of this can be found in Husserl's analysis of perceptual intentionality. Although Husserl does argue that perceptual intentionality is direct, his analysis also reveals that it involves and is enabled by a number of complex kinaesthetic and temporal processes.

said to grasp the other's intentions or emotions directly if the other's bodily behaviour constitutes those very intentions and emotions. If it does not constitute them, then clearly by perceiving the former one cannot perceive the latter. But if it does constitute them, then the proposal basically amounts to a form of (unacceptable) behaviourism (Jacob 2011: 531).

Prima facie, there is something rather odd about accusing a phenomenologically informed proposal like this one of behaviourism. After all, one of the characteristic features of a phenomenological approach to consciousness has been its recurrent emphasis on the importance of subjectivity and the first-personal character of consciousness. No phenomenologist has ever accepted the claim that mental terms or concepts ought either to be translated into behavioural concepts or eliminated. I would consequently rephrase the central question. Contrary to what Jacob is claiming, I don't think the question is whether bodily expressivity exhausts our mental life. Rather, the point of controversy concerns whether bodily expressivity has intrinsic psychological significance, or whether whatever psychological significance it has is derived. Jacob seems to think that bodily expressivity owes whatever psychological significance it has exclusively to the fact that it stands in a certain causal relationship to various hidden mental states. This is what is being disputed by the phenomenologists, who all resist the lean construal of behaviour that the behaviourists were favouring (Leudar and Costall 2004: 603).

In any case, the suggestion has obviously never been to identify or reduce mental states to behaviour or behavioural dispositions. There is more to the mind than its publicly accessible behavioural manifestation—and this holds true not only for complex abstract beliefs, but even for simple volitions and basic emotions. But from the fact that some aspects of a given subject's mental state are not directly accessible to others, one cannot infer that no aspect of a given subject's mental state is directly accessible to others. It is perfectly legitimate to say that one is able to grasp empathically another's mental state even if there are aspects of that state that aren't empathically accessible. Thus, we shouldn't conflate the claim that it is possible to understand empathically the other's emotions or intentions with the claim that it is possible to understand empathically all aspects of the other's emotions or intentions. This incidentally also holds true for ordinary object perception. There is a difference between seeing a table and seeing the whole table. I can see a table even if I cannot see all its parts and properties.

It might be objected that there is a crucial disanalogy between the two cases. It is true that I can see a table even if I don't see all its parts, but in order for me to see the table, I still have to see a sufficiently characteristic part of it. And the problem is that the truly defining and distinguishing feature of mental states, namely, their phenomenal character, will always remain inaccessible to others. However, there are various reasons why one ought to resist this line of reasoning. First of all, and this, of course, is the point that Scheler has been pushing most vociferously, it is by no means obvious that the phenomenal character of a subject's experience is entirely off limits to everybody else. When empathically grasping the anger, exhaustion, frustration, admiration, or joy of another, I am not simply registering or detecting that the other is in some mental state while having no clue about what it is like for him or her to be in that state. What it is like for me to empathize with another's joy is quite different from what it is like for me to empathize with another's frustration or exhaustion. And even when there are limits to what I can empathically grasp (I cannot empathically grasp what it is like to taste shoe polish), some dimensions of the other's experience might remain accessible to me; I might, for instance, be able to apprehend the intensity of the experience, or whether it is a pleasant or an unpleasant one. Secondly, our understanding of various conative and affective states, our understanding of what it means to desire or fear something, to be angry, ashamed, or jealous, quite naturally includes a reference to their bodily, expressive, and behavioural aspects, and if asked to provide definitions of said phenomena, it would be quite odd merely to focus on and mention their phenomenal character. In fact, according to a currently influential approach, emotions are component processes and include subjective feelings, expressive motor behaviour, cognitive appraisal, physiological arousal, and action readiness (Niedenthal et al. 2006: 6–7). It could, of course, be retorted that a definition ought precisely to focus on the necessary and sufficient conditions, and that play-acting and stoic suppression have shown expressive behaviour to be neither necessary nor sufficient. But surely such cases are the exceptions rather than the norm. It is quite hard to see why we should conclude from such cases alone that expressive and intentional behaviour lack intrinsic psychological significance.[14] Moreover, isn't the underlying assumption, that unexpressed experiences are just like expressed experiences, that is, that experiences would remain precisely the same even without bodily and linguistic expressions, challenged by empirical evidence? Many studies show that when subjects are induced to adopt specific facial expressions or postures, they experience the corresponding emotions. Likewise, when people's bodily expressivity is inhibited, they report diminished emotional experience. Thus, according to the so-called facial feedback hypothesis, facial expressions can affect and modulate the intensity of an already existing emotion, just as they might give rise to the corresponding emotional experience (Niedenthal 2007; Laird 2007). To suppress or remove the expressive aspect of the emotion consequently seems to change the phenomenal character of the emotional experience itself.

---

[14] In addition, one might also insist on the need for a further differentiation. Whereas Mitchell Green argues that one 'who expresses anguish without being anguished is performing an act that is express*ive* of anguish without expressing *her* anguish' (Green 2007: 26), Overgaard has defended a disjunctive account, and argued that 'the difference between the person who genuinely vents her anger and the person feigning anger is not that in the former case, there is the angry behaviour plus a feeling of anger, while in the latter case, there is only the behaviour (or rather, that plus an intention to deceive, say). Rather, even if the two behaviours are movement-for-movement indistinguishable to an outside spectator, they are *different kinds* of processes. In the one case, the visible behaviour is a person's coming to grips with the world as infuriating; in the other it is not' (Overgaard 2012: 476).

In her dissertation Stein wrote that an unexpressed emotion is an incomplete emotion (Stein 2008: 57). She spoke of the expression as an experiential externalization of the emotion and argued that the two 'form a natural unity' (Stein 2008: 87) and are 'related by nature and meaning, not causally' (Stein 2008: 59). The view that the expressive relation that obtains between mental phenomena and behaviour is stronger than that of a mere contingent causal connection is also defended by Merleau-Ponty, who in a text dating from 1948 wrote as follows:

Imagine that I am in the presence of someone who, for one reason or another, is extremely annoyed with me. My interlocutor gets angry and I notice that he is expressing his anger by speaking aggressively, by gesticulating and shouting. But where is this anger? People will say that it is in the mind of my interlocutor. What this means is not entirely clear. For I could not imagine the malice and cruelty which I discern in my opponent's looks separated from his gestures, speech and body. None of this takes place in some otherworldly realm, in some shrine located beyond the body of the angry man. It really is here, in this room and in this part of the room, that the anger breaks forth. It is in the space between him and me that it unfolds. I would accept that the sense in which the place of my opponent's anger is on his face is not the same as that in which, in a moment, tears may come streaming from his eyes or a grimace may harden on his mouth. Yet anger inhabits him and it blossoms on the surface of his pale or purple cheeks, his blood-shot eyes and wheezing voice. (Merleau-Ponty 2004: 83–4)

Such ideas are by no means unique to the philosophers from the phenomenological tradition, but are also to be found in other thinkers of that time. In *Philosophie der symbolischen Formen*, for instance, Cassirer defends the view that the understanding of expressive phenomena is primitive and that it is more basic than the understanding of sensory phenomena or knowledge of proper objects (Cassirer 1957: 63, 65). According to Cassirer, Scheler's great achievement was to have shown the phenomenological weaknesses of both the theory of analogy and the theory of projective empathy. Both theories failed to appreciate that the expressive dimension is a genuinely original phenomenon. But to miss this is to close off all access to the world of inner experience; it is to cut the bridge that alone could lead us into the realm of the *thou*. Indeed, as Cassirer continues,

Any attempt to replace the *primary* function of expression by other higher functions, whether intellectual or aesthetic, leads only to inadequate substitutes, which can never achieve what is demanded of them. Such higher functions can only be effective insofar as they already presuppose the primary stratum of the experience of expression in its absolutely original form. (Cassirer 1957: 87)

Cassirer asks us to be wary of any theory that makes the phenomena of expression be dependent upon a subsequent act of interpretation. Such an account is in fact reversing the order of data. It first kills off perception by making it into a complex of mere sensory contents, in order then to reanimate it by an act of projection (Cassirer 1957: 65). What we must do is to reverse the order and direction of enquiry:

Instead of asking by what processes of logical inference or of aesthetic projection the physical *becomes* psychical, it must follow perception back to the point where it is not a perception of things but purely a perception of expression, and where, accordingly, it is inside and outside in one. (Cassirer 1957: 84; translation modified)

Were we to deny that some expressions and bodily movements are psychologically meaningful and socially salient from the very start, were we to opt for what McCulloch has called a 'behaviour-rejecting mentalism' (McCulloch 2003: 94), we would also face various versions of the problem of other minds. One version would run as follows: If behaviour per se were psychologically meaningless, if it could be adequately accounted for in terms of a purely physical analysis, like the falling of snowflakes or the shifting of a mobile in the wind, what should then motivate us to seek a psychological explanation of it? And wouldn't we be caught in circularity if we inferred the underlying mental states on the basis of the observed behaviour, on the one hand, and appealed to the underlying mental states in order to gather the meaning of the behaviour, on the other (Malle 2005: 27)? Another version would be the so-called conceptual problem of other minds. If my self-experience were, in the primary instance, of a purely mental nature, that is, if my bodily behaviour did not figure essentially in my self-ascription of (some) psychological states, while my ascription of mental states to others was based solely on their bodily behaviour, what, then, would guarantee that we are, in fact, ascribing states of the same type to self and to others? How would we ever come to be in possession of a truly general concept of mind that is equally applicable to different subjects (Merleau-Ponty 2012: 391; Davidson 2001: 207; Avramides 2001: 135, 224)? Rather than attempting to solve the problem of other minds by arguing that the inferential move from overt behaviour to covert inner states is, in fact, justified, a more promising strategy would be to reject the sceptic's conception of what is given.

Expressions and expressive phenomena are complex topics, and a more adequate account would require a far more detailed investigation than I am able to offer here. Let me just once again emphasize that it would be a mistake to limit or restrict such an investigation to automatic and involuntary expressions. On a standard definition, expressions refer to verbal and non-verbal behaviour, such as facial expressions, gestures, bodily posture, or vocalization, by means of which mental states are revealed and displayed or communicated to others (Niedenthal et al. 2006: 116). Consequently, we should not forget that much of our daily interaction involves the use of voluntary expressions for communicative purposes, and not only can the communicative efficacy of our natural forms of expression benefit from being stylized, dramatized, or otherwise modified, our very expressive *and* experiential repertoire can also be dramatically expanded through the use of such conventions.

The moment we shift the focus of investigation to include voluntary and conventional expressions, we obviously need to factor in that we might also fail to express our thoughts, feelings, and intentions adequately. But if we succeed, we manifest those states and make them accessible to others. Importantly, however, they will only be accessible and comprehensible to those who possess the necessary background knowledge. So even if the use of such conventional expressions might allow for new forms of accessibility, we are no longer talking about a basic or primitive type of interpersonal understanding.

As ought to be clear by now, I am not defending the claim that everything is open to view or that others are totally transparent. I am not arguing that *every* aspect of the mental life of others is directly accessible, but merely that the phenomenological proposal according to which we can be directly acquainted with some aspects of the mental life of others is a proposal that contemporary research on social cognition ought to take seriously. As we have seen, it has been claimed that such a view is hugely controversial in that it commits one to behaviourism (Jacob 2011: 531). I do not think this criticism is correct. Moreover, I think the view is far more widespread than the critics realize. Not only have a number of philosophers from a variety of different traditions recently been entertaining similar ideas (Rudd 2003; Overgaard 2005; Cassam 2007; Green 2007; Newen and Schlicht 2009; Smith 2010; Stout 2010), but consider also Michael Tomasello's proposal that social cognition takes three forms. We can understand others (1) as animate beings, (2) as intentional agents, and (3) as mental agents. In Tomasello's view, the ontogenetic relevance of this tripartition is straightforward. Whereas infants are able to distinguish animate beings from non-animate beings from birth, they are able to detect intentionality, in the sense of goal-directed behaviour, from around 9–12 months of age, as evidenced in phenomena such as joint attention, gaze following, joint engagement, and imitative learning; and they become aware of others as mental agents with beliefs that might differ from their own at around 4–5 years of age. Why does the last step take so much longer, on Tomasello's view? On the one hand, he calls attention to the different role of expressive behaviour. Whereas the animacy of others is directly expressed in their behaviour, intentionality is also expressed in actions, but is at the same time somewhat divorced from them, since on occasion it may remain unexpressed or be expressed in different ways. Finally, when it comes to thoughts and beliefs, these might lack natural behavioural expressions altogether (Tomasello 1999: 179), which is what makes them so much more difficult to grasp. Now, one might certainly question Tomasello's choice of terms (the distinction between intentional agents and mental agents is problematic in that it might suggest both that there is nothing mindful about goal-directed actions and that there is no intentionality to thoughts and beliefs), as well as his proposed developmental time frame (compare, for instance, Onishi and Baillargeon 2005), but his distinction between different levels of social understanding, including his focus on the infant's innate, automatic, and pre-reflective ability to tune in to and respond to the expressive behaviour of others (supposedly including early sensitivity to emotional expressions), seems quite compatible with the view defended here. On the other hand, Tomasello argues that the more advanced form of social cognition emerges as late as it does because it depends on prolonged real-life social interaction (Tomasello 1999: 198). In order to understand that other people have beliefs about the world that differ from their own, children need to engage in discourses where these different perspectives become clearly apparent, be it in disagreements, misunderstandings, requests for clarification, or reflective dialogues (Tomasello 1999: 176, 182). As Bernhard Waldenfels once remarked, a dialogue is by nature polycentric. When I am engaged in a dialogue, the other is addressing me, and I am consequently experiencing reality simultaneously from a multiplicity of perspectives. The experience of this simultaneity differs from and precedes my ability to adopt imaginatively the perspective of the other (Waldenfels 1971: 203). Now, Tomasello is certainly right in pointing to the fact that our understanding of others gradually becomes more sophisticated, and that there are dimensions of the mind that are not as readily accessible as others. Moreover, he is also right in pointing to the cultural and social dimension of this developmental process. Rather than being the result of an automatic maturation of certain innate cognitive modules, it seems plausible to view these more sophisticated forms of social cognition as abilities that develop in tandem with increasingly complex forms of social interaction.

One conclusion to draw from these findings is that social cognition comes in many different forms, and that some are present from quite early on. Indeed, trying to explain everything about social cognition using a single sort of mechanism or process is, as Nichols and Stich put it, a bit like trying to fit a round peg into an irregular trapezoidal hole (Nichols and Stich 2003: 101). One should consequently be wary of monolithic approaches, since they tend to ignore those forms that the theory in question cannot explain.

Not surprisingly a debate has sprung up regarding whether it might be possible to explain some of the findings in a more parsimonious way, that is, in a way that doesn't ascribe any so-called mind-reading capacities to the infant. Perhaps the infant isn't really reasoning about unobservable mental states, but is merely very good at behaviour-reading, that is, sensitive to observable behaviour and capable of reasoning about such behaviour (for instance, in a way that allows it to predict and anticipate certain outcomes) (Apperly 2011: 151). However, this dispute about whether infants are really mind-reading or merely behaviour-reading seems premissed on the assumption that intersubjectivity, social understanding, and other-directed intentionality all come down to some form of mind-reading that necessarily involves reference to purely interior and private states, that is, states that are not visible in meaningful actions and expressive behaviour. Given such a concept of mentality, there are good reasons to believe that children will only be able to master the capacity at a relatively late stage. But the obvious and crucial question is why one would want to opt for such a narrow mentalistic understanding of the mind in the first place. Phenomenologists have in general taken an embodied approach to questions of understanding others and the problem of intersubjectivity. We begin from the recognition that the body of the other presents itself quite differently from any other physical entity, and accordingly that our perception of the other's bodily presence is unlike our perception of ordinary physical objects.

It is revealing that Jacob, in presenting his criticism of the phenomenological account of empathy, writes that an agent's intentional behaviour or expressive behaviour can be said to 'betray' the intention or emotion that caused the agent's movements (Jacob 2011: 534). To use the term 'betray' in this context evokes the impression that we ought to take, say, poker play, where a player's twitching eye might be said to betray his nervousness, as the paradigmatic case of social under-standing. Would we also say that the scream of the non-anaesthetized patient on the surgeon's table is mere behaviour and must be sharply distinguished from the real pain, though it betrays it, or that the mother's embrace betrays her affection, though it must be sharply distinguished from the latter? Does it really make sense to divide phenomena such as a frown, a kiss, or a smile neatly into their psychological and behavioural aspects? Doesn't the caress embody the affection rather than merely being a causal effect of it? We might readily agree that there is more to, say, affection than what is visibly displayed, but at the same time hold that an affection that remains entirely invisible is somewhat incomplete.

I would suggest that a more fortuitous route to explore is one that takes us beyond the dichotomy of behaviour-reading and mind-reading (Sinigaglia 2008), and ultim-ately dispenses with the whole reading imagery. Moving beyond that dichotomy changes the nature of the challenge. The decisive question is no longer how to bridge the gap between visible but mindless behaviour and invisible but disembodied mentality, but to understand the link between early forms of perceptually grounded empathy and more sophisticated forms of interpersonal understanding. To under-stand this link might itself pose many challenges, but to adopt a terminology from philosophy of mind, the challenges would belong to the easy problems, rather than the hard problem, of social cognition. As Merleau-Ponty puts it, the problem of knowing how I can come to understand the other is infinitely less difficult to solve if the other is understood primarily as an intentional comportment in the world, as a way of intending and grasping the world that surrounds us, than if she is understood as a radically alien psyche (Merleau-Ponty 1964a: 117).

12

Subjectivity and Otherness

In this part of the book, I have argued that an examination of empathy can throw light on the self–other relationship, and that important insights are to be found in the classical phenomenological investigations. In closing, let me mention some implications of the preceding discussion that link up with topics discussed in Part I, and highlight one important limitation of my analysis.

The primary goal of my probe into the early phenomenological exploration of empathy was not to contribute to a terminological dispute by settling how the term ought to be defined and used, but rather to point to some of the insights that can be garnered from that exploration—insights that remain of relevance for the contemporary discussion of social cognition. These would include an emphasis on the multifaceted character of interpersonal understanding, a recognition of our basic sensitivity to the mindedness of others, and, of course, a highlighting of the extent to which we can be directly acquainted with the other's experiences. It is debatable whether an acceptance of these points will necessitate a major overhaul of existing theories, but even if it doesn't, it could still motivate new and divergent interpretations of some of the empirical findings as well as a reconsideration of what should count as paradigmatic cases of social cognition.

As should have become clear, I have some sympathy with the general idea that who I am is also a question of what matters to me, and is therefore something that cannot be settled independently of my own self-understanding. However, I don't think this approach can stand alone. It needs to be supplemented by an account that does more justice to the first-person perspective. This is why I have argued that it is mandatory to operate with a more primitive and fundamental notion of self than the one endorsed by the narrativists—a notion that cannot be captured in terms of narrative structures. In a parallel move, I also think that there is a crucial dimension of what it means to be other that is bound to be missed by the narrative approach. This can be illustrated by returning to Schapp. For Schapp, human life is a life that is caught up in stories; it is nothing apart from these stories, and such stories provide the only possible access to oneself and to others (Schapp 2004: 123, 126, 136, 160). More specifically, he claims that what is essential about others is their stories. The encounter with the other in flesh and blood, the concrete face-to-face encounter, doesn't add anything significant, doesn't point beyond the narrative. In fact, and sticking to the metaphor, Schapp argues that the face also tells stories, and that meeting somebody face to face is like reading a book. It is when we know these stories that we know the other person. To know or meet somebody in person is merely to encounter new stories or have the old stories confirmed (Schapp 2004: 105–6). This approach might be criticized for entailing what could be called a domestication of otherness: you reduce the other to that which can be captured in narratives. But it thereby fails to realize that the other is precisely characterized by an otherness which resists or exceeds whatever narratives we bring to bear on him or her.

One obvious question to ask is whether there is a systematic link between these two limitations of the narrative approach. The answer seems straightforward. The reason why the other is characterized by a certain dimension of transcendence, the reason why the other is an other, is precisely because he or she is also an experiential self, with his or her own irreplaceable first-person perspective. Indeed, rather than preventing or obstructing a reasonable account of intersubjectivity, I would consider a strong commitment to the first-personal character of consciousness, that is, to the for-me-ness of experience, a necessary requirement for any such account.

Some have claimed that the only way to solve the problem of intersubjectivity and avoid a threatening solipsism is by conceiving of the difference between self and other as a founded and derived difference, a difference arising out of an undifferentiated anonymous life. However, as should have become clear by now, this 'solution' does not solve the problem of intersubjectivity, it dissolves it. To speak of a fundamental anonymity prior to any distinction between self and other obscures that which has to be clarified, namely, intersubjectivity understood as the relation between subjectivities. On the level of this fundamental anonymity there is neither individuation nor selfhood, but nor is there any differentiation, otherness, or transcendence, and there is consequently room for neither subjectivity nor intersubjectivity. To put it differently, the fundamental anonymity thesis threatens not only our concept of a self-given subject; it also threatens our notion of an irreducible other. Thus, rather than impeding a satisfactory account of intersubjectivity, an emphasis on the inherent and essential individuation of experiential life must be seen as a prerequisite for getting the relation and difference between self and other right. One of the recurrent ideas found in both classical and more recent accounts of empathy has been the idea that empathy presupposes a felt separation between self and other, presupposes a preservation rather than an overcoming or elimination of the self–other differentiation. Indeed, as we have seen, for the phenomenologists, empathy is precisely characterized as a form of intentionality that involves a marked self-transcendence, a confrontation with something decisively other. A basic presupposition in this line of reasoning is a commitment to an egological account of consciousness. For that reason, any resolutely non-egological account of consciousness, and this would obviously include various Buddhist no-self accounts, might be faulted for its incapacity to account convincingly for empathy (and, by extension, compassion). Compare by way of illustration the two following statements:

An enlightened being is strictly impartial, showing equal love and compassion for all sentient beings. But how can we make sense of this if there *is* a deep difference—if only an experiential one—between my suffering and yours? How can I view someone's suffering as just *someone's* suffering, rather than as my suffering or yours, if, in fact, there is a deep difference between us? To make sense of this, we must suppose that as an enlightened being, I would no longer conceive of someone as 'me' in a deep sense. I would no longer experience myself *as* myself but as an anonymous 'someone'. (Fink 2012: 295)

Hence sympathy does not proclaim the essential identity of persons, as Schopenhauer and von Hartmann allege, but actually presupposes a pure essential *difference* between them...if, as we saw, it is the very office of true sympathy to dissipate the solipsistic illusion by apprehending the equivalent status of the other person *as* such, it cannot be at the same time a dim perception of the fact that neither of us really exists, but only some third party, of whom we are merely the functions. (Scheler 2008: 65–6; translation modified)

It should be clear from the previous discussion why I would side with Scheler on this point. The connection between selfhood and empathy—and a nice formulation of a core tenet in the phenomenological account of the latter—can be found in another quotation from Scheler, which incidentally is one that Husserl, Stein, and Schutz could all accept without any qualms:

That we cannot be aware of an experience without being aware of a self is something which is directly based upon the intuitable intrinsic connection between individual and experience...It is a corollary of this that the other person has—like ourselves—a sphere of absolute personal privacy, which can never be given to us. But that 'experiences' occur there is given for us *in* expressive phenomena—again, not by inference, but directly, as a sort of primary 'perception'. It is *in* the blush that we perceive shame, *in* the laughter joy. To say that 'our only initial datum is the body' is completely erroneous. This is true only for the doctor or the scientist, i.e. for man in so far as he abstracts *artificially* from the expressive phenomena, which have an altogether primary givenness. (Scheler 2008: 9–10)

As I briefly alluded to in Chapter 10.1, however, the focus on expressivity and empathy is not entirely uncontroversial within phenomenology. Strong reservations can, for instance, be found in Heidegger, who argues that one will remain committed to a serious misconception of the nature of the self if one seeks to understand intersubjectivity on the basis of empathy:

If this word [empathy] is at all to retain a signification, then it is only because of the assumption that the 'I' is at first in its ego-sphere and must then subsequently enter the sphere of another. The 'I' does not first break out...since it already is outside, nor does it break into the other, since it already encounters the other outside. (Heidegger 2001: 145)

According to this understanding of the concept, the notion of empathy is introduced in order to explain how one (isolated) subject can encounter and understand another (isolated) subject. Even if the empathic approach does not commit the same mistakes as the argument from analogy, and even if it can be freed from any projectivist tendencies, it still misconstrues the nature of intersubjectivity, since it takes it to be first and foremost a thematic encounter between individuals, where one is trying to grasp the inner emotions or experiences of the other (this connotation is particularly evident in the German term *Einfühlung*). As Heidegger points out, the very attempt to grasp thematically the experiences of others is the exception rather than the rule. Under normal circumstances, we understand each other well enough through our shared engagement in the common world. In fact, as existing-in-the-world we are constantly dependent upon others, and their coexistence is co-implied in our daily activities. Heidegger even argues that Dasein at the same time, with equal originality, and by ontological necessity is both being-among (*Sein bei*) entities within the world and being-with (*Mitsein*) other Dasein (Heidegger 1975: 394), and that this holds true regardless of whether others are de facto present. As the influential phenomenological psychiatrist Ludwig Binswanger would subsequently put it:

By presenting this ontological connection, Heidegger has banished entire libraries on the problem of empathy, the problem of perceiving the foreign as such, the problem of the 'constitution of the foreign I', and so on, to the realm of history, for what the latter want to furnish proof of and explain is always already presupposed in the proof and the explanations; the presupposition itself can neither be explained nor proven, but rather only ontologically–phenomenologically 'disclosed'. (Binswanger 1953: 66)

Gurwitsch expresses similar reservations. He readily acknowledges the importance of expressive phenomena, but he criticizes Scheler for having been too one-sided in his approach, and then argues that the realm of expressive phenomena is neither the only, nor the primary, dimension to be considered if we wish to understand what it is that enables us to encounter other human beings as humans (Gurwitsch 1979: 33). In his view, we do not primarily, and ordinarily, encounter others as thematic objects of cognition. Rather, we encounter them in the world in which our daily life occurs, or to be more precise, we encounter others in worldly situations, and our way of being together and understanding each other is co-determined in its meaning by the situation at hand (Gurwitsch 1979: 35–6, 95, 106). To exemplify, Gurwitsch analyses a situation in which two workers are cobbling a street. In this work situation, one worker lays the stones while the other knocks them into place. Each worker is related to the other in his activity and comportment. When one worker understands the other, the understanding in question does not involve grasping some hidden mental occurrences. There is no problem of other minds. There is no problem of how one isolated ego gets access to another isolated ego. Rather, both workers understand each other in virtue of the roles they play in the common situation (Gurwitsch 1979: 104, 108, 112).

Heidegger and Gurwitsch both emphasize the social and cultural embeddedness of intersubjective understanding. However, it is not at all clear why one cannot acknowledge—as Schutz, for instance, did—that our typical understanding of others is contextual, while still insisting on the relevance of empathy and the importance of the face-to-face encounter. Moreover, the phenomenologists who do work on empathy do not conceive of it as a process where one tries to worm one's way into the other's inner realm, nor for that matter as some kind of bridge-building between two essentially closed-off interiorities. On the contrary, and this was highlighted by both Stein and Husserl, when I empathically understand the other, the other is given to me not as a pure nucleus of experience, but as a centre of intentionality, as a different perspective on the very world that I also inhabit. Rather than facing the other as an isolated object, her intentionality will pull me along and make me co-attend her worldly objects. As Merleau-Ponty would later put it, 'My gaze falls upon a living body performing an action and the objects that surround it immediately receive a new layer of signification: they are no longer merely what I could do with them, they are also what this behavior is about to do with them' (Merleau-Ponty 2012: 369). At the same time, Heidegger's own approach seems to be confronted with some important limitations. As Sartre pointed out early on, to downplay or ignore the face-to-face encounter and to emphasize the extent to which our everyday being-with-one-another is characterized by anonymity and substitutability—as Heidegger puts it, the others are those among whom one is, but from whom 'one mostly does *not* distinguish oneself' (Heidegger 1986: 118)—is to lose sight of the real issue and nexus of intersubjectivity: the encounter and confrontation with a radical otherness.[1] The same criticism can be applied to Heidegger's claim that Dasein is essentially characterized by its being-with, since this misinterprets our original relationship to the other as an 'oblique interdependence' rather than as a 'frontal opposition' (Sartre 2003: 270). According to Sartre, any convincing account of intersubjectivity must respect the irreducible difference between self and other, must respect the *transcendence* of the other. Any attempt to bridge the gap between the self and the other by emphasizing their similarity, undifferentiatedness, and a prior interconnectedness is, according to Sartre, in constant danger of lapsing into a monism that in the end would be indistinguishable from solipsism.

But Sartre's criticism doesn't stop there. Whereas the phenomenological empathy theorists took one of the decisive tasks to consist in an analysis of the specific intentional structure of empathy and investigated to what extent it is possible to experience the other in a way that preserves her transcendence and otherness, Sartre took this line to be misguided, and instead proposed a reversal of the direction of enquiry. According to Sartre, it is crucial to distinguish between the other, whom I perceive, and the other, who perceives me; that is, it is crucial to distinguish between the other as object and the other as subject. What is truly unique about meeting another is that I am thereby encountering somebody who is able to perceive and objectify *me*. The other is exactly the one before whom I can appear as an object. Thus, rather than focusing upon the other as a specific object of empathy, Sartre argues that the more original and authentic intersubjective relation is to be found in

---

[1] For a more extensive discussion of Sartre's criticism of Heidegger, see Zahavi (1996).

the experience of being the other's object. Only in this way can the other be fully or purely present as a subject. The original presence of the other as such is hence his or her presence as 'the one who looks at me' (Sartre 2003: 293; compare 2003: 280, 294).

Sartre's highlighting of the alterity and transcendence of the other was subsequently radicalized by Levinas, who also took the problem of intersubjectivity to be primarily a problem of the encounter with radical otherness. He explicitly denied that any form of intentionality (including empathy) would ever enable such an encounter. Intentionality is for Levinas a process of objectification and it only lets us meet the other by reducing the other to something it is not, namely, an object. Levinas consequently argued that a true encounter with the other is an encounter with that which cannot be conceptualized or categorized. 'If one could possess, grasp, and know the other, it would not be other' (Levinas 1987: 90). It is an encounter with an ineffable and radical exteriority. The other is not conditioned by anything in my power, but can only offer itself from without, independently of all systems, contexts, and horizons as a kind of epiphanic visitation or revelation (Levinas 1979: 65). In a characteristic move, Levinas further argued that the authentic encounter with the other, rather than being perceptual or epistemic, is *ethical* in nature (Levinas 1979: 47).

Sartre's and Levinas's own accounts of intersubjectivity have not gone unchallenged. One common objection is that I never encounter others in isolation, but always in a context. I meet others in the situational framework of a history with a beginning and a direction. Furthermore, Sartre's excessively confrontational characterization of our encounter with others—one is either objectifying the other or being objectified by the other—has also frequently been faulted (see Zahavi 2002). But although both Sartre and Levinas might for their part be said to miss certain features of interpersonal coexistence, I also think they manage to highlight something important about our encounter with others. This is a feature that isn't merely somewhat absent from Heidegger's account, and by and large ignored by those who seek to construe interpersonal understanding primarily in terms of projection and imitation, but also, and in this context most importantly, something that my own preceding investigation of empathy hasn't done sufficient justice to. Intersubjectivity is a relation between subjects; it is a subject–subject relation. But for me to relate to another as subject is for me to relate to somebody with a first-person perspective of his or her own. We encounter others as such when we encounter them as experiencing subjects, and this means as subjects that have a perspective not just upon the world of objects, but upon us too.

This is where the reservation mentioned earlier sets in. To employ Schutz's distinction between a one-sided and a reciprocal thou-orientation, the previous discussion has primarily been focusing on the former, where empathic understanding of the other occurs without any kind of reciprocation on the part of the other. But that certainly seems to miss something quite crucial about the self–other relation. To quote Chris Frith:

Communication, when we confront each other face-to-face, is not a one-way process from me to you. The way you respond to me alters the way I respond to you. This is a communication loop.... This is the big difference from my interactions with the physical world. The physical world is utterly indifferent to my attempts to interpret it. But when two people interact face-to-face, their exchange of meaning is a cooperative venture. The flow is never just one-way. (Frith 2007: 175)

We consequently ought to recognize that there is much more to a developed phenomenology of intersubjectivity and social life than what can be addressed through an analysis of empathy. This, however, is something that virtually all phenomenologists have recognized (Zahavi 2001), and the preceding investigation was never intended as a comprehensive account of a phenomenology of intersubjectivity. Rather, my focus on empathy was motivated by three other concerns. First of all, I wanted to show that an endorsement of an experiential account of self does not entail a denial of the possibility of being directly acquainted with the experiential life of others; it does not entail a commitment to a highly mediated inferentialist account of social understanding. Quite the contrary, in fact, since I have argued that an emphasis on the inherent and essential first-personal character of experiential life is a prerequisite for getting the distinctiveness of other-experience right. Secondly, by focusing on empathy, it was possible to engage constructively with the contemporary discussions of social cognition in order to show how insights found in the phenomenological tradition could contribute to and enrich that debate (and vice versa). Thirdly, and perhaps most importantly, although a focus on empathy might be limited in the sense that thematic encounters with others by no means exhaust the role and contribution of intersubjectivity, it remains a necessary springboard for what is to follow, namely, an investigation of a particular socially mediated form of self(-experience) that involves iterative empathy. To put it differently, the focus on the thematic face-to-face encounter with the other has paved the way for Part III, which will offer some analyses of the self as social object. Although it will be impossible to provide anything like a comprehensive investigation of this vast topic, the following investigations will still allow for a highlighting of an interpersonal dimension of self (which, while being constitutively dependent upon others, and while taking us beyond the experiential self, must nevertheless be distinguished from the narratively extended self), and also include some concluding remarks about more reciprocal forms of self–other interdependence.

PART III

The Interpersonal Self

13

The Self as Social Object

13.1 Neuroscientific complications

Let me start this final part of my investigation by returning to a topic that I touched upon in Chapter 1. As I pointed out then, the exploration of the self is no longer a prerogative of philosophers. Researchers from many different empirical disciplines, including neuroscience, are currently investigating the development, structure, function, and pathology of the self. Not surprisingly, one of the stated goals of a neuroscientific investigation of the self has been to identify and locate its neural correlate. In a survey article entitled 'Is Self Special? A Critical Review of Evidence from Experimental Psychology and Cognitive Neuroscience', Gillihan and Farah, two neuroscientists, discussed the different suggestions that neuroscience had recently been offering. Their conclusion was somewhat discouraging in that different researchers had pointed to quite different areas in the brain (Gillihan and Farah 2005).

What might explain this lack of consensus? One of the outcomes of Part I was that a satisfactory account of the self has to recognize its multifaceted character. The self is a multidimensional and complex phenomenon, and if we are to do justice to its complexity, various complementary accounts have to be integrated. Given this situation, and given the coexistence of a multiplicity of complementary and competing notions of self in the current theoretical debate, it does not make very much sense to discuss where the neural correlate of self is located if one does not at the same time make it clear which concept of self one is operating with, and why one takes one's point of departure in precisely this concept rather than in another. Indeed, one reason for the lack of consensus documented by Gillihan and Farah might precisely be that various experimentalists operate with different notions of self. Another reason is the frequent absence of any explicit discussion and clarification of the very notion of self that one is employing. Indeed, to quote Klein, 'most investigators sidestep these difficulties, relying on their readers' familiarity with the term "self", derived from years of knowledge by acquaintance, to confer a sense of confidence (in my opinion, false) that he or she knows to what the author refers' (Klein 2010: 173). However, a lack of clarity in the concepts used will lead to a lack of clarity in the questions posed, and thus also to a lack of clarity in the design of the experiments supposed to provide an answer to the questions. In the following, let me exemplify and substantiate this verdict by taking a closer look at the neuroscientific study of facial self-recognition. The motivation for this particular choice is not only that it can serve as a clear demonstration of the need for interdisciplinary collaboration when it comes to the study of the self, but also that it will introduce themes that will further guide us towards the main topic of Part III: a socially mediated and constituted self(-experience). More specifically, I shall argue that the self-experience that facial self-recognition exemplifies is not as socially impoverished as it has often been made out to be.

13.2 Facial self-recognition and mirrors

In articles and books such as 'Where in the Brain Is the Self?', 'Where Am I? The Neurological Correlates of Self and Other', and *The Face in the Mirror: How We Know Who We Are*, Keenan's (and colleagues') search for the neural location of self led to the study of facial self-recognition. The assumption has typically been that if there are areas in the brain that show more pronounced activity when one recognizes one's own face (compared to what happens when one recognizes other familiar faces), then the respective areas in the brain must constitute, or at least be a central part of, the neural correlate of self. One of the recurrent findings reported by Keenan is right frontal lateralized activation for self-face recognition—there is more than twice the activity for self-faces compared to familiar faces (Feinberg and Keenan 2005: 673)—and Keenan has claimed that this empirical evidence provides support for what he calls 'the right hemisphere model of self-awareness' (Platek et al. 2004: 119). When reading the various publications, one is immediately struck by the almost complete absence of an actual working definition of both self and self-awareness. In *The Face in the Mirror*, however, it is acknowledged that a definition might be in place, and it is proposed that self-awareness amounts to higher-order consciousness and meta-cognition (Keenan et al. 2003, pp. xi, xx, 54, 57). At the same time, however, it is also stated that consciousness might be used as a synonym for self-awareness (Keenan et al. 2003, pp. xix, xxi). As we shall see in a moment, these definitions are far from innocuous.

One initial question to ask is why self-face recognition is considered so significant? Why should it tell us something important about self? It is not difficult to see that Keenan's investigation of facial self-recognition is indebted to an older and still highly influential paradigm in developmental psychology and comparative psychology, namely, the attempt to subject children, chimpanzees, elephants, dolphins, and most recently magpies to the mirror self-recognition task in order to test for the presence of self-awareness. Indeed, this debt is explicitly admitted by Keenan, who points to Gordon Gallup's classical work, in particular his articles published in 1970 and 1982, for providing the theoretical framework (Platek et al. 2004: 114).

In Gallup's by now famous experiments, chimpanzees who had been exposed to mirrors for ten days, thereby making them familiar with the reflecting properties of the mirror, were sedated and, while unconscious, were marked with an odourless dye on the upper part of one eyebrow and the opposite ear. Back in the cage and fully recovered, they were observed for thirty minutes to account for any spontaneous touches of the marked area. Then the mirror was reintroduced and the chimpanzees were observed for mark-directed behaviour. Gallup reports that the number of incidences of mark-directed behaviour rose from one during the post-anaesthesia mirrorless period to four to ten in the period where the mirror was reintroduced (Gallup 1970). According to Gallup's interpretation, passing the mirror mark test testifies to mirror self-recognition, thereby providing empirical and operational evidence for the presence of conceptual self-awareness (Gallup 1977: 337). More specifically, for Gallup, a prerequisite for successfully passing the mirror self-recognition test and correctly interpreting the source of the reflection as oneself is that the creature in question is in possession of a 'concept of self' (Gallup 1970: 87).

On Gallup's view, mirror self-recognition testifies to the perfect match between the observer and the observed. As he puts it, the 'unique feature of mirror-image stimulation is that the identity of the observer and his reflection in a mirror are necessarily one and the same' (Gallup 1977: 334). It is consequently important to emphasize that mirror exposure on Gallup's account does not give rise to self-consciousness. Rather, the capacity to correctly *infer* the identity between the observer and the reflection presupposes that the observing organism is already in possession of a sense of self-identity. As Gallup puts it, the mirror simply represents a means of explicating what the observing creature already knows.

Gallup did not merely stress the link between mirror self-recognition and self-awareness, however. He also took the passing of the mirror mark test to be a litmus test for the possession of consciousness. In the article 'Self-Awareness and the Emergence of Mind in Primates', Gallup claimed that consciousness is bidirectional. It allows one to attend outwardly to things in the world, but also to attend inwardly and to monitor one's own mental states. To that extent, consciousness covers and includes both awareness and self-awareness (Gallup 1982: 242). This claim is further developed in the article 'Do Minds Exist in Species Other than Our Own?', where Gallup claimed that conscious experience necessarily presupposes self-awareness and that creatures who lack the ability to monitor their own mental states also lack a conscious mind. Either one is aware of being aware, or one is unaware of being aware, and the latter amounts to being unconscious (Gallup 1985: 638). On the basis of this line of reasoning, Gallup concluded that although most organisms behave *as if* they are conscious and minded, prior to the emergence of self-awareness as evidenced from their ability to pass the mirror self-recognition task, they are mindless. They lack conscious experience, and only possess unconscious sensations, pains, etc. (Gallup 1982: 242; 1985: 638). Some might object that the absence of evidence for self-awareness is hardly evidence of absence of self-awareness, but Gallup has been quick to ridicule this worry by arguing that the same logic applies to Santa Claus and the Tooth Fairy (Gallup 1985: 632).

Gallup's considerations are obviously related to the ongoing theory of mind debate. This is also brought out in passages where Gallup linked the possession of a mind (and the ability to monitor one's own mental states) to the ability to infer and impute mental states to others. He claimed that the ability to impute mental states to others presupposes the capacity to monitor such states on the part of the individual making the imputation (to that extent other-experience depends on reflective self-experience) (Gallup 1982: 243), and he consequently argued that we can use the presence of the former as evidence for the presence of the latter (Gallup 1985: 634).

Although Keenan does not explicitly endorse such a view, his own definitions seem to point in the same direction. Having defined self-awareness in terms of reflective meta-cognition, and having said that consciousness is a synonym for such self-awareness, it follows that creatures incapable of such reflective meta-cognition also lack consciousness. Keenan's initial definition consequently commits him to a controversial higher-order representational account of consciousness according to which a creature only enjoys conscious experiences if it has the ability to reflect upon its own mental states.

Perhaps Keenan would refrain from such a view. At least, they are not implications he explicitly draws and endorses. So let us return to his central claim. Keenan repeatedly claims that the ability to pass the mirror self-recognition test demonstrates the capacity for self-awareness. But how strong is this correlation supposed to be? There is hardly any doubt that he opts for a strong claim, which would also match Gallup's view on the matter. This is why Keenan claims that the passing of the mirror test is highly correlated with every indicator of self-awareness, and that the absence of mirror self-recognition is correlated with an absence of other self-aware behaviours (Keenan et al. 2003: 22).[1] It is not obvious, however, that Keenan's own findings really support these claims. Take the case of people suffering from the delusional misidentification symptom known as 'mirror sign', which he also discusses. People afflicted with this delusion misidentify themselves in the mirror, although they

---

[1] Incidentally, Keenan very much sees his own account as being in line with the theory of mind approach of autism researchers such as Baron-Cohen, Frith, and Happé, and he explicitly writes that the empirical findings indicate a lack of self-awareness in individuals with autism (Keenan et al. 2003: 209). In support of this, Keenan refers to an older study that indicated that children with autism had difficulties passing the mirror test (Spiker and Ricks 1984). As a matter of fact, the study in question did report that 69 per cent of the examined children showed evidence of mirror self-recognition, and as another study from 1984 concluded: 'autistic children do not show specific deficits in self-recognition. Even at a relatively young age, most of the autistic children studied showed clear evidence of self-recognition on the mirror-image task' (Dawson and McKissick 1984: 392). A similar conclusion—regarding the ability of children with autism to pass the mirror self-recognition task—is also reached by more recent research (Reddy et al. 2010). What is striking, however, and I shall come back to that shortly, is that children with autism who do pass the mirror test tend to be neutral in their affective expressions and rarely show the signs of coyness or embarrassment that are so typical of normal children. They seem to lack, as Peter Hobson writes, a sense of themselves as potential objects of other people's evaluation. In fact, their removal of the red mark (or yellow sticker) does not seem to be motivated by a concern with how they look to other people (Hobson 1990: 174; 2002: 89; Hobson et al. 2006: 42).

typically retain the capacity to recognize others in the mirror (Postal 2005). As a consequence they are incapable of passing the mirror self-recognition test, and the reason for this incapacity is specifically related to problems with self-recognition, and isn't simply due to some form of prosopagnosia. If one were to take Keenan seriously, people such as these would also lack self-awareness and the capacity for self-reflection, and that is hardly the case.

More importantly, it is not difficult to come up with quite general objections to the idea that our ability to identify a visual representation of our own face should constitute a particular central or fundamental form of self-awareness. Although facial self-recognition might testify to the existence of a form of self-awareness, the failure to recognize one's own face certainly does not prove the absence of every form of self-awareness. To put it differently, the absence of facial self-recognition might be perfectly compatible with the presence of other (less sophisticated) forms of self-awareness. Indeed, as I see it, one decisive problem facing Gallup and Keenan's interpretation of the mirror test is that they both employ an overly narrow and restrictive definition of self-experience and consequently underestimate how complex and varied it really is. Not only do they fail to consider the possibility that phenomenal consciousness might involve self-consciousness in the weak sense that there is something it is like for the subject to have the experience, that is, that the first-personal character of phenomenal consciousness amounts to a low-level form of self-consciousness (compare Chapter 2), but Gallup's explicit conclusion has dramatic (and highly counter-intuitive) implications for our ascription of experiences, that is, mental episodes with a phenomenal character, to infants and all those animals that cannot pass the mirror self-recognition task. On a certain construal of higher-order representation theory, Gallup's view might be comprehensible, but he never provides the theoretical arguments to support this view, and higher-order representational accounts of consciousness have in any case come under increasing criticism in recent years (Zahavi 2004a, 2005; Kriegel and Williford 2006). Furthermore, Gallup and Keenan both seem to ignore the possibility that infants might have a sense of their own bodies as organized and environmentally embedded entities long before they are able to pass any mirror self-recognition tasks, and hence an early embodied sense of themselves in perception and action. Thus, as many developmental psychologists have pointed out, from shortly after birth infants already discriminate what pertains to the self and what pertains to someone else interacting with them (Rochat 2001: 30–1, 41). One obvious question to ask is whether we would be able to recognize our own mirror image at all, which presumably relies on detection of the cross-modal match and temporal contingency between our own bodily movements and the movements of the mirror image, if we were not already proprioceptively aware of our *own* bodily movements and postures. Would it not be much harder to recognize oneself in the mirror if one lacked bodily self-awareness? There are even those who claim that this bodily self-awareness constitutes the fundamental requirement. Mitchell, for instance, has argued that mirror self-recognition merely requires a kinaesthetic sense of one's own body (subjective self-awareness), a capacity for kinaesthetic–visual matching, and an understanding of mirror correspondence (Mitchell 1997a: 31; 1997b: 41). Likewise, Katherine Loveland has argued that mirror self-recognition might have more to do with appreciating the properties of reflecting surfaces than with understanding anything about selfhood (Loveland 1986). If so, it would obviously invalidate Gallup and Keenan's claim that mirror self-recognition requires a capacity for introspection. But that claim is in any case dubious, since, as Mitchell remarks, it is quite unclear what mental state a creature is supposed to attend to in recognizing itself in the mirror (Mitchell 1997a: 23). Finally, the claim that mark-directed behaviour is evidence for mirror self-recognition is not uncontested. The fact that some children, after witnessing a mark on their mother's nose, touch their own nose indicates that the passing of the mirror test might be a false positive (Mitchell 1993: 304).

All of this is not to say that mirror self-recognition is insignificant. The question, though, is whether Keenan and before him Gallup have realized its proper significance. As already mentioned, Gallup took mirror self-recognition to testify to the perfect match between the observer and the observed. As he put it, 'The unique feature of mirror-image stimulation is that the identity of the observer and his reflection in a mirror are necessarily one and the same' (Gallup 1977: 334). In addition, he repeatedly emphasized the distinction between social responsiveness and self-directed mirror behaviour, and claimed that in recognizing one's mirror image one ceased to respond socially to it (Gallup 1970: 86). Is that really correct?

It is striking how one-dimensional mirror self-recognition is for Gallup. Creatures are either capable or incapable of accomplishing the task. No attempt is made to differentiate further the kind of mirror experience we find in creatures capable of passing the test; that is, on Gallup's account there is no significant difference between the mirror self-experience undergone by human beings and that undergone by chimpanzees. However, we should not overlook that mirror self-experience from a developmental perspective, rather than amounting to a climactic moment, is a continuous and multi-level experience (O'Neill 1989: 70; Rochat 2003). In fact, it is particularly important to recognize that the infant's behaviour and affective reaction to the mirror undergoes marked and dramatic changes (Amsterdam 1968, 1972; Tomasello 1999). As reported by Beulah Amsterdam in her classical studies, three main developmental periods unfold between the ages of 3 and 24 months. The first period is characterized by mainly sociable behaviours towards the specular image. Infants between 3 and 12 months old tend to treat their own image as a playmate. This kind of behaviour was found in over 85 per cent of the tested infants. Around 13 months of age a second period starts, during which 90 per cent of the infants showed a marked increase in withdrawal behaviours: the infants would cry, or hide from or avoid looking at the mirror. Towards the end of this period, from around 20 months, Amsterdam reported that 75 per cent of the children also started to display signs of embarrassment and coyness when confronted with the mirror. Finally, towards the end of the second year, a third period starts, in which the children are able to pass the mirror self-recognition test. These changes reveal the complex interplay of cognitive and affective progress that takes place during this early period of child development (Amsterdam and Levitt 1980). To understand and assess the significance and import of mirror self-experience fully these changes have to be accounted for.

To start unearthing the complex nature of mirror self-experience, let me return to Merleau-Ponty's long essay *Les Relations avec autrui chez l'enfant*, which I alluded to in Chapter 6. As we saw then, Merleau-Ponty argues that a proper solution to the problem of how we can relate to and understand others will require a redefinition of the traditional notions of psyche and body. It is precisely in this context that he then starts to analyse mirror self-experience and argues that the mirror (and other reflecting surfaces) furnishes the child with a visual presentation of her own body that is very different from what she can obtain on her own (Merleau-Ponty 1964a: 125). Thus, the mirror does not simply provide redundant information; it does not just replicate knowledge already possessed. Hitherto the child has never seen her own face or the visual gestalt of her entire body. The mirror not only permits the child to perceive her own facial features; it also affords the child a very different apprehension of her own bodily unity than what is available from interoceptive, proprioceptive, and exteroceptive sources (Merleau-Ponty 1964a: 119, 126). Merleau-Ponty initially talks of this new unifying appearance of the body in terms of an objectification (Merleau-Ponty 1964a: 119), and describes how the child's encounter with her own specular image can make her aware of her own insularity and separation by presenting her with her body as a clearly delineated object (Merleau-Ponty 1964a: 119). Merleau-Ponty next proceeds to investigate this objectification more carefully. For the child to recognize the specular image as her own is for her to become a spectator of herself. It is to adopt a perspective or viewpoint on herself that equals what others can adopt on her. It is to recognize—and here it might be necessary to differentiate several developmental steps more carefully than Merleau-Ponty did—that one is visible to oneself and to others as well (Merleau-Ponty 1964a: 136). In short, the mirror permits the child to see herself as she is seen by others, and might bring about the explicit realization that she is given to others with the same visual appearance that she is being confronted with in the mirror. Merleau-Ponty writes:

At the same time that the image makes possible the knowledge of oneself, it makes possible a sort of alienation. I am no longer what I felt myself, immediately, to be; I am that image of myself that is offered by the mirror. To use Dr. Lacan's terms, I am 'captured, caught up' by my spatial image. Thereupon I leave the reality of my lived *me* in order to refer myself constantly to the ideal, fictitious, or imaginary *me*, of which the specular image is the first outline. In this sense I am torn from myself, and the image in the mirror prepares me for another still more serious alienation, which will be the alienation by others. For others have only an exterior image of me, which is analogous to the one seen in the mirror. Consequently others will tear me away from my immediate inwardness much more surely than will the mirror. (Merleau-Ponty 1964a: 136)

Let me try to unpack the guiding idea. Merleau-Ponty's central claim is that mirror self-experience exemplifies a troubled form of self-knowledge. To recognize oneself in the mirror does not simply involve an identification of the felt me which is here and the perceived me which is there; rather, it also and more importantly involves the dawning and unsettling realization that the felt me has an exterior dimension that can be witnessed by others (Merleau-Ponty 1964a: 129, 140). In short, the decisive and unsettling impact of mirror self-experience is not that I succeed in identifying the mirror image as myself. Rather, what is at stake here is the realization that I exist in an intersubjective space. I am exposed and visible to others. Consider that the face I see reflected in the mirror is also the face others see when I interact with them. Indeed, one of the reasons why people spend so much time before a mirror engaged in impression management is precisely because of the high social valence of one's face. When seeing myself in the mirror, I am seeing myself as others see me. I am confronted with the appearance I present to others. In fact, not only am I seeing myself as others see me, I am also seeing myself as if I were an other; that is, I am adopting an alienating perspective on myself.[2] The enigmatic and uncanny character of mirror self-experience is precisely due to this intermingling of self and other. It is me that I see in mirror, but the me I see hasn't quite the same familiarity and immediacy as the me I know from immediate experience. The me that I see in the mirror is distant and yet close; it is felt as another, and yet as myself. As Philippe Rochat puts it, 'inspecting oneself in a mirror and recognizing that it is "Me" out there is very much an "out-of-the-body experience"' (Rochat 2010: 334). Even though the specular image might indeed look like any other person, it retains its unbreakable link to me. I cannot get rid of this exteriority, since it shows up every time I look in the mirror. One explanation why the infant's initial delight when facing her specular image is replaced by wariness and embarrassment is the emergence of this more complex and more ambivalent form of self-experience, with its odd mix of the familiar and the alien.

More needs to be said in defending this claim. In particular, one has to consider the relation between successful mirror self-recognition in humans and in non-human animals. However, it is not at all obvious that the two can be equated, and that mirror self-recognition in chimpanzees or magpies corresponds to the cognitive and affective self-consciousness manifested in children passing the test (Rochat and Zahavi 2011). For now, all I wish to deny is that the recognition of a visual representation of one's own face is a paradigmatic and fundamental instance of self-consciousness, and that in the case of children, it is as socially and culturally impoverished as it has often been made out to be. Far from amounting to a primitive and basic type of self-experience, far from simply confirming an already existing self-identity, the recognition of one's own specular image is a rather sophisticated type of mediated

---

[2] It is noteworthy that both Husserl and Stein claim that recognition of our own mirror image presupposes empathy (Husserl 1952: 148; 1973b: 509; Stein 2008: 71).

self-recognition, one that takes place across distance and separation. Moreover, contrary to what Gallup is claiming, when humans recognize their own mirror image they don't cease to respond socially to it (Gallup 1970: 86). Even recognizing something as apparently simple as an image of oneself is more complicated than just contrasting self and other. It involves the appropriation of an objectification of oneself, and thus entails a critical tension between experiencing oneself as object and experiencing oneself as subject (Legrand 2007). This is nothing but a special case of a much more complicated pattern of how people in interaction with others experience and develop themselves.

A couple of intriguing studies by Rochat, Broesch, and colleagues support this interpretation. In one study, they compared responses to the classic mirror mark test in over two hundred children from 18 to 72 months of age growing up in highly contrasted cultural and socio-economical contexts (middle-class United States, rural Kenya, Fiji, Grenada, rural Peru, and Canada). What they discovered was marked differences. In rural and more traditional contexts, children showed significantly less touching or removing of the mark, typically facing their own specular image frozen, subdued, and avoidant. In a sample of eighty-two children from a rural village in Kenya, for example, only two passed the mirror test by touching or removing the mark they discovered on their face (Broesch et al. 2011: 1022). The authors argue that the children in all likelihood realized that it was themselves in the mirror, but that they were unsure of an acceptable response and therefore dared not touch or remove the unexpected mark. If this is correct, it would not only show that a failure to pass the mark test might be a false negative. It would also suggest that children who 'passed' the test by inhibiting their behaviour would possess a special kind of self-consciousness, namely, an awareness of their own identity in relation to the adults who surrounded them (Broesch et al. 2011: 1026). The extent to which the child's mirror self-experience and ability to pass the mirror mark test depends on normative pressure and social conformity was further demonstrated in another study, where the self-recognition of eighty-six children between 14 and 52 months old was assessed using the mirror mark test in two different social contexts: either the child was the only one with a mark on his face, or the experimenter and all the adults surrounding the child during the test also wore the same mark on their forehead. Far more children passed the mirror mark test by touching and removing the mark when they were the only one with the mark. When everybody around them was also marked, children showed significantly more hesitation in touching and removing the mark (a yellow 'post-it' sticker) on their forehead, often putting it back in an apparent attempt to conform with the social norm established in the testing room. These findings also illustrate the role of socio-affective factors in the development of mirror self-experience. When the child begins to manifest explicit self-recognition in mirrors, it is rarely merely with reference to his own embodied self, but is also with reference to how others might perceive and evaluate him. In short, mirror self-experience in typically developing children does not develop independently of the child's awareness of his social surroundings, but includes social awareness and a concern with self-presentation and public appearance (Rochat et al. 2012: 1496; see also footnote 1). To test facial self-recognition is consequently not to test the self per se, but to test and probe a quite specific dimension of self, namely, the self as social object. This angle and limitation is something that has not been sufficiently considered by the standard interpretation.

One possible objection to this criticism might run as follows: In Gallup and Keenan one finds occasional positive references to the work of Cooley and Mead (Gallup 1977: 335; Keenan et al. 2003: 41), who both explicitly and persistently discussed the self as social object. Cooley famously argued that the human self is an interpersonal entity and as such dependent upon social interactions with others. Along similar lines, and as earlier mentioned, Mead argued that one can only become self-conscious (in the sense of becoming an object to oneself) in an indirect manner, namely, by adopting the attitudes of others towards oneself, and that this is something that can only happen within a social environment (Mead 1962: 138). In support of the Cooley–Mead hypothesis, Gallup even referred to studies of chimpanzees reared in isolation who failed to exhibit self-directed behaviour in mirror situations even after extensive exposure. As a further test of the importance of social experience, two of the original chimpanzees were given three months of group experience, after which time self-recognitory responses began to appear. Gallup suggested that it was the chimpanzees' opportunity to view themselves from the other's point of view that made the difference (Gallup 1977: 336). It is consequently important to notice that whereas Keenan's work is indebted to Gallup's, Gallup's own account of self-recognition is precisely influenced by ideas found much earlier in Mead and Cooley (see Gallup et al. 1971; Gallup 1975, 1983). On closer examination, however, Gallup's references to Mead and Cooley are quite puzzling, since his own account flatly contradicts their views (for a careful analysis, see Mitchell 1997a). Whereas Cooley and Mead argued that self-knowledge presupposes knowledge of others and that the self-concept derives from one's taking the perspective of another towards oneself (Cooley 1912: 246; Mead 1962: 138), Gallup and Keenan both defend the view that knowledge of others presupposes knowledge of self and a developed self-concept. Whereas Gallup wrote that the ability to impute mental states to others presupposes the capacity to monitor such states on the part of the individual making the imputation (Gallup 1982: 243), Keenan argues that it is because I know my own thoughts that I can predict or infer another person's mental state (Keenan et al. 2003: 78).

As should have become clear by now, the neuroscientific study of facial self-recognition relies on a theoretical framework with a long (and partly distorted) history. When it comes to its own more principled reflections on, and analyses of, central concepts such as consciousness, self-awareness, and self—which have shaped the design of the experiment and continue to influence the interpretation of the empirical findings—these are clearly inadequate and in many ways committed to controversial theses. Rather than obviating the need for careful conceptual analysis, neuroscientific research on the neural correlates of self-recognition and self-experience is obviously in need of the latter. The complexity of the self and self-consciousness necessitates interdisciplinary collaboration—collaboration across the divide between theoretical analysis and empirical investigation. To think that a single discipline, be it philosophy or neuroscience, should have a monopoly on the investigation of the self is merely an expression of both arrogance and ignorance.

In various publications, Keenan and colleagues have claimed that the search for the localization of the self in the brain has been the goal of consciousness research for centuries (Feinberg and Keenan 2005: 661), and that this problem remains one of the great mysteries of science, philosophy, and psychology (Keenan et al. 2003: 99). In the article entitled 'Where in the Brain Is the Self?', however, the authors are careful to modify the initial claim by conceding not only that modules of the brain do not exist in isolation, and that one has to view the brain in its entirety, but also that it might be more appropriate and correct to opt for the more modest claim that the right hemisphere is dominant for certain aspects of self, rather than making the stronger claim that the self resides in the right hemisphere (Feinberg and Keenan 2005: 673, 675). I obviously agree. It is indeed far better to label the search for the neural correlates of self a search for those neural structures and mechanisms that enable self-recognition and self-experience than to describe it as an attempt to locate the self in the brain. The latter claim is tantamount to a category mistake (and here I would side with philosophers such as Dennett and Hacker who are otherwise frequently in disagreement; Dennett 1992; Bennett and Hacker 2003). For that reason, the answer to the question 'Where in the brain is the self?' can only be 'Nowhere'. To say that the self is nowhere in the brain is, however, not to say that 'nobody ever was or had a self' (Metzinger 2003: 1). One might deny that the self is a kind of thing that can be localized in the brain without denying the reality of the self.

14

Shame

On many standard readings, shame is an emotion that targets and involves the self in its totality. In shame, the self is affected by a global devaluation: it feels defective, objectionable, condemned. But what does the fact that we feel shame tell us about the nature of self? Does shame testify to the presence of a self-concept, a (failed) self-ideal, and a capacity for critical self-assessment, or does it rather, as some have suggested, point to the fact that the self is in part socially constructed (Calhoun 2004: 145)? Should shame primarily be classified as a self-conscious emotion or is it, rather, a distinct social emotion, or is there something misleading about these alternatives? In the following, I shall explore these questions and ultimately suggest that a closer study of complex emotions like shame can add important facets to our understanding of self and help to bridge the two notions of self I discussed in Part I, the minimalist notion of an experiential self and the richer notion of a narratively extended self.

14.1 Shame and self-consciousness

Emotions come in many different forms and shapes. Emotion research has spent much time investigating what Paul Ekman called the basic six: joy, fear, sadness, surprise, anger, and disgust (Ekman 2003). Allegedly these emotions emerge early in human development, they have a biological basis and a characteristic facial expression, and they are culturally universal. It is obvious, however, that these basic or primary emotions do not exhaust the richness of our emotional life. Think merely of more complex emotions like embarrassment, envy, shame, guilt, pride, jealousy, remorse, or gratitude. According to Michael Lewis, one useful way of classifying the different emotions is by operating with a distinction between self-conscious and non-self-conscious emotions. Whereas primary emotions do not involve self-consciousness, the more complex emotions do (Lewis 2007: 136). Indeed, on Lewis's account, the latter group of emotions involves elaborate cognitive processes, they all come about through self-reflection, and they all involve and require a concept of self. Thus, a developmental requirement for experiencing such emotions is that the child is in possession of a self-concept or a self-representation, which according to Lewis only happens from around 18 months of age. Lewis further distinguishes two groups of self-conscious emotions. Both groups involve self-exposure and objective self-consciousness, that is, self-reflection, but whereas the first involves non-evaluative exposure, the second involves both self-exposure and evaluation. The first group emerges around 18 months and includes emotions like embarrassment and envy. The second group emerges around 36 months. It includes shame and guilt and requires the ability to appropriate and internalize standards, rules, and goals, and to evaluate and compare one's behaviour vis-à-vis such standards (Lewis 2007: 135).

When Lewis speaks of self-consciousness or self-awareness, what precisely does he have in mind? Lewis operates with a distinction between subjective self-awareness and objective self-awareness. On his account, all living systems from the simplest to the most complicated regulate and monitor themselves. Some of the examples he provides concern the way a body tracks the level of carbon dioxide in the blood, or the way in which T-cells differentiate themselves from foreign protein (Lewis 2003: 279). For Lewis, this self-regulation and self–other differentiation require a certain amount of subjective self-awareness but we are dealing here with a form of self-awareness that remains unconscious (Lewis 1992: 16, 27).[1]

All living systems possess subjective self-awareness; only very few attain the level of objective self-awareness, which denotes a much higher representational complexity. The moment this level is attained, however, experiences and emotions become conscious. Only from that moment are they like something to or for us. Thus, on Lewis's account, it is only when we consciously reflect upon ourselves, only when we direct our attention inwards and internally attend to our own mental states as objects of attention, that they become conscious (Lewis 1992: 29). Lewis illustrates this idea with the following example: A loud noise may put me in a state of fright. However, I only consciously experience the state of fright if I reflect upon it. Prior to reflection, the fright remains unconscious. Considered from a developmental point of view, Lewis claims that prior to the emergence of objective self-consciousness, that is, before the infant develops a self-concept and an objective self-representation, she might have emotional states, but none of these states are conscious (Lewis 2004: 273–4), just as she doesn't have any other conscious experiences.

Increasing cognitive capacities allow for objective self-awareness and thereby, according to Lewis, also for self-conscious emotions like embarrassment, empathy, and envy. When joined with an even more sophisticated cognitive apprehension of standards, rules, and goals, self-conscious evaluative emotions like pride, guilt, and shame become possible, and Lewis ends up defining the latter as an intense negative emotion that is elicited when one experiences failure relative to a standard, feels responsible for the failure, and believes that the failure reflects a damaged self. Whereas he considers the issue of public failure to be relevant to the emotion of

---

[1] Perhaps it would have been better if Lewis had talked of non-conscious self-regulation and self-differentiation rather than of unconscious subjective self-awareness. It is somewhat difficult to make sense of the idea that leucocytes possess subjective self-awareness.

embarrassment, he denies its relevance when it comes to emotions like shame, guilt, and pride (Lewis 1998: 127).

Consider now, by contrast, the account of shame proposed by Rom Harré. Briefly put, Harré has argued that whereas embarrassment is occasioned by the realization that others have become aware that what one has been doing has been a breach of convention and the code of manners, shame is occasioned by the realization that others have become aware that what one has been doing has been a moral infraction (Harré 1990: 199).

I find both of these proposals problematic. Although we might readily agree that embarrassment is less shattering and painful than shame, that it is more obviously related to awkward social exposure (due to an open fly button, a loud stomach noise, inappropriate clothing, etc.) than to the violation of important personal values, Harré's definitions and neat distinction are unsatisfactory. Not only does he put too much emphasis on the presence of an actual audience—as if one can't feel ashamed when being alone, as if one only feels shameful because one has been found out—his sharp distinction between moral infraction and breach of convention also seems questionable. As a case in point, consider the following vignette reported by Jacoby: A boy had been on a field trip with his class and was on a train on the way back. He got acute diarrhoea, but since the toilet was occupied, he eventually defecated in his pants—something that was noticed and ridiculed by the entire class (Jacoby 1994: 7). As Jacoby goes on to explain, this episode turned out to be quite a traumatic experience for the child, and even as an adult he remained deeply affected by it. It seems wrong to categorize this experience as a momentary feeling of embarrassment, but on the other hand, neither does it seem plausible to categorize it as a moral transgression. Although one can be ashamed of moral infractions, one can certainly also be ashamed of things that have nothing to do with ethics. Indeed, shame doesn't have to be brought about by something one wilfully does. One can feel ashamed of a physical disability or of one's parentage or skin colour. Thus, rather than linking shame and embarrassment to an infraction of moral values and social conventions respectively (an attempt that also flies in the face of the fact that the same event can be felt as either shameful or embarrassing by different people), I think an initially more plausible criterion for demarcation is one that links shame, but not embarrassment, to a global decrease of self-esteem or self-respect and a painful awareness of personal flaws and deficiencies. This would also match well with an observation by Galen Strawson: whereas past embarrassments can easily furnish funny stories to tell about oneself, past shames and humiliations do so rarely if at all (Strawson 1994).[2]

---

[2] As Strawson has subsequently pointed out, childhood shames might be some of the rare exceptions. Might we not in retrospect find it amusing that such trifles could back then have been felt as shameful? I suspect, however, that the ability to feel amusement about such past shames is conditional upon us no longer identifying as strongly with our past self.

As for Lewis's account, there is much with which one can take issue. Consider, for instance, his distinction between primary and secondary emotions. Lewis writes:

I suggest that emotions can be classified in relation to the role of the self. The elicitation of fear, joy, disgust, surprise, anger, sadness, and interest does not require introspection or self-reference. Therefore, let us consider these emotions as one set. The elicitation of jealousy, envy, empathy, embarrassment, shame, pride, and guilt does require introspection or self-reference. These emotions constitute another set.... Thus, I propose that the difference between primary and secondary emotions is that the secondary emotions involve self-reference. Secondary emotions will be referred to as *self-conscious emotions*; shame is a self-conscious emotion. (Lewis 1992: 19–20)

Is it true that primary emotions are non-self-conscious, and that they lack a reference to self? I think this claim can be disputed in at least two ways. The first way is to endorse a notion of pre-reflective self-consciousness. If one does that, as I think one should, it makes no sense to single out the complex emotions as self-conscious emotions, since all emotions, in so far as the subject experiences them first-personally, are self-conscious. Of course, Lewis might object that the subject does not consciously experience emotions like fear, anger, and joy, at least not prior to taking them as objects of reflection. By arguing in this manner, by taking objective self-consciousness to be a precondition for phenomenal consciousness, he is committed to the view that animals and infants who lack higher-order representational skills will also lack experiences with phenomenal character; there will be nothing it is like for them to experience pain, exhaustion, frustration, etc. But although he is not alone in holding such a view—as we have already seen, it is a view he shares with Gallup and Carruthers—it has little to recommend it.

The second way to question Lewis's distinction is by arguing that emotions—in an even more accentuated manner than perceptions or cognitions—are self-involving. Consider that we respond emotionally to that which matters to us, to that which we care about, to that towards which we are not indifferent. In that sense, one might argue that emotions involve appraisals of what has importance, significance, value, and relevance to oneself. This holds true not merely for complex emotions like guilt, shame, or pride, but certainly also for emotions like joy, disgust, anger, and fear. If this is correct, the claim would not be that there are no significant differences between emotions like anger and fear and emotions like shame and repentance. It would just be doubtful whether the relevant difference has anything to do with whether the emotions are self-conscious or self-involving or not.

But where then should one search for the difference? One rather obvious possibility would be to claim that the different emotions are self-involving in different ways, be it because the self is the focus of attention in some of these emotions, or because some of the emotions are self-constituting in some more significant sense of the term.

Consider again the title of Lewis's book *Shame: The Exposed Self*. This is how Lewis explains the subtitle: 'The subtitle of this book is *The Exposed Self*. What is an exposed self and to whom is it exposed? The self is exposed to itself, that is, we are capable of viewing ourselves. A self capable of self-reflection is unique to humans' (Lewis 1992: 36). In short, Lewis defines the exposure in question as one of being exposed to oneself. That is, when he talks of the exposed self, he is referring to our capacity for self-reflection. But is this not to miss the crucial point? Compare by contrast the following remark by Darwin: 'It is not the simple act of reflecting on our own appearance, but the thinking what others think of us, which excites a blush' (Darwin 2009 [1872]: 345). One problem with a definition of shame like Lewis's that focuses exclusively on an individual's own negative self-assessment is that it becomes difficult to differentiate shame from other negative self-evaluations, such as self-disappointment or self-criticism. Another problem with this highlighting of our visibility to ourselves is that it seems to overlook an important type of shame, namely, the kind of shame that is induced by a deflation and devaluation of our public appearance and social self-identity, by the exposure of a discrepancy between who we claim to be and how we are perceived by others. Any account of shame ought to explain why personal flaws that are recognized and tolerated in private as minor shortcomings might be felt as shameful the moment they are publicly exposed.

But my criticisms of Lewis and Harré seem to point in opposite directions. I blame Harré for exaggerating the need for an actual audience, and Lewis for downplaying the importance of sociality. How do these criticisms go together? Let us move onwards and consider some alternative views on shame found in phenomenology.

14.2 Varieties of shame

As we saw in Chapter 2, Sartre distinguishes two types of self-consciousness: a pre-reflective and a reflective. The first has priority since it can prevail independently of the latter, whereas reflective self-consciousness always presupposes pre-reflective self-consciousness. In the third part of *L'Être et le néant* Sartre complicates matters in so far as he now argues that there is a third type of self-consciousness that is intersubjectively mediated, that is, it has the other as its condition of possibility. Sartre claims that there are modes of consciousness that although remaining strictly for-itself, that is, characterized by pre-reflective self-consciousness, nevertheless point to a very different type of ontological structure. More specifically he makes the somewhat enigmatic claim that there are modes of consciousness which, although they are mine, nevertheless reveal to me a being which is my being without being-for-me (Sartre 2003: 245). To understand better what Sartre is up to, let us consider the example he himself introduces, namely, the feeling of shame.

According to Sartre, shame is a form of intentional consciousness. It is a shameful apprehension of something, and this something happens to be myself. I am ashamed of what I am, and to that extent shame also exemplifies a self-relation. As Sartre points out, however, shame is not primarily and originally a phenomenon of reflection. I can reflect upon my failings and feel shame as a result, just as I might reflect upon my feeling of shame, but I can feel shame prior to engaging in reflection. Shame is initially, as he puts it, 'an immediate shudder which runs through me from head to foot without any discursive preparation' (Sartre 2003: 246). Indeed and more significantly, in its primary form shame is not a feeling I can simply elicit on my own through reflection; rather, shame is shame of oneself before the other (Sartre 2003: 246, 312). It presupposes the intervention of the other, not merely because the other is the one before whom I feel ashamed, but also and more significantly because that of which I am ashamed is only constituted in and through my encounter with the other. Thus, although shame exemplifies a self-relation, we are on Sartre's account dealing with an essentially mediated form of self-relation, one where the other is the mediator between me and myself. To put it differently, rather than being primarily a self-reflective emotion involving negative self-evaluation, shame is, for Sartre, an emotion that reveals our relationality, our being-for-others. Sartre would consequently deny that shame is either merely a self-conscious emotion or merely a social emotion. On his account, it is both.

Shame makes me aware of not being in control and of having my foundation outside myself. The other's gaze confers a truth upon me that I do not master, and over which I am, in that moment, powerless (Sartre 2003: 260). Thus, to feel shame, according to Sartre, is to recognize and accept the other's evaluation, if ever so fleetingly. It is to identify with the object that the other looks at and judges (Sartre 2003: 246, 287, 290). Moreover, for Sartre, it makes no difference whether the evaluation of the other is positive or not, since it is the very objectification that is shame-inducing. He writes:

Pure shame is not a feeling of being this or that guilty object but in general of being *an* object; that is, of *recognizing myself* in this degraded, fixed, and dependent being which I am for the Other. Shame is the feeling of an *original fall*, not because of the fact that I may have committed this or that particular fault but simply that I have 'fallen' into the world in the midst of things and that I need the mediation of the Other in order to be what I am. (Sartre 2003: 312)

In shame, I recognize the other as the subject through whom I acquire objecthood. On Sartre's view, however, this recognition takes a rather peculiar form. Although I experience that the other furnishes me with the self-identity of an object—the gaze of the other petrifies my freedom and reduces me to a fixed set of determinations, I *am* the way the other sees me and I am nothing but that—the precise nature of this object will always elude my grasp. I can neither control nor know with certainty how I am assessed by others. Why? In part, because I am fundamentally incapable of adopting his view. I cannot objectify myself as mercilessly as the other does, since I lack the required self-distance. So although the feeling of shame reveals to me that I exist for and am visible to others, although it reveals to me that I am (partly) constituted by the other, and that a dimension of my being is one that the other provides me with, it is according to Sartre a dimension of myself that I cannot know or intuit in the same way as others can. It is consequently no wonder that Sartre calls my being-for-others an *ecstatic* and *external* dimension of being, and speaks of the *existential alienation* occasioned by my encounter with the other (Sartre 2003: 286, 292, 320).

Although Sartre's analysis of shame is the most well-known phenomenological account, his analysis is neither the first nor the most extensive phenomenological one. In 1933 Erwin Straus published a short but suggestive article entitled 'Die Scham als historiologisches Problem', and twenty years earlier Max Scheler wrote a long essay entitled *Über Scham und Schamgefühl*.[3] One reason for looking at Straus and Scheler is that they both add to, as well as challenge, Sartre's analysis. Moreover, in the last few years Scheler's account has received something of a revival, and has been assessed positively in recent books by, for instance, Nussbaum (2004) and Deonna et al. (2011).

One commonality between Straus and Scheler is that they both emphasize the need for a differentiation between various types of shame. Sartre's focus is almost exclusively on *honte*, but French distinguishes between *honte* and *pudeur*, whereas German distinguishes between *Schande* and *Scham*. Both meanings can also be found in the entry on shame in the *Oxford English Dictionary*. The *OED* distinguishes the painful emotion arising from the consciousness of something dishonouring or disgraceful in one's own conduct from our sense of shame, that is, our perception of what is improper or disgraceful. As for Scheler and Straus, they both argue against the view that shame is a negative and repressive emotion per se, one we should aim to remove from our lives (compare Schneider 1987), and they would consequently disagree with Tangney and Dearing's general characterization of shame as an 'extremely painful and ugly feeling that has a negative impact on interpersonal behavior' (2002: 3). Straus for his part distinguishes between a protective form of shame, which involves sensitivity to and respect for boundaries of intimacy, and a concealing form of shame, which is more concerned with maintaining social prestige (Straus 1966: 220). To exemplify what Straus might have in mind when talking of the protective form of shame, consider the situation in which you feel ashamed as a result of having intimate details about your life revealed publicly. You might feel ashamed even if the audience doesn't react critically, but simply as a result of the exposure itself. Addressing the same phenomenon, Bollnow links shame to the desire to protect the most private and intimate core of ourselves from the violation that public scrutiny might cause (Bollnow 2009: 67, 91).

---

[3] In addition to Sartre and Scheler, Levinas is another major figure in phenomenology who early on addressed the issue of shame. His first analysis was published in a text entitled *De l'évasion* from 1935. In his later work *Totalité et infini* from 1961, Levinas argued that shame is a response to the ethical encounter with the other who interrupts and disrupts my tranquillity by putting me and my unjustified and arbitrary freedom into question (Levinas 1979: 83–4).

As for Scheler, he not only thinks the feeling of shame can in some instances be pleasurable, but more importantly, he considers a sensitivity to and capacity for shame ethically valuable and links it to the emergence of conscience—it is, as he points out, no coincidence that Genesis explicitly relates shame to knowledge of good and evil (Scheler 1957: 142). Scheler's first point, regarding the pleasurable quality of shame, is connected to a distinction he makes that matches the one made by Straus. Scheler distinguishes the anticipating and protecting shame of the blushing virgin, which, on his view, is characterized by lovely warmth, from the painful experience of repenting shame (*Schamreue*), a burning shame that is backward-looking and full of piercing sharpness and self-hatred (Scheler 1957: 140). As for the second point, Scheler emphasizes that when we are ashamed of something, the shame reaction must be seen in the light of a normative commitment that existed prior to the situation about which one is ashamed (Scheler 1957: 100). The feeling of shame occurs precisely because of the discrepancy between the values one continues to endorse and the actual situation. Indeed, shame anxiety, the fear of shaming situations, might be considered a guardian of dignity. It puts us on guard against undignified behaviour that would place us (and others) in shaming situations.[4] As Plato pointed out in the *Laws*, shame is what will prevent or inhibit a man from doing what is dishonourable (Plato 1961: 647a). Indeed, the very notion of shamelessness suggests that the possession of a sense of shame is a moral virtue, and its absence an incapacitating trait. Rather than being inherently debilitating, shame might also, in short, play a constructive role in moral development, and not only because it can aid socialization by promoting social conformity, but because it can disrupt my self-complacency, modify my self-understanding, and in the long run motivate me to reorient my way of living (Steinbock 2014).[5] In addition, Scheler argues that the occurrence of shame testifies to the presence of a certain self-respect and self-esteem; it is only because one expects oneself to have worth that this expectation can be disappointed and give rise to shame (Scheler 1957: 141; see also Taylor 1985: 80–1; Nussbaum 2004: 184).

Scheler would agree with the idea that shame is an essentially self-involving emotion, but he explicitly rejects the claim that shame is essentially a social emotion, one that by necessity involves others. Rather, Scheler claims that there is a self-directed form of shame which is just as fundamental as the shame one can feel in the presence of others, and argues that the core feature of shame is that it points to the clash or discrepancy between our higher spiritual values on the one hand and our

---

[4] The following example might illustrate this. You are on a train and looking for the toilet. When you find it and enter, you discover that it is already being used by an elderly woman who must have forgotten to lock the door. If you possess a sense of shame, you will not only retreat immediately, but also search for another toilet in order to spare the woman the experience of re-encountering you when she exits.

[5] Even if shame anxiety can play a role in the process of socialization, it can obviously also be debilitating by killing initiative: If I do not do anything, I do not risk potential shameful exposure. Likewise, it is hard to see anything positive in the so-called 'toxic shame' felt by some sexually abused children.

animal nature and bodily needs on the other (Scheler 1957: 68, 78). This is also why Scheler claims that shame is a distinctly human emotion, one that neither God nor animals could have. It is, in his view, a fundamental human emotion, one characterizing the *conditio humana* (Scheler 1957: 67, 91). More recently, Nussbaum has followed up on this and has argued that shame is on the scene before we become aware of what is normal within a particular social value system, and that it most fundamentally concerns the tension between our aspirations and ideals on the one hand and our awareness of our finitude and helplessness on the other. Shame is an emotional response to the uncovering and display of our weakness, our defects, and our imperfections (Nussbaum 2004: 173), one that precedes any particular learning of social standards, although societies obviously have room to shape the experience of shame differently by teaching different views of what is an appropriate occasion for shame (Nussbaum 2004: 173, 185).

It is hardly insignificant that shame has frequently been associated with nakedness and that the etymology of the word 'shame' can be traced back to the Old High German term *scama* and to the pre-Germanic *skem*, which mean to cover. Likewise, the Greek term for genitalia, *aidoia*, is related to one of the Greek terms for shame, *aidos* (Nussbaum 2004: 182; see also Konstan 2003). One might add that the German term for shame, *Scham*, also refers to the genitals, as does the Danish term for labia, *skamlæber*, which literally means lips of shame. According to Scheler, one reason why nakedness has traditionally been associated with shame, one reason why we seek to cover our sexual organs, is precisely because they are symbols of animality, mortality, and neediness (Scheler 1957: 75). Consider how the loss of control over one's bodily functions, as in sickness or old age, might be felt as shameful, just as it might be shame-inducing to realize that one is being observed while defecating. As Sartre would later argue, the fear of being surprised in a state of nakedness is a symbolic manifestation of original shame. The body symbolizes our defenceless state as objects. To put on clothes is to attempt to hide one's object-state; it is to claim the right of seeing without being seen, that is, to be a pure subject (Sartre 2003: 312).

14.3 Others in mind

At this point, we need to get clearer on what role others play. To claim that shame only occurs in situations where a discrediting fact about oneself is exposed to others is not convincing. One can certainly feel shame when alone; that is, shame does not require an actual observer or audience. One may also feel ashamed of something even if one can be certain that it will for ever remain secret. But does that mean that a reference to others is inessential, and that an account of shame can dispense with the social dimension? Let us not be too hasty. Let us consider some alleged cases of non-social shame.

1. You have a congenital facial disfigurement and you feel shame when you see yourself in the mirror.
2. You have done something you believe should not be done (or failed to do something you believe ought to be done). In such a situation, you might indeed feel ashamed afterwards. You might feel guilty about the specific deed in question, but you might also feel ashamed of simply being the kind of person who could do (or fail to do) such a thing.[6]
3. You feel ashamed of who you have become when compared to who you were; that is, you feel ashamed of not living up to your capacities, of having betrayed your potential.
4. You have made a firm decision not to touch alcohol again. In a moment of weakness, however, you indulge your urge and commence on a drinking binge that eventually leaves you senseless. When you emerge from your stupor, you feel ashamed of your lack of self-control, of your surrender to what you consider base instincts.
5. You are together with a group of peers. They start to discuss a political issue and quickly a racist consensus emerges that you strongly disagree with. However, shame anxiety prevents you from expressing your dissenting opinion in order not to be ridiculed or ostracized. Afterwards, however, when alone, you are deeply ashamed of your cowardly attitude.

These examples certainly demonstrate that the feeling of shame does not require the presence of an actual observer. However, this is hardly something that Sartre would deny. Just consider his famous example of the voyeur who is looking through a keyhole and suddenly hears steps behind him. He shudders as a wave of shame sweeps over him, but when straightening up and looking down the corridor, he realizes that it was a false alarm. There is nobody there (Sartre 2003: 301). Sartre's interpretation of this is not that shame is after all something I can attain on my own. Rather, he argues that the feeling of shame refers me to the other-as-subject, and that the other-as-subject can be present even when the other-as-object is absent. There are various things to be said for and against this analysis.[7] For now, I just want to

---

[6] According to widespread convention, the difference between shame and guilt is that the former is about shortcomings whereas the latter is about wrongdoings. In guilt, the focus is on specific actions of the self, whereas the focus of shame is on the self as such. However, to insist that shame and guilt must be distinguished is not, of course, to deny that they can often occur together.

[7] When Sartre advances the claims that the look is merely the concrete occasion of my original being-for-others (Sartre 2003: 441), that the other is present everywhere as that through which I become an object, and that this fundamental relation to the other is the condition of possibility for my particular experience of the concrete other (which is why the concrete encounter with a particular other is described as a mere empirical variation of my fundamental being-for-others) (Sartre 2003: 303–4), it is difficult not to reproach him for advocating the very kind of apriorism that he was criticizing in Heidegger's account of *Mitsein* (for a more extensive discussion, see Zahavi 1996: 114–17). More generally speaking, although there are many valuable insights to be found in Sartre's analysis of intersubjectivity, there is also a good deal to disagree with. This would include Sartre's excessively negative assessment and characterization of our

emphasize that Sartre concedes that one can feel shame when alone. But as Bernard Williams pointed out, to overlook the importance of the imagined other is just silly (Williams 1993: 82).[8] In many cases where the shame-experiencing subject is physically alone and not in the presence of others, he or she will have internalized the perspective of the others; he or she will have others in mind (Rochat 2009). Moreover, the distinctive character of the shame experience frequently includes the conviction that others would not have done or been like that. To fail at a task that nobody else is able to succeed at, and that nobody expects you to succeed at, is less likely to result in shame. The imagined other might consequently figure not only as a critical observer, but also as a point of contrast or comparison. Consider, as a case in point, the first example. Although the disfigured person who feels shame when looking in the mirror is alone, I think a natural interpretation would be that the shame experience in question is connected to the fact that the person considers the disfigurement a stigma, as something that excludes him or her from normality.

Objections to this line of reasoning, however, can be found in various writings by Gabriele Taylor and by Julien Deonna and Fabrice Teroni. In her book *Pride, Shame, and Guilt: Emotions of Self-Assessment*, Taylor initially argues that Sartre's account of shame is too simplistic in that it only covers a limited range of cases (Taylor 1985: 59). To some extent, I would agree with this assessment, just as I also think that Sartre's analysis could have profited from a more meticulous differentiation between the members of the so-called shame family of emotions: shame, embarrassment, humiliation, etc. According to Taylor, shame is crucially related to a shift in the agent's perspective on himself or herself—a shift that specifically occasions the realization of an adverse discrepancy between the agent's assumptions about himself until now and the perspective offered by a more detached observer (Taylor 1985: 66). According to Taylor, this shift is typically brought about by the realization that one is or could be the object of another's attention. In contrast to Sartre, however, the other is, for Taylor, merely a means to this shift. Although the adverse judgement—and for Taylor shame is a rather sophisticated type of self-consciousness in that it amounts to a reflective self-evaluation (Taylor 1985: 67)—is brought about by the realization of how one's position is or may be seen from an observer's point of view, there is in the final self-directed judgement no reference to such a point of view. The final judgement concerns oneself only. One is degraded absolutely and not just relative to a specific observer or audience (Taylor 1985: 68). For Taylor, this points to one of the

encounter with others. After all, for Sartre, shame is not just one emotion among others, but the emotion that best captures and most fundamentally characterizes our relation to others.

[8] As Williams continues, the internalized other need not be a particular individual, or the representative of some socially significant group; rather, the other may also be identified in ethical terms. He might be conceived as one whose reactions I would respect. Some might claim that if the other is identified in such terms, then he is no longer an other. But, as Williams argues, this is the wrong conclusion. Although the other does not have to be an identifiable individual, he is still potentially somebody rather than nobody and somebody other than me (Williams 1993: 84).

important differences between shame and embarrassment. In embarrassment, the focus is on the agent's appearance to others, on the impression he makes on others in a given situation. Given that the concern is always with one's own position vis-à-vis others, embarrassment is a more social emotion than shame. But, according to Taylor, this is also what makes it a less painful and shattering experience. Given that the focus is merely on how one presents oneself in a specific context vis-à-vis a given audience, the embarrassment can be alleviated by changing the situation and context, whereas shame concerns an absolute failure, an adverse judgement of the person as a whole, which is why it typically persists even after the shame-inducing situation has changed or ceased (Taylor 1985: 70–6).

Although in the course of her analysis Taylor can point to examples of shame where the social dimension is less perspicuous, although she can come up with counter-examples that don't easily fit Sartre's model—for instance, by referring to an artist who feels ashamed because his current work doesn't match the quality of his earlier creations (Taylor 1985: 58)—this doesn't in and of itself show that Sartre's account fails to capture a central type of shame. Indeed, I think one problem with Taylor's model is that she commits the same kind of mistake as Sartre and offers us an account with too few distinctions.

Before I proceed to cash out this criticism in more detail, let me first consider Deonna and Teroni's objections as well. Deonna and Teroni insist that we ought to distinguish carefully between different definitions of what a social emotion amounts to. Is the claim that (1) the object of shame is specifically social, its object being either somebody else or our own social standing, or (2) that the values involved in shame are acquired through contact with others, or (3) that shame always requires taking an outside perspective on ourselves, or (4) that shame always takes place in a social context? Deonna and Teroni basically reject all these proposals. It is, on their view, quite implausible to claim that there is always an actual or imagined audience when we feel shame; nor, on their view, is it correct to claim that shame is always connected to a perceived threat to our social standing or with the management of our social image (Deonna and Teroni 2009: 39; 2011). Although this might indeed be the case when it comes to what they term 'superficial shame', what they call 'deep shame' is something we feel as a result of personal failure quite regardless of the evaluation by others, for instance, when reflecting on our own morally repugnant behaviour (Deonna and Teroni 2011: 201). For a concrete and extreme example, consider a case discussed by Hutchinson. It concerns Léopard, who committed atrocities during the Rwanda genocide. Several years later, Léopard is interviewed while in prison, and he recounts how he has come to feel deep shame, despite the fact that this has led to mockery and ridicule from his comrades (Hutchinson 2008: 141–3). It would indeed be far-fetched to explain Léopard's shame as the result of his comrades' negative evaluation. Deonna and Teroni next concede that the values involved in shame might be socially acquired, but they argue that this would hardly be sufficient to warrant the claim that shame is essentially a social emotion, since the acquisition of values involved in other non-social emotions is equally social (Deonna and Teroni 2011: 195). Finally, Deonna and Teroni take up the issue of perspective change. It is, they write, impossible to be ashamed of what one is wholly immersed in. In that sense, shame does involve the critical perspective of an evaluator. But they deny that the evaluator has to be another, or that the shift in perspective has to be motivated by others. Rather, and here they come quite close to Lewis's view, the shift of perspective is merely a question of a shift from an unreflective doer to a reflective evaluator (Deonna and Teroni 2011: 203).

What is their positive proposal? In their view, shame involves a negative evaluative stance towards oneself. It is motivated by an awareness of a conflict between a value one is committed to and a (dis)value exemplified by what one is ashamed of (Deonna and Teroni 2011: 206). They consequently propose the following definition of shame:

Shame is the subject's awareness that the way he is or acts is so much at odds with the values he cares to exemplify that it appears to disqualify him from his very commitment to the value, that is he perceives himself as unable to exemplify it even at a minimal level. (Deonna and Teroni 2009: 46)

More specifically, they argue that a subject will feel shame only if the following three conditions are met:

[1] She comes to take a trait or an action of hers to exemplify the polar opposite of a self-relevant value. [2] She apprehends this as indicating a distinctive incapacity with respect to the demands of this particular value. [3] This incapacity is distinctive in the sense that it consists in the incapacity to exemplify, even minimally, this value. (Deonna et al. 2011: 103)

How should we assess these various objections and non-social definitions? One initial concern is that the definition provided by Deonna and Teroni, which mainly targets highly elaborate, self-directed judgemental forms of shame, seems to be so cognitively demanding that it would rule out not only something like pre-reflective shame, but also anything like infantile shame. Another worry might be that shame is less about one's failure to exemplify a self-relevant value than it is about exemplifying a self-relevant defect; that is, what is shame-inducing is not the distance from an ideal self but the closeness to an undesired self (Lindsay-Hartz et al. 1995: 277; Gilbert 1998: 19).

Both Taylor and Deonna and Teroni are very concerned with coming up with a definition of shame that covers all possible cases. To some extent, this is, of course, a perfectly respectable endeavour, but such a focus also runs the risk of presenting us with too undifferentiated a picture of the emotion. It may offer us a definition that blinds us to important distinctions. I doubt anybody would deny that shame is a multifaceted phenomenon, but as we have already seen, some would go further and insist on the need for a distinction between different irreducible forms of shame. Some would distinguish disgrace shame and discretion shame, concealing shame and protective shame, natural shame and moral shame, envy shame and shame jealousy, or bodily shame and psychical shame, to mention just a few of the available candidates (see, for instance, Ausubel 1955: 382; Bollnow 2009: 55–7; Smith et al. 2002: 157; Gilbert 2003: 1215; Rawls 1972: 444). Furthermore, we should not forget that shame belongs to a family of interrelated emotions. It is not difficult to come up with examples where the demarcation gets somewhat fuzzy. The fact that the same event can be felt as humiliating, shameful, or embarrassing by different people doesn't make things easier. Ultimately, I think Susan Miller is quite right when she argues that since concepts like shame or embarrassment are not as effortlessly applied to experiences as concepts like door or table are applied to objects, it might be best not to assume that the study of shame is the study of an absolutely clear and well-bounded category of experience (Miller 1985: 28).

Given this situation, I shall refrain from the bold but perhaps also overly ambitious task of offering a clear-cut definition of shame, one that specifies its necessary and sufficient features. My goal in the following will be somewhat more modest. Rather than attempting to disprove that there are non-social types of shame, my primary claim will be that there are other, and arguably more prototypical, forms of shame that cannot adequately be understood in non-social terms, and that an attempt to provide a non-social definition of shame is consequently bound to miss something quite significant. Consider for a start—and in the following my main focus will be on disgrace shame—the following five situations:

1. When writing your latest article, you make extensive use of passages found in an essay by a little-known and recently deceased scholar. After your article has been published, you participate in a public meeting where you are suddenly accused of plagiarism. You emphatically deny it, but the accuser, your departmental nemesis, produces incontrovertible proof.

2. You are met with the contempt of your new classmates when you show up at a high school party in out-of-fashion clothes.

3. You apply for a position and have been bragging to your friends that you are sure to get it, but after the job interview, and while in the company of your friends, you are informed by the appointing committee that you are far from being even qualified for the job.

4. You have been having a row with your unruly 5-year-old daughter and you finally lose your patience and slap her. Right away, you experience guilt, but then you suddenly realize that the principal of the kindergarten has been observing the whole scene.

5. You have started a new romantic relationship. After a while, in a moment of intimacy, you reveal your sexual preferences. Your disclosure is met by your partner's incredulous stare.[9]

---

[9] As Nussbaum points out, the more intimate we become with others, the more we expose ourselves, the more vulnerable we also become to shame (Nussbaum 2004: 216).

If we consider these five situations, and if we grant that they are likely to give rise to an experience of shame (rather than, say, embarrassment) in some people, how plausible is it then to claim that concrete others are quite accidental to the emotion in question—at most a mere trigger for its emergence—and that the very same experience of shame could have occurred in a private setting? I do not find such a suggestion plausible at all.[10] I am not denying that we can sit in judgement on ourselves and as a result come to feel shame, but I think that this kind of repenting, self-reflective shame, with its accompanying feeling of self-disappointment, self-misery, or even self-loathing, has a somewhat different intentional structure and phenomenality than the overpowering feeling of shame that one can experience in the presence of others.[11] In the latter case, there is a heightened feeling of exposure and vulnerability, and an accompanying wish to hide and disappear, to become invisible, to sink into the ground. There is also a characteristic narrowing of focus. You cannot carefully attend to details in the environment while being subjected to that kind of shame. Rather, the world recedes and the self stands revealed. In his own analysis, Sartre highlights the way the gaze of the other disrupts my control of the situation (Sartre 2003: 289). Rather than simply existing bodily, rather than simply being absorbed in my various projects and interacting confidently with the environment, I become painfully aware of my bodily facticity and exposure. In fact, the acute experience of shame might give rise to something akin to bodily paralysis. The behavioural manifestation of shame—slumped posture, downward head movement and gaze-avoidance, covering of the face—also emphasizes the centripetality of the emotion. The experience of shame is an experience of self, but it is one that is thrust upon us. We are in the spotlight whether we want it or not. It is one that overwhelms us and which is initially almost impossible to avoid, escape, or control. As Nietzsche puts it in *Morgenröte*:

The feeling 'I am the mid-point of the world!' arises very strongly if one is suddenly overcome with shame; one then stands there as though confused in the midst of a surging sea and feels dazzled as though by a great eye which gazes upon us and through us from all sides. (Nietzsche 1997: 166)

---

[10] The same obviously holds true for something like vicarious shame. It is noteworthy that the *Oxford English Dictionary* in defining shame specifically includes a reference to those situations in which shame arises from the consciousness of something dishonouring, ridiculous, or indecorous in the conduct of those whose honour or disgrace one regards as one's own.

[11] In an intriguing study, Smith and colleagues asked participants to read hypothetical accounts of an event that could have happened to a person like themselves. They were told to try to imagine what the central person in the account would be thinking and feeling. Then, after reading the accounts, participants were tested to measure their sense of this person's experience. In one test, the different accounts involved a protagonist who committed a moral transgression, and the story then varied according to three conditions (privacy, or implicit or explicit public exposure). In the first condition, the transgression took place in private. In the second condition, the transgressor either saw or was reminded of someone who would have disapproved of the transgression; and in the final condition, the transgression was actually witnessed by another. The findings showed unequivocally that explicit public exposure intensified the experience of shame when compared to the privacy condition. If the transgression involved a violation of personal standards, the feeling of shame was also significantly higher in the implicit exposure condition when compared to the privacy condition (Smith et al. 2002).

This kind of shame also disrupts the normal temporal flow. Whereas repenting self-reflective shame is retrospective and past-oriented, and whereas shame anxiety—which in any case might be more of a disposition than an occurrent feeling—is by and large anticipatory and future-oriented, the interpersonal experience of shame that I am currently focusing on might best be characterized in terms of a 'frozen now' (Karlsson and Sjöberg 2009: 353). The future is lost, and the subject is fixed in the present moment. As Sartre writes, in shame I experience myself as trapped in facticity, as being irremediably what I am (rather than as someone with future possibilities, as someone who can become otherwise), as defencelessly illuminated by an absolute light (with no protective privacy) (Sartre 2003: 286, 312). Whereas guilt is primarily focused on the negative effects on others, includes a wish to undo the deed, and might motivate reparative actions, the acute feeling of interpersonal shame does not leave room for the exploration of future possibilities of redemption.

As already mentioned, Taylor has argued that shame (in contrast to embarrassment) involves an absolute sense of degradation, and not just one that is relative to a specific observer or audience. Whereas one might feel embarrassed vis-à-vis specific others, that is, whereas embarrassment might be relative to specific others, and whereas one might seek comfort for this embarrassment and even joke about it with friends and confederates, the experience of shame is different. Not only is shame difficult to communicate,[12] but we lack the inclination to let others in on it (in order to obtain their sympathy and consolation). Moreover, although shame might be induced by our encounter with a specific other, we are not merely shamed vis-à-vis him or her. Our relationship to everybody is affected. To that extent, shame is a far more isolating experience than embarrassment. However, instead of seeing this as evidence for the fact that others play no significant role (which would be Taylor's interpretation), I find it more plausible to claim that shame, rather than simply involving a global decrease of self-esteem and self-confidence, is also essentially characterized by the way it affects and alters our relationship to and connectedness with others in general. In addition, as we shall soon see, others might play a crucial role in the very development of the emotion.

14.4 Standards and evaluations

In his analysis, Sartre highlights the impact of the gaze. The nature of the look can, however, vary enormously. As Straus points out, the look of the voyeur is as different from the looks exchanged by lovers as the medical palpation is from the gentle caress (Straus 1966: 219). Sartre's analysis can consequently be criticized for being

---

[12] Based on her clinical experience, Miller recounts how the speech of a person who attempts to talk about shame might be fragmented at first as a struggle takes place between the impulse to disclose and the impulse to conceal (Miller 1985: 36).

somewhat one-sided. More importantly, however, shame can be triggered not only by the look of others, but also by their wilful overlooking. In his intriguing study 'Invisibility', Axel Honneth discusses different acts of wilful non-perception ranging from

the harmless inattention displayed in forgetting to greet an acquaintance at a party, through the absent-minded ignorance of the master of the house vis-à-vis the cleaning lady, whom he overlooks because of her social meaninglessness, all the way to the demonstrative 'looking through' that the black person affected can understand only as a sign of humiliation. (Honneth 2001: 112)

Honneth points to infancy research that suggests that there is a range of adult facial expressions such as the loving smile, the extended hand, the benevolent nod, that will let the child know that he is the recipient of attention and devotion, and then argues that the child, by being the recipient of such prelinguistic expressions, becomes socially visible. By contrast, wilful non-perception, making a person socially invisible, is to deny recognition to that person (Honneth 2001). The fact that we can feel ashamed because we are overlooked and ignored by others suggests that there might be some significant relation between shame and the need for and perceived absence of such recognition. In recent psychoanalytic theorizing, it has been proposed that shame is a reaction to the absence of approving reciprocity (Ikonen and Rechardt 1993: 100).[13] If so, it would situate shame right at the core of our interpersonal life. Whereas embarrassment typically involves a sense of unwanted and unwelcome attention, shame has more to do with the loss of social recognition as such. As Velleman puts it, whereas 'the subject of embarrassment feels that he has egg on his face, the subject of shame feels a loss of face—the difference being precisely that between presenting a target for ridicule and not presenting a target for social interaction at all' (Velleman 2001: 49). Whereas the mockery of others can give rise to embarrassment, and whereas their anger or indignation can give rise to guilt, their contempt and rejection is more likely to occasion shame—at least as long as we respect the people in question and desire their reciprocal respect.

Aristotle pointed out in the *Rhetoric* that the people we feel shame before are those whose opinion of us matters to us (Aristotle 1984: 1384[a]25). Indeed, it is rarely the case that the identity of the audience is irrelevant. To have one's frailties exposed to one's beloved is very different from having them exposed to people in whose presence one does not feel safe or loved. Not only might it make a difference whether the witness is a close family member, somebody who is part of your social network, or a total stranger (especially if the person in question does not know who you are either), but hierarchy and social status can also play a role. An under par

---

[13] Given such a proposal it should not come as a surprise that some psychoanalysts would interpret the infant's reaction to the still-face experiment (see Chapter 14.5) as a primitive shame response (Nathanson 1987: 22; Broucek 1991: 31).

performance in public will be experienced as more shameful if noticed by somebody with more rather than less social status than you. Compare, for instance, the situation in which a pianist makes mistakes when practising a piece alone with the situation in which he makes mistakes at a public recital with the composer in attendance. However, as Hilge Landweer has observed, the status and authority of the witness make a difference to the intensity of the experience of shame. If the witness expects and values your competence, and if she is sufficiently qualified to be able to notice your failure, her presence can also change the character and intensity of the shame, even if she might be less competent and have a lower social status than yourself (Landweer 1999: 94).

As we have seen, Sartre argued that shame in the first instance is shame of oneself before the other, and that this involves an acceptance of the other's evaluation (Sartre 2003: 246, 287). This highlighting of the entailed acceptance matches well with an observation made by Karlsson and Sjöberg, namely, that that which is revealed in shame, although highly undesirable, is nevertheless experienced as disclosing the truth about oneself (2009: 350).

Such claims have, however, been disputed by various authors, who by contrast have stressed the *heteronomous* character of shame. John Deigh, for instance, has argued that we must 'admit cases of shame felt in response to another's criticism or ridicule in which the subjects do not accept the other person's judgment of them and so do not make the same judgment of themselves' (Deigh 1983: 233; compare Wollheim 1999: 152). Cheshire Calhoun has even argued that it is a mark of moral maturity to feel ashamed before those with whom one shares a moral practice, even when one disagrees with their moral criticisms (Calhoun 2004: 129). By arguing in this manner, Calhoun criticizes those who claim that 'mature agents only feel shame in *their own eyes*, and only for falling short of their own, autonomously set standards' (Calhoun 2004: 129).

It is not obvious that such a use of the notions *autonomous* and *heteronomous* is really clarifying. When siding with Sartre, and when arguing that one only feels shame if one accepts the involved evaluation, I am obviously not suggesting that one only feels shame when falling short of one's own autonomously set standards. The relevant question is not whether the standards are set autonomously in the sense of being set completely independently of others (to quote Walsh, 'it is naive to suppose that human beings act in total isolation from their fellows, or to think that they bring virgin minds to their actions, minds which in no sense bear the impress of their associations with other men'; Walsh 1970: 8), but whether the feeling of shame entails an endorsement of those standards, regardless of their origin. In short, the real point of disagreement is not over whether others might impose certain external standards on the subject—this is hardly disputed by anyone—but whether the subject needs to endorse the evaluation in order to feel shame. Now, Calhoun further argues that any strategy that roots 'the power to shame in the agent's endorsement of the shamer's evaluations will have trouble capturing shame's distinctively social character'

(2004: 135), since it ultimately reduces 'the other before whom we feel shame to a mirror of ourselves' (2004: 129). But why should we accept this reasoning? Might an internalization of the other's evaluation not involve the acceptance of new standards? If so, it is hardly a question of making the other a mirror of oneself.

We need, however, to distinguish more carefully between the other's evaluation and the underlying value. Consider the following example: When giving mouth-to-mouth respiration to a girl after you have saved her from drowning, passers-by accuse you of taking advantage of the girl. Since you have a clear conscience, you do not accept the evaluation, but you do share the underlying value: that it is wrong sexually to exploit a defenceless girl. According to Castelfranchi and Poggi, you will in this case feel ashamed in the eyes of others without feeling ashamed before yourself (Castelfranchi and Poggi 1990: 238). Is this suggestion convincing? Does it really make sense to speak of cases of shame where one is ashamed in the eyes of others but not in one's own? It is obviously possible that others can think one ought to be ashamed when one is not, but that is not what Castelfranchi and Poggi have in mind. Rather, and to repeat, they think that one might feel shame without feeling it in one's own eyes. I am somewhat sceptical about this proposal. I think it would be more correct to interpret the case in question as a case involving embarrassment rather than shame.

Why? Primarily because I think shame, in contrast to embarrassment, involves a sense of a flawed self and is linked to a global decrease of self-esteem, and I do not think the situation in question—in which one does not share the other's evaluation and knows it to be false—would occasion such a decrease. Another reason could be the following. As Bollnow has observed, embarrassment has to do with uncertainty vis-à-vis others, which is why you do not feel embarrassed when alone. Importantly, this uncertainty, this feeling of embarrassment, is something you typically feel as an annoying hindrance, as something you wish you could push aside and leave behind. Shame, by contrast, is different. Although it is painful, it is not felt as an irritating limitation, but as something that has to be obeyed and respected (Bollnow 2009 [1947]: 66, 69). I doubt the situation described by Castelfranchi and Poggi would occasion such a feeling.

Perhaps some might object to this assessment and insist that the situation could in fact be shame-inducing. I agree that under some circumstances it could indeed, but even then, it would not support the interpretation of Castelfranchi and Poggi, since the feeling of shame would still be conditional upon the acceptance of the others' evaluation. How could that possibly be the case? Well, what if you were struck by the girl's beauty during your attempt to resuscitate her, and felt attracted by her, and even had the fleeting thought that her lips were voluptuous. Had that been the case, I think one might possibly feel ashamed by the accusation of the passers-by. It would sow doubt in one's own mind: was there perhaps after all an illicit element of arousal involved? To make the case for this interpretation, consider a slight variation of the story. In order to save the woman, you have to risk your own life, since you are a very poor swimmer. After struggling to bring her to safety, and after commencing the attempt to resuscitate her, passers-by accuse you of attempting to exploit the situation in order to steal her valuables. In this case, the accusation is so far-fetched that it is very unlikely to be accepted by the accused, and as a result, I find it quite implausible to claim that it would be shame-inducing. If anything, a more likely reaction would be strong indignation.

Consider by comparison the following case. In some countries, women are expected to wear a niqab; failing to do so will be met with stern disapproval. I don't think it is very likely that such disapproval would be shame-inducing to a woman who was thoroughly secular, and who did not at all respect the disapproving others. But what if she did respect them; what if their recognition did matter to her? Might she then not feel ashamed when faced with their disapproval, and would this not support Calhoun's view? I am not sure it would. Rather than seeing such a situation as proof that one can feel ashamed even if one rejects the relevant standards and disagrees with the evaluation, I think a more likely explanation for why the woman might feel shame would be because she realized that she was causing offence to those she respected; that part of the evaluation she did accept.

But are there not, some might continue to insist, situations in which one might feel ashamed even if one rejects the relevant standards, disagrees with the evaluation, and despises the evaluator? Consider the relation between shame and humiliation. Humiliation usually involves a temporary alteration of status—one is put in a lowered or degraded position—rather than a more enduring change of identity. Moreover, it usually comes about not because you yourself are doing anything, but because somebody else is doing something to you. In that sense, it usually requires another agent, one with power over you. To humiliate someone is to assert and exert a particular insidious form of control over the person in question, since one seeks to manipulate the person's self-esteem and self-assessment. In fact, and this is the central point, the person who is being humiliated might often have difficulties keeping his identity uncontaminated by the humiliated status. He might feel soiled and burdened with an unwanted identity, and might even begin to blame himself and feel responsible for the status. In such cases, shame will also follow (Miller 1985: 44). This, I think, might be part of the reason why people who have been sexually abused might feel shame, though they are obviously the victims and not the perpetrators.[14] In some cases, however, humiliation and shame can come apart. In some cultures, it

---

[14] Arguing like this is not to deny that a scenario like the following might be possible: Somebody is humiliating me, and I subsequently feel ashamed: not because I accept and internalize the other's derogatory evaluation, but because by finding myself in the humiliating situation, and by accepting it, say, out of fear of physical punishment, I come to exemplify a cowardice that I despise. Conceding that something like this could very well happen is neither to accept Calhoun's view, nor is it to abandon the real thrust behind Sartre's claim. Whereas it should be obvious why the former is not the case, it might be less clear why the latter holds true. Despite appearance, however, the scenario is really an example of a self-reflective form of shame, and Sartre has never denied the possibility of such shame, and is not claiming that that kind of shame also necessarily involves the acceptance of the other's evaluation.

might be humiliating to be treated as an equal by a person of lower status, but although you might feel humiliated by this, it does not entail that you accept the evaluation. It does not lead to the global decrease of self-esteem that I take to be a necessary feature of shame. For a literary example of this, consider Mark Twain's story about the prince and the pauper. When Prince Edward takes the place of Tom the beggar, he is obviously confronted again and again with a clash between his own self-appraisal and the way he is perceived by others. Although the way others assess him is far more negative and derogatory than his own self-assessment, this tension is not shame-inducing. Why not? Because Edward's own self-assessment is in no way threatened or undermined by the way he is perceived by others. They might treat him as a beggar, but he knows he is of royal blood. Edward would only experience shame if he accepted the others' assessment. Whereas people believe (in some cases quite wrongly, of course) that their shame is deserved and justified, they do not necessarily believe they deserve their humiliation. This is also why humiliation frequently involves a focus on the harmful and unfair other, and why it might be accompanied by a desire for revenge (Gilbert 1998).

14.5   Developmental considerations

At this point let me return to the question regarding the developmental onset of shame. As we have seen, Lewis argues that shame only emerges from around the end of a child's third year. On his account, the child must possess objective self-consciousness and a self-concept if shame is to occur. In addition, she must also have the ability to recognize, appropriate, and internalize standards, rules, and goals, and to evaluate and compare her behaviour vis-à-vis such standards (Lewis 2007: 135). A somewhat similar view has been defended by Zinck and Newen, who argue that shame requires a mini-theory as a constitutive element, and that this mini-theory includes a concept of self, a cognitive evaluation of the situation, beliefs about concrete social relations to individuals as well as about general social norms, and expectations or hopes concerning the future (Zinck and Newen 2008: 14). By contrast, Scheler claims that shame is present in early forms from birth onwards (1957: 107), and similar views can be found in many psychoanalytical accounts (Broucek 1991; Nathanson 1994). For our present purposes, it is not of paramount importance to determine precisely how early shame appears; rather, the significant question concerns whether or not shame really does presuppose the possession of a concept of self and a capacity for reflective self-consciousness, or whether it might rather presuppose empathy and a sensitivity to the evaluating perspective of the other.

Lewis not only denies that the latter holds true; he also argues that such sensitivity is itself dependent upon the possession of a concept of self. Indeed, Lewis explicitly denies early forms of other-awareness, including empathy and emotional sharing, since they all presuppose what the infant lacks, namely, a conceptual self–other distinction (Lewis 1987: 431). Lewis is not the only one who has argued for such a dependency. In her work, Doris Bischof-Köhler has also attempted to link shame and empathy to the possession of a self-concept. What is her argument? Bischof-Köhler follows the convention by arguing that empathy is distinguished from emotional contagion in virtue of its preservation of the self–other differentiation. Although empathy, on her account, requires that the empathizer vicariously shares the emotion of the target (which makes empathy different from a more detached cognitive perspective taking), the emotion in question always retains its quality of belonging to the other: it is other-centred (Bischof-Köhler 2012: 41). In so far as such a self–other distinction is one of the requirements for empathy, according to Bischof-Köhler the latter must also presuppose the possession of a self-concept, since an individual is only aware of itself as separate and distinct from others in virtue of such a concept. What exactly does Bischof-Köhler understand by self-concept? For her, a self-concept refers to the conceptual knowledge we have of ourselves as objects, or to put it more precisely, to possess a self-concept is to have the capacity to objectify oneself and to recognize one's outwardly appearance, one's exteriority, as (part of) oneself (Bischof-Köhler 1991: 254). Prior to such a self-objectification, the infant will certainly possess subjective self-experiences (and here Bischof-Köhler endorses a less radical view than Lewis), but the infant will lack the ability to discriminate psychologically between self and other; she will remain unaware of others as distinct and separate subjects of experience, and therefore remain stuck in emotional contagion (Bischof-Köhler 1991: 254, 260). On Bischof-Köhler's account, empathy consequently requires a special kind of objectifying self-recognition. The same holds true for shame, which can be seen as an emotional reaction to such a self-objectification (Bischof-Köhler 1989: 165), and incidentally also for mirror self-recognition, which is why Bischof-Köhler claims that there is a straightforward correlation between the presence of empathy and the ability to pass the mirror self-recognition task. Thus, in the end, the possession of a self-concept turns out to be a critical precondition for empathy, shame, and mirror self-recognition.[15]

---

[15] Bischof-Köhler argues that this hypothesis is confirmed by experimental findings, since none of the studied children who failed to recognize their own mirror image showed behaviour that qualified as empathic (Bischof-Köhler 1991: 266). How did Bischof-Köhler measure empathy? Her design involved a group of children aged 16–24 months. One by one, and accompanied by their mothers, these children would encounter a grown-up playmate who brought along a teddy bear. After a while, the playmate 'accidentally' made the teddy bear lose one of its arms. The playmate started to mourn and sob, and then verbally expressed her grief by saying, 'My teddy is broken.' Meanwhile, the teddy and its arm lay on the floor in front of the child. If the child then attempted to change the situation of the playmate by trying to console her, by attempting to repair the teddy bear, or by securing help from the child's mother, it would be classified as an empathizer (1991: 261–2). Bischof-Köhler consequently targets prosocial intervention in her experimental setup and claims that this is the only feasible operationalization of empathy at the developmental stage in question (1991: 260). This is somewhat surprising, given that Bischof-Köhler herself is well aware that empathy and compassion must be distinguished, and that empathy is not necessarily prosocial (1991: 259). Furthermore, in her work Bischof-Köhler actually distinguishes two different ways of eliciting empathy. It can be induced either by the expressive behaviour of the other

These views have not remained unchallenged. A number of authors have argued that the possession of a self-concept as well as the possession of conceptual self-knowledge, rather than being a precondition for intersubjectivity, presupposes social interaction. As Tomasello and Hobson, for instance, have argued, concepts are generalizable and applicable to more than one instance of whatever they pick out. To learn a concept of self means to learn that it applies to oneself and to others. It is to see the similarity between self and other (Hobson et al. 2006: 132). But we don't notice this similarity simply by scrutinizing our own experiences. Rather, it is by taking or adopting the perspective of the other on herself that the infant comes to see herself as like others, as one among others, and thereby comes to be in possession of a true self-concept (Tomasello 1993: 181). Thus, in contrast to Lewis, who defends a four-step developmental trajectory—(1) I know, (2) I know I know, (3) I know you know, and (4) I know you know I know (Lewis 2011)—the claim of Hobson and Tomasello is not only that the infant is aware of herself in relation to others before she is able reflectively to take herself as an object, but also that a self-concept, rather than being a precondition for social understanding and intersubjectivity, arises out of intersubjectivity and is a product of cultural learning. It is consequently only creatures that are social or interpersonal in a special way that will be able to form such self-concepts (Tomasello 1993: 174; Hobson et al. 2006: 132–3).[16] More specifically, Tomasello and Hobson have both advanced the thesis that acculturated forms of cognition are characterized by the individual's ability to understand something through the perspectives of others (Tomasello 1993, 2001; Hobson 1993, 2002). Not only does the increased flexibility of perspective taking—the ability to adopt multiple perspectives on the same item simultaneously—allow for a more complex understanding, but the internalization of the view of the other on oneself eventually gives rise to the ability critically to self-monitor one's own behaviour and cognition.

(expression-induced empathy) or by the situation of the other (situation-induced empathy), and she regards the former to be the more primitive and basic form of empathy (1991: 248) and the latter to involve a more sophisticated kind of involuntary perspective change (1991: 269). On her own admission, however, her experimental setup most likely targets situation-induced empathy (1991: 269). What is actually measured by Bischof-Köhler is consequently the correlation between mirror self-recognition and the presence of a prosocial intervention that occurs as a result of situation-induced empathy. But the absence of such an intervention seems quite compatible with the presence of a more primitive form of expression-induced empathy that doesn't result in prosocial intervention, and if that is the case, it is hard to argue that the experimental findings show that empathy in general presupposes a self-concept and the ability to self-objectify. In addition, as Draghi-Lorenz and colleagues have pointed out, younger infants, who would fail to qualify as empathizers on Bischof-Köhler's test, are incapable of independent motility, and since the distressed person is beyond their reach, and they often have limited knowledge about how to help someone who is distressed, their inactivity cannot be taken as evidence for the absence of empathic concern and compassion (Draghi-Lorenz et al. 2001: 266).

[16] It is important to emphasize that this is a claim about normal development. It is not supposed to rule out that there might be other compensatory ways to form a self-concept, which, for instance, are employed by children with autism (Hobson 1993; Loveland 1993).

By adopting the perspective of the other, we can, in short, gain sufficient self-distance to permit a critical self-questioning (Tomasello 1999: 172, 198; Hobson 2002).

Much arguably depends on what precisely one takes a self-concept and conceptual self-knowledge to amount to. Tomasello and Hobson seem to opt for a more demanding definition than Bischof-Köhler, so the safest strategy might again be to insist on the need for a differentiated model. Philippe Rochat has argued that infants, through their interaction with objects, and through the exploration of the perceptual consequences of their own action, are already engaged in a process where they externalize their own feelings of vitality, and that this process might be construed as an early objectification of self (Rochat 1995: 62) and hence, if we follow Bischof-Köhler, as an early self-conceptualization. As Rochat then continues, however, the contribution of this process is in all likelihood minimal when compared to the objectification of self that stems from social interaction (Rochat 1995: 64).

But what kind of other-experiences does the pre-verbal infant possess that could afford this peculiar form of socially mediated self-experience? Let us look at some relevant developmental research.

Consider the notion of 'primary intersubjectivity' introduced by Trevarthen in order to designate the young infant's ability to engage in dyadic, affectively charged exchanges and interactions with other people (Trevarthen 1979). As already mentioned, infants are sensitive to eye contact from birth onwards. Newborns look longer and more frequently at a face with direct compared to averted eye gaze, just as they also look longer at a face with open eyes compared to one with closed eyes (Farroni et al. 2002). Even very early on, infants can react negatively to (too much) attention, and will also react with distress if attempts to disengage fail (Stern 1985). Prolonged eye contact is an amazingly powerful stimulus—and it obviously remains so in adulthood. At 2–3 months old, an infant will start to engage in proto-conversations with other people by smiling and vocalizing, and will demonstrate a capacity to vary the timing and intensity of communication with her partner. The purpose of this early interaction seems to be the interaction itself, with the participants affectively resonating with one another. Somewhat later, the infant will enter into what Trevarthen calls 'secondary intersubjectivity'. She now not only notices events in the world, and people and their actions, but is able to combine the two—to notice how other people interact with the world, and increasingly, how others can pay attention to the *same* bits of the world that the infant is engaged with (Trevarthen and Hubley 1978). The emergence of triadic joint attention is often considered the precursor to the development of full-blown human social cognition and social interaction. It plays an important role in the acquisition of language (in order to learn a new word the infant must understand what the adult is focusing on when using that word), whereas language on its part allows for a far more sophisticated and refined form of joint attention: the sharing of thought.

But what exactly is joint attention? There is widespread consensus that joint attention is not simply a question of two unrelated people simultaneously looking at the same thing, nor is it sufficient that the attention of one of them is causally influenced by the eye direction of the other, a phenomenon that can be observed in dogs, goats, and ravens. For joint attention to occur, the attentional focus of two people (or more) shouldn't merely run in parallel: it must be joint in the sense that it is shared; that is, it must involve an awareness of attending together. This is precisely what makes joint attention quite unlike any kind of experience one might have on one's own. Prototypical instances of joint attention include not only cases where the child is passively attending to the other, but also cases where the infant through acts of protodeclarative pointing actively invites another to share his focus of attention. In either case, the infant will often look back and forth between adult and object and use the feedback from his or her face to check whether joint attention has been realized. Importantly, the jointness of the attention is not primarily manifest in the mere gaze alternation, but in the shared affect that, for instance, is expressed in knowing smiles. One proposal has been that interpersonally coordinated affective states may play a pivotal developmental role in establishing jointness (Hobson and Hobson 2011: 116). Another suggestion has been to see joint attention as a form of communicative interaction. On this proposal, it is communication, which, for instance, can take the form of a meaningful look (that is, it does not have to be verbal), that turns mutually experienced events into something truly joint (Carpenter and Liebal 2011: 168).

It remains controversial how early joint attention kicks in. It has frequently been claimed that infants only start to become aware of others' attention when they are around 9–12 months of age, as evidenced by their increasing ability to engage in social referencing, imitative learning, etc. As Vasudevi Reddy has pointed out, however, when exemplifying forms of joint attention and social referencing there has been a tendency to focus on triangulations that involved an object spatially separated from both adult and infant. But thereby one might overlook various other forms of joint attention, including those where the object of the joint attention is other people, or objects close to our bodies, or objects that are part of our bodies, or simply and most centrally, those situations where the object of the other's attention is the infant him- or herself (Reddy 2008: 97–8). As Reddy points out, if infants only started to become aware of others' attention around the end of the first year of life, why should they then engage in complex face-to-face exchanges with others much earlier, namely, from 2–3 months of age? If the latter does not involve awareness that the other person is attending to them, what could it signify (Reddy 2008: 91)?[17] According to Reddy, infants are aware of others' attention initially and in the first

---

[17] Whereas Tomasello concedes that human infants are social creatures from the very start—he even calls them ultra-social—and also accepts that at around 2–3 months of age they start to interact dyadically with other people, expressing emotions back and forth in turn-taking sequences, he also insists that these forms of early social interaction do not yet amount to real intersubjectivity, which on his account only starts to emerge from around 9 months of age, and which he directly relates to the infant's understanding of others as subjects of experience (Tomasello 1999: 59–62). Tomasello consequently operates with a

instance when it is directed at themselves—she takes this to be the most powerful experience of attention that any of us will ever have—and she argues that infants only subsequently become aware of others' attention when directed to other things in the world, be it frontal targets, objects in hand, or distal targets (Reddy 2008: 92, 98). On her view, infants consequently exhibit an expanding awareness of others' attention from around 2–4 months of age. They respond to the others' attention with interest, pleasure, or distress, they call attention to themselves by making utterances, and seem to expect people to work actively with them in order to sustain and regulate the face-to-face interaction, as has been documented for instance in the *still-face experiment*. In that experiment, an adult initially engages with the infant in a normal face-to-face interaction. This is followed by a period where the adult becomes unresponsive and poses a stationary expression (still-face). The still-face episode is then generally followed by an additional period of normal face-to-face interaction. Infants as young as 2 months of age manifest a robust still-face response: they are sensitive to such interruptions of social interactions, and not only do they attempt to re-engage their social partner by smiling, vocalizing, and gesturing, but when this fails they display eye contact avoidance and distress (Tronick et al. 1978). The general interpretation of such findings is not only that something in the gaze of the other is perceived by the infant as significant enough to arouse strong emotional reactions, but also that they have expectations about the way the face-to-face interactions should proceed, and about the nature of appropriate interactive responses from social partners (Rochat and Striano 1999). It is partly because of findings like these that Reddy denies that the infant only discovers the attention of the other in late infancy, and instead argues that it is already experienced emotionally by the infant from early infancy onwards (Reddy 2008: 144).

Regardless of whether one dates the onset of true joint attention to 2–3 months or 9–12 months, regardless of how one views the relation between dyadic joint attention (occasionally called mutual attention) and triadic joint attention, the investigations of joint attention are of obvious relevance for the social cognition debate. For one, they call some of the more conservative estimates regarding its developmental onset into question. After all, infants as young as 2 months old appear to react to some of its partner's psychological (rather than merely behavioural) properties by showing clear responses to the other's attention and affect. Now, this is not, of course, to say that the infant already enjoys a reflective or conceptual understanding of the other's perspective. But they might, as Barresi and Moore have put it, have an experience of sharing before they understand what it is to share experiences, just as they might have an experience of the other's attention, as a certain kind of affordance for social interaction, before they begin to understand the concept of attention (Barresi and Moore 1993: 513). Likewise, the child's ability to adopt the other's perspective

distinction between sociality and intersubjectivity which I find potentially confusing and less informative than Trevarthen's distinction between primary and secondary intersubjectivity.

precedes and shouldn't be conflated with the later and more sophisticated ability to confront and compare different perspectives (Moll and Meltzoff 2012: 394).

The investigation of joint attention suggests that to a large extent we come to understand others by sharing objects and events with them. Moll and colleagues have argued that young infants in situations of joint engagements where they are being directly addressed by the adult and involved in her actions are able to learn things and display skills they otherwise could not (Moll et al. 2007: 883). Such findings obviously call into question the assumption that an observer placed behind a one-way mirror is on a par with someone who interacts with those she seeks to interpret (compare Butterfill 2013). Indeed, it has been suggested that infants come to learn about the social world, not 'from "he's" or "she's" whom they observe dispassion-ately from the outside' but 'from "you's" with whom they interact and engage in collaborative activities with joint goals and shared attention' (Moll and Meltzoff 2012: 398). This would incidentally match well with a point made previously by Husserl and Stein, who not only emphasized the interrelation between the experience of others and the constitution of a shared world, but who also argued that our empathic experience of others typically involves co-attending to their intentional objects (see Chapter 10.3.4). It would also echo ideas found in Schutz, who argued that the we-relationship involves sharing a context where our respective streams of consciousness are interlocked and that in such situations we can enjoy a form of other-understanding that is not based on theory or imagination (see Chapter 10.4). Indeed, why should you engage in imaginative or inferential exercises in order to understand the perspective of the other if the latter is manifest to you qua co-attender (Roessler 2005: 231)?

It is partly in the light of findings like these that Draghi-Lorenz and colleagues have taken issue with Lewis's account of primary (basic) and secondary (self-conscious) emotions, and criticized him for dismissing offhand evidence suggesting the presence of emotions like jealousy and coyness during the first year of life. On their view, rather than being based on sound empirical findings, this dismissal is based on a priori assumptions about the late emergence of both self-experience and intersubjectivity (Draghi-Lorenz et al. 2001). This is not to deny the reality of developmental change and maturation. Children have a richer and more sophisti-cated experiential life than young infants. The point is simply to acknowledge that there are developmental precursors to these more complex experiences. The presence of emotions such as shyness, embarrassment, and coyness, and acts of clowning, showing off, and teasing, indicates that during the first year of life the infant already has a sense of herself as the target of the other's evaluation, and that that evaluation matters to her (Tomasello 1999: 90; Hobson 2002: 82; Reddy 2008: 126–7, 137, 143). In fact, rather than arguing that self-conscious emotions presuppose a self-concept and involve a reflective self-assessment, rather than calling the emotions in question self-conscious emotions, it might be better to call them self–other-conscious emotions, since they make us aware of a relational being: they concern the self-in-relation-to-the-other (Reddy 2008: 145). In their developmentally primary form, they are emotions that reveal the exposed and interpersonal nature of the self; they are regulated by the visibility of self as an object of the other's attention. This is obviously a quite different, but in my view far more pertinent, understanding of what the exposed nature of the self amounts to than the explanation offered by Lewis.

14.6 The shamed self

Despite the lack of a precise and unequivocal definition of shame, enough has been elucidated in the preceding analysis to allow for a response to the questions I started out with: What does the fact that we feel shame tell us about the nature of self? What kind of self is affected in shame?

In Part I, I defended a minimalist notion of self and argued that the experiential self plays a foundational role. At the same time, however, I also emphasized that there are limits to what this notion of the self can account for. It is a thin notion of selfhood; it is a self lacking in depth. One reason for delving into this extended discussion of shame was precisely in order to illustrate the limitations of the notion of an experiential self. Shame testifies to our exposure, vulnerability, and visibility, and is importantly linked to such issues as concealment and disclosure, sociality and alienation, separation and interdependence, difference and connectedness. The shamed self is not simply the experiential core self; or to put it more accurately, a self that can be shamed is a more complex (and complicated) self than the minimalist experiential self.

As mentioned earlier, Deonna and Teroni employ a distinction between superficial and deep shame (2011: 201) and argue that only the former concerns our social identity. Their very choice of terms strongly suggests that they take the inner core of our being, our real identity, to be pre- or asocial, whereas they consider the social dimension of our identity to be only skin deep, a mere matter of appearance. In arguing like this, they are getting very close to a view articulated in the following passage:

Everyone who when before himself is not more ashamed than he is before all others will, if he is placed in a difficult position and is sorely tried in life, end up becoming a slave of people in one way or another. What is it to be more ashamed before others than before oneself but to be more ashamed of seeming than of being? (Kierkegaard 1993: 53)

It is only a small step from such a view to the claim that we ought to turn away from the social order and our contingent social identity if we wish to discover our real authentic self: who we truly are. Despite my criticism of social constructivism, I very much hope it is clear by now that my own defence of an experiential self is in no way committed to such a romantic idea. Although I do hold that there is a core dimension of our selfhood that is presocial, I dispute that it is this experiential notion of self that is at stake in deep shame.

Perhaps a reference to Mead might clarify matters further. As mentioned earlier, according to Mead we are selves not by individual right, but in virtue of our relation to one another. For Mead, the problem of selfhood is primarily the problem of how an individual can get experientially outside himself in such a way as to become an object to himself. In his view, one can only become an object to oneself indirectly, namely, by adopting the attitudes of others towards oneself, and this is something that can only happen within a social environment (Mead 1962: 138). Mead further argues that the individual's adoption of the attitude of the other towards itself allows not only for self-consciousness, but also for self-criticism, self-control, and self-unity. By adopting the attitude of the other towards itself, the individual, as Mead writes, can bring 'himself, as an objective whole, within his own experiential purview; and thus he can consciously integrate and unify the various aspects of his self, to form a single consistent and coherent and organized personality' (Mead 1962: 309).

In Sartre's analysis of shame, we have found related ideas. For Sartre, shame reveals to me that I exist for, and am visible to, others. Sartre also characterizes my being-for-others as an ecstatic and external dimension of being, and speaks of the *existential alienation* occasioned by my encounter with the other. The other's gaze makes me aware of my body as something on which others' points of view bear. This is why Sartre speaks of my body as something that escapes me on all sides and as a perpetual 'outside' of my most intimate 'inside' (Sartre 2003: 375). To apprehend myself from the perspective of the other is to apprehend myself as seen in the midst of the world, as a thing among things with properties and determinations that I am without having chosen them. The gaze of the other thrusts me into worldly space and time. I am no longer given to myself as the temporal and spatial centre of the world. I am no longer simply here, but next to the door, or on the couch; I am no longer simply now, but too late for the appointment (Sartre 2003: 287, 291, 451, 544).

Sartre was not the first phenomenologist to entertain ideas of these kinds, however. Husserl occasionally calls attention to a special and highly significant form of self-consciousness, namely, the one that involves me experiencing the other as experiencing myself. According to Husserl, this case of iterative empathy, where my indirect experience of another coincides with my self-experience, can be described as a situation where I see myself through the eyes of the other (Husserl 1959: 136–7). When I realize that I can be given for the other in the same way as the other is given for me, that is, when I realize that I myself am another to the other, my self-apprehension is transformed accordingly. It is only when I apprehend the other as apprehending me, and take myself as other to the other, that I apprehend myself in the same way that I apprehend them and become aware of the same entity that they are aware of, namely, myself as a person (Husserl 1954: 256; 1973b: 78). Thus, to exist as a person is, for Husserl, to exist socialized in a communal horizon, where one's bearing to oneself is appropriated from the others (Husserl 1973b: 175; 1954: 315; 1952: 204–5; 1973c: 177, 603). Husserl occasionally distinguishes two types of alienating self-apprehensions. Through another subject, I can learn to apprehend myself as a person among persons, that is, I can learn to adopt a *personalistic* attitude towards myself. However, I can also learn to conceive of myself as a causally determined object among objects, that is, learn to adopt a *naturalistic* attitude towards myself. By assuming the objectifying perspective of the other on myself, I learn to apprehend myself both as a person or human being, that is, as a socialized subject of the kind studied by the humanities and social sciences, and as a psyche or psychophysical entity, that is, as a naturalized subject of the kind studied by the natural sciences (Husserl 1959: 71; 1952: 142–3, 174–5). Neither of these attitudes is immediately accessible; both entail a fundamental change of attitude towards oneself that is occasioned by the other. It is the other that teaches me to apprehend myself from a third-person perspective as the bearer of cultural and natural properties. As Husserl said, I cannot experience my own intersubjective *Realitätsform* directly, but only mediated through empathy, which, he then adds, leads to self-alienation (Husserl 1952: 90, 111, 200; 1973a: 342, 462; 1973b: 418; 1973c: 19, 589, 634).

I am not claiming that Mead, Sartre, and Husserl would agree on everything. In fact, one important difference between them is that whereas Mead distinguishes sharply between consciousness and self-consciousness and even claims that prior to the emergence of self-consciousness, we experience our own feelings and sensations as parts of the environment rather than as our own (Mead 1962: 171), Husserl and Sartre would both argue that our experiential life is characterized by a primitive form of self-consciousness from the very start. Despite this important difference, however, I think all three of them are highlighting the extent to which certain forms of self (-experience) are constitutively dependent upon others. They all call attention to the dramatic way our awareness of, and subsequent adoption of, the other's attitude towards ourselves contributes to our development as selves.

Consider, once again, the distinction between the notions of experiential self and narrative self. It should be obvious that we are dealing with two notions placed at each end of the scale. On the one hand, we have a minimal take on self that seeks to cash it out in terms of the first-person perspective. On the other hand, we have a far richer normatively guided notion that firmly situates the self in culture and history. Whereas the minimal notion captures an important but presocial aspect of our experiential life, the narrative notion most certainly does include the social dimension, but it does so by emphasizing the role of language. Given the difference between the two notions, it is natural to wonder about the developmental trajectory. How do we get from one to the other? A possible answer that simultaneously suggests that the notions of experiential self and narrative self are in need of a supplement is to consider prelinguistic forms of sociality with a direct impact on the formation and development of the self. To be more specific, my suggestion would be that our experience of and subsequent adoption of the other's attitude towards ourselves, that is, our coming to understand ourselves through others, contributes to the consti-tution of a new dimension of selfhood, one that brings us beyond the experiential self, while not yet amounting to a full-blown narratively extended self.[18] It is in this context that the whole range of self–other-conscious emotions becomes relevant. Studying them allows us to explore what, following Ulric Neisser, we might call the *interpersonal self*, that is, the self in its relation to and interaction with others (Neisser 1991: 203–4). In contrast to the experiential self, the interpersonal self is clearly a socially constituted self. We come to be the social selves we are, not only by experiencing ourselves in our interaction with and emotional response to others, but also by experiencing and internalizing the other's perspective on ourselves. This interpersonal self will feed into and is an important precursor to the subsequent development of a more normatively enriched and diachronically extended narrative self, and can thereby serve as an important bridge between the two previously discussed dimensions of self. But it also and significantly has crucial presuppositions of its own, including (and this is obviously reflected in the very structure of this book) the possession of a first-person perspective and a capacity for empathy.

If we now return to the topic of shame, my claim is *not* that shame is a necessary condition of possibility for interpersonal selfhood, and that subjects who for one reason or another lack shame experiences will fail to develop as interpersonal selves. I am also not denying what should be rather obvious, namely, that many shame experiences are culturally nested and presuppose narrative capacities. In its developmentally primary form, however, shame precedes the learning of particular social standards. It is a powerful example of a self-conscious emotion that reveals the exposed and social (in)visibility of the self. This is also why I would dispute that 'what is distinctive of shame is the presence of a specific kind of *intrapersonal* evaluation, an evaluative perspective the subject takes upon himself' (Deonna et al. 2011: 135). I do not think one can capture what is distinctive about shame simply by focusing on the fact that the shamed subject is thrown back upon itself. As Seidler points out, and I think this constitutes an essential insight: 'The shamed subject is "entirely self-present" and simultaneously "beside itself"' (Seidler 2001: 25–6). This, I think, is also Sartre's basic idea. Sartre takes shame to involve an existential alienation. I would agree with this—at least if one understands it as amounting to a decisive change of perspective on oneself. In some cases, the alienating power is a different subject, and Sartre's description of our pre-reflective feeling of shame when confronted with the evaluating gaze of the other is an example of this. In other cases, the feeling of shame occurs when we sit in judgement on ourselves. But in this case as

---

[18] Let me add that both Sartre and Mead would argue that the adoption of the other's perspective on oneself very much continues to flourish in our use of language. Whereas Sartre writes that language expresses my being-for-others in a pre-eminent way, since it confers significance upon me that others have already found words for (Sartre 2003: 377, 395), Mead argues that the language process is essential for the development of the self, and that its critical importance stems from the fact that communication requires the individual to take the attitude of the other towards himself. As Mead puts it, a person who is saying something is saying to himself what he says to others; otherwise he wouldn't know what he was talking about (Mead 1962: 69, 135, 142, 147).

well, there is a form of exposure and self-alienation, a kind of self-observation and self-distancing. To put it differently, in the company of others the experience of shame can occur pre-reflectively since the alien perspective is co-present. When alone, the experience of shame will take a more reflective form, since the alien perspective has to be provided through a form of reflective self-distancing.

I would consequently maintain that shame contains a significant component of *alterity*.[19] This is obvious in those cases where the experience of shame arises as a reaction to the evaluation of others, but even past-oriented self-reflective shame and future-oriented shame anxiety contain this aspect. This is so not only because of the self-distancing and doubling of perspectives involved, but also because others influence the development and formation of our own standards. To that extent, the evaluating perspectives of others may play a role in the structure of the emotion even if they are not factually present or explicitly imagined (Landweer 1999: 57, 67). More importantly, however, even if one could argue that the kind of shame you might feel when failing to meet your own standards is not socially mediated in any direct fashion (it is not as if you only feel shameful because you are losing face or that other people's evaluations are always part of what shame us), we shouldn't overlook the question concerning the relation between *intra*personal and *inter*personal shame. I have not only rejected the claim that the latter can be reduced to or explained on the basis of the former, but would also argue that intrapersonal shame is subsequent to (and conditioned by) interpersonal shame. It is my empathic awareness of the other's attention and my subsequent internalization of that foreign perspective that eventually allows me to gain the self-distance that is required for the kind of critical self-evaluation that can lead to decreased self-esteem. As Sartre writes, 'although certain complex forms derived from shame can appear on the reflective plane, shame is not originally a phenomenon of reflection. In fact no matter what results one can obtain in solitude by the religious *practice* of shame, it is in its primary structure shame *before somebody*' (Sartre 2003: 245). In short, I think prototypical shame experiences provide vivid examples of other-mediated forms of self-experience, and this is why I would contest that the self-relation we find in shame is as self-contained and inward-directed as Lewis and Deonna and Teroni claim.

One obvious way to explore the validity of this claim further would be to look at shame in individuals with autism. Given the social impairments of the latter, given their lack of concern with how they appear to others, given their difficulties of conceiving of themselves as selves in the minds of others, the prediction would be that they would lack normal shame experiences. Unfortunately, very little systematic research has so far been done on the topic. In a study from 2006, however, Hobson

---

[19] There are other ways to explore the alterity internal to the self than by looking at shame. As I argued in my book *Self-Awareness and Alterity*, a closer look at the temporal and bodily character of consciousness suggests that even the most basic form of pre-reflective self-consciousness contains an incipient element of alterity.

and colleagues asked parents of young children with autism whether the children showed shame. According to their findings, none of the children with autism was reported to manifest shame unambiguously, in contrast to the majority of the children in the control group. A few children with autism were reported to show some ambiguous signs of shame, but there is even some uncertainty about whether in these tentative cases the parents were really reporting shame rather than guilt, as the following example might illustrate:

Yes, when he's done something wrong, he'll hide the fact and he says: 'You're gonna shout at me, you're gonna shout at me'...he's aware if he's done something, and there is going to be a punishment linked to it. I think he's more scared of the consequences than the actual doing the damage, that's what I think. (Hobson et al. 2006: 66)

There is much more to be said about the many faces of shame (not to speak of the many other facets of the social self). A more comprehensive account would require further investigations of, for instance, its developmental trajectory (how early does it emerge; how much does infantile shame, if it exists, resemble adult shame; what role does it play in adolescence and in other periods of life when one struggles with issues of independence and interdependence?), its relation to personality traits (what is the link between self-confidence and shame vulnerability?), and its cultural specificity (to what extent do the shame-inducing situations, the very experience of shame, and the available coping strategies vary from culture to culture?). It is hardly insignificant that emotions like shame are more culture-specific than the basic emotions, and that a cultural perspective might indeed be indispensable for an understanding of the full complexity of these emotions.[20]

---

[20] Chinese, for instance, is supposed to contain 113 shame-related terms, and has special terms for 'losing face', 'truly losing face', 'losing face terribly', 'being ashamed to death', and 'being so ashamed that even the ancestors of eight generations can feel it' (Edelstein and Shaver 2007: 200). For further considerations concerning what a cultural psychology of shame might look like, see Shweder (2003).

15

You, Me, and We

In an article from 1995, Meltzoff and Moore distanced themselves from two historically influential views on the status of the self in infancy. According to the first, that of Piaget, there is no initial bridge between self and other; rather, the child only comes to discover the existence of others as separate entities at a relative late stage. According to the second, that of social constructivism, infants are initially selfless and only come to acquire selfhood through social interaction (Meltzoff and Moore 1995: 88). The alternative offered by Meltzoff and Moore bears a remarkable affinity to the view I have offered in the preceding chapters and might even serve as a concise summary of one of my main points:

The newborn brings innate structure to his or her first interactions with people, and yet interactions with other individuals profoundly alter the notion of self. The challenge for a theory of self-development is to specify this innate structure and the way that it is subsequently reorganized. A theory of development that mischaracterizes the newborn is flawed; a model of the innate that ignores development misses the human capacity for reconceiving things, even our self. (Meltzoff and Moore 1995: 88)

In this concluding chapter, I shall not offer more in terms of summary and recapitulation. Rather, I shall end by looking forward. There is much more to the relation between, and intertwinement of, self and other than what I have been able to cover in the preceding chapters. Let me conclude by considering how the basic framework I have been developing might be used to elucidate the structure of the *we*.

One of the still-controversial questions in the social ontology debate concerns the status of the we. Who is the subject of we-intentionality? When looking at the available answers, it shouldn't come as a surprise that one's account of the we and of the first-person plural often depends on one's account of the self and of the first-person singular.

Consider, for example, the normative account of personal identity according to which personal identity is more a matter of normative commitments than of a unified first-person perspective. It is when I allow normative principles to govern my will, it is when I endorse, embrace, and affirm them, that I make them my own and thereby decide who to be. As Carol Rovane puts it, 'wherever there is a commitment to living up to the normative requirements that define individual rationality, there is an individual person' (Rovane 2012: 20). Rovane defends a voluntarist conception of personal identity, according to which it is up to rational agents to determine their own identities by drawing the boundaries within which they deliberate. On her view, it is consequently by committing themselves to take certain attitudes as the normative basis from which to reason and act, it is by living a life in accordance with self-imposed guidelines, that rational agents come to have their own distinct points of view and, thereby, their own identities. Importantly, for Rovane such commitments can also arise within a group of human beings, thereby giving rise to 'a *group person* that comprises all of those human beings' (Rovane 2012: 21). Rovane's normative account thus entails the possibility of group personhood, since the identity-constituting acts of appropriation can and may occur within different boundaries, thereby giving rise to persons of different sizes. Through the intentional efforts of the individual participants, a new group identity can be forged, one that can and ought to be treated like any individual person. Indeed, Rovane explicitly argues that a group possesses the same distinctive ethical significance as ordinary individual persons (Rovane 2012: 29).

This normative route to the we is one option. Another route is the methodological individualism we find in Searle. On Searle's view there is no such thing as a group-mind of which our minds are fragments. Rather, all intentionality, and this includes we-intentionality, must be located in the minds of individuals. Thus, whenever people share an intention, each individual has his or her own intention, and there is no such thing as one (token) intention that is shared by the participants in any straightforward sense of the term. On this proposal, we-intentionality does not involve a single shared intentional state, but several individual states that differ from states exhibiting quite ordinary intentionality in virtue of having a special form. Thus, Searle has argued that we-intentionality is an intention inside the mind of a single individual with the form *we intend*, and claimed that an individual can we-intend even if no other agent exists. Searle consequently allows for solipsistic we-intentionality and has insisted that an individual might possess we-intentionality even if he is nothing but a brain in a vat (Searle 2002: 96).

Searle might in general be more concerned with phenomenal consciousness than Rovane, but this is not to say that his account and the methodological individualism he favours is necessarily in line with views found in the phenomenological tradition. In the introduction to *The Construction of Social Reality*, Searle remarks that the great 'philosophers-sociologists' from the early twentieth century lacked the adequate tools, especially a sufficiently developed theory of intentionality, to tackle the question concerning the we-perspective (Searle 1995, p. xii). Searle refers to the work of Weber, Simmel, and Durkheim, but forgets Schutz, whose dissertation *Der sinnhafte Aufbau der sozialen Welt* from 1932 has more affinities with Searle's project than merely the title. What we find in Schutz, and in the phenomenological tradition that he is part of, is not only quite sophisticated analyses of intentionality, self, and intersubjectivity, but also a targeted investigation of we-intentionality and its contribution to the constitution of social reality. One obvious question to consider is whether phenomenology might offer an account of the we that is more relational than Searle's while retaining an experiential first-person basis, that is, without its becoming quite as normative as Rovane's account.

Consider the work of David Carr. In his article 'Cogitamus Ergo Sumus: The Intentionality of the First-Person Plural', Carr asks whether it makes sense to speak of the group as a collective subject. His answer is affirmative, and he suggests that phenomenology will support such a verdict. Take, for instance, those cases where, rather than ascribing an experience or an action to myself or to you, I ascribe it to us, that is, to a we, as in the case where my son and I return from a trip and, when seeing a common friend, I shout 'We saw it! We found the hedgehog!' In such a case, the experience isn't simply given to me as my experience, but as ours; the action isn't simply given to me as my action, but as our action.

There are admittedly many uses of the first-person plural. In some cases, the locution 'we saw the hedgehog' might imply nothing more than a common object. If each of us saw the hedgehog at different times or even at the same time, but without knowing of each other's presence, we can without any loss replace 'we saw the hedgehog' with 'I saw the hedgehog and you saw the hedgehog'. But in other cases, we say 'we' in order to express our identification with and membership of a group (Carr 1986a: 525). If we found the hedgehog together, and if each of us was aware that the other was also seeing it, something important would be lost by the distributive reformulation, since the use of 'we' was intended to capture more than simply the fact that there was a common object. We found the hedgehog together, and although I didn't see the animal through my son's eyes, its having been seen by him is part of the experience I have of it. And as Carr makes clear, it is not just me that has this kind of composite experience. My son has it as well. Thus, each of us has a complex experience that integrates and encompasses several perspectives at once. That complex experience can only be attributed to one sort of subject, the plural subject, the we. It cannot be attributed to a single individual. Importantly, one of the reasons why it cannot is precisely because the experience incorporates phases and perspectives that are not directly available to that individual (Carr 1986a: 526). This is a significant point, since Carr hereby clearly emphasizes the difference between a we (which necessarily involves a preservation and even acknowledgement of plurality and difference) and some kind of larger-scale I (Carr 1986a: 532).

On Carr's account, the we is the label for a distinct way of being with others, a distinct form of social existence. The we is consequently and very importantly not some entity that is observed from without, but rather something I experience from within in virtue of my membership and participation. When adopting the we-perspective, we do not leave the first-person point of view behind; rather, we merely exchange its singular for its plural form. Carr next emphasizes how a consideration of the first-person plural or we-subject opens up a whole new description of social existence and action. The experiences and actions of social groups need no longer be viewed as third-person phenomena, but can precisely be considered from the participant's perspective (Carr 1986a: 530). It is consequently important to distinguish objective group membership from being part of a we. One might by birth (right) be a member of a certain group (family, class, nation, ethnicity, etc.) regardless of whether one knows or cares about it, just as outsiders might classify one as a member of a certain group quite independently of one's own view on the matter. But this kind of group membership doesn't amount to a we. For a we to emerge, the members have to identify with and participate in the group. It is their attitudes towards each other (and towards themselves) that are important (Carr 1986b: 161). Saying this is by no means to say that the identification with and participation in the we always happens voluntarily. The point is merely that in important ways it involves rather than bypasses the self-understanding and first-person perspective of the involved parties.

One way to summarize Carr's account might be by saying that for him we-intentionality is both relational and irreducible. On such an account, we-intentionality has no single owner (neither an individual nor a group-mind), but is rather something that emerges in and is maintained by the interaction of the participating individuals. That is, we-intentionality necessarily has plural ownership. It cannot exist independently of individual intentions, but nor can it be reduced to the latter.

I have more sympathy for this proposal than for Searle's and Rovane's, but something is left rather underdetermined and unaddressed by all three accounts, namely, the question regarding the cognitive and affective presuppositions for we-intentionality. At one point, Searle admits that one of the central presuppositions is a 'biologically primitive sense of the other person as a candidate for shared intentionality' (Searle 1990: 415). Likewise, Carr suggests that an individual can be enlisted into a we-subject by becoming a member of a community of experiencers, and that this requires a certain amount of identification with the group in question. But if we-intentionality involves some kind of identification and/or sharing with others, what kind of other-awareness does it presuppose? This is a question that neither Searle nor Carr (nor Rovane for that matter) addresses.

At this point, it is easy to profit from the discussion found in Parts II and III. Consider first the developmental research on joint attention. It has sometimes been claimed that young children fail to appreciate the separateness of subjects of experience, and that their awareness of mental states involves an undifferentiated *we*, not decomposable into *I* and *you*. If this is intended to mean that infants' understanding of others' psychological properties is such as to leave no room for any divergence between their own and others' points of view, early joint attention interactions provide, as Roessler has pointed out, straightforward counter-evidence, since the whole point of proto-declaratives is to bring someone else's focus of attention in line with one's own (Roessler 2005: 247).

Consider next the distinction between emotional contagion, empathy, and experiential sharing. Whereas the first two do not constitute or amount to any we-perspective, experiential sharing might get us closer to what we are after. As we have already seen, there are good reasons to reject the view that empathy involves sharing. But what about experiential sharing proper? To use some terms recently proposed by Szanto, experiential sharing has a plurality requirement as well as an integrity requirement (Szanto 2015). Sharing has nothing to do with fusion, nor with a merged unity.[1] Sharing involves a plurality of subjects, but it also involves more than mere summation or aggregation: there also has to be a special kind of integration. Experiential sharing isn't merely individual experience plus reciprocal knowledge; rather, what we are after is a situation in which the experiences of the individuals are co-regulated and constitutively bound together, that is, where the individuals only have the experiences they have in virtue of their reciprocal relation to each other. In addition, there also seems to be some need for a felt togetherness (Walther 1923: 33), that is, some kind of identification with each other.[2]

Since experiential sharing involves a component of other-understanding and an entailed preservation of difference and plurality, it clearly differs from emotional contagion. It also differs from empathy, however, precisely by virtue of the co-regulation and reciprocity. Consider a situation in which my friend and I are enjoying a movie together. Not only do we each perceive and enjoy the movie, but we also empathically experience that the other is jointly attending to and enjoying the movie, which is something that affects the structure and quality of our own enjoyment. As Schutz writes, we are then 'living in *our* common stream of consciousness' (Schutz 1967: 167). Rather than entailing a metaphysical fusion, what Schutz has in mind here is the fact that our respective streams of consciousness in such situations

---

[1] It might be objected that this construal flatly contradicts Scheler's position in *Wesen und Formen der Sympathie*, where one finds the following passage: 'The father and the mother stand beside the dead body of a beloved child. They feel in common the "same" sorrow, the "same" anguish. It is not that A feels this sorrow and B feels it also, and moreover that they both know they are feeling it. No, it is a *feeling-in-common*. A's sorrow is in no way "objectual" for B here, as it is, e.g. for their friend C, who joins them, and commiserates "with them" or "upon their sorrow". On the contrary, they feel it together, in the sense that they feel and experience in common, not only the self-same value-situation, but also the same keenness of emotion in regard to it. The sorrow, as value-content, and the grief, as characterizing the functional relation thereto, are here *one and identical*' (Scheler 2008: 12–13; translation modified). It might be tempting to interpret Scheler as saying that emotional sharing exemplifies a situation in which one token experience is shared by two individuals in the sense that they both have first-personal access to the very same experience in question. But in so far as such a view would seem to entail that the two individuals, at least with regard to the experiential episode in question, had merged or fused and become one, one might ask whether the notion of a dually owned or shared token state might not be fundamentally incoherent. Here is one reason, however, why this might in any case be a misinterpretation of Scheler. Slightly later in *Wesen und Formen der Sympathie*, Scheler returns to the example of the grieving parents, and then writes that 'the process of feeling in the father and the mother is given separately in each case; only what they feel—the one sorrow— and its value-content, is immediately present to them as identical' (Scheler 2008: 37). If the process of feeling is given separately to the father and the mother, it is certainly not obvious that Scheler should be defending the view that the same token experience is shared by several individuals.

[2] This requirement must be added in order to rule out obvious counter-examples, including cases that involve constitutively interdependent experiences that clearly do not qualify as shared. Consider, for instance, the case of the sadistic rapist whose enjoyment feeds off and is constitutively dependent on the terror of the victim and vice versa.

are *interlocked* to such an extent that each of our respective experiences are coloured by our mutual involvement (Schutz 1967: 167, 180).

One thing that should emerge from these very hasty remarks is that we-intentionality seems to presuppose and involve both self-consciousness and other-consciousness. This obviously stands in contrast to any proposal according to which the we is a primitive and unconditioned phenomenon. However, it is one thing to say that a we-perspective retains rather than abolishes the difference between self and other. What needs to be better understood is the kind of relation that has to obtain between self and other in order to allow for the emergence of a we. Let me make one final suggestion, namely, that we-intentionality proper also involves a distinct kind of reciprocity, one that requires the ability to adopt what has been termed a *second-person perspective*.

Recall Schutz's discussion of the thou-orientation. Schutz's distinction between a one-sided 'social observation' and the reciprocal engagement that we find in the face-to-face encounter (Schutz 1967: 165–6, 173) pre-empts recent discussions in the social cognition debate about the nature of the second-person perspective. As I have already mentioned, during the last few years there has been an ongoing debate about whether the two dominant mainstream positions in the theory of mind debate, the theory-theory (in its different versions) and the simulation theory (in its different versions), are exhaustive and adequate when it comes to capturing fundamental forms of social cognition. It has occasionally been argued that a limitation of both of the traditional positions is that they privilege either the first-person perspective (this would be one version of the simulation theory) or the third-person perspective (this would be the theory-theory) and that what we really need is a theory that explicitly targets the second-person perspective. However, there is still quite some disagreement about what exactly a second-person perspective amounts to. One influential account can be found in a target article in *Behavioral and Brain Sciences* written by Schilbach and colleagues. For them, the second-person perspective concerns the issue of directly interacting with and emotionally engaging with others (rather than simply observing them from a distance). Thus, the second-person perspective is contrasted with what is called the 'spectatorial stance' (Schilbach et al. 2013). One aspect that might not have been sufficiently highlighted in the contribution of Schilbach and his colleagues, however, is the role of reciprocity. Perhaps the most unique feature of the second-person perspective isn't the action part, isn't the fact that one is aware of others' mental states as a result of engaging and interacting with them, but rather the reciprocal relation (de Bruin et al. 2012; Fuchs 2013). It could be argued that the second-person perspective involves a relation between you and me, where the unique feature of relating to you as you is that you also have a second-person perspective on me, that is, you take me as your you. To that extent, there cannot be a single you: there always has to be at least two. In short, to adopt the second-person perspective is to engage in a subject–subject (you–me) relation where I am aware of the other and at the same time implicitly aware of myself in the accusative, as attended to or addressed by the other (Husserl 1973b: 211).[3]

One implication of this would obviously be that Schutz is wrong when he refers to social observation as a one-sided thou-orientation. Simply singling somebody out by paying attention to the person in question, simply attributing consciousness to somebody that I directly experience, is not yet, contrary to what Schutz is saying, to engage in a thou-orientation, since there cannot be any thou-orientation if there is no reciprocation on the part of the other.

Now, surely this idea needs to be fleshed out further. But my suggestion is that if we wish to obtain a better understanding of the we, we ought to look closer at the you, since the second-person singular might be crucial for an understanding of the first-person plural. To adopt the second-person perspective and to stand in a you-relation to somebody else is at the same time to modify and enrich your own self-experience. But this is precisely one of the requirements. In order to join in and participate in a we-experience, you cannot just make do with your ordinary self-experience; nor is it enough simply to observe others being engaged in actions that you could also accomplish. What you need is a certain amount of self-alienation—to decrease your distance from, and make you more like, the others. You need to experience the others' perspectives on you, you need to be aware of them as being aware of you and see yourself through their eyes, so that you can come to experience yourself in the same manner as you experience them. When that happens, you can become aware of yourself as one of them or, rather and more accurately, you can become aware of yourself as one of us. This latter self-experience does not replace your pre-reflective self-consciousness: it supplements it.

As already indicated, this is not an idea that is entirely foreign to classical phenomenology. Consider the following quotation from Schutz:

I take up an Other-orientation toward my partner, who is in turn oriented toward me. Immediately, and at the same time, I grasp the fact that he, on his part, is aware of my attention to him. In such cases I, you, *we*, live in the social relationship itself, and that is true in virtue of the intentionality of the living Acts directed toward the partner. I, you, we, are by this means carried from one moment to the next in a particular attentional modification of the state of being mutually oriented to each other. The social relationship in which we live is constituted, therefore, by means of the attentional modification undergone by my Other-orientation, as I immediately and directly grasp within the latter the very living reality of the partner as one who is in turn oriented toward me. (Schutz 1967: 156–7)

Schutz also insists that the we-relationship, rather than being reflectively available within the face-to-face situation, is something that is pre-reflectively lived through (Schutz 1967: 170). If we wish to think about and thematically observe our relation-ship and the experiences we have together, we must withdraw from each other and thereby step out of the face-to-face relationship (Schutz 1967: 167).

---

[3] Incidentally, this is also why it might be better to talk of a you–me relation than of an I–thou relation.

If we move to Husserl, in various research manuscripts he argues that something momentous happens, something that goes beyond empathy, the moment I turn towards and start to address the other. As he puts it, when I seek to influence the other, and when the other is aware that he is being addressed and when he reciprocates, and when both of us become aware that we are being experienced and understood by the other, we are dealing with communicative acts through which a higher interpersonal unity, a we, is established, and through which the world acquires the character of a truly social world (Husserl 1973c: 472; 1952: 192–4). Husserl consequently emphasizes the centrality of communication and dialogue, and also highlights the importance of reciprocity when it concerns the emergence of the we. In some of his texts, he calls attention to a special form of self-consciousness that comes about by adopting the perspective of the other on oneself. It is no wonder that Husserl often asserts that this type of self-apprehension, where I am reflected through others, is characterized by a complex and indirect intentional structure. But as he also makes clear, it is only then that I am, for the first time and in the proper sense, an I over against an other, and thereby in a position to say 'we' (Husserl 1952: 242, 250).

Although Husserl's description of the process might make it sound overly complicated, it is not obvious that we are dealing with a process that only occurs late in development. Or, to put it differently, we shouldn't forget that the most advanced form of second-person perspective taking has developmental precursors. Over the years, Peter Hobson has argued that the process of 'identifying-with' plays a very early and pivotal role in human development by structuring 'social experience with polarities of self-other differentiation as well as connectedness' (Hobson 2008: 386). In a co-authored paper, the process in question is further described as follows: 'to identify with someone else is to relate to the actions and attitudes of someone else from the other's perspective or stance, in such a way that a person assimilates the other's orientation toward the world, including toward the self, so that this orientation becomes a feature of the person's own psychological repertoire' (Hobson and Hobson 2007: 415). Importantly, Hobson also considers identifying-with to be crucially involved in affective sharing, and he argues that young infants' affective engagement with others already provides them with interpersonal experiences that encompass an interplay between similarity and difference, connectedness and differentiation (Hobson 2007: 270, cf. Reddy 2008).

On the account I am proposing, the we(-experience) is not prior to or equiprimordial with self(-experience) or other(-experience). Rather, prototypical forms of we-intentionality are founded upon empathy and joint attention and require a special reciprocal second-person perspective. The self–other differentiation, the distinction between self and other, consequently precedes the emergence of, and is retained in, the we. Let me emphasize that this is not a reductive claim. The claim is not that the latter can be reduced to the former or that it can be exhaustively accounted for by means of an analysis of the you–me relation. The claim is merely that the you–me relation is a necessary component.

In fact, it might be important to distinguish the being-for-one-another (*Füreinan-dersein*) and the being-with-one-another (*Miteinandersein*). Whereas the you–me relation can be dyadic, the we typically involves a triadic structure, where the focus is on a shared object or project. Not only can there be cases of intense you–me interaction, such as strong verbal disagreements or arguments, where there is not yet (or no longer) a we present, but even in more conciliatory situations, paying too much attention to the other might disrupt the shared perspective. The couple who are enjoying the movie together can serve as a good illustration of this. Their focus of attention is on the movie and not on each other. Thus, the we is often present and lived through pre-reflectively in actions and experiences before it is thematized reflectively (Schmid 2005: 99). However, this is not to say that the sharing of experience is independent of and precedes any awareness of the other, as Schmid also seems to suggest (Schmid 2005: 138). We shouldn't make the mistake of equating consciousness with thematic or focal consciousness. After all, I can remain aware of my partner even if I am not thematically aware of her, and I find it exceedingly hard to make sense of the notion of shared experiences if other-aware-ness in any form whatsoever is entirely absent.

So far, however, I have been focusing on the kind of we that emerges in the face-to-face interaction and which entails an awareness of the other as a distinct individual. But we also ought to recognize that this rather ephemeral form of we, which is bound to the here and now, is only one type of we. On the one hand, we can find far more impersonal, anonymous, and linguistically mediated forms of we-intentionality. Consider, for instance, the case where a physicist declares 'We finally discovered a Higgs boson-like particle' although she herself was in no way directly involved in the CERN experiment, or the resistance fighter who when facing the firing squad yells 'We will defeat you', thereby identifying with a group that will postdate his own existence. It would be important to determine here what role various processes of identification play in such forms of we-intentionality, and also whether these more impersonal forms of we-intentionality are simply parasitic on the supposedly more basic and fundamental form of face-to-face-based we-intentionality, or whether they have their own originality and irreducibility.[4] On the other hand, it has been argued that there are forms of we-intentionality that are more primitive than the form I have been focusing on. Consider, for instance, forms of action coordination that take place quite independently of any other-directed intentionality or joint plans, as when agents start to act as a single coordinated entity because they are driven by the same perceptual cues and motor routines. Examples that come to mind are cases where an audience claps in unison, where pedestrians fall into the same walking

---

[4] Even if the former were the case, it obviously wouldn't entail that one would necessarily have to have had concrete you–me relations with all those individuals who are members of the group that one identifies with. The point would rather be that one would have to have had some you–me relations before one could engage in the more anonymous form of we-intentionality.

pattern, or where two people in rocking chairs involuntarily synchronize their rocking frequencies (Knoblich et al. 2011). If such emergent action coordination qualifies as a form of we-intentionality, it is doubtful whether it can be analysed along the lines suggested above. One option would consequently be to introduce and operate with a more minimalist form of we-intentionality. Another option, which I am considerably more attracted to, is to concede that emergent action coordination might indeed be quite basic, but then insist that it has more in common with motor mimicry and contagion than with genuine sharing, which is why it ultimately doesn't amount to or constitute a genuine case of we-experience.

As in the case of shame, there is so much more to be said about the we. Consider, for instance, the claim by Turner and his colleagues that 'it is where intergroup differences tend to be perceived as larger than intragroup differences that we tend to categorize self as "we" instead of "I" and see the included other(s) as similar rather than different' (Turner et al. 1994: 457). In short, what is the role of the *they*, and to what extent does the tendency to experience oneself as part of we, as one of us, increase when confronted with outgroup members and contrasting groups? These are important questions that I cannot pursue further here, but I hope this short concluding discussion of the we has nevertheless exemplified the theoretical usefulness of the preceding investigation of self and other. I would agree with those who claim that results from the domains of social cognition and social ontology can put pressure on certain basic assumptions in the philosophy of mind. Findings in the former domains might force us to revise or even reject certain overly solipsistic and disembodied accounts of mind and self if the latter should turn out to be incompatible with the existence of genuine we-phenomena. I agree with this, but I would reject the proposal that the way forward, when it comes to developing a satisfactory account of the we, is to jettison altogether notions such as subject, subjectivity, I, you, me, self, other. To do that would not only be to throw out the proverbial baby with the bathwater; it would also suggest a commitment to the very Cartesian conception of the subject that one was allegedly trying to overcome.

References

I have quoted from English translations where available. If no translations are available I have provided one myself (with the help of numerous colleagues).

Since the translations of Husserl and Heidegger typically contain the page number of the original in the margin, the page number given is to the original edition. (The translations of Husserl's *Logische Untersuchungen* and *Die Krisis der europäischen Wissenschaften und die transzendentale Phänomenologie* unfortunately lack this feature, so when quoting from these works, I have chosen to add the corresponding English page number in square brackets.) In such cases, both the original text and the English translation are given here in the list of References.

When I refer to Stein's doctoral dissertation, I shall be using the new critical edition of *Zum Problem der Einfühlung*. However, the page numbers referred to are those of the first edition. They can be found in the margin of the critical edition, as well as in the English translation.

Square brackets indicate the year of the original publication (or composition) of a historically significant work.

Albahari, M. (2006), *Analytical Buddhism: The Two-Tiered Illusion of Self* (New York: Palgrave Macmillan).

Albahari, M. (2009), 'Witness-Consciousness: Its Definition, Appearance and Reality', *Journal of Consciousness Studies*, 16/1: 62–84.

Althusser, L. (1971), *Lenin and Philosophy and Other Essays* (New York: Monthly Review Press).

Amsterdam, B. K. (1968), 'Mirror Behavior in Children under Two Years of Age', Ph.D. thesis (University of North Carolina); order no. 6901569, University Microfilms, Ann Arbor, Mich., 48106.

Amsterdam, B. K. (1972), 'Mirror Self-Image Reactions before Age Two', *Developmental Psychobiology*, 5: 297–305.

Amsterdam, B. K., and Levitt, M. (1980), 'Consciousness of Self and Painful Self-Consciousness', *Psychoanalytic Study of the Child*, 35: 67–83.

Andrews, K. (2009), 'Understanding Norms without a Theory of Mind', *Inquiry*, 52/5: 433–48.

Apperly, I. (2011), *Mindreaders: The Cognitive Basis of 'Theory of Mind'* (Hove: Psychology Press).

Aristotle (1984) [*c*.340 BCE], *Rhetoric*, in *The Complete Works of Aristotle II*, ed. J. Barnes (Princeton: Princeton University Press).

Atkins, K. (2004), 'Narrative Identity, Practical Identity and Ethical Subjectivity', *Continental Philosophy Review*, 37/3: 341–66.

Atkinson, A. P. (2007), 'Face Processing and Empathy', in T. F. D. Farrow and P. W. R. Woodruff (eds.), *Empathy in Mental Illness* (Cambridge: Cambridge University Press), 360–85.

Ausubel, D. P. (1955), 'Relationships between Shame and Guilt in the Socializing Process', *Psychological Review*, 62/5: 378–90.

Avramides, A. (2001), *Other Minds* (London: Routledge).

Aydede, M. (2003), 'Is Introspection Inferential?', in B. Gertler (ed.), *Privileged Access: Philosophical Accounts of Self-Knowledge* (Aldershot: Ashgate), 55–64.

Baker, L. R. (2000), *Persons and Bodies* (Cambridge: Cambridge University Press).

Baron-Cohen, S. (1989), 'Are Autistic Children "Behaviorists"? An Examination of their Mental–Physical and Appearance–Reality Distinctions', *Journal of Autism and Developmental Disorders*, 19/4: 579–600.

Baron-Cohen, S. (1995), *Mindblindness: An Essay on Autism and Theory of Mind* (Cambridge, Mass.: MIT Press).

Baron-Cohen, S. (2005), 'Autism-"Autos": Literally, a Total Focus on the Self?', in T. E. Feinberg and J. P. Keenan (eds.), *The Lost Self: Pathologies of the Brain and Identity* (Oxford: Oxford University Press), 166–80.

Barresi, J., and Moore, C. (1993), 'Sharing a Perspective Precedes the Understanding of that Perspective', *Behavioral and Brain Sciences*, 16/3: 513–14.

Barrett, L. F., Mesquita, B., and Gendron, M. (2011), 'Context in Emotion Perception', *Current Directions in Psychological Science*, 20/5: 286–90.

Bate, S., Cook, S. J., Mole, J., and Cole, J. (2013), 'First Report of Generalized Face Processing Difficulties in Möbius Sequence', *PLoS ONE*, 8/4: e62656; doi:10.1371/journal.pone.0062656.

Battaly, H. D. (2011), 'Is Empathy a Virtue?', in A. Coplan and P. Goldie (eds.), *Empathy: Philosophical and Psychological Perspectives* (Oxford: Oxford University Press), 277–301.

Bayne, T. (2010), *The Unity of Consciousness* (Oxford: Oxford University Press).

Bayne, T. (2013), 'Précis of *The Unity of Consciousness*', *Philosophy and Phenomenological Research*, 86/1: 200–8.

Becchio, C., Manera, V., Sartori, L., Cavallo, A., and Castiello, U. (2012), 'Grasping Intentions: From Thought Experiments to Empirical Evidence', *Frontiers in Human Neuroscience*, 6: 1–6.

Bennett, M. R., and Hacker, P. M. S. (2003), *Philosophical Foundations of Neuroscience* (Oxford: Blackwell).

Benveniste, É. (1966), *Problèmes de linguistique générale I* (Paris: Gallimard).

Bergson, H. (1910) [1889], *Time and Free Will: An Essay on the Immediate Data of Consciousness* (London: George Allen and Unwin).

Bermúdez, J. L. (2011), 'Bodily Awareness and Self-Consciousness', in S. Gallagher (ed.), *The Oxford Handbook of the Self* (Oxford: Oxford University Press), 157–79.

Binswanger, L. (1953) [1942], *Grundformen und Erkenntnis menschlichen Daseins* (Zurich: Max Niehans).

Bischof-Köhler, D. (1989), *Spiegelbild und Empathie: Die Anfänge der sozialen Kognition* (Bern: Verlag Hans Huber).

Bischof-Köhler, D. (1991), 'The Development of Empathy in Infants', in M. E. Lamb and H. Keller (eds.), *Infant Development: Perspectives from German Speaking Countries* (Hillsdale, NJ: Lawrence Erlbaum), 245–73.

Bischof-Köhler, D. (2012), 'Empathy and Self-Recognition in Phylogenetic and Ontogenetic Perspective', *Emotion Review*, 4/1: 40–8.

Blackburn, S. (1995), 'Theory, Observation and Drama', in M. Davies and T. Stone (eds.), *Folk Psychology: The Theory of Mind Debate* (Oxford: Blackwell), 274–90.

Blanke, O., and Metzinger, T. (2009), 'Full-Body Illusions and Minimal Phenomenal Selfhood', *Trends in Cognitive Sciences*, 13/1: 7–13.

Bodhi, B. (ed.) (1993), *A Comprehensive Manual of Abhidharma* (Seattle: Buddhist Publication Society).

Boghossian, P. A. (2003), 'Content and Self-Knowledge', in B. Gertler (ed.), *Privileged Access: Philosophical Accounts of Self-Knowledge* (Aldershot: Ashgate), 65–82.

Bollnow, O. F. (2009) [1947], *Die Ehrfurcht: Wesen und Wandel der Tugenden* (Würzburg: Königshausen and Neumann).

Borg, E. (2007), 'If Mirror Neurons Are the Answer, What Was the Question?', *Journal of Consciousness Studies*, 14/8: 5–19.

Botterill, G. (1996), 'Folk Psychology and Theoretical Status', in P. Carruthers and P. K. Smith (eds.), *Theories of Theories of Mind* (Cambridge: Cambridge University Press), 105–18.

Broesch, T., Callaghan, T., Henrich, J., Murphy, C., and Rochat, P. (2011), 'Cultural Variations in Children's Mirror Self-Recognition', *Journal of Cross-Cultural Psychology*, 42/6: 1018–29.

Broucek, F. J. (1991), *Shame and the Self* (New York: Guilford Press).

Bruner, J. (2003), *Making Stories: Law, Literature, Life* (Cambridge, Mass.: Harvard University Press).

Bruner, J. S., and Sherwood, V. (1976), 'Peekaboo and the Learning of Rule Structures', in J. S. Bruner, A. Jolly, and K. Sylva (eds.), *Play: Its Role in Evolution and Development* (London: Penguin Books), 277–85.

Butterfill, S. (2013), 'Interacting Mindreaders', *Philosophical Studies*, 165/3: 841–63.

Byrne, A. (2005), 'Introspection', *Philosophical Topics*, 33: 79–104.

Byrne, A. (2009), 'Experience and Content', *Philosophical Quarterly*, 59/236: 429–51.

Byrne, A. (2012), 'Knowing What I Want', in J. Liu and J. Perry (eds.), *Consciousness and the Self: New Essays* (Cambridge, Mass.: Cambridge University Press), 165–83.

Calder, A. J., Keane, J., Cole, J., Campbell, R., and Young, A. W. (2000), 'Facial Expression Recognition by People with Moëbius Syndrome', *Cognitive Neuropsychology*, 17/1–3: 73–87.

Calhoun, C. (2004), 'An Apology for Moral Shame', *Journal of Political Philosophy*, 12/2: 127–46.

Campbell, J. (1999), 'Schizophrenia, the Space of Reasons, and Thinking as a Motor Process', *The Monist*, 82/4: 609–25.

Campos, J. J. (2007), 'Foreword', in J. L. Tracy, R. W. Robins, and J. P. Tangney (eds.), *The Self-Conscious Emotions: Theory and Research* (New York: Guilford Press), pp. ix–xii.

Carpenter, M., and Liebal, K. (2011), 'Joint Attention, Communication, and Knowing Together in Infancy', in A. Seemann (ed.), *Joint Attention: New Developments in Psychology, Philosophy of Mind, and Social Neuroscience* (Cambridge, Mass.: MIT Press), 159–81.

Carr, D. (1986a), 'Cogitamus Ergo Sumus: The Intentionality of the First-Person Plural', *The Monist*, 69/4: 521–33.

Carr, D. (1986b), *Time, Narrative, and History* (Bloomington: Indiana University Press).

Carr, D. (1991), 'Discussion: Ricœur on Narrative', in D. Wood (ed.), *On Paul Ricœur: Narrative and Interpretation* (London: Routledge), 160–73.

Carruthers, P. (1996a), *Language, Thought and Consciousness: An Essay in Philosophical Psychology* (Cambridge: Cambridge University Press).

Carruthers, P. (1996b), 'Autism as Mind-Blindness: An Elaboration and Partial Defence', in P. Carruthers and P. K. Smith (eds.), *Theories of Theories of Mind* (Cambridge: Cambridge University Press), 257–73.

Carruthers, P. (1998), 'Natural Theories of Consciousness', *European Journal of Philosophy*, 6/2: 203–22.

Carruthers, P. (2000), *Phenomenal Consciousness: A Naturalistic Theory* (Cambridge: Cambridge University Press).

Carruthers, P., and Smith, P. K. (1996), 'Introduction', in P. Carruthers and P. K. Smith (eds.), *Theories of Theories of Mind* (Cambridge: Cambridge University Press), 1–8.

Cassam, Q. (1997), *Self and World* (Oxford: Clarendon Press).

Cassam, Q. (2007), *The Possibility of Knowledge* (Oxford: Oxford University Press).

Cassirer, E. (1957) [1929], *The Philosophy of Symbolic Forms III* (New Haven: Yale University Press).

Castelfranchi, C., and Poggi, I. (1990), 'Blushing as a Discourse: Was Darwin Wrong?', in W. R. Crozier (ed.), *Shyness and Embarrassment: Perspectives from Social Psychology* (Cambridge: Cambridge University Press), 230–51.

Caston, V. (2006), 'Comment on A. Thomasson, "Self-Awareness and Self-Knowledge"', *Psyche*, 12/2: 1–15.

Clark, A. (2003), *Natural-Born Cyborgs: Minds, Technologies, and the Future of Human Intelligence* (New York: Oxford University Press).

Cooley, C. H. (1912), *Human Nature and the Social Order* (New Brunswick, NJ: Transaction Books).

Crick, F. (1995), *The Astonishing Hypothesis* (London: Touchstone).

Csibra, G. (2010), 'Recognizing Communicative Intentions in Infancy', *Mind and Language*, 25/2: 141–68.

Currie, G. (2008), 'Some Ways to Understand People', *Philosophical Explorations*, 11/3: 211–18.

Currie, G. (2011), 'Empathy for Objects', in A. Coplan and P. Goldie (eds.), *Empathy: Philosophical and Psychological Perspectives* (Oxford: Oxford University Press), 82–95.

Dainton, B. (2000), *Stream of Consciousness: Unity and Continuity in Conscious Experience* (London: Routledge).

Dainton, B. (2004), 'The Self and the Phenomenal', *Ratio*, 17/4: 365–89.

Dainton, B. (2008), *The Phenomenal Self* (Oxford: Oxford University Press).

Damasio, A. (1999), *The Feeling of What Happens* (San Diego: Harcourt).

Darwall, S. (1998), 'Empathy, Sympathy, Care', *Philosophical Studies*, 89/2–3: 261–82.

Darwin, C. (2009) [1872], *The Expression of the Emotions in Man and Animals* (Cambridge: Cambridge University Press).

Davidson, D. (2001), *Subjective, Intersubjective, Objective* (Oxford: Oxford University Press).

Dawson, G., and McKissick, F. C. (1984), 'Self-Recognition in Autistic Children', *Journal of Autism and Developmental Disorders*, 14/4: 383–94.

De Bruin, L., van Elk, M., and Newen, A. (2012), 'Reconceptualizing Second-Person Interaction', *Frontiers in Human Neuroscience*, 6: 1–14.

Decety, J., Echols, S., and Correll, J. (2010), 'The Blame Game: The Effect of Responsibility and Social Stigma on Empathy for Pain', *Journal of Cognitive Neuroscience*, 22/5: 985–97.

Decety, J., Jackson, P. L., and Brunet, E. (2007), 'The Cognitive Neuropsychology of Empathy', in T. F. D. Farrow and P. W. R. Woodruff (eds.), *Empathy in Mental Illness* (Cambridge: Cambridge University Press), 239–60.

Decety, J., Michalska, K. J., and Akitsuki, Y. (2008), 'Who Caused the Pain? An fMRI Investigation of Empathy and Intentionality in Children', *Neuropsychologia*, 46/11: 2607–14.

Deigh, J. (1983), 'Shame and Self-Esteem: A Critique', *Ethics*, 93/2: 225–45.

Dennett, D. (1987), *The Intentional Stance* (Cambridge, Mass.: MIT Press).

Dennett, D. (1991), *Consciousness Explained* (Boston: Little, Brown).

Dennett, D. (1992), 'The Self as the Center of Narrative Gravity', in F. S. Kessel, P. M. Cole, and D. L. Johnson (eds.), *Self and Consciousness: Multiple Perspectives* (Hillsdale, NJ: Lawrence Erlbaum), 103–15.

Deonna, J. A., and Teroni, F. (2009), 'The Self of Shame', in M. Salmela and V. Mayer (eds.), *Emotions, Ethics, and Authenticity* (Amsterdam: John Benjamins).

Deonna, J. A., and Teroni, F. (2011), 'Is Shame a Social Emotion?', in A. Konzelman-Ziv, K. Lehrer, and H. B. Schmid (eds.), *Self-Evaluation: Affective and Social Grounds of Intentionality* (Dordrecht: Springer), 193–212.

Deonna, J. A., Rodogno, R., and Teroni, F. (2011), *In Defense of Shame* (New York: Oxford University Press).

De Preester, H. (2008), 'From Ego to Alter Ego: Husserl, Merleau-Ponty and a Layered Approach to Intersubjectivity', *Phenomenology and the Cognitive Sciences*, 7/1: 133–42.

Derrida, J. (1967), *L'Écriture et la différence* (Paris: Éditions du Seuil).

De Vignemont, F. (2009), 'Affective Mirroring: Emotional Contagion or Empathy?', in S. Nolen-Hoeksema, B. Frederikson, G. R. Loftus, and W. A. Wagenaar (eds.), *Atkinson and Hilgard's Introduction to Psychology*, 15th edn (Florence, Ky.: Cengage Learning), 787.

Dilthey, W. (2002) [1910], *The Formation of the Historical World in the Human Sciences* (Princeton: Princeton University Press).

Draghi-Lorenz, R., Reddy, V., and Costall, A. (2001), 'Re-thinking the Development of "Non-Basic" Emotions: A Critical Review of Existing Theories', *Developmental Review*, 21/3: 263–304.

Dretske, F. (1973), 'Perception and Other Minds', *Nous*, 7/1: 34–44.

Dretske, F. (1995), *Naturalizing the Mind* (Cambridge, Mass.: MIT Press).

Dretske, F. (1999), 'The Mind's Awareness of Itself', *Philosophical Studies*, 95/1–2: 103–24.

Dretske, F. (2003), 'How Do You Know You Are Not a Zombie?', in B. Gertler (ed.), *Privileged Access: Philosophical Accounts of Self-Knowledge* (Aldershot: Ashgate), 1–13.

Dreyfus, G. (2011), 'Self and Subjectivity: A Middle Way Approach', in M. Siderits, E. Thompson, and D. Zahavi (eds.), *Self, No Self? Perspectives from Analytical, Phenomenological, and Indian Traditions* (Oxford: Oxford University Press), 114–56.

Dreyfus, H., and Kelly, S. D. (2007), 'Heterophenomenology: Heavy-Handed Sleight-of-Hand', *Phenomenology and the Cognitive Sciences*, 6/1–2: 45–55.

Dreyfus, H. L. (2005), 'Overcoming the Myth of the Mental: How Philosophers Can Profit from the Phenomenology of Everyday Expertise', *Proceedings and Addresses of the American Philosophical Association*, 79/2: 47–65.

Dreyfus, H. L. (2007a), 'The Return of the Myth of the Mental', *Inquiry*, 50/4: 352–65.

Dreyfus, H. L. (2007b), 'Response to McDowell', *Inquiry*, 50/4: 371–7.

Dreyfus, H. L. (2013), 'The Myth of the Pervasiveness of the Mental', in J. K. Schear (ed.), *Mind, Reason, and Being-in-the-World: The McDowell–Dreyfus Debate* (London: Routledge), 15–40.

Drummond, J. (2004), '"Cognitive Impenetrability" and the Complex Intentionality of the Emotions', *Journal of Consciousness Studies*, 11/10–11: 109–26.

Duddington, N. (1918), 'Our Knowledge of Other Minds', *Proceedings of the Aristotelian Society*, 19: 147–78.

Dullstein, M. (2012), 'Direct Perception and Simulation: Stein's Account of Empathy', *Review of Philosophy and Psychology*, 4/2: 333–50.

Edelstein, R. S., and Shaver, P. R. (2007), 'A Cross-Cultural Examination of Lexical Studies of Self-Conscious Emotions', in J. L. Tracy, R. W. Robins, and J. P. Tangney (eds.), *The Self-Conscious Emotions: Theory and Research* (New York: Guilford Press), 194–208.

Eisenberg, N. (1986), *Altruistic Emotion, Cognition, and Behaviour* (Hillsdale, NJ: Lawrence Erlbaum).

Ekman, P. (2003), *Emotions Revealed: Understanding Faces and Feelings* (London: Weidenfeld and Nicolson).

Epley, N., and Waytz, A. (2009), 'Mind Perception', in S. T. Fiske, D. T. Gilbert, and G. Lindsay (eds.), *The Handbook of Social Psychology* (New York: John Wiley), 498–541.

Farroni, T., Csibra, G., Simion, F., and Johnson, M. H. (2002), 'Eye Contact Detection in Humans from Birth', *Proceedings of the National Academy of Sciences of the United States of America*, 99/14: 9602–5.

Fasching, W. (2009), 'The Mineness of Experience', *Continental Philosophy Review*, 42/2: 131–48.

Fasching, W. (2011), '"I Am of the Nature of Seeing": Phenomenological Reflections on the Indian Notion of Witness-Consciousness', in M. Siderits, E. Thompson, and D. Zahavi (eds.), *Self, No Self? Perspectives from Analytical, Phenomenological, and Indian Traditions* (Oxford: Oxford University Press), 193–216.

Feinberg, T. E., and Keenan, J. P. (2005), 'Where in the Brain Is the Self?', *Consciousness and Cognition*, 14/4: 661–78.

Fink, C. K. (2012), 'The "Scent" of a Self: Buddhism and the First-Person Perspective', *Asian Philosophy*, 22/3: 289–306.

Finkelstein, D. H. (2003), *Expression and the Inner* (Cambridge, Mass.: Harvard University Press).

Flanagan, O. (1992), *Consciousness Reconsidered* (Cambridge, Mass.: MIT Press).

Foucault, M. (1990) [1976], *The History of Sexuality: An Introduction* (New York: Vintage Books).

Frankfurt, H. (1988), *The Importance of What We Care About: Philosophical Essays* (Cambridge: Cambridge University Press).

Frith, C. (2007), *Making up the Mind: How the Brain Creates Our Mental Worlds* (Malden, Mass.: Blackwell).

Frith, U. (2003), *Autism: Explaining the Enigma* (Oxford: Blackwell).

Frith, U., and Happé, F. (1999), 'Theory of Mind and Self-Consciousness: What Is It Like to Be Autistic?', *Mind and Language*, 14/1: 82.

Fuchs, T. (2013), 'The Phenomenology and Development of Social Perspectives', *Phenomenology and the Cognitive Sciences*, 12/4: 655–83.

Fuchs, T., and De Jaegher, H. (2009), 'Enactive Intersubjectivity: Participatory Sense-Making and Mutual Incorporation', *Phenomenology and the Cognitive Sciences*, 8/4: 465–86.

Gallagher, S. (1997), 'Mutual Enlightenment: Recent Phenomenology in Cognitive Science', *Journal of Consciousness Studies*, 4/3: 195–214.

Gallagher, S. (2000), 'Self-Reference and Schizophrenia: A Cognitive Model of Immunity to Error through Misidentification', in D. Zahavi (ed.), *Exploring the Self* (Amsterdam: John Benjamins), 203–39.

Gallagher, S. (2003), 'Self-Narrative in Schizophrenia', in T. Kirchner and A. David (eds.), *The Self in Neuroscience and Psychiatry* (Cambridge: Cambridge University Press), 336–57.

Gallagher, S. (2005), *How the Body Shapes the Mind* (Oxford: Oxford University Press).

Gallagher, S. (2007), 'Simulation Trouble', *Social Neuroscience*, 2/3–4: 353–65.

Gallagher, S., and Miyahara, K. (2012), 'Neo-Pragmatism and Enactive Intentionality', in J. Schulkin (ed.), *Action, Perception and the Brain: Adaptation and Cephalic Expression* (Basingstoke: Palgrave Macmillan), 117–46.

Gallagher, S., and Zahavi, D. (2008), *The Phenomenological Mind: An Introduction to Philosophy of Mind and Cognitive Science* (New York: Routledge).

Gallese, V. (2001), 'The "Shared Manifold" Hypothesis: From Mirror Neurons to Empathy', *Journal of Consciousness Studies*, 8/5–6: 33–50.

Gallese, V. (2003a), 'The Manifold Nature of Interpersonal Relations: The Quest for a Common Mechanism', *Philosophical Transactions: Biological Sciences*, 358/1431: 517–28.

Gallese, V. (2003b), 'The Roots of Empathy: The Shared Manifold Hypothesis and the Neural Basis of Intersubjectivity', *Psychopathology*, 36/4: 171–80.

Gallese, V. (2005), 'Embodied Simulation: From Neurons to Phenomenal Experience', *Phenomenology and the Cognitive Sciences*, 4/1: 23–48.

Gallese, V. (2007a), 'Before and Below "Theory of Mind": Embodied Simulation and the Neural Correlates of Social Cognition', *Philosophical Transactions: Biological Sciences*, 362/1480: 659–69.

Gallese, V. (2007b), 'Embodied Simulation: From Mirror Neuron Systems to Interpersonal Relations', *Empathy and Fairness: Novartis Foundation Symposium*, 278: 3–19.

Gallese, V. (2008), 'Empathy, Embodied Simulation, and the Brain: Commentary on Aragno and Zepf/Hartmann', *Journal of the American Psychoanalytic Association*, 56/3: 769–81.

Gallese, V. (2009), 'Mirror Neurons, Embodied Simulation, and the Neural Basis of Social Identification', *Psychoanalytic Dialogues*, 19/5: 519–36.

Gallese, V., and Goldman, A. (1998), 'Mirror Neurons and the Simulation Theory of Mind-Reading', *Trends in Cognitive Sciences*, 2/12: 493–501.

Gallese, V., Keysers, C., and Rizzolatti, G. (2004), 'A Unifying View of the Basis of Social Cognition', *Trends in Cognitive Sciences*, 8/9: 396–403.

Gallup, G. G. (1970), 'Chimpanzees: Self-Recognition', *Science*, 167/3914: 86–7.

Gallup, G. G. (1975), 'Towards an Operational Definition of Self-Awareness', in R. H. Tuttle (ed.), *Socioecology and Psychology of Primates* (Paris: Mouton), 309–41.

Gallup, G. G. (1977), 'Self-Recognition in Primates: A Comparative Approach to the Bidirectional Properties of Consciousness', *American Psychologist*, 32: 329–38.

Gallup, G. G. (1982), 'Self-Awareness and the Emergence of Mind in Primates', *American Journal of Primatology*, 2/3: 237–48.

Gallup, G. G. (1983), 'Toward a Comparative Psychology of Mind', in R. L. Mellgren (ed.), *Animal Cognition and Behavior* (Amsterdam: North-Holland), 473–510.

Gallup, G. G. (1985), 'Do Minds Exist in Species Other than Our Own?', *Neuroscience and Biobehavioral Reviews*, 9/4: 631–41.

Gallup, G. G., McClure, M. K., Hill, S. D., and Bundy, R. A. (1971), 'Capacity for Self-Recognition in Differentially Reared Chimpanzees', *Psychological Record*, 21: 69–74.

Ganeri, J. (2007), *The Concealed Art of the Soul: Theories of Self and Practices of Truth in Indian Ethics and Epistemology* (Oxford: Oxford University Press).

Ganeri, J. (2012), *The Self: Naturalism, Consciousness, and the First-Person Stance* (Oxford: Oxford University Press).

Geiger, M. (1911), 'Über das Wesen und die Bedeutung der Einfühlung', in F. Schumann (ed.), *Bericht über den IV. Kongress für experimentelle Psychologie* (Leipzig: Barth Verlag), 29–73.

Gergely, G. (2007), 'The Social Construction of the Subjective Self: The Role of Affect-Mirroring, Markedness, and Ostensive Communication in Self-Development', in L. Mayes, P. Fonagy, and M. Target (eds.), *Developmental Science and Psychoanalysis: Integration and Innovation* (London: Karnac), 45–82.

Gilbert, P. (1998), 'What Is Shame? Some Core Issues and Controversies', in P. Gilbert and B. Andrews (eds.), *Shame: Interpersonal Behavior, Psychopathology, and Culture* (New York: Oxford University Press), 3–38.

Gilbert, P. (2003), 'Evolution, Social Roles, and the Differences in Shame and Guilt', *Social Research*, 70/4: 1205–30.

Gillihan, S. J., and Farah, M. J. (2005), 'Is Self Special? A Critical Review of Evidence from Experimental Psychology and Cognitive Neuroscience', *Psychological Bulletin*, 131/1: 76–97.

Goldie, P. (2000), *The Emotions: A Philosophical Exploration* (Oxford: Oxford University Press).

Goldie, P. (2012), *The Mess Inside: Narrative, Emotion, and the Mind* (Oxford: Oxford University Press).

Goldman, A. I. (1992), 'Empathy, Mind, and Morals', *Proceedings and Addresses of the American Philosophical Association*, 66/3: 17–41.

Goldman, A. I. (1995), 'Interpretation Psychologized', in M. Davies and T. Stone (eds.), *Folk Psychology: The Theory of Mind Debate* (Oxford: Blackwell), 74–99.

Goldman, A. I. (2006), *Simulating Minds* (New York: Oxford University Press).

Goldman, A. I. (2012), 'Theory of Mind', in E. Margolis, R. Samuels, and S. P. Stich (eds.), *The Oxford Handbook of Philosophy of Cognitive Science* (New York: Oxford University Press), 402–24.

Goldman, A. I., and Sripada, C. S. (2005), 'Simulationist Models of Face-Based Emotion Recognition', *Cognition*, 94/3: 193–213.

Gopnik, A. (1993), 'How We Know Our Minds: The Illusion of First-Person Knowledge of Intentionality', *Behavioral and Brain Sciences*, 16: 1–14.

Gopnik, A. (1996), 'Theories and Modules: Creation Myths, Developmental Realities, and Neurath's Boat', in P. Carruthers and P. K. Smith (eds.), *Theories of Theories of Mind* (Cambridge: Cambridge University Press), 169–83.

Gopnik, A., and Wellman, H. M. (1995), 'Why the Child's Theory of Mind Really Is a Theory', in M. Davies and T. Stone (eds.), *Folk Psychology: The Theory of Mind Debate* (Oxford: Blackwell), 232–58.

Gordon, R. (1986), 'Folk Psychology as Simulation', *Mind and Language*, 1/2: 158–71.

Gordon, R. (1995), 'Sympathy, Simulation, and the Impartial Spectator', *Ethics*, 105/4: 727.

Gray, K., and Schein, C. (2012), 'Two Minds vs. Two Philosophies: Mind Perception Defines Morality and Dissolves the Debate between Deontology and Utilitarianism', *Review of Philosophy and Psychology*, 3/3: 405–23.

Green, M. S. (2007), *Self-Expression* (Oxford: Oxford University Press).

Grünbaum, T., and Zahavi, D. (2013), 'Varieties of Self-Awareness', in K. W. M. Fulford, M. Davies, R. Gipps, G. Graham, J. Sadler, G. Stanghellini, and T. Thornton (eds.), *The Oxford Handbook of Philosophy and Psychiatry* (Oxford: Oxford University Press), 221–39.

Gurwitsch, A. (1941), 'A Non-Egological Conception of Consciousness', *Philosophy and Phenomenological Research*, 1/3: 325–38.

Gurwitsch, A. (1966), *Studies in Phenomenology and Psychology* (Evanston: Northwestern University Press).

Gurwitsch, A. (1979) [c.1932], *Human Encounters in the Social World* (Pittsburgh: Duquesne University Press).

Habermas, J. (1984), *Vorstudien und Ergänzungen zur Theorie des kommunikativen Handelns* (Frankfurt am Main: Suhrkamp).

Hacking, I. (1995), *Rewriting the Soul: Multiple Personality and the Sciences of Memory* (Princeton: Princeton University Press).

Harré, R. (1990), 'Embarrassment: A Conceptual Analysis', in W. R. Crozier (ed.), *Shyness and Embarrassment: Perspectives from Social Psychology* (Cambridge: Cambridge University Press), 181–204.

Hart, J. G. (2009), *Who One Is, Book I: Meontology of the 'I': A Transcendental Phenomenology* (Dordrecht: Springer).

Hatfield, E., Rapson, R. L., and Le, Y.-C. (2009), 'Emotional Contagion and Empathy', in J. Decety and W. Ickes (eds.), *The Social Neuroscience of Empathy* (Cambridge, Mass.: MIT Press), 19–30.

Heidegger, M. (1975) [1927], *Die Grundprobleme der Phänomenologie*, Gesamtausgabe, vol. 24 (Frankfurt am Main: Vittorio Klostermann).

Heidegger, M. (1986) [1927], *Sein und Zeit* (Tübingen: Max Niemeyer Verlag); trans. J. Stambaugh as *Being and Time* (Albany, NY: SUNY, 1996).

Heidegger, M. (1993), *Grundprobleme der Phänomenologie (1919/1920)*, Gesamtausgabe, vol. 58 (Frankfurt am Main: Vittorio Klostermann).

Heidegger, M. (1994) [1921–2], *Phänomenologische Interpretationen zu Aristoteles: Einführung in die phänomenologische Forschung*, Gesamtausgabe, vol. 61 (Frankfurt am Main: Vittorio Klostermann).

Heidegger, M. (2001) [1928–9], *Einleitung in die Philosophie*, Gesamtausgabe, vol. 27 (Frankfurt am Main: Vittorio Klostermann).

Henry, M. (1963), *L'Essence de la manifestation* (Paris: PUF).

Henry, M. (1965), *Philosophie et phénoménologie du corps* (Paris: PUF).

Herschbach, M. (2008), 'Folk Psychological and Phenomenological Accounts of Social Perception', *Philosophical Explorations*, 11/3: 223–35.

Hobson, J., and Hobson, R. P. (2007), 'Identification: The Missing Link between Joint Attention and Imitation?' *Development and Psychopathology*, 19: 411–31.

Hobson, R. P. (1990), 'On the Origins of Self and the Case of Autism', *Development and Psychopathology*, 2/2: 163–81.

Hobson, R. P. (1993), *Autism and the Development of Mind* (Hove: Psychology Press).

Hobson, R. P. (2002), *The Cradle of Thought* (London: Macmillan).

Hobson, R. P. (2007), 'Communicative Depth: Soundings from Developmental Psychopathology', *Infant Behavior & Development*, 30: 267–77.

Hobson, R. P. (2008), 'Interpersonally Situated Cognition', *International Journal of Philosophical Studies*, 16/3: 377–97.

Hobson, R. P., and Hobson, J. (2011), 'Joint Attention or Joint Engagement? Insights from Autism', in A. Seemann (ed.), *Joint Attention: New Developments in Psychology, Philosophy of Mind, and Social Neuroscience* (Cambridge, Mass.: MIT Press), 115–36.

Hobson, R. P., Chidambi, G., Lee, J., and Meyer, J. (2006), *Foundations for Self-Awareness: An Exploration through Autism* (Oxford: Blackwell).

Hodges, S. D. (2005), 'Is How Much You Understand Me in Your Head or Mine?', in B. F. Malle and S. D. Hodges (eds.), *Other Minds: How Human Bridge the Divide between Self and Others* (New York: Guilford Press), 298–309.

Hodges, S. D., and Wegner, D. M. (1997), 'Automatic and Controlled Empathy', in W. Ickes (ed.), *Empathic Accuracy* (New York: Guilford Press), 311–39.

Hoffman, M. L. (2001), *Empathy and Moral Development: Implications for Caring and Justice* (Cambridge: Cambridge University Press).

Hollan, D. (2012), 'Emerging Issues in the Cross-Cultural Study of Empathy', *Emotion Review*, 4/1: 70–8.

Honneth, A. (2001), 'Invisibility: On the Epistemology of "Recognition"', *Proceedings of the Aristotelian Society, Supplementary Volumes*, 75/1: 111–39.

Honneth, A. (2008), *Reification: A New Look at an Old Idea* (Oxford: Oxford University Press).

Hopkins, G. M. (1959) [1880], 'Commentary on the Spiritual Exercises of St Ignatius Loyola', in *The Sermons and Devotional Writings of Gerard Manley Hopkins*, ed. C. J. Devlin (London: Oxford University Press).

Hume, D. (2000) [1739], *A Treatise of Human Nature* (Oxford: Oxford University Press).

Husserl, E. (1932), MS B I 14, unpublished manuscript, Husserl Archives Leuven.

Husserl, E. (1950) [1931], *Cartesianische Meditationen und Pariser Vorträge*, ed. S. Strasser, Husserliana 1 (The Hague: Martinus Nijhoff); pages 3–39 trans. P. Koestenbaum as *The Paris Lectures* (The Hague: Martinus Nijhoff, 1964); pages 43–183 trans. D. Cairns as *Cartesian Meditations: An Introduction to Phenomenology* (The Hague: Martinus Nijhoff, 1960).

Husserl, E. (1952) [c.1912–28], *Ideen zu einer reinen Phänomenologie und phänomenologischen Philosophie*, book 2, *Phänomenologische Untersuchungen zur Konstitution*, ed. M. Biemel, Husserliana 4 (The Hague: Martinus Nijhoff); trans. R. Rojcewicz and A. Schuwer as *Ideas Pertaining to a Pure Phenomenology and to a Phenomenological Philosophy*, book 2, *Studies in the Phenomenology of Constitution* (Dordrecht: Kluwer Academic Publishers, 1989).

Husserl, E. (1954) [1936], *Die Krisis der europäischen Wissenschaften und die transzendentale Phänomenologie: Eine Einleitung in die phänomenologische Philosophie*, ed. W. Biemel, Husserliana 6 (The Hague: Martinus Nijhoff); pages 1–348, 357–86, 459–62, 473–5, 508–16 trans. D. Carr as *The Crisis of European Sciences and Transcendental Phenomenology: An Introduction to Phenomenological Philosophy* (Evanston, Ill.: Northwestern University Press, 1970).

Husserl, E. (1959), *Erste Philosophie (1923/24)*, vol. ii, *Theorie der phänomenologischen Reduktion*, ed. R. Boehm, Husserliana 8 (The Hague: Martinus Nijhoff).

Husserl, E. (1962), *Phänomenologische Psychologie: Vorlesungen Sommersemester 1925*, ed. W. Biemel, Husserliana 9 (The Hague: Martinus Nijhoff); pages 3–234 trans. J. Scanlon as *Phenomenological Psychology: Lectures, Summer Semester, 1925* (The Hague: Martinus

Nijhoff, 1977); pages 237–349, 517–26 ed. and trans. T. Sheehan and R. E. Palmer as *Psychological and Transcendental Phenomenology and the Confrontation with Heidegger (1927–1931)* (Dordrecht: Kluwer Academic Publishers, 1997).

Husserl, E. (1966a), *Zur Phänomenologie des inneren Zeitbewusstseins (1893–1917)*, ed. R. Boehm, Husserliana 10 (The Hague: Martinus Nijhoff); trans. J. B. Brough as *On the Phenomenology of the Consciousness of Internal Time (1893–1917)* (Dordrecht: Kluwer Academic Publishers, 1991).

Husserl, E. (1966b), *Analysen zur passiven Synthesis: Aus Vorlesungs- und Forschungsmanuskripten, 1918–1926*, ed. M. Fleischer, Husserliana 11 (The Hague: Martinus Nijhoff).

Husserl, E. (1971) [c.1912], *Ideen zu einer reinen Phänomenologie und phänomenologischen Philosophie*, book 3, *Die Phänomenologie und die Fundamente der Wissenschaften*, ed. M. Biemel, Husserliana 5 (The Hague: Martinus Nijhoff).

Husserl, E. (1973a), *Zur Phänomenologie der Intersubjektivität: Texte aus dem Nachlass*, vol. i, *1905–1920*, ed. I. Kern, Husserliana 13 (The Hague: Martinus Nijhoff).

Husserl, E. (1973b), *Zur Phänomenologie der Intersubjektivität: Texte aus dem Nachlass*, vol. ii, *1921–1928*, ed. I. Kern, Husserliana 14 (The Hague: Martinus Nijhoff).

Husserl, E. (1973c), *Zur Phänomenologie der Intersubjektivität: Texte aus dem Nachlass*, vol. iii, *1929–1935*, ed. I. Kern, Husserliana 15 (The Hague: Martinus Nijhoff).

Husserl, E. (1973d), *Ding und Raum: Vorlesungen 1907*, ed. U. Claesges, Husserliana 16 (The Hague: Martinus Nijhoff); trans. R. Rojcewicz as *Thing and Space: Lectures of 1907* (Dordrecht: Kluwer Academic Publishers, 1997).

Husserl, E. (1974) [1929], *Formale und transzendentale Logik: Versuch einer Kritik der logischen Vernunft*, ed. P. Janssen, Husserliana 17 (The Hague: Martinus Nijhoff).

Husserl, E. (1976) [1913], *Ideen zu einer reinen Phänomenologie und phänomenologischen Philosophie*, book 1, *Allgemeine Einführung in die reine Phänomenologie*, ed. K. Schuhmann, Husserliana 3/1–2 (The Hague: Martinus Nijhoff); trans. F. Kersten as *Ideas Pertaining to a Pure Phenomenology and to a Phenomenological Philosophy*, book 1, *General Introduction to a Pure Phenomenology* (The Hague: Martinus Nijhoff, 1982).

Husserl, E. (1980), *Phantasie, Bildbewusstsein, Erinnerung: Zur Phänomenologie der anschaulichen Vergegenwärtigungen. Texte aus dem Nachlass (1898–1925)*, ed. E. Marbach, Husserliana 23 (Dordrecht: Kluwer Academic Publishers).

Husserl, E. (1984a) [1901], *Logische Untersuchungen*, vol. ii, *Untersuchungen zur Phänomenologie und Theorie der Erkenntnis*, ed. U. Panzer, Husserliana 19 (The Hague: Martinus Nijhoff); trans. J. N. Findlay as *Logical Investigations I* (London: Routledge, 2001).

Husserl, E. (1984b), *Einleitung in die Logik und Erkenntnistheorie: Vorlesungen 1906/07*, ed. U. Melle, Husserliana 24 (Dordrecht: Martinus Nijhoff).

Husserl, E. (1985) [1939], *Erfahrung und Urteil*, ed. L. Landgrebe (Hamburg: Felix Meiner).

Husserl, E. (1993), *Die Krisis der europäischen Wissenschaften und die transzendentale Phänomenologie*, supplementary volume, *Texte aus dem Nachlass 1934–1937*, ed. R. N. Smid, Husserliana 29 (Dordrecht: Kluwer Academic Publishers).

Husserl, E. (1994), *Briefwechsel IV*, ed. K. and E. Schuhmann, Husserliana Dokumente III/4 (Dordrecht: Kluwer Academic Publishers).

Husserl, E. (2001), *Die Bernauer Manuskripte über das Zeitbewusstsein (1917/18)*, ed. R. Bernet and D. Lohmar, Husserliana 33 (Dordrecht: Kluwer Academic Publishers).

Husserl, E. (2002a), *Logische Untersuchungen*, supplementary volume, vol. i, *Entwürfe zur Umarbeitung der VI. Untersuchung und zur Vorrede für die Neuauflage der Logischen Untersuchungen (Sommer 1913)*, ed. U. Melle, Husserliana 20/1 (Dordrecht: Kluwer Academic Publishers).

Husserl, E. (2002b), *Einleitung in die Philosophie: Vorlesungen 1922/23*, ed. B. Goossens, Husserliana 35 (Dordrecht: Kluwer Academic Publishers).

Husserl, E. (2003), *Transzendentaler Idealismus: Texte aus dem Nachlass (1908–1921)*, ed. R. Rollinger, Husserliana 36 (Dordrecht: Kluwer Academic Publishers).

Husserl, E. (2004), *Einleitung in die Ethik: Vorlesungen Sommersemester 1920 und 1924*, ed. H. Peucker, Husserliana 37 (Dordrecht: Kluwer Academic Publishers).

Husserl, E. (2005), *Logische Untersuchungen*, supplementary volume, vol. ii, *Texte für die Neufassung der VI. Untersuchung. Zur Phänomenologie des Ausdrucks und der Erkenntnis (1893/94–1921)*, ed. U. Melle, Husserliana 20/2 (Dordrecht: Springer).

Husserl, E. (2006), *Späte Texte über Zeitkonstitution (1929–1934): Die C-Manuskripte*, ed. D. Lohmar, Husserliana Materialien 8 (Dordrecht: Springer).

Hutchinson, P. (2008), *Shame and Philosophy: An Investigation in the Philosophy of Emotions and Ethics* (Basingstoke: Palgrave Macmillan).

Hutto, D. (2008), 'Articulating and Understanding the Phenomenological Manifesto', *Abstracta*, Special Issue II, 10–19.

Iacoboni, M. (2007), 'Existential Empathy: The Intimacy of Self and Other', in T. F. D. Farrow and P. W. R. Woodruff (eds.), *Empathy in Mental Illness* (Cambridge: Cambridge University Press), 310–21.

Iacoboni, M. (2009), *Mirroring People: The Science of Empathy and How We Connect with Others* (New York: Picador).

Iacoboni, M. (2011), 'Within Each Other: Neural Mechanisms for Empathy in the Primate Brain', in A. Coplan and P. Goldie (eds.), *Empathy: Philosophical and Psychological Perspectives* (Oxford: Oxford University Press), 45–57.

Ikonen, P., and Rechardt, E. (1993), 'The Origin of Shame and its Vicissitudes', *Scandinavian Psychoanalytic Review*, 16/2: 100–24.

Ingarden, R. (1994) [1921], *Frühe Schriften zur Erkenntnistheorie* (Tübingen: Max Niemeyer).

Jackson, F. (1999), 'All That Can Be at Issue in the Theory-Theory Simulation Debate', *Philosophical Papers*, 28/2: 77–96.

Jacob, P. (2008), 'What Do Mirror Neurons Contribute to Human Social Cognition?', *Mind and Language*, 23/2: 190–223.

Jacob, P. (2011), 'The Direct-Perception Model of Empathy: A Critique', *Review of Philosophy and Psychology*, 2/3: 519–40.

Jacoby, M. (1994), *Shame and the Origins of Self-Esteem: A Jungian Approach* (London: Routledge).

James, W. (1890), *The Principles of Psychology*, vols. i–ii (London: Macmillan).

Janzen, G. (2008), *The Reflexive Nature of Consciousness* (Amsterdam: John Benjamins).

Jaspers, K. (1959) [1913], *Allgemeine Psychopathologie* (Berlin: Springer).

Jeannerod, M., and Pacherie, E. (2004), 'Agency, Simulation and Self-Identification', *Mind and Language*, 19/2: 113–46.

Johnson, S. C. (2000), 'The Recognition of Mentalistic Agents in Infancy', *Trends in Cognitive Sciences*, 4/1: 22–8.

Jopling, A. (2000), *Self-Knowledge and the Self* (London: Routledge).

Kahneman, D., and Tversky, A. (1982), 'The Simulation Heuristic', in D. Kahneman, P. Slovic, and A. Tversky (eds.), *Judgment under Uncertainty: Heuristics and Biases* (New York: Cambridge University Press), 201–8.

Karlsson, G., and Sjöberg, L. G. (2009), 'The Experiences of Guilt and Shame: A Phenomenological–Psychological Study', *Human Studies*, 32/3: 335–55.

Kearney, R. (1984), *Dialogues with Contemporary Continental Thinkers* (Manchester: Manchester University Press).

Keenan, J. P., Gallup, G. G., and Falk, D. (2003), *The Face in the Mirror: How We Know Who We Are* (New York: HarperCollins).

Kenny, A. (1988), *The Self* (Milwaukee, Wis.: Marquette University Press).

Keysers, C. (2011), *The Empathic Brain: How the Discovery of Mirror Neurons Changes Our Understanding of Human Nature* (Los Gatos, Calif.: Smashwords Edition).

Kierkegaard, S. (1993) [1847], *Upbuilding Discourses in Various Spirits*, trans. H. V. Hong and E. H. Hong (Princeton: Princeton University Press).

Klawonn, E. (1987), 'The "I": On the Ontology of First Personal Identity', *Danish Yearbook of Philosophy*, 24: 43–76.

Klawonn, E. (1990a), 'On Personal Identity: Defence of a Form of Non-Reductionism', *Danish Yearbook of Philosophy*, 25: 41–61.

Klawonn, E. (1990b), 'A Reply to Lübcke and Collin', *Danish Yearbook of Philosophy*, 25: 89–107.

Klawonn, E. (1991), *Jeg'ets ontologi: en afhandling om subjektivitet, bevidsthed og personlig identitet* (Odense: Odense Universitetsforlag).

Klawonn, E. (1998), 'The Ontological Concept of Consciousness', *Danish Yearbook of Philosophy*, 33: 55–69.

Klein, S. B. (2010), 'The Self: As a Construct in Psychology and Neuropsychological Evidence for its Multiplicity', *Wiley Interdisciplinary Reviews: Cognitive Science*, 1/2: 172–83.

Klein, S. B. (2012), 'The Self and its Brain', *Social Cognition*, 30/4: 474–518.

Klein, S. B., and Nichols, S. (2012), 'Memory and the Sense of Personal Identity', *Mind*, 121/483: 677–702.

Knoblich, G., Butterfill, S., and Sebanz, N. (2011), 'Psychological Research on Joint Action: Theory and Data', in B. H. Ross (ed.), *The Psychology of Learning and Motivation* (Burlington: Academic Press), 59–101.

Konstan, D. (2003), 'Shame in Ancient Greece', *Social Research*, 70/4: 1031–60.

Kopelman, M. D. (1999), 'Varieties of False Memory', *Cognitive Neuropsychology*, 16/3–5: 197–214.

Korsgaard, C. M. (2009), *Self-Constitution: Agency, Identity, and Integrity* (Oxford: Oxford University Press).

Kriegel, U. (2003a), 'Consciousness as Intransitive Self-Consciousness: Two Views and an Argument', *Canadian Journal of Philosophy*, 33/1: 103–32.

Kriegel, U. (2003b), 'Consciousness, Higher-Order Content, and the Individuation of Vehicles', *Synthese*, 134/3: 477–504.

Kriegel, U. (2004), 'Consciousness and Self-Consciousness', *Monist*, 87/2: 182–205.

Kriegel, U. (2009), *Subjective Consciousness: A Self-Representational Theory* (Oxford: Oxford University Press).

Kriegel, U., and Williford, K. (eds.) (2006), *Consciousness and Self-Reference* (Cambridge, Mass.: Cambridge University Press).

Laird, J. D. (2007), *Feelings: The Perception of Self* (Oxford: Oxford University Press).

Landweer, H. (1999), *Scham und Macht: Phänomenologische Untersuchungen zur Sozialität eines Gefühls* (Tübingen: Mohr Siebeck).

Lane, T. (2012), 'Toward an Explanatory Framework for Mental Ownership', *Phenomenology and the Cognitive Sciences*, 11/2: 251–86.

Lavelle, J. S. (2012), 'Theory-Theory and the Direct Perception of Mental States', *Review of Philosophy and Psychology*, 3/2: 213–30.

Legrand, D. (2007), 'Pre-Reflective Self-as-Subject from Experiential and Empirical Perspectives', *Consciousness and Cognition*, 16/3: 583–99.

Legrand, D. (2011), 'Phenomenological Dimensions of Bodily Self-Consciousness', in S. Gallagher (ed.), *The Oxford Handbook of the Self* (Oxford: Oxford University Press), 204–27.

Leslie, A. M. (1987), 'Children's Understanding of the Mental World', in R. L. Gregory (ed.), *The Oxford Companion to the Mind* (Oxford: Oxford University Press), 139–42.

Leudar, I., and Costall, A. (2004), 'On the Persistence of the "Problem of Other Minds" in Psychology: Chomsky, Grice and Theory of Mind', *Theory and Psychology*, 14/5: 601–21.

Levinas, E. (1979) [1961], *Totality and Infinity*, trans. A. Lingis (The Hague: Martinus Nijhoff).

Levinas, E. (1987) [1948], *Time and the Other*, trans. R. A. Cohen (Pittsburgh: Duquesne University Press).

Levinas, E. (2003) [1935], *On Escape*, trans. B. Bergo (Stanford: Stanford University Press).

Levine, J. (2001), *Purple Haze: The Puzzle of Consciousness* (Oxford: Oxford University Press).

Lewis, M. (1987), 'Social Development in Infancy and Early Childhood', in J. Osofsky (ed.), *Handbook of Infant Development*, 2nd edn (New York: Wiley), 419–93.

Lewis, M. (1992), *Shame: The Exposed Self* (New York: Free Press).

Lewis, M. (1998), 'Shame and Stigma', in P. Gilbert and B. Andrews (eds.), *Shame: Interpersonal Behavior, Psychopathology, and Culture* (New York: Oxford University Press), 126–40.

Lewis, M. (2003), 'The Development of Self-Consciousness', in J. Roessler and N. Eilan (eds.), *Agency and Self-Awareness* (Oxford: Oxford University Press), 275–95.

Lewis, M. (2004), 'The Emergence of Human Emotions', in J. M. Haviland-Jones (ed.), *Handbook of Emotions*, 2nd edn (New York: Guilford Press), 265–80.

Lewis, M. (2007), 'Self-Conscious Emotional Development', in J. L. Tracy, R. W. Robins, and J. P. Tangney (eds.), *The Self-Conscious Emotions: Theory and Research* (New York: Guilford Press), 134–49.

Lewis, M. (2011), 'The Origins and Uses of Self-Awareness; or, The Mental Representation of Me', *Consciousness and Cognition*, 20/1: 120–9.

Lichtenberg, G. C. (2000) [1800–6], *The Waste Books*, trans. R. J. Hollingdale (New York: New York Review of Books).

Lind, S. E. (2010), 'Memory and the Self in Autism: A Review and Theoretical Framework', *Autism*, 14/5: 430–56.

Lindsay, D. S., and Johnson, M. K. (1991), 'Recognition Memory and Source Monitoring', *Bulletin of the Psychonomic Society*, 29/3: 203–5.

Lindsay-Hartz, J., de Rivera, J., and Mascolo, M. F. (1995), 'Differentiating Guilt and Shame and their Effects on Motivations', in J. P. Tangney and K. W. Fischer (eds.), *Self-Conscious Emotions: The Psychology of Shame, Guilt, Embarrassment and Pride* (New York: Guilford Press), 274–300.

Lipps, T. (1900), 'Aesthetische Einfühlung', *Zeitschrift für Psychologie und Physiologie der Sinnesorgane*, 22: 415–50.

Lipps, T. (1905), *Die ethischen Grundfragen* (Hamburg: Leopold Voss Verlag).

Lipps, T. (1907a), 'Das Wissen von fremden Ichen', in T. Lipps (ed.), *Psychologische Untersuchungen I* (Leipzig: Engelmann), 694–722.

Lipps, T. (1907b), 'Ästhetik', in P. Hinneberg (ed.), *Systematische Philosophie* (Berlin: Verlag von B. G. Teubner), 351–90.

Lipps, T. (1909), *Leitfaden der Psychologie* (Leipzig: Verlag von Wilhelm Engelmann).

Locke, J. (1975) [1690], *An Essay concerning Human Understanding* (Oxford: Clarendon Press).

Lohmar, D. (2006), 'Mirror Neurons and the Phenomenology of Intersubjectivity', *Phenomenology and the Cognitive Sciences*, 5/1: 5–16.

Loveland, K. A. (1986), 'Discovering the Affordances of a Reflecting Surface', *Developmental Review*, 6/1: 1–24.

Loveland, K. A. (1993), 'Autism, Affordances, and the Self', in U. Neisser (ed.), *The Perceived Self: Ecological and Interpersonal Sources of Self-Knowledge* (Cambridge: Cambridge University Press), 237–53.

Lurz, R.W. (2003), 'Neither HOT nor COLD: An Alternative Account of Consciousness', *Psyche*, 9/1: 1–18.

Lusthaus, D. (2002), *Buddhist Phenomenology: A Philosophical Investigation of Yogacara Buddhism and the Ch'eng Wei-shih Lun* (London: Routledge).

Lyyra, P. (2009), 'Two Senses for "Givenness of Consciousness"', *Phenomenology and the Cognitive Sciences*, 8/1: 67–87.

McCulloch, G. (2003), *The Life of the Mind: An Essay on Phenomenological Externalism* (London: Routledge).

MacIntyre, A. (1985), *After Virtue: A Study in Moral Theory* (London: Routledge).

MacKenzie, M. (2008), 'Self-Awareness without a Self: Buddhism and the Reflexivity of Awareness', *Asian Philosophy*, 18/3: 245–66.

MacKenzie, M. D. (2007), 'The Illumination of Consciousness: Approaches to Self-Awareness in the Indian and Western Traditions', *Philosophy East and West*, 57/1: 40–62.

Maclaren, K. (2008), 'Embodied Perceptions of Others as a Condition of Selfhood: Empirical and Phenomenological Considerations', *Journal of Consciousness Studies*, 15/8: 63–93.

McNeill, W. E. S. (2012), 'On Seeing that Someone Is Angry', *European Journal of Philosophy*, 20/4: 575–97.

Malle, B. F. (2005), 'Three Puzzles of Mindreading', in B. F. Malle and S. D. Hodges (eds.), *Other Minds: How Human Bridge the Divide between Self and Others* (New York: Guilford Press), 26–43.

Mar, R. A. (2011), 'The Neural Bases of Social Cognition and Story Comprehension', *Annual Review of Psychology*, 62/1: 103–34.

Margolis, J. (1988), 'Minds, Selves, and Persons', *Topoi*, 7/1: 31–45.

Matsumoto, D., and Willingham, B. (2009), 'Spontaneous Facial Expressions of Emotion of Congenitally and Noncongenitally Blind Individuals', *Journal of Personality and Social Psychology*, 96/1: 1–10.

Mead, G. H. (1962) [1934], *Mind, Self and Society: From the Standpoint of a Social Behaviorist* (Chicago: University of Chicago Press).

Meltzoff, A. N., and Moore, M. K. (1995), 'A Theory of the Role of Imitation in the Emergence of Self', in P. Rochat (ed.), *The Self in Infancy: Theory and Research* (Amsterdam: Elsevier), 73–93.

Menary, R. (2008), 'Embodied Narratives', *Journal of Consciousness Studies*, 15/6: 63–84.

Merleau-Ponty, M. (1964a), *The Primacy of Perception* (Evanston, Ill.: Northwestern University Press).

Merleau-Ponty, M. (1964b) [1960], *Signs*, trans. R. C. McClearly (Evanston, Ill.: Northwestern University Press).

Merleau-Ponty, M. (2010), *Child Psychology and Pedagogy: The Sorbonne Lectures 1949–1952*, trans. T. Welsh (Evanston, Ill.: Northwestern University Press).

Merleau-Ponty, M. (2012) [1945], *Phenomenology of Perception*, trans. D. A. Landes (London: Routledge).

Merleau-Ponty, M. (2004) [1948], *The World of Perception*, trans. O. Davis (London: Routledge).

Metzinger, T. (2003), *Being No One* (Cambridge, Mass.: MIT Press).

Metzinger, T. (2011), 'The No-Self Alternative', in S. Gallagher (ed.), *The Oxford Handbook of the Self* (Oxford: Oxford University Press), 279–96.

Miller, S. (1985), *The Shame Experience* (London: Analytic Press).

Minkowski, E. (1997) [1928], 'Du symptome au trouble générateur', in *Au-delà du rationalisme morbide* (Paris: Éditions l'Harmattan), 93–124.

Mitchell, J. P. (2008), 'Contributions of Functional Neuroimaging to the Study of Social Cognition', *Current Directions in Psychological Science*, 17/2: 142–6.

Mitchell, R. W. (1993), 'Mental Models of Mirror-Self-Recognition: Two Theories', *New Ideas in Psychology*, 11/3: 295–325.

Mitchell, R. W. (1997a), 'Kinesthetic–Visual Matching and the Self-Concept as Explanations of Mirror-Self-Recognition', *Journal for the Theory of Social Behaviour*, 27/1: 17–39.

Mitchell, R. W. (1997b), 'A Comparison of the Self-Awareness and Kinesthetic–Visual Matching Theories of Self-Recognition: Autistic Children and Others', *Annals of the New York Academy of Sciences*, 818/1: 39–62.

Mohanty, J. N. (1972), *The Concept of Intentionality* (St Louis: Green).

Moll, H., and Meltzoff, A. N. (2012), 'Joint Attention as the Fundamental Basis of Understanding Perspectives', in A. Seemann (ed.), *Joint Attention: New Developments in Psychology, Philosophy of Mind, and Social Neuroscience* (Cambridge, Mass.: MIT Press), 393–413.

Moll, H., Carpenter, M., and Tomasello, M. (2007), 'Fourteen-Month-Olds Know What Others Experience Only in Joint Engagement', *Developmental Science*, 10/6: 826–35.

Moran, R. (2001), *Authority and Estrangement: An Essay on Self-Knowledge* (Princeton: Princeton University Press).

Murray, L., and Trevarthen, C. (1985), 'Emotional Regulation of Interactions between Two-Month-Olds and their Mothers', in T. M. Field and N. A. Fox (eds.), *Social Perception in Infants* (Norwood, NJ: Ablex), 177–97.

Nathanson, D. L. (1987), 'A Timetable for Shame', in D. L. Nathanson (ed.), *The Many Faces of Shame* (New York: Guilford Press), 1–63.

Nathanson, D. L. (1994), *Shame and Pride: Affect, Sex and the Birth of Self* (New York: W. W. Norton).

Neisser, U. (1988), 'Five Kinds of Self-Knowledge', *Philosophical Psychology*, 1/1: 35–59.

Neisser, U. (1991), 'Two Perceptually Given Aspects of the Self and their Development', *Developmental Review*, 11/3: 197–209.

Neisser, U. (1993), 'The Self Perceived', in U. Neisser (ed.), *The Perceived Self: Ecological and Interpersonal Sources of Self-Knowledge* (New York: Cambridge University Press), 3–21.

Newen, A., and Schlicht, T. (2009), 'Understanding Other Minds: A Criticism of Goldman's Simulation Theory and an Outline of the Person Model Theory', *Grazer Philosophische Studien*, 79/1: 209–42.

Nichols, S., and Stich, S. (2003), *Mindreading: An Integrated Account of Pretence, Self-Awareness, and Understanding of Other Minds* (Oxford: Oxford University Press).

Niedenthal, P. M. (2007), 'Embodying Emotion', *Science*, 316/5827: 1002–5.

Niedenthal, P. M., Krauth-Gruber, S., and Ric, F. (2006), *Psychology of Emotions: Interpersonal, Experiential, and Cognitive Approaches* (New York: Psychology Press).

Nietzsche, F. W. (1997) [1881], *Daybreak: Thoughts on the Prejudices of Morality* (Cambridge: Cambridge University Press).

Nussbaum, M. C. (2004), *Hiding from Humanity: Disgust, Shame and the Law* (Princeton: Princeton University Press).

Olson, E. T. (1998), 'There Is No Problem of the Self', *Journal of Consciousness Studies*, 5/5–6: 645–57.

O'Neill, J. (1989), *The Communicative Body: Studies in Communicative Philosophy, Politics and Sociology* (Evanston, Ill.: Northwestern University Press).

Onishi, K. H., and Baillargeon, R. (2005), 'Do 15-Month-Old Infants Understand False Beliefs?', *Science*, 308/5719: 255–8.

Overgaard, S. (2003), 'The Importance of Bodily Movement to Husserl's Theory of Fremderfahrung', *Recherches Husserliennes*, 19: 55–66.

Overgaard, S. (2005), 'Rethinking Other Minds: Wittgenstein and Lévinas on Expression', *Inquiry*, 48/3: 249–74.

Overgaard, S. (2007), *Wittgenstein and Other Minds: Rethinking Subjectivity and Intersubjectivity with Wittgenstein, Levinas, and Husserl* (London: Routledge).

Overgaard, S. (2012), 'Other People', in D. Zahavi (ed.), *The Oxford Handbook of Contemporary Phenomenology* (Oxford: Oxford University Press), 460–79.

Parnas, J., and Sass, L. A. (2011), 'The Structure of Self-Consciousness in Schizophrenia', in S. Gallagher (ed.), *The Oxford Handbook of the Self* (Oxford: Oxford University Press), 521–46.

Peacocke, C. (2012), 'Subjects and Consciousness', in A. Coliva (ed.), *The Self and Self-Knowledge* (Oxford: Oxford University Press), 74–101.

Petit, J.-L. (1999), 'Constitution by Movement: Husserl in Light of Recent Neurobiological Findings', in J. Petitot, F. Varela, B. Pachoud, and J.-M. Roy (eds.), *Naturalizing Phenomenology* (Stanford: Stanford University Press), 220–44.

Platek, S. M., Keenan, J. P., Gallup Jr, G. G., and Mohamed, F. B. (2004), 'Where Am I? The Neurological Correlates of Self and Other', *Cognitive Brain Research*, 19/2: 114–22.

Plato (1961) [c.bce 348], *Laws*, in *The Collected Dialogues of Plato*, ed. E. Hamilton and H. Cairns (Princeton: Princeton University Press), 1225–1513.

Postal, K. S. (2005), 'The Mirror Sign Delusional Misidentification Syndrome', in T. E. Feinberg and J. P. Keenan (eds.), *The Lost Self: Pathologies of the Brain and Identity* (Oxford: Oxford University Press), 131–46.

Praetorius, N. (2009), 'The Phenomenological Underpinning of the Notion of a Minimal Core Self: A Psychological Perspective', *Consciousness and Cognition*, 18/1: 325–38.

Premack, D., and Woodruff, G. (1978), 'Does the Chimpanzee Have a Theory of Mind?', *Behavioral and Brain Sciences*, 1/4: 515.

Prinz, J. (2012), 'Waiting for the Self', in J. Liu and J. Perry (eds.), *Consciousness and the Self: New Essays* (Cambridge: Cambridge University Press), 123–49.

Prinz, W. (2003), 'Emerging Selves: Representational Foundations of Subjectivity', *Consciousness and Cognition*, 12/4: 515–28.

Prinz, W. (2012), *Open Minds: The Social Making of Agency and Intentionality* (Cambridge, Mass.: MIT Press).

Radke-Yarrow, M. R., Zahn-Waxler, C., and Chapman, M. (1983), 'Children's Prosocial Dispositions and Behavior', in P. H. Mussen (ed.), *Handbook of Child Psychology IV: Socialization, Personality, and Social Development* (New York: Wiley), 469–546.

Ramachandran, V. S. (2000), 'Mirror Neurons and Imitation Learning as the Driving Force behind the Great Leap Forward in Human Evolution', <http://edge.org/conversation/mirror-neurons-and-imitation-learning-as-the-driving-force-behind-the-great-leap-forward-in-human-evolution> (accessed 9 Jan. 2014).

Ratcliffe, M. (2006), 'Phenomenology, Neuroscience, and Intersubjectivity', in H. L. Dreyfus and M. A. Wrathall (eds.), *A Companion to Phenomenology and Existentialism* (Oxford: Blackwell), 329–45.

Ratcliffe, M. (2007), *Rethinking Commonsense Psychology* (London: Palgrave Macmillan).

Ratcliffe, M. (2014), *Experiences of Depression: A Study in Phenomenology* (Oxford: Oxford University Press).

Rawls, J. (1972), *A Theory of Justice* (Oxford: Clarendon Press).

Reddy, V. (2008), *How Infants Know Minds* (Cambridge, Mass.: Harvard University Press).

Reddy, V., Williams, E., Costantini, C., and Lan, B. (2010), 'Engaging with the Self: Mirror Behaviour in Autism, Down Syndrome and Typical Development', *Autism*, 14/5: 531–46.

Reid, T. (1863) [1785], *Essays on the Intellectual Powers of Man*, in *The Works of Thomas Reid*, ed. W. Hamilton, 2 vols. (Edinburgh: Maclachlan and Stewart).

Reid, V. M., and Striano, T. (2007), 'The Directed Attention Model of Infant Social Cognition', *European Journal of Developmental Psychology*, 4/1: 100–10.

Ricœur, P. (1988) [1985], *Time and Narrative III*, trans. K. Blamey and D. Pellauer (Chicago: University of Chicago Press).

Rizzolatti, G., and Craighero, L. (2004), 'The Mirror-Neuron System', *Annual Review of Neuroscience*, 27/1: 169–92.

Robbins, P., and Jack, A. I. (2006), 'The Phenomenal Stance', *Philosophical Studies*, 127/1: 59–85.

Rochat, P. (1995), 'Early Objectification of the Self', in P. Rochat (ed.), *The Self in Infancy: Theory and Research* (Amsterdam: Elsevier), 53–72.

Rochat, P. (2001), *The Infant's World* (Cambridge, Mass.: Harvard University Press).

Rochat, P. (2003), 'Five Levels of Self-Awareness as they Unfold Early in Life', *Consciousness and Cognition*, 12/4: 717–31.

Rochat, P. (2009), *Others in Mind: Social Origins of Self-Consciousness* (Cambridge: Cambridge University Press).

Rochat, P. (2010), 'Emerging Self-Concept', in J. G. Bremner and T. D. Wachs (eds.), *The Wiley-Blackwell Handbook of Infant Development*, vol. i, *Basic Research*, 2nd edn (Oxford: Blackwell), 320–44.

Rochat, P., and Striano, T. (1999), 'Social-Cognitive Development in the First Year', in P. Rochat (ed.), *Early Social Cognition: Understanding Others in the First Months of Life* (Hillsdale, NJ: Lawrence Erlbaum), 3–34.

Rochat, P., and Zahavi, D. (2011), 'The Uncanny Mirror: A Re-Framing of Mirror Self-Experience', *Consciousness and Cognition*, 20/2: 204–13.

Rochat, P., Broesch, T., and Jayne, K. (2012), 'Social Awareness and Early Self-Recognition', *Consciousness and Cognition*, 21/3: 1491–7.

Roessler, J. (2005), 'Joint Attention and the Problem of Other Minds', in N. Eilan, C. Hoerl, T. McCormack, and J. Roessler (eds.), *Joint Attention: Communication and Other Minds* (Oxford: Oxford University Press), 230–59.

Rosenthal, D. M. (1997), 'A Theory of Consciousness', in N. Block, O. Flanagan, and G. Güzeldere (eds.), *The Nature of Consciousness* (Cambridge, Mass.: MIT Press), 729–53.

Rosenthal, D. M. (2002), 'Explaining Consciousness', in D. J. Chalmers (ed.), *Philosophy of Mind: Classical and Contemporary Readings* (New York: Oxford University Press), 406–21.

Rousse, B. S. (2013), 'Heidegger, Sociality, and Human Agency', *European Journal of Philosophy*; doi: 10.1111/ejop.12067.

Rovane, C. (2012), 'Does Rationality Enforce Identity?', in A. Coliva (ed.), *The Self and Self-Knowledge* (Oxford: Oxford University Press), 17–38.

Rowlands, M. (2013), 'Sartre, Consciousness, and Intentionality', *Phenomenology and the Cognitive Sciences*, 12/3: 521–36.

Royce, J. (1898), *Studies of Good and Evil* (New York: D. Appleton).

Rudd, A. (2003), *Expressing the World: Skepticism, Wittgenstein, and Heidegger* (Chicago: Open Court).

Rudd, A. (2012), *Self, Value, and Narrative: A Kierkegaardian Approach* (Oxford: Oxford University Press).

Sacks, O. (1995), *An Anthropologist on Mars* (London: Picador).

Sartre, J.-P. (1948), 'Conscience de soi et connaissance de soi', *Bulletin de la Société française de philosophie*, 42: 49–91.

Sartre, J.-P. (1957) [1936], *The Transcendence of the Ego*, trans. F. Williams and R. Kirkpatrick (New York: Noonday Press).

Sartre, J.-P. (2003) [1943], *Being and Nothingness: An Essay in Phenomenological Ontology*, trans. H. E. Barnes (London: Routledge).

Sass, L. A., and Parnas, J. (2003), 'Schizophrenia, Consciousness, and the Self', *Schizophrenia Bulletin*, 29/3: 427–44.

Saxe, R., Carey, S., and Kanwisher, N. (2004), 'Understanding Other Minds: Linking Developmental Psychology and Functional Neuroimaging', *Annual Review of Psychology*, 55: 87–124.

Schacter, D. (1996), *Searching for Memory: The Brain, the Mind, and the Past* (New York: Basic Books).

Schapp, W. (2004) [1953], *In Geschichten verstrickt* (Frankfurt am Main: Vittorio Klostermann).

Schear, J. K. (2009), 'Experience and Self-Consciousness', *Philosophical Studies*, 144/1: 95–105.

Schechtman, M. (1996), *The Constitution of Selves* (Ithaca: Cornell University Press).

Schechtman, M. (2001), 'Empathic Access: The Missing Ingredient in Personal Persistence', *Philosophical Explorations*, 4/2: 95–111.

Schechtman, M. (2007), 'Stories, Lives, and Basic Survival: A Defense and Refinement of the Narrative View', in D. Hutto (ed.), *Narrative and Understanding Persons* (Cambridge: Cambridge University Press), 155–78.

Schechtman, M. (2011), 'The Narrative Self', in S. Gallagher (ed.), *The Oxford Handbook of the Self* (Oxford: Oxford University Press), 394–418.

Scheler, M. (1957) [1913], *Über Scham und Schamgefühl*, in *Schriften aus dem Nachlass*, vol. i, *Zur Ethik und Erkenntnislehre* (Bern: Francke Verlag).

Scheler, M. (2008) [1913/1923], *The Nature of Sympathy* (London: Transaction).

Schilbach, L., Timmermans, B., Reddy, V., Costall, A., Bente, G., Schlicht, T., and Vogeley, K. (2013), 'Toward a Second-Person Neuroscience', *Behavioral and Brain Sciences*, 36/4: 393–414.

Schmid, H. B. (2005), *Wir-Intentionalität: Kritik des ontologischen Individualismus und Rekonstruktion der Gemeinschaft* (Freiburg: Karl Alber).

Schneider, C. D. (1987), 'A Mature Sense of Shame', in D. L. Nathanson (ed.), *The Many Faces of Shame* (New York: Guilford Press), 194–213.

Schutz, A. (1962), *Collected Papers II: The Problem of Social Reality* (The Hague: Martinus Nijhoff).

Schutz, A. (1967) [1932], *Phenomenology of the Social World* (Evanston, Ill.: Northwestern University Press).

Schutz, A. (1975), *Collected Papers III: Studies in Phenomenological Philosophy* (The Hague: Martinus Nijhoff).

Searle, J. R. (1990), 'Collective Intentions and Actions', in P. Cohen, J. Morgan, and M. E. Pollack (eds.), *Intentions in Communication* (Cambridge, Mass.: MIT Press), 401–16.

Searle, J. R. (1995), *The Construction of Social Reality* (New York: Free Press).

Searle, J. R. (1999), 'The Future of Philosophy', *Philosophical Transactions of the Royal Society of London*, 354/1392: 2069–80.

Searle, J. R. (2002), *Consciousness and Language* (Cambridge: Cambridge University Press).

Searle, J. R. (2005), 'The Self as a Problem in Philosophy and Neurobiology', in T. E. Feinberg and J. P. Keenan (eds.), *The Lost Self: Pathologies of the Brain and Identity* (Oxford: Oxford University Press), 7–19.

Seeley, W. W., and Miller, B. L. (2005), 'Disorders of the Self in Dementia', in T. E. Feinberg and J. P. Keenan (eds.), *The Lost Self: Pathologies of the Brain and Identity* (Oxford: Oxford University Press), 147–65.

Seidler, G. H. (2001), *Der Blick des Anderen: Eine Analyse der Scham* (Stuttgart: Klett-Cotta).

Seigel, J. (2005), *The Idea of the Self: Thought and Experience in Western Europe since the Seventeenth Century* (Cambridge: Cambridge University Press).

Shoemaker, S. (1996), *The First-Person Perspective and Other Essays* (Cambridge: Cambridge University Press).

Shweder, R. A. (2003), 'Toward a Deep Cultural Psychology of Shame', *Social Research*, 70/4: 1109–30.

Siderits, M. (2011), 'Buddhas as Zombies: A Buddhist Reduction of Subjectivity', in M. Siderits, E. Thompson, and D. Zahavi (eds.), *Self, No Self? Perspectives from Analytical, Phenomeno-logical, and Indian Traditions* (Oxford: Oxford University Press), 308–31.

Singer, T., Seymour, B., O'Doherty, J., Kaube, H., Dolan, R. J., and Frith, C. D. (2004), 'Empathy for Pain Involves the Affective but not Sensory Components of Pain', *Science*, 303/5661: 1157–62.

Singer, T., Seymour, B., O'Doherty, J. P., Stephan, K. E., Dolan, R. J., and Frith, C. D. (2006), 'Empathic Neural Responses Are Modulated by the Perceived Fairness of Others', *Nature*, 439/7075: 466–9.

Sinigaglia, C. (2008), 'Mirror Neurons: This Is the Question', *Journal of Consciousness Studies*, 15/10–11: 70–92.

Smith, A. (2002) [1759], *The Theory of Moral Sentiments* (Cambridge: Cambridge University Press).

Smith, A. D. (2003), *Routledge Philosophy Guidebook to Husserl and the Cartesian Meditations* (London: Routledge).

Smith, J. (2010), 'Seeing Other People', *Philosophy and Phenomenological Research*, 81/3: 731–48.

Smith, R. H., Webster, J. M., Parrott, W. G., and Eyre, H. L. (2002), 'The Role of Public Exposure in Moral and Nonmoral Shame and Guilt', *Journal of Personality and Social Psychology*, 83/1: 138–59.

Snow, N. E. (2000), 'Empathy', *American Philosophical Quarterly*, 37/1: 65–78.

Sorabji, R. (2006), *Self: Ancient and Modern Insights about Individuality, Life and Death* (Oxford: Clarendon Press).

Spaulding, S. (2010), 'Embodied Cognition and Mindreading', *Mind and Language*, 25/1: 119–40.

Spiker, D., and Ricks, M. (1984), 'Visual Self-Recognition in Autistic Children: Developmental Relationships', *Child Development*, 55/1: 214.

Stein, E. (2000) [1922], *Philosophy of Psychology and the Humanities*, trans. M. C. Baseheart and M. Sawicki (Washington, DC: ICS).

Stein, E. (2008) [1917], *Zum Problem der Einfühlung* (Freiburg: Herder); trans. W. Stein as *On the Problem of Empathy* (Washington, DC: ICS, 1989).

Steinbock, A. J. (2014), *Moral Emotions: Reclaiming the Evidence of the Heart* (Evanston, Ill.: Northwestern University Press).

Stern, D. N. (1985), *The Interpersonal World of the Infant* (New York: Basic Books).

Stich, S., and Nichols, S. (1995), 'Folk Psychology: Simulation or Tacit Theory?', in M. Davies and T. Stone (eds.), *Folk Psychology: The Theory of Mind Debate* (Oxford: Blackwell), 123–58.

Stich, S., and Nichols, S. (1997), 'Cognitive Penetrability, Rationality and Restricted Simulation', *Mind and Language*, 12/3–4: 297–326.

Stokes, P. (2014), 'Crossing the Bridge: The First-Person and Time', *Phenomenology and the Cognitive Sciences*, 13: 295–312.

Stout, R. (2010), 'Seeing the Anger in Someone's Face', *Proceedings of the Aristotelian Society, Supplementary Volumes*, 84/1: 29–43.

Straus, E. W. (1966) [1933], 'Shame as a Historiological Problem', in *Phenomenological Psychology: The Selected Papers of Erwin W. Straus* (New York: Basic Books), 217–24.

Strawson, G. (1994), 'Don't Tread on Me', *London Review of Books*, 16/19: 11–12.

Strawson, G. (2000), 'The Phenomenology and Ontology of the Self', in D. Zahavi (ed.), *Exploring the Self* (Amsterdam: John Benjamins), 39–54.

Strawson, G. (2004), 'Against Narrativity', *Ratio*, 17/4: 428–52.

Strawson, G. (2009), *Selves: An Essay in Revisionary Metaphysics* (Oxford: Oxford University Press).

Strawson, G. (2011), 'The Minimal Subject', in S. Gallagher (ed.), *The Oxford Handbook of the Self* (Oxford: Oxford University Press), 253–78.

Strawson, P. F. (1959), *Individuals: An Essay in Descriptive Metaphysics* (London: Methuen).

Stueber, K. R. (2006), *Rediscovering Empathy: Agency, Folk Psychology, and the Human Sciences* (Cambridge, Mass.: MIT Press).

Szanto, T. (2015), 'Husserl on Collective Intentionality', in A. Salice and H. B. Schmid (eds.), *Social Reality* (Dordrecht: Springer).

Taguchi, S. (2006), *Das Problem des 'Ur-Ich' bei Edmund Husserl: Die Frage nach der selbstverständlichen 'Nähe' des Selbst* (Dordrecht: Springer).

Tangney, J. P., and Dearing, R. L. (2002), *Shame and Guilt* (New York: Guilford Press).

Taylor, C. (1989), *Sources of the Self* (Cambridge, Mass.: Harvard University Press).

Taylor, G. (1985), *Pride, Shame, and Guilt: Emotions of Self-Assessment* (Oxford: Clarendon Press).

Theunissen, M. (1977) [1965], *Der Andere* (Berlin: Walter de Gruyter).

Thiel, U. (2011), *The Early Modern Subject: Self-Consciousness and Personal Identity from Descartes to Hume* (Oxford: Oxford University Press).

Thomasson, A. L. (2000), 'After Brentano: A One-Level Theory of Consciousness', *European Journal of Philosophy*, 8/2: 190.

Thomasson, A. L. (2006), 'Self-Awareness and Self-Knowledge', *Psyche*, 12/2: 1–15.

Thompson, E. (2001), 'Empathy and Consciousness', *Journal of Consciousness Studies*, 8/5–7: 1–32.

Thompson, E. (2007), *Mind in Life: Biology, Phenomenology, and the Sciences of the Mind* (Cambridge, Mass.: Harvard University Press).

Titchener, E. B. (1909), *Lectures on the Experimental Psychology of Thought-Processes* (New York: Macmillan).

Tomasello, M. (1993), 'On the Interpersonal Origins of Self-Concept', in U. Neisser (ed.), *The Perceived Self: Ecological and Interpersonal Sources of Self-Knowledge* (New York: Cambridge University Press), 174–84.

Tomasello, M. (1999), *The Cultural Origins of Human Cognition* (Cambridge, Mass.: Harvard University Press).

Tooby, J., and Cosmides, L. (1995), Foreword to S. Baron-Cohen, *Mindblindness: An Essay on Autism and Theory of Mind* (Cambridge, Mass.: MIT Press), pp. xi–xviii.

Trevarthen, C. (1979), 'Communication and Cooperation in Early Infancy: A Description of Primary Intersubjectivity', in M. M. Bullowa (ed.), *Before Speech: The Beginning of Interpersonal Communication* (New York: Cambridge University Press), 321–47.

Trevarthen, C., and Hubley, P. (1978), 'Secondary Intersubjectivity: Confidence, Confiding and Acts of Meaning in the First Year', in A. Lock (ed.), *Action, Gesture and Symbol: The Emergence of Language* (London: Academic Press), 183–229.

Tronick, E., Als, H., Adamson, L., Wise, S., and Brazelton, T. B. (1978), 'Infants' Response to Entrapment between Contradictory Messages in Face-to-Face Interaction', *Journal of the American Academy of Child and Adolescent Psychiatry*, 17: 1–13.

Turner, J. C., Oakes, P. J., Haslam, S. A., and McGarty, C. (1994), 'Self and Collective: Cognition and Social Context', *Personality and Social Psychology Bulletin*, 20/5: 454–63.

Tye, M. (1995), *Ten Problems of Consciousness* (Cambridge, Mass.: MIT Press).

Tye, M. (2003), *Consciousness and Persons* (Cambridge, Mass.: MIT Press).

Tye, M. (2009), *Consciousness Revisited: Materialism without Phenomenal Concepts* (Cambridge, Mass.: MIT Press).

Varela, F., and Shear, J. (1999), 'First-Person Methodologies: What, Why, How?', *Journal of Consciousness Studies*, 6/2–3: 1–14.

Velleman, J. D. (2001), 'The Genesis of Shame', *Philosophy and Public Affairs*, 30/1: 27–52.

Vischer, R. (1873), *Über das optische Formgefühl: Ein Beitrag zur Ästhetik* (Leipzig: Hermann Credner).

Waldenfels, B. (1971), *Das Zwischenreich des Dialogs: Sozialphilosophische Untersuchungen in Anschluss an Edmund Husserl* (The Hague: Martinus Nijhoff).

Waldenfels, B. (1989), 'Erfahrung des Fremden in Husserls Phänomenologie', *Phänomenologische Forschungen*, 22: 39–62.

Walsh, W. H. (1970), 'Pride, Shame and Responsibility', *Philosophical Quarterly*, 20/78: 1–13.

Walther, G. (1923), 'Zur Ontologie der sozialen Gemeinschaften', in E. Husserl (ed.), *Jahrbuch für Philosophie und phänomenologische Forschung VI* (Halle: Niemeyer), 1–158.

Waytz, A., and Mitchell, J. P. (2011), 'Two Mechanisms for Simulating Other Minds: Dissociations between Mirroring and Self-Projection', *Current Directions in Psychological Science*, 20/3: 197–200.

Whalen, P. J., Shin, L. M., McInerney, S. C., Fischer, H., Wright, C., and Rauch, S. L. (2001), 'A Functional MRI Study of Human Amygdala Responses to Facial Expressions of Fear Versus Anger', *Emotion*, 1/1: 70–83.

Wicker, B., Keysers, C., Plailly, J., Royet, J.-P., Gallese, V., and Rizzolatti, G. (2003), 'Both of Us Disgusted in My Insula: The Common Neural Basis of Seeing and Feeling Disgust', *Neuron*, 40/3: 655–64.

Williams, B. A. O. (1973), *Problems of the Self* (Cambridge: Cambridge University Press).

Williams, B. A. O. (1993), *Shame and Necessity* (Berkeley: University of California Press).

Wittgenstein, L. (1980), *Remarks on the Philosophy of Psychology*, vol. ii, ed. G. H. von Wright and H. Nyman, trans. C. G. Luckhardt and M. A. E. Aue (Oxford: Blackwell).

Wittgenstein, L. (1982), *Last Writings on the Philosophy of Psychology*, vol. i, ed. G. H. von Wright and H. Nyman, trans. C. G. Luckhardt and M. A. E. Aue (Oxford: Blackwell).

Wittgenstein, L. (1992), *Last Writings on the Philosophy of Psychology*, vol. ii, ed. G.H. von Wright and H. Nyman, trans. C. G. Luckhardt and M. A. E. Aue (Oxford: Blackwell).

Wollheim, R. (1999), *On the Emotions* (New Haven: Yale University Press).

Yamaguchi, I. (1982), *Passive Synthesis und Intersubjektivität bei Edmund Husserl* (The Hague: Martinus Nijhoff).

Young, K., and Saver, J. L. (2001), 'The Neurology of Narrative', *SubStance*, 30/1–2: 72–84.

Zahavi, D. (1996), *Husserl und die transzendentale Intersubjektivität: Eine Antwort auf die sprachpragmatische Kritik* (Dordrecht: Kluwer Academic Publishers).

Zahavi, D. (1999), *Self-Awareness and Alterity: A Phenomenological Investigation* (Evanston, Ill.: Northwestern University Press).

Zahavi, D. (2001), 'Beyond Empathy: Phenomenological Approaches to Intersubjectivity', *Journal of Consciousness Studies*, 8/5–7: 151–67.

Zahavi, D. (2002), 'Intersubjectivity in Sartre's *Being and Nothingness*', *Alter*, 10: 265–81.

Zahavi, D. (2003), 'Inner Time-Consciousness and Pre-Reflective Self-Awareness', in D. Welton (ed.), *The New Husserl: A Critical Reader* (Bloomington: Indiana University Press), 157–80.

Zahavi, D. (2004a), 'Back to Brentano?', *Journal of Consciousness Studies*, 11/10–11: 66–87.

Zahavi, D. (2004b), 'Phenomenology and the Project of Naturalization', *Phenomenology and the Cognitive Sciences*, 3/4: 331–47.

Zahavi, D. (2005), *Subjectivity and Selfhood: Investigating the First-Person Perspective* (Cambridge, Mass.: MIT Press).

Zahavi, D. (2007a), 'Perception of Duration Presupposes Duration of Perception—or Does It? Husserl and Dainton on Time', *International Journal of Philosophical Studies*, 15/3: 453–71.

Zahavi, D. (2007b), 'Expression and Empathy', in D. D. Hutto and M. Ratcliffe (eds.), *Folk Psychology Re-Assessed* (Dordrecht: Springer), 25–40.

Zahavi, D. (2007c), 'Killing the Straw Man: Dennett and Phenomenology', *Phenomenology and the Cognitive Sciences*, 6/1–2: 21–43.

Zahavi, D. (2008), 'Simulation, Projection and Empathy', *Consciousness and Cognition*, 17/2: 514–22.

Zahavi, D. (2010a), 'Inner (Time-)Consciousness', in D. Lohmar and I. Yamaguchi (eds.), *On Time: New Contributions to the Husserlian Phenomenology of Time* (Dordrecht: Springer), 319–39.

Zahavi, D. (2010b), 'Naturalized Phenomenology', in S. Gallagher and D. Schmicking (eds.), *Handbook of Phenomenology and Cognitive Science* (Dordrecht: Springer), 2–19.

Zaki, J., and Ochsner, K. (2012), 'The Cognitive Neuroscience of Sharing and Understanding Others' Emotions', in J. Decety (ed.), *Empathy: From Bench to Bedside* (Cambridge, Mass.: MIT Press), 207–26.

Zeedyk, M. S. (2006), 'From Intersubjectivity to Subjectivity: The Transformative Roles of Emotional Intimacy and Imitation', *Infant and Child Development*, 15/3: 321–44.

Zinck, A., and Newen, A. (2008), 'Classifying Emotion: A Developmental Account', *Synthese*, 161/1: 1–25.

Index of Names

Index of Subjects